# Issues and
# Problems in Teacher
# Education

# Issues and Problems in Teacher Education

## AN INTERNATIONAL HANDBOOK

EDITED BY

## Howard B. Leavitt

FOREWORD BY

Arthur W. Foshay

GREENWOOD PRESS
NEW YORK • WESTPORT, CONNECTICUT • LONDON

**Library of Congress Cataloging-in-Publication Data**

Issues and problems in teacher education : an international handbook /
    edited by Howard B. Leavitt : foreword by Arthur W. Foshay.
        p.    cm.
    Includes bibliographical references and index.
    ISBN 0–313–25991–7 (alk. paper)
    1. Teachers—Training of.   2. Teachers—Training of—Case studies.
3. Comparative education.   I. Leavitt, Howard B.
LB1707.I85   1992
370'.71—dc20        91–33503

British Library Cataloguing in Publication Data is available.

Library of Congress Catalog Card Number: 91–33503
ISBN: 0–313–25991–7

First published in 1992

Greenwood Press, 88 Post Road West, Westport, CT 06881
An imprint of Greenwood Publishing Group, Inc.

Printed in the United States of America

The paper used in this book complies with the
Permanent Paper Standard issued by the National
Information Standards Organization (Z39.48–1984).

10 9 8 7 6 5 4 3 2 1

# CONTENTS

# FOREWORD

When we look beyond our borders, most of us try to perceive similarities and differences. We behave like tourists: we notice that the cities of Europe also have traffic problems, that some of our foods are available there, that public entertainment is quite similar, but that many Europeans already know a foreign language or two. When those of us who have taught children visit schools in other countries, we notice that most of the same subjects are offered, that teachers stand before classes, that the students use textbooks, and so on. In an important sense, we have never left home.

In this handbook we are invited to assume a different posture. Each of the country studies is written by someone directly involved in teacher education. Each of them, therefore, is written from the insider's viewpoint. The writers are concerned with their own situations, not ours; they are not interested in the similarities and differences between them and us. In this work we are invited to look at teacher education, not as tourists, but as natives. We are asked to overlook, for the time being, our professional parochialism.

In so doing, the reader finds that even what appear to be similar problems are different. For example, many of the reports indicate that teacher education has a low status in the university and that teachers tend to have lower status than other university-trained professionals in their communities. But the term *status* has different connotations in Nigeria and Germany, in the Gulf Emirates and the United Kingdom. In some countries, for example, the fact that the teacher is better educated than his or her parents threatens the status of the father of the family. In others, verbal fluency is associated with deception. The problem of retaining good teachers in the classroom is virtually universal since the rewards of status and income are greater elsewhere, but the situations underlying this problem differ greatly from one country to another. In some developing countries there is no employment for those with advanced education. It finally dawns on us that the specifics of such problems are superficial; they reflect underlying culture- and country-specific environments.

The thoughtful reader is thus drawn to conclude that each of the problems and issues in teacher education is nested in a local culture, a local polity, a local history. If we get beyond being merely curious about other peoples in other lands, we will find ourselves looking afresh at our own version of these problems and issues.

Teacher educators know very well that the beliefs and practices in the classroom are central to the culture, politics, and economy of a country. The fact that these are in large part determined, not by teacher educators, but by the larger situations in which teachers do their work emerges from these accounts with great force. In Egypt, for example, a long series of attempts has been made to bring about universal education and to develop a teaching force large enough and good enough to achieve this goal. Yet Egypt continues to export most of its best trained teachers. In Oman, the substantial reforms recently undertaken have collided with one local frustration after another, yet the writer of that account continues to be optimistic.

A considerable part of today's world is in turmoil. Third World countries are attempting to recover their own independent identities and to escape from their colonial pasts; yet vestiges of Europe remain in their status systems and confound their reforms in teacher education. East Germany had developed what appear to be some sound approaches to universal education amidst its stifling authoritarian governmental structures, but these approaches are being overlooked in a time of breathless change as the two Germanies unite. In the United States, a somewhat organized attempt is being made to do away with formal teacher preparation, with conflicting consequences. In England, the problems of teacher education appear to be a product of certain aspects of their national history. Each country follows its own path.

What is to be learned from this volume? First, a study of issues and problems associated with teacher education in other countries can provide a good perspective on one's own issues and problems. Second, the preparation of teachers remains central to a country's well-being. Those in education have known this since the seventeenth century, but those in power have not. Only now is it being generally recognized—though for different reasons in different places. Third, teaching is a complicated, difficult thing to do with one's life. Like the other helping professions, teaching is blamed for faults not of its making. Fourth, the practice of teaching remains an ill-understood undertaking, and therefore is often prey to outside pressures that become fads. Fifth, despite these uncertainties and difficulties, there remains a corps of devoted people, some of whom are the authors of these reports, who are determined to bring about constructive change in the education of teachers.

—Arthur W. Foshay, Professor Emeritus
Teachers College, Columbia University

# ACKNOWLEDGMENTS

The task of locating scholars around the world who are willing and able to prepare country studies on issues in teacher education has involved locating a very large number of key informants with many international contacts. These international contacts often turned out to be, not potential authors, but simply further sources of advice on recommended authors knowledgeable about the policy problems and issues of teacher education in the light of history and the social, political, and economic milieu in which they are found.

The twenty-one contributors to this book represent the end result of a time-consuming process involving the activation of a worldwide network of professional contacts.

I am deeply indebted to my advisory board which was a constant source of advice on contacts and also, as individuals, helped review the individual manuscripts as they came in. Members of the advisory board at the University of Massachusetts at Amherst were: Barbara Burn, Director, International Programs; Marilyn Haring-Hidore, Dean, School of Education; and Louis Fischer, Professor of Foundations of Education. Other members were Arthur Foshay, Professor Emeritus, Teachers College, Columbia University; William Gardner, Dean, School of Education, University of Minnesota; John Goodlad, Director of the Center for Educational Renewal, University of Washington; David Imig, Director, American Association of Colleges for Teacher Education; Harry Judge, Director Emeritus, Department of Educational Studies, Oxford University; Harry Passow, Professor, Department of Curriculum, Teachers College, Columbia University; and Ralph Tyler, Professor Emeritus, University of Chicago.

I am also indebted to persons in key organizations with strong international activities. These are Sheldon Shaeffer at the Canadian International Development and Research Centre; George Atiyeh at the United States Library of Congress; and Adrian Verspoor as well as Marlene Lockheed, both at the World Bank.

Other individuals whose cooperation I wish to acknowledge are Babs Fafunwa, Nigerian Minister of Education; Hans Weiler, School of Education, Stanford University; Val Rust, School of Education, University of California, Los Angeles; Arie Shoval, Israeli Ministry of Education and Culture; William Lauroesch, Chair, Division of Policy and Administration; and Phillip Eddy, Professor, Foundations of Education, both of the School of Education, University of Massachusetts, Amherst.

I also wish to acknowledge the cooperation of my son, John Leavitt, President of the October Communications Corporation of Newton, Massachusetts, for facilitating the process of extensive faxing to and from countries worldwide. I wish to thank Angela Fraley Foshay for help in editing the manuscripts.

Finally, I want to acknowledge the help of my wife, Margaret, an experienced editor in her own right, who helped with editing during the six-week period when the editor was suffering the nuisance of wearing a cast on the right arm to protect a broken wrist.

# INTRODUCTION

This reference volume provides a survey of the major issues and problems in teacher education today in a representative group of twenty-one countries around the world. Key political, economic, social, and educational factors affecting teacher education against an historical background are examined. This is truly an international overview of current issues and problems, policies, approaches and trends, and future outlooks because, with one exception (that of the Soviet Union), all the country studies were written by native scholars and experts.

During these times of rapid social change and world uncertainties, this survey views systems of teacher education in the various countries as moving and changing entities where efforts to resolve problems are changing constantly.

This reference is designed for deans of schools, colleges, and departments of education; directors of teacher education programs; government officials concerned with the field of education; and teachers as well as students of comparative and teacher education.

Despite the large differences between countries, issues and problems of teacher education from country to country are remarkably similar. An examination of other countries' issues brings an international perspective to decision and policy making in one's own country. This is likely to produce a broader, more detached viewpoint toward one's own problems. An international awareness can reveal that the problems faced in one country are shared by others, even though their resolution may differ. In addition, the handbook helps the reader understand how various social, economic, and educational factors, especially historical antecedents, shape educational systems and make us more aware of the factors impacting on our own system.

The handbook defines the key terms *issues*, *problems*, and *teacher education* as follows:

*Issues*: Ideas, policies, practices, and concepts under discussion or in dispute.

*Problems*: Questions raised for inquiry, consideration, or solution.

*Teacher Education*: The deliberate preparation and upgrading of teaching personnel from preservice through in-service education.

## EIGHT MAJOR ISSUES IN TEACHER EDUCATION

An analysis of these twenty-one country studies reveals eight major issues and problems in the promotion of teacher education.

### Recruitment

What conditions can be created to permit the recruitment of the most promising teaching talent in light of strong competition from other vocations and professions?

Thirteen of the twenty-one countries describe this issue as critical: the six Arab Gulf States, Australia, China, Egypt, Malawi, Spain, the United States, and the Soviet Union.

### Content of Preservice Teacher Education

What should be the balance between academic and professional studies? In light of the nearly universal preference for siting teacher education in universities, how can the tension be resolved between the university ideal of knowledge for the sake of pure scholarship and the professional use of knowledge for practical application?

This curriculum issue is the single most frequently reported problem among the twenty-one countries. Only one country, Malaysia, failed to mention it as a critical problem—critical because of the extreme difficulty in reconciling the need for scholarship and the need for practical knowledge in the education of teachers.

### Governance and Quality Control

To what extent should the jurisdiction of teacher education and quality control be the province of a central government rather than that of state or local administrations?

This basic issue of centralized versus decentralized control of teacher education is a burning problem fraught with political overtones, as reported in fourteen countries: the six Arab Gulf States, Australia, Brazil, Canada, China, England/ Wales, Germany, Japan, and Nigeria.

## Research

To what extent should research be undertaken to create new knowledge as against applying it for the development of policy?

Six countries—Australia, Brazil, Canada, Egypt, Malawi, and Malaysia—describe the uncertainty in deciding to what ends research in teacher education should be directed.

## Professionalism

To what extent can teacher education promote professionalism in the teaching profession in the face of society's treatment of teaching as a semiprofession because of, among other things, the lack of a strong knowledge base, limited autonomy to make professional decisions, and accountablity to superiors rather than to the profession?

Virtually every country cites this problem at least indirectly, while seven (Brazil, Egypt, Japan, Nigeria, Spain, the United States, and the Soviet Union) describe the issue at some length.

## Teacher Educators

To what extent should the activities of teacher educators reflect their connection with the higher education traditions of research and scholarship as against their responsibilities for preparing teachers to teach and inducting them into the profession?

Although many countries decry the ineffectiveness of some of the instruction provided in teacher preparation programs, two countries, Malawi and the United States, describe this issue as a major one.

## In-service Education

What priorities should be established for promoting the different types of in-service education, for example, induction of new teachers; courses for certification and promotion, upgrading professional knowledge, and upgrading the teaching speciality; programs based on individual teacher problems; programs for preparing teachers for school reform; correspondence and education television courses for rural teachers, and so on? To what extent should courses be optional or required, theory or practice oriented, planned by teachers or administrators, located in or out of schools?

Virtually every country lists this issue as a critical one to be resolved because of the difficulty of coordinating preservice and in-service education as well as providing a coherence to countless programs of differing types, organized by countless institutions, and aiming at a countless variety of goals.

### Development of Native, Indigenous Teacher Education

To what extent can countries, especially the former colonial nations, develop their own educational policies, practices, and institutions while modifying or eliminating unwanted foreign influence?

This issue is listed by thirteen countries, among them Canada which is concerned about undue U.S. influence, and Germany, uncertain about the results of unification. The other countries are the six Arab Gulf States, Brazil, China, Egypt, Malawi, Malaysia, and Nigeria.

## WORLDWIDE TRENDS IN TEACHER EDUCATION

The following common trends or themes have emerged from an analysis of the multination contributions to this volume.

With only a few exceptions, the preparation of teachers is being increasingly brought under the province of universities where future teachers are able to draw upon the full intellectual resources of higher education on a par with other professions. Qualifications for teaching are generally increasing throughout the world. The two most significant elements in this trend are the requirements for a university degree and practical experience in classroom teaching before certification. Also notable is a widespread trend toward requiring substantial school-based experience as part of the preservice teacher education program. This has inevitably necessitated the involvement of secondary and elementary school personnel in the preparation of teachers.

As access to education increases throughout most of the world, there is a growing recognition that the increased diversity of students' background and ability is making teaching a far more complex enterprise, with serious implications for teacher education. An increased emphasis on in-service education in a large number of countries has occurred for upgrading unqualified teachers already in service as well as for introducing new subject matter. This is a byproduct of the explosion of knowledge. In addition, many countries are introducing teacher education for teachers of preschool education, even though in many countries these institutions are privately supported.

The problem of recruiting, training, and retaining teachers of science, mathematics, computer science, and certain vocational subjects has become a worldwide problem, solutions to which are increasingly being sought through attempts to collaborate with industry and business. The uncritical acceptance of imported foreign models for teacher education is rapidly coming to an end as countries, especially the former colonies, are developing their own models embedded in local culture.

There is also a growing realization, especially in countries where financial constraints have been the most severe, that research in teacher education should become action-oriented and serve policy issues related to higher quality programs at greater cost effectiveness. Finally, a trend toward the use of innovative methods to upgrade the quality of untrained and undertrained teachers in remote rural areas is characteristic of a growing number of countries. Of particular note are the programs that utilize educational television, student correspondence, and radio.

## FUTURE PROSPECTS

In the future, more attention will likely be paid to the status of teachers and their professional education because of two trends that are operating simultaneously worldwide. At a time when teaching is becoming more complicated and more demanding, the competition from other professions is increasingly draining away promising talent, especially women. In order to decrease the sizable number of teacher candidates who typically drop out of teaching during the first year or two, many countries can be expected to establish carefully designed induction programs sponsored by both university and school.

It is uncertain whether the professional practice of teaching will gain the prestige of other professions. Although educational researchers have attempted with some success to identify a theoretical knowledge base for teaching, many still believe that teaching is conducted according to intuition, experience, and common-sense knowledge.

The development of special semiautonomous professional institutions may gradually come into existence. These would maintain strong links with universities and at the same time with school systems but avoid domination by either. In such institutions it would be theoretically possible to award professor-practitioners equal status as professor-theoreticians. In addition, the balance between research for the discovery of new knowledge could be carefully balanced against the need for action research, policy research, and evaluation of educational practice.

Finally, as the communication links and social contacts between countries of the world become stronger and stronger with each passing year, educators will likely recognize, more than ever, the value of learning from the experience of others. Research to accurately define the relevance of experience in other countries will be undertaken more frequently to make this sharing possible.

## REFERENCES

American Association of Colleges for Teacher Education. *Educating a Profession*. Washington, D.C.: The Association, 1985.

Beebe, C. E. *The Quality of Education in Developing Countries*. Cambridge, Mass.: Harvard University Press, 1966.

Braun, Joseph, ed. *Reforming Teacher Education: Issues and New Directions*. New York: Garland Publishing, 1989.

Butts, Freeman. "Teacher Education and Modernization." In George Bereday, ed., *Essays in World Education*. New York: Oxford University Press, 1969.

Cameron, J., et al., eds. *International Handbook of Educational Systems*. New York: John Wiley, 1983.

Cruikshank, Donald. *Models for the Preparation of America's Teachers*. Bloomington, Ind.: Phi Delta Kappa Educational Foundations, 1985.

Dunkin, M. J., ed. *The International Encyclopedia of Teaching and Teacher Education*. Oxford: Pergamon Press, 1987.

Goodings, Richard, et al., eds. *Changing Priorities in Teacher Education*. New York: Nichols Publishing Co., 1982.

Goodlad, John. *Teachers for Our Nation's Schools*. San Francisco: Jossey-Bass, 1990.

Gumbert, Edgar B., ed. *Fit to Teach: Teacher Education in International Perspective*, Atlanta: Georgia State University, 1990.

Haddad, Wadi. *Teacher Training: A Review of World Bank Experience*. Washington, D.C.: World Bank, 1985.

Houston, W. Robert, ed. *Handbook of Research on Teacher Education*. New York: Macmillan Publishing Co., 1990.

Howey, Kenneth R., and William Gardner, *The Education of Teachers*. New York: Longman, 1983.

Hoyle, Eric, and Jacquetta Megarry, eds. *Professional Development of Teachers: World Yearbook of Education 1980*. New York: Nichols Publishing Co., 1980.

Husen, Torsten, and T. Neville Postlewaite, eds. *The International Encyclopedia of Education*. New York: Pergamon Press, 1985.

Knowles, Asa, ed. *The International Encyclopedia of Higher Education*. New York: Jossey-Bass, 1977.

Lasley, Thomas, ed. *Issues in Teacher Education*, Vol II, Washington, D.C.: American Association of Colleges for Teacher Education, 1986.

Lomax, Donald, ed. *European Perspectives in Teacher Education*. New York: John Wiley Publishers, 1976.

Lynch, James, and David Plunkett. *Teacher Education and Cultural Change*. London: Allen and Unwin, 1973.

Postlewaite, Neville, ed. *Encyclopedia of Comparative Education and National Systems of Education*. New York: Pergamon Press, 1988.

Rust, Val, and Per Dalin. *Teachers and Teaching in the Developing World*. New York: Garland Publishing, 1990.

# Issues and
# Problems in Teacher
# Education

# 1

## ARAB GULF STATES

### TAHER RAZIK

The Arab Gulf States—Saudi Arabia, Qatar, Oman, Bahrain, Kuwait, and the United Arab Emirates—rest in the strategic geopolitical pivot of the Middle East. These nations border the Arabian Gulf and stand as sentinels to the crucial Gulf of Hormuz through which hundreds of oil tankers bearing the peninsula rich crude travel each day. This strategic location, as well as the rapid internal social development that is occurring in each of these states, is creating an increased need for effective educational systems. Furthermore, the rapidly changing economies of these nations, catalyzed by the massive development of natural resources during the last fifty years, feed the need for a highly skilled workforce that is concomitantly aligned with the social and religious values of the Arab leaders in these states. Therefore, the institutions charged with the education of teachers at all levels are being pressured by the leadership of the respective countries to provide effective teacher preparation that will serve as a vehicle for social change.

### ISSUES AND PROBLEMS

A myriad of complex challenges now face the educational planners in the Arab Gulf States. These planners must find expedient answers to the following questions if they hope to assist their respective nation's ministries in the development of their peoples.

### Issue 1: How Can an Adequate Number of Native-born Teachers Be Recruited and Retained in the Teacher Workforce?

This question evolves from the perplexing effects of a rapidly diversifying economy. Throughout the region, youth who have the opportunity to go to school are choosing to enter the high-paying occupations that have been generated by the exploding technology. In states where schools are agents of both change and of cultural and religious value transmission, the constant importation of foreign teachers has become costly. Furthermore, the higher the number of imported teachers, the higher the possibility of problems in the system arising as a result of cultural differences. With high-tech and business positions luring the best qualified candidates from postsecondary and college cohorts, the region is experiencing a ''brain-drain'' of its potential teacher resources. The states need native-born teachers who can easily enter classrooms without having to negotiate cultural and language differences. Natives of the states can also better identify the needs of native learners and more easily develop long-term educational plans that the ministries need as they face the pressures of the twenty-first century.

### Issue 2: How Can Students Be Educated to Meet the Specific Personnel Needs of the Region, in Both Science and High Tech and in Human Services?

The current workforce needs far exceed the supply of trained workers. This problem impinges on teacher education in both economic terms and in terms of teacher preparation. Without an adequate supply of trained teachers at all levels, students now flooding the schools in the region will not receive opportunities to learn enough content in the sciences or human services (teaching, health care, and social services) to serve in the changing societies. Teachers with minimal training in some areas are forced to be purveyors of highly technical curricula and, at the same time, to meet a human values agenda. The human values agenda is comprised of the cross-disciplinary concern for developing literate citizenries in the region. It is hoped that increased literacy will result in greater societal development leading to the eradication of poverty in the region. Literacy here refers both to the acquisition of skills and knowledge and the concomitant development of students' commitment to an overall responsible development of resources. This dilemma underpins recent changes in the teacher preparation programs in some of the states. Programs are evolving which require preservice teachers to master a specific subject area prior to teaching.

### Issue 3: How Can Teachers Be Prepared to Adapt to the Learners' Needs in the Constantly Changing Socioeconomic Milieu That Affects Their Classrooms?

Since the educational systems in this region are still young, teachers, with few exceptions, are not yet formally trained to evaluate and modify their work

to meet the changing needs of their students. The development of natural resources in the area has altered the societies tremendously. In countries where
people have lived for generations as witnesses to sequential social and economic
change, adjustment to the type of changes that technology has wrought has been
difficult. Teachers need to be versatile as they address the changes in society.
Developing preparatory programs that balance strong subject content with courses
in pedagogical skills has been difficult because of the constant impact of social
and technological change.

The rapid application of technology has necessitated adding special courses
in some teacher preparation programs. These courses, however, have been largely
offered in universities responsible for educating students in the scientific professions. Thus, the teachers benefiting from these courses are largely those associated with higher education. Teachers in most of the states' public systems
struggle with the dilemma of providing technological literacy in many of the
same ways that American teachers do today. Faced with a limited supply of
computer hardware, they attempt to acquaint students with use of the computer
as a small step in providing them with technological awareness. The macro-
impact of technology is economic in these countries. Consequently, greater
urbanization is occurring, and mass communication systems are being developed.
No single impact of technology is earmarked for specific content in teacher
preparation programs. Instead, in a variety of ways, the Gulf State governments
provide staff development programs for teachers in the hope of addressing issues
that arise in conditions of rapid change.

### Issue 4: How Can Teachers Be Prepared to Assume Differential Staffing Roles that Are Crucial to the Ongoing Development of Schools in the Region?

As the number of schools grows in this region and as the economy diversifies
and creates new personnel needs, teachers need to be prepared to assume roles
in differentially staffed situations. Some of the countries are using systems
planning models for education. These models require continuous feedback and
evaluation of all aspects of schooling. Because of the labor shortage, teachers
are asked to participate in these processes, and they require training to do so
effectively. Teachers in the twenty-first century will be required to assume roles
of curriculum planners, school administrators, and supervisors as the bureaucratic
nature of the systems grows.

### Issue 5: How Can Teacher Education Best Capitalize on the Talents of Women Who Are Just Beginning to Enter the Public Workplace?

During the past decade many women in most of the Arab Gulf States have
begun to enter the public workplace as teachers. Since teaching is one of the
few acceptable positions for women to assume, it has given them the opportunity

to leave their homebound lives en masse. Although females still account for only 40 percent of the total in-school population in the region today, it is estimated that they will account for over 50 percent of the teacher workforce by 1995. These women are highly qualified academic candidates; as of 1990 female students across the region were scoring higher in all areas of study than their male counterparts. This fact and the social structures that bar women from seeking other types of employment in business, industry, or high tech can be the key to improving both the quality and the quantity of the teacher workforce. Ironically, special analysis of this predicament and careful planning which results in giving women equal access to teacher education programs with strong content in curriculum and methodology could be the answer to the personnel shortage in many fields. Paradoxically, in a region where women have culturally held the inferior public position, they may hold the power to serve as change agents.

### Issue 6: How Can Teacher Education Contribute to the Specific Human Development Interests of Each Nation?

The Gulf Cooperation Council (GCC), a cooperative organization consisting of Saudi Arabia, Qatar, Oman, Bahrain, Kuwait, and the United Arab Emirates, has called for the total development of their people as a means of further developing resources, the revenues of which should guarantee a dignified standard of living for all. Without a diversified cadre of teachers, the goals of the GCC cannot possibly be met. Resources are available for building schools and procuring materials and importing teachers. Since importing teachers from neighboring countries is not a favorable practice from the economic and cultural viewpoint, the states are attempting to funnel resources toward the development of a native corps of teachers. By building this native corps, the states hope to give more permanence and overall effectiveness to their planning. However, since education is labor-intensive, a native supply of teachers is essential. If teacher education programs are developed in light of the national goals for development and if adequate rewards and status are a part of those programs, greater human development may have a chance of occurring. This concern for educational development stems from the reaction against the restrictions foreign colonial governments placed on education in the past. Now, as these nations initiate their own course of development, they are seeking to provide general education for all. Since rapid urbanization is underway and isolation is still occurring in rural areas, systems developed several years ago to prepare teachers have become obsolete. Therefore, national educational agendas are being realigned to give preservice teachers an opportunity to develop a wider range of skills and perspective on their mission. For the region as a whole just barely over 50 percent of the eligible school-aged children are now enrolled in schools (Unesco, 1981). With thousands of students still isolated from schooling and rapid change occurring which is altering schooling conditions, the preparation of teachers has been targeted as a key to providing ongoing development efforts.

For example, adult illiteracy has been a major problem in the region which needs a skilled labor force. Teachers are being prepared to adjust their methodologies to child and adult learners who occupy their classrooms.

### Issue 7: Where Does Teacher Education Fit in the Scheme of Higher Education?

Each of the Arab Gulf States has at least one university; Saudi Arabia now has seven universities. Several of the states have systems of universities and colleges that have grown up since World War II. In some states teacher education has fallen under university planning and supervision. In most states the ministries of education have been responsible for formulating programs to respond to immediate workforce and development needs. As the states' educational systems grow and as more skilled teachers are required, teacher education may most legitimately be housed in higher education. Higher education in the region has been more concerned about providing programs for training in the money-producing sectors of business, industry, science, and technology. Realizing the magnitude of the nations' educational needs has in some cases forced the university and college systems to incorporate schools for teacher training. There is an acute personnel shortage in higher education, however, and the wide disparity in the economic development among the states may be directly related to the number of graduates produced within a given state and the number of degreed professors serving in the respective state's higher education system. The state of higher education may still be too fragile to accommodate a strong focus on education.

## A CONTEXT FOR UNDERSTANDING THESE ISSUES

These questions can be best understood initially by placing them within the understanding of the history of teacher education within the region as a whole. Teacher education in this part of the Arabian peninsula has developed slowly during the last three or four decades. No models for teacher preparation were unilaterally developed owing to the foreign domination and underdeveloped economies of these countries prior to World War II. Since a relatively small number of schools existed in the region forty years ago, teachers were drawn from the foreign teacher ranks of Egypt, Jordan, Sudan, Tunisia, Morocco, and Iraq. Until the last twenty years, in fact, very few teachers were professionally educated in the Arab Gulf States. Most educational resources were devoted to developing training programs for the other occupations connected with the production and export of oil. Political and business leaders in these states were largely sent abroad to Egypt, Europe, or America to study. However, as the states' participation in the international market increased and as they recognized the incredible power that the magnitude of their oil resources gave them, they became aware of the crucial need for native-born personnel. This recognition was not tied to mere business maneuvers or economic necessity; rather, it co-incided with the governments' belief that the development of the natural resources could only be justified and stabilized by the full development of human resources. Therefore, the states gradually began to design comprehensive educational programs aimed at the total eradication of illiteracy and the creation of strong elementary, secondary and postsecondary school systems.

The practical problems of developing these initial comprehensive systems were complex. At varying degrees and at varying times during the last forty years, the states were preparing to extend public education to huge numbers of students who had no family history of schooling. The result was obviously a large increase in the number of students and the simultaneously critical shortage of teachers for those students. Originally, the states designed teacher training programs to prepare teachers for immediate entry into the elementary classroom. Young students who had successfully completed preparatory school (junior high school) were recruited into teacher training institutes. Here, the preservice teacher was provided with three years of instruction covering issues of curriculum and pedagogy.

Secondary teachers have traditionally been trained in colleges of education at the university level. Originally, teacher training institutes were created in Kuwait, Saudi Arabia, and Oman to train elementary teachers. Students who had completed preparatory school attended the institute for three years and then were allowed to teach at the elementary level in these countries. Secondary school graduates, who had concentrated on education courses in their secondary education, could attend the teacher training institute for one year and then enter elementary teaching positions. This plan was practical; the teacher training institutes prepared a number of native teachers for the initial influx of students into elementary schools. Now, intermediate colleges with two-year teacher training programs have grown from the early teacher training institutes. These intermediate colleges exist in most of the Arab Gulf States to provide training for elementary level teachers.

The intermediate colleges offer specialized educational coursework and field experience to teaching candidates. The curriculum of the intermediate college programs centers on developing teachers' skills to accommodate the changing conditions in their societies. As the school systems have matured, so, too, has the teacher preparation system in the GCC. In the GCC today, a varied mix of teacher training institutes, intermediate teachers' colleges, and four-year college programs are now functioning as vehicles for teacher preparation.

Nevertheless, in spite of an increased number of preparation programs, the demand for teachers still far exceeds the supply. In 1990 the states collectively estimate that only 50 percent of the elementary teachers, 35 percent of the preparatory teachers, and 25 percent of the secondary teachers are native-born. Across the states, ministries of education are seeking to recruit teachers by offering financial and scholarship incentives. In the face of rapidly diversifying economies with an ample supply of high-paying jobs in business and industry, these ministries are concerned that the current teacher recruits are not high academic achievers. The ministries fear that if this continues as a trend, education will suffer directly from the brain-drain and the development of the states' people and natural resources will similarly weaken. One factor that is easing the teacher shortage in this region is the increased number of women entering the profession.

While each of the Arab Gulf States has developed its own comprehensive educational system geared to meet the generic demands of the respective nation, there are many commonalities in these systems. Teachers currently prepared in one state can easily find work in another. Each of the states has paired a quasi-religious educational mission rooted in the Muslim faith: to develop the individual person with dignity as the key to developing state policy which safeguards civil rights, with the secular mission of educating citizens in areas of literacy, technical skill, and professional expertise that both domestic and international political economies demand.

The demands put on these systems during the past fifteen years specifically have multiplied exponentially, since the world market demand for petroleum products has grown and since the Middle East has been torn by political warfare.

Ironically, the same wealth, oil, which makes these Arab Gulf States place in the wealthiest third of the twenty-one-nation Arab League, intensifies the need for rapid development of the human resources in the region. This fact was publicly and formally recognized when Saudi Arabia, Qatar, Kuwait, Bahrain, the United Arab Emirates, and Oman joined in the agreement to form the Gulf Cooperation Council in 1981. This council was originally set up to ally the states in an agreement to cooperate in a wide variety of issues including defense, security, business, environmental protection, human development, education, industry, agriculture, foreign trade, arts and culture, science and technology, commerce, communication, tourism, and legislation. During the past nine years the council has strengthened the ties of cooperation among the states and has been the major catalyst for the promotion of common systems in each of the fields of concern. In education this has meant setting up joint efforts for planning and implementation of programs both to teach more of the region's children and adults and to teach teachers. The GCC has a vested interest in the training of teachers; its identity, which is strongly tied to the development of the Arab world, relies on a native teaching force that can express the dual mission. Therefore, cooperative ventures in education receive widespread concern and support of the council.

Previous economic and social structures and the unique history of each of these states have compounded the development of social and educational service delivery systems whose growth can keep pace with the growth in the diversified economy. Societies that have dealt with change previously as a slow, sequential process could afford to take their time to build schools and develop teacher training systems almost as an afterthought to progress. Now, with the immediacy of change, the states must quickly build systems that will both ease the teacher shortage and provide quality education for all.

While all the above information provides a frame for the picture of teacher education in the GCC, we would be remiss not to reveal some of the specific trends in the respective states. The same issues impinge on teacher education throughout the region; however, each state has addressed those issues in different ways according to the direction of leadership and economic resources. The brief "verbal snapshots" below provide a more fine-grained description of some of the individual state's predicaments.

## GENERAL BACKGROUND

### Saudi Arabia

The Kingdom of Saudi Arabia occupies four-fifths of the Arabian Peninsula. It is the motherland of Islam and the homeland to a population of 8.2 million. Long recognized for its tremendous reserves of oil and natural gas, Saudi Arabia has enjoyed a wealthy, stable share of the international market. This stability is accounted for by the strong monolithic value system that permeates the Saudi society and by the fact that among the Arab Gulf States Saudi Arabia was the first to receive the influx of foreign teachers during the decade immediately following World War II. However, as the industry becomes more complex, the state, like its neighbors to the east—Bahrain, Oman, Qatar, and the United Arab Emirates—faces a critical personnel shortage in scientific and technical fields. Under a new five-year development plan, the state is projecting a diversified economy that will even press the shortage to a more critical point. By the year 2000 Saudi planners estimate that the size of their student population will have multiplied by eight times its size in 1980 (Unesco, 1981). This enrollment will require an eightfold increase in the number of teachers.

While public education is available to all in Saudi Arabia, at all schooling levels, deeply rooted religious and social structures have constricted the total growth of an education system that is efficient. Saudis abide by the practice of separation of the sexes in schools and at the workplace. Therefore, girls and boys are educated separately. Girls who aspire to become teachers must attend teacher training institutes, colleges, or universities that are open to girls only. Subsequently, they may only teach in all-girls' schools. Should a specific teacher shortage arise in a boys' or girls' school, teaching by a member of the opposite sex is provided via videotape. Without changing this structure, the Saudi Arabian Ministry of Education may face a more difficult challenge than the other area states in providing an adequate supply of teachers. While a separate Directorate of Education of Girls and Women exists within the Ministry of Education, the historical tradition of allocating more resources to male education still occurs. With the regional trend indicating that more women are attempting to become teachers as a means of breaking away from their homebound lifestyles, the Saudi Arabian system is somewhat archaic. As the need for a more highly skilled workforce spirals, this state may continue to rely heavily on expatriates from other Arab countries as its teachers.

In a nation that has the highest projected increase in gross national product (GNP) of all the twenty-one states in the Arab League, it is ironic that the education and teacher education systems are still ensnared in the religious tradition. Teacher education here requires that candidates be loyal to this separate-but-equal philosophy. As reported above, the regional achievement scores indicate that women are surpassing men academically at all levels. If the Saudi Arabian system remains as it is—and there is little reason to believe that it will change given the strict adherence within the nation to conservative Islamic practice—this state may be missing its chance to capitalize on the willingness of women to become a crucial ingredient in the efforts to eradicate illiteracy and serve in skilled labor-shortage areas.

## Kuwait

The second state to establish schools for teacher education was Kuwait which began seriously to develop oil resources in the early 1950s. Prior to the Iraqi invasion of Kuwait in 1990, these resources had been dedicated to increased development of public education and human services. Because of this emphasis and because of careful planning, Kuwait enjoyed a literacy rate of over 50 percent. While this figure may seem low by American standards, it is outstanding in a region where half of the twenty-one Arab League nations have literacy rates below 25 percent (World Bank, 1981).

The size of Kuwait's pre-war population, 1.9 million, also enabled its Ministry of Education to plan education systems carefully. Kuwait had long been a center for international industry and banking. Hence, it had required a highly skilled labor force. Prior to the invasion, the Kuwaiti population figures included at least 1 million non-Kuwaiti people who had emigrated to the area for work. Teacher education programs were a part of colleges supported by the government. There are still many unemployed, illiterate Kuwaitis who require literacy education. However, this is not the focus of teacher training programs. Kuwait's teachers are trained largely to continue upward mobility of students now enrolled in the school system. Prior to the invasion, Kuwait had a strong, progressive educational system. This organization and structure is now being activated as Kuwait rebuilds for an independent future.

## Bahrain

The second state in the Gulf Cooperation Council which enjoys a high literacy rate is Bahrain. Its small population of 400,280 includes approximately 145,000 non-Bahrainians who have come to work in the most diversified of the economies on the peninsula. The state is actually located on an archipelago of islands in the Arabic Sea where a wide variety of industries have been developed to reduce the total dependence on oil. The Bahrainian Ministry of Education carefully planned for teacher preparation in the early 1960s. The earliest program for teacher education required candidates to study for two years in a postpreparatory or secondary teaching institute; these teachers were then sent to teach in elementary and secondary schools. In 1978, however, the Ministry responded to the government's plan for diversified development by instituting new programs of preparation that require all teachers to have a minimum of a bachelor's degree prior to teaching. This new requirement coincided with the creation of a college of education at the University of Bahrain. This college is devoted to training teachers for different levels of professional service, training supervisors for teachers, and providing staff development resources for the ongoing training and retraining of teachers so that they can meet the classroom and marketplace demands of the diversifying economy. The college program is holistic and specialized; students learn the rudiments of pedagogy and also major in a content area that they will teach in public school.

By raising the requirements for teachers, the Bahrainian Ministry of Education is hoping to professionalize teaching and make it an attractive career choice for its youth who are easily attracted to the high-paying jobs readily available in industry and business in this state. The college of education also provides advanced training for teachers beyond the bachelor's degree level. These raised standards have also served to attract more young women into higher education in Bahrain. The procurement of a B.A. and the availability of teaching jobs enable women to move out of their homebound lives and into the mainstream of the workplace. Since Bahrain cannot yet afford to provide free access to higher education to all its citizens, the competition for placements in the college of education is strong and currently guarantees a quality supply of teachers. The country's educational resources are still largely spent on the provision of free public schooling for elementary and secondary students. While foreign-born teachers continue to serve across these levels, the university's move should lead to higher recruitment of teaching candidates.

### Qatar and the United Arab Emirates

Qatar and the United Arab Emirates share a similar system of education and teacher education. Both states can provide free public education at all levels to all their citizens. However, this is being done at a heavy cost of transporting foreign teachers from other Arab and non-Arab countries to these two states. The United Arab Emirates has a population of 1.9 million; Qatar has a small population of 200,000. Recent studies at universities in both states indicate that a decreasing number of students are opting to assume teaching careers. This is creating a special shortage of male teachers, who still largely assume administrative roles in schools throughout the Arab region. Again, women are enrolling in teacher training institutes and colleges, and then entering the classroom as a means of gaining some social mobility. Teachers in both states do not enjoy the status that comes from high-paying jobs that abound in the countries. The faculty of education of the University of Qatar specifically reported in 1979 that the teacher education programs were not drawing the type of candidates desired owing to a lack of monetary rewards following college study (Razik, 1986). Yet, here, too, an increase in the number of women in the profession could change that conclusion by the year 2000. It remains to be seen what effect the enrollment of more women in teacher education programs at the college level in these two countries will have on the programs in general.

## Oman

The most recently developed program for education and teacher education in the GCC occurred in the Sultanate of Oman. Since this nation's story is both intriguing and significant as a case for modeling planning for the GCC, more explanation will be given here. Oman rests on the far eastern shore of the peninsula, where the Arabic Sea meets the Gulf of Hormuz. It occupies the second largest land mass in the GCC and has an estimated population of 1.5 million. Whereas other GCC members experienced significant social, political, and economic changes during the past several decades, Oman was virtually in what Omanis call the "dark ages" (Phillips, 1977). The current sultan, Qaboos bin Said, came into power in 1970 after a coup that exiled his father. When Sultan Qaboos came to power, the nation was extremely underdeveloped. Many Omani people lived as their ancestors had done for centuries as desert nomads, subsistence farmers or fishermen, or worked as laborers in the other Gulf States. In 1970 no more than three schools existed, having 909 students and a teaching staff of 30 (Razik, 1984). These three schools served primary education and were located in the urban center, Muscat. Basically, no education system was in place. In earlier eras, ruling families had sent their children abroad to be schooled. The advent of Sultan Qaboos as a well-educated leader with a vision for human and natural resource development in 1970 has changed this scenario drastically. Through his leadership a Ministry of Education was established in 1970 to begin a series of five-year plans for the development of schools and, concurrently, teacher preparation programs. At that point the sultan stated that education is the foundation of a brighter future for children and the country; it is also the means of helping older people come to terms with the rapid changes which development will bring (Hawley, 1979). This vision has been translated into a philosophy that guides the Ministry of Education and that is dominated by a strong Islamic faith. The five tenets of this philosophy are the beliefs (1) that education is a universal right of all people; (2) that education should develop the individual's unique potential; (3) that education should be constructed as a vehicle for supplying the necessary national workforce; (4) that education can help the individual recognize his own human rights, respect the rights of others, and safeguard the rights of the Arab nations; and finally, (5) that students need to learn positive ways to spend their lifetime and energies for their own development and for the progress of their fellows. The Ministry of Education accepts this philosophy as a guiding worldview in their planning for all levels of schooling. Since they hope to operationalize this vision in their schools, they build teacher education programs on the same vision.

Vision and philosophy notwithstanding, the Omani ministry faced a phenomenal task in 1970. Virtually, they were building their educational system with no historical basis. While this made early communication about the value of education difficult, it also provided an exciting opportunity to mold the system as deliberately as possible in light of manifold barriers. The first five-year plan addressed the development of primary and secondary schools and centers for adult literacy study. The second five-year plan (1980) addressed the quality of educational facilities and programs, diversification of secondary programs, balancing educational opportunities in spite of geographical barriers, and planning for a higher education system. Within the first five years 176 schools were opened; by 1985 there were a total of 588 schools with an enrollment of 235,000 students. In the 1989–1990 school year, there were 759 schools enrolling 327,131 students (Ministry of Education, 1990). In a nation where very few people had ever attended school, these numbers are remarkable especially given the underdeveloped conditions of the country manifest in a lack of roads, communication networks, hospitals, and social services. When education was touted as a means of achieving an improved quality of life for the individual and the nation, a hunger to learn swept throughout Oman. Citizens built some of their own schools, using the thatched reeds and rudimentary resources of their native districts if the government could not immediately supply building resources. Some early schools were a configuration of canvas tents that provided shelter for teachers and their large classes of new students. The sultan's strong support for schools as a means of developing and safeguarding the dignity of his individual citizens, and the further development of the nation as a prosperous and peaceful power in the GCC, drew hundreds of Omani parents to enroll their children in schools. Adults, too, have enrolled in adult learning centers with programs for vocational training and illiteracy eradication. Clearly, through the sultan's leadership, education in Oman was earmarked and maintained as a national priority.

What was occurring in terms of Omani teacher education at this time? Many teachers in Oman were expatriates again from other Arab and non-Arab nations. The teacher count in the nation for 1989–1990 was 14,113, of which only 3,390 were Omani. To supplement these ranks the Ministry of Education built two-year teaching institute programs that allowed those students who had completed junior high school to take a three-year training course and then teach at the primary level. By the early 1980s the ministry had developed a variety of secondary school concentrations that included teacher training. These concentrations were geared to prepare students to meet the personnel needs of the expansive development occurring in the country. In 1984–1985 new intermediate teachers' colleges, like those in other GCC states, were established to develop educational professionals. The focus of the Omani institutes is to train teachers who can give stronger subject area courses in primary education. Since many primary students were not originally meeting the requirements of the new school programs, training specifically for primary programs is deemed essential for student retention in schools. In addition, teacher training institutes, like those previously described, recruit preparatory and secondary graduates and prepare them for elementary teaching roles. As of 1989, the Omani intermediate teachers' colleges require two-year programs of study for secondary school graduates who wish to teach in the elementary public system. These teachers' colleges are providing stronger academic and pedagogical preparation for candidates. Secondary teachers are required to have a bachelor's degree from a college or university prior to teaching. While this results in a flow of young teachers into the system who may not be fully ready to teach, it does insure that some native personnel with some teaching preparation are in the field to meet the drastically increased numbers of students. By the year 2000 the number of students in the Omani public system will have grown by 170 percent of what it is today (World Bank, 1981). This translates to a 170 percent increase in the number of teachers needed, too. By strengthening the preparation program at the intermediate college level and by encouraging a positive image of teaching as a profession at the secondary school level, the Ministry of Education hopes to increase the numbers of native Omani teachers.

In 1986, just sixteen years after the end of the Omani dark ages, the Sultan Qaboos University was opened to meet the nation's need for a center of higher education. The university includes a faculty of education dedicated to planning for the needs of preparatory and secondary schools. This university is constantly grappling with the national personnel shortage issues and has focused its resources on providing strong technical, health, and scientific programs. In the meantime teacher preparation on the primary level is managed by the Ministry of Education which is able to provide leadership in planning school programs. The ministry also capitalizes on the resources provided through contracted international consultants who provide expertise in educational planning.

The Oman case is significant because it represents an intensified situation embodying all the issues mentioned previously. The sultan's leadership and his plans for developing Omani human potential has manifested itself in equal opportunities for all in education. Males and females are taught and given equal access to the university. The government will find the financial means to support any capable secondary graduate's desire to attend the university. However, the university can only accommodate students who score in the top 15 percent of their national class. This results in a highly qualified pool of university students; the first class of two hundred students of the college of education graduated in 1990. These graduates assumed teaching positions in preparatory and secondary schools. With a continued graduating enrollment of this or a larger size, the ministry is assured of a steady influx of university-trained educators in the future. The intermediate teachers' colleges are now expanding; by 1995 the ministry plans to have a total of eighteen of these colleges—nine for men and nine for women—to train local teachers. These colleges are now being established in the nine educational districts in order to provide more access for nonurban candidates.

The Ministry of Education in Oman is also providing teacher training courses to those college graduates who choose teaching careers in secondary school but who have not taken education courses as a part of their bachelor's degree programs. This in-service training in curriculum delivery and classroom management complements the college graduates' preparation in the subject areas. The in-service training also provides a vehicle for fielding an increased number of college graduates with potential for teaching careers. By keeping the training of teachers housed in these intermediate colleges, the focus of the university education college has been on research and development of the national system of schools. The intermediate teachers' colleges can realign their curricula to meet the needs of specific urban and rural situations in a more direct manner than the university faculty can do at this point. Oman has streamlined its teacher training in order to get native teachers into the schools; like the region as a whole, by the year 2000 more than 50 percent of the teachers will be women. This is particularly significant in this country which had adhered to strict, religiously defined sex roles prior to the sultan's assumption of power in 1970. Therefore, women are entering the workforce both as a result of social changes and as role models for other women. As teachers share a new role, women may very well be agents of change to a greater degree in the future of this country. Currently, the intermediate teachers' colleges do not specifically address any issues about women in the workforce; the expectations for men and women are the same. Yet, the influx and presence of women in the system at a time when more men are leaving teaching to pursue more financially lucrative positions in the market will undoubtedly color the nature of education and teacher education in the next decades.

In conclusion, the development of education in Oman is an intriguing case study of a developing nation whose natural and human resources are inextricably linked.

**CONCLUSION**

Educational planning is at a critical point in the Arab Gulf States. Great strides have been made in terms of the overall development of the public education system. However, the progress is always shadowed by the awareness that the systems in place are still not reaching the total educable population, nor are they totally eradicating illiteracy in the GCC states. The efforts of the GCC are outstanding, however, because they represent the leaders' attempts to put their religious faith and philosophical concern for the development of people at the forefront of their economic plans. It is wise to recognize that the two types of development are inseparable and that maintaining the peace of this specific region will depend on a symbiosis of the two undertakings.

In order to project a greater emphasis on the value of education in the region, the Arab Thought Forum—an intellectual organization and a nongovernmental cooperative venture in the Arab nations—convened in Jordan in March 1990 to produce an action plan for educational development in the Arab world. This document, now in its final revision and already endorsed by all Arab nations, is called "The Education of Arab Nations in the 21st Century: Catastrophe or Hope?" The document urges a unified effort to develop public education for children in grades K–12. It calls for establishing educational systems that are built around curricula designed to develop the whole person intellectually, socially, emotionally, and spiritually. It also calls for the infusion of values of national citizenship and regional loyalty and adherence to Islamic practices of respect for the individual. This document recognizes the strategic role of education as a vehicle for improving the quality of life of the peoples in the region and for strengthening the mission of peaceful development of the Arab community. The document may catalyze the same type of proactive debate in the Arab region as the American document, *A Nation at Risk*, did in the United States during the 1980s. The members of the Arab nations see the document as a means of centering education on the development of the whole person. Thus teacher education programs must be developed with a similar focus.

Interestingly, the GCC states face some problems today in teacher education which are similar to problems in American teacher education. There are no foolproof research paradigms that can be operationalized into teacher education programs in the various GCC states. The sheer size of the teacher preparation enterprise, pressured by the diverse, critical personnel needs, has required educational planners to base their proposals on the "best fit" of several teacher education models to the changing societies. The GCC states do not have the luxury of debating which models for teacher preparation are most effective. Instead, teacher educators hope to instill a commitment to teaching as a lifelong career, a belief that teaching in a rapidly changing society requires lifelong learning on the part of the teacher, a self-belief that gives teaching status on an individual level, in societies where high-status, high-money opportunities are now widespread, and a belief that teacher education is based on a legitimate academic knowledge base.

Thus far, research in education in the GCC has centered primarily on sociological issues. For example, GCC ministries of education have commissioned studies concerning who is coming to certain schools and why, or concerning trends and personnel correlations. School effectiveness is now a concern being woven into teacher preparation programs. Hence, the creation of the intermediate teachers' colleges has allowed the ministries of education to provide candidates with more teaching skills aimed at improving student performance.

A style of futures research will be an important tool that the GCC will continue to employ in teacher education planning. This style of research combines quantitative and qualitative analyses in order to monitor the systemic issues as educational systems grow in a developing nation. Because of the centralized ministries in each country, and the limited bureaucracy (i.e., a national versus a local system), the long-range planning can be more easily implemented. However, the long-range plans must constantly bend to the impact of social change. By increasing high-quality systemic analyses of the public education systems in the GCC and the allied teacher education systems, the increase in quality matches between the content of teacher education programs and the ever-changing field of practice may occur.

Teacher education at the university level in the GCC will continue to feel the pressure of attempts to balance the personnel needs of other higher education disciplines with those in education.

In spite of all the challenges that confront the creators of teacher education in the GCC states, the future looks promising given the strong political and economic support for education in general. With the continued commitment of groups like the Arab Thought Forum and the GCC itself, education will progress. This region's commitment to planned human development may offer the world a few new models of teacher education in the coming decades.

## REFERENCES

Development Council. *Second Five-Year Development Plan*. Muscat: Sultanate of Oman, 1980.

Hawley, D. *Oman and Its Renaissance*. London: Stacey International, 1979.

Ministry of Education and Youth. *Statistical Yearbook 1989–1990*. Muscat: Sultanate of Oman, 1990.

Phillips, W. *Unknown Oman*. London: Longman Press, 1977.

Razik, T. "Innovations in Teacher Training in the Arab Gulf States." Washington, D.C.: International Council on Education for Teaching, June 1986.

Razik, T. *The Internal Efficiency of the Omani Educational System: A Study of Educational Wastage,* Muscat: Sultanate of Oman, Ministry of Education and Youth. 1984.

Unesco *Worldbook*, Paris, 1981.

World Bank. *World Bank Development Report*, Washington, D.C.: 1981.

# 2

# AUSTRALIA

## R. D. TRAILL

This chapter provides the reader with a viewpoint on the issues that confront teacher educators in Australia, together with a comment on how these issues are being addressed. The early sections of this chapter are devoted to outlining the overall system of education that has developed in this country and the influence it has on the education of teachers for and within that system. The historical background and traditions have also helped shape current issues and practices in current Australian teacher education. These influences are discussed briefly.

Seven major issues confront teacher educators in Australia.

*How should teacher education be structured?* Should preservice teacher education be made available at undergraduate, graduate, or both levels? Closely linked with this issue is that concerning the length of training: a concerted move has been made to restrict early childhood and primary (elementary) programs to a three-year undergraduate degree. Does this provide adequate time for such teachers to develop a grasp of the content they will teach, an appropriate background in curriculum and instruction and in education studies, and sufficient supervised practicum experiences?

*How should the entrants to teacher education be selected?* Do teacher education programs effectively monitor the entry qualifications of their new students? Currently, academic achievements at the end of secondary school education are used as the main filter. Should other characteristics and qualities be required of those seeking a career in teaching? Which selection procedures can best accommodate such criteria?

*Is it feasible to establish national standards for teacher registration?* Is it feasible to have a common set of registration standards for teachers which cover the requirements of all the separate state education systems within Australia?

What role does the accreditation of teacher education programs play in any effort to standardize such requirements?

*What is a desirable balance for teacher education programs between academic and education areas?* Within programs of teacher education what balance should be established between the competing demands of background studies in the disciplines to be taught, education and curriculum studies, and the practicum?

*How might societal needs be reflected within teacher education programs?* How can the needs of the community be acknowledged within programs preparing teachers to work in schools? How inclusive can the curriculum of teacher education become? What are some of the significant indicators in Australia of such societal needs?

*How can the articulation of pre- and in-service education be best achieved?* What mechanisms can be developed to link pre- and in-service teacher education in order to create a continuum of such professional development? How can institutions of higher education play a role?

*Is research changing the directions of Australian teacher education?*

These seven issues provide an overview of major concerns at the forefront of debate in Australia on teacher education. They are discussed in further detail later in this chapter, together with a projection of some emerging issues that will likely be of concern in later years. What is the setting for such issues?

## GENERAL BACKGROUND

Australia was first settled some 40,000 years ago through migration from Asia, thus forming the basis of the country's indigenous population. In 1788 European settlement commenced when Great Britain took possession of the country with the principal intention of using it as a penal colony. Since that time, the population has grown to 16,531,929 (June 1988 census), with the indigenous population totaling 227,645, or approximately 1.5 percent of the total population.

In the 1800s Australia developed as a series of separate colonies, but in 1901 these federated to form the Commonwealth of Australia. There are now seven states—New South Wales, Victoria, Queensland, South Australia, West Australia, Northern Territory, and Tasmania—and most Commonwealth activities are located in the city of Canberra within the Australian Capital Territory. In this federal government structure, powers are distributed between the Commonwealth and the state governments; for the purposes of this country study education is identified as a state power. However, because of its financial powers the Commonwealth government does play an active role in education, for example, it makes special grants to the states for specific educational purposes.

## THE EDUCATIONAL SYSTEM

### Areas of Responsibility

The separate states and the Australian Capital Territory each have their own administrative structure for education. In addition, there is a significant non-government school sector, the schools of which largely operate within the same curriculum and examination frameworks as the government school systems. Technical and further education is almost wholly provided by government. Tertiary education is now funded by the Commonwealth government, and public schools and technical and further education facilities are funded by state governments with financial support from the Commonwealth. Nongovernment schools are subsidized by both state and Commonwealth governments. Universities and other tertiary institutions are controlled by individual councils and have a substantial degree of independence.

Local government agencies play no part in educational administration and have no formal role in decision-making processes. Community involvement has generally been through parent groups that have played a large part in supplementary fund raising for individual schools as well as influencing policy at state and national levels. More recently, this involvement has also been through school boards where parents and teachers participate in making a range of policy decisions on school matters.

As stated previously, in constitutional terms education is primarily a responsibility of the states. Nevertheless, the Commonwealth government provides financial assistance to education in the states and has a direct constitutional responsibility for financial assistance to students, for funding research, and for providing education in the Commonwealth territories. The Commonwealth also conducts educational activities incidental to its responsibilities in areas such as defense, health, immigration, and social services. In fact, the Commonwealth government has become significantly involved in funding all aspects of education and, as a consequence, in influencing national education priorities.

### The Size of the System

In July 1987 there were 10,079 schools operating in Australia; of these, 7,575 were government schools and 2,504 were nongovernment schools. The number of full-time students attending these schools in July 1987 totaled 3,004,883, comprising 2,196,742 in government schools and 808,141 in the nongovernment school sector. The number of teaching staff at government and nongovernment schools in July 1987 comprised 184,731 full-time and 26,759 part-time staff.

The retention rate of secondary school students to Year 12 was 49 percent in 1986. Approximately 20 percent proceed to postsecondary studies. Until 1988 this schooling was provided through three main types of institutions: universities, colleges of advanced education, and colleges of technical and further education.

However, in the latter part of 1988 the Commonwealth government tabled a white paper that signified the merger of universities and colleges of advanced education into a unified system. At the time of writing, these mergers are taking place throughout the Australian higher education system.

## THE SYSTEM OF TEACHER EDUCATION

### Early History

In order to fully comprehend the present-day teacher education program in Australia, it is necessary to describe how the preparation of teachers has developed from the time of the early European settlement of the country at the end of the eighteenth century. The first teachers in Australia migrated from the United Kingdom or assumed the task of teaching the colony's children on the basis of a previous position that required them to possess knowledge of basic skills in reading, arithmetic, and the like. Such teachers, apart from being poorly trained (if indeed "trained" at all), were poorly paid and generally held in fairly low esteem by the early colonists.

The first efforts to introduce a form of teacher training in Australia were made when teachers newly arrived from the United Kingdom introduced the monitorial system into local schools. This system involved the instruction of very large groups of children (sometimes in parts of England these groups had numbered in the hundreds) by one teacher who was assisted by a number of trainee teachers, or monitors, as they were then known. This system was gradually replaced by a movement away from mass instruction through teaching with the assistance of monitors, to a pupil-teacher system. Here, the teacher was assisted by his or her better pupils who in turn received lessons from the teacher, both before and after school, on how to teach. The pupil-assistants sat for examinations each year, and if they were able to pass them, went to a teacher training institution. After a brief time at such a center, and further examinations, they duly qualified as assistant teachers. Other pupil-assistants were not so fortunate: places in training centers were limited, and many pupil-assistants, after withstanding the rigors of training by their teachers, were not able to become acknowledged as "trained" teachers.

As the population of the various colonies increased, however, the demands for more trained teachers also increased. Not only was there a demand for more teachers, but also a demand came for the teachers to be more adequately trained. As a result, larger centers for the training of teachers began to emerge in the various colonies. The first such center was established in Adelaide, South Australia, in 1876. As these training centers developed, the old pupil-teacher and monitor systems generally disappeared.

As Australia moved further into the twentieth century, it became accepted that students who intended to become primary teachers should complete a period of secondary education (the period varying from state to state and undergoing changes as the years passed), and then go to a training college for periods ranging from a few months to a maximum period of two years, depending again on the state in which the intending teacher resided. Prospective secondary teachers were commonly expected to complete further years of secondary education up to the maximum years of study available, and then go to a university to undertake a degree, followed by a professional training program. This pattern, with minor variations over the years in the different states, would exist in Australia until the 1960s.

### New Patterns

The 1950s witnessed a marked increase in pupil enrollments in schools, which in turn led to an increase in the number of teachers needed to staff Australian schools. The need for more teachers was also exacerbated by moves to decrease class sizes, to raise the school-leaving age, and to provide a range of specialist teacher services. A need emerged for more newly trained teachers to move into the profession from the various training institutions. For example, the number of students-in-training grew from a total of 11,329 in 1957 to 16,179 in 1961 and increased even further to 22,257 by 1964. Consequently, additional colleges were created to provide programs for the students. From the end of World War II until the early 1970s, the number of teachers' colleges rose five times.

Such a period of increased numbers of students and of institutions inevitably led to problems. Many of the problems related to the types of facilities made available in the colleges, many of which had been established in already existing buildings with inadequate conversions to suit their new functions. With regard to these problems, a federal government committee stated:

For the colleges generally, there have been serious consequences of the urgent measures taken to cope with the demand for more teachers: larger classes and heavier staff teaching loads; overcrowding in staff offices; pressure on existing library, gymnasium (if any) and laboratory resources; inadequate amenities for students; poorly equipped science laboratories and industrial arts workshops; lack of special studios for art and music and special rooms for individual subject departments to provide for the increasing proportion of college students preparing to teach in secondary schools. There have arisen problems relating to the administration and supervision of students' work in the schools (Traill, p. 8).

Aggravating this situation was the tendency of each of the states, through their respective education departments, to develop different policies relating to the training of teachers. This tendency especially affected the amount of finance made available to teacher education. As a result, where particular states did not make sufficient funds available, buildings and facilities were of a much lower standard than those in states whose policies directed more toward the training of teachers.

All these factors were brought to a peak in 1965 by the report of a government committee that had been established to inquire into the patterns of tertiary education in Australia. This document, commonly known as the Martin Report (1965), made the following recommendations relating to teacher education: (1) additional resources, both state and Commonwealth, should be devoted to the urgent task of increasing the supply of teachers in Australia; (2) the minimum standard of entrance to a course of preparation for teaching should be the university-entrance level; (3) within the next six or seven years, the length of the minimum course of preparation for teaching should be increased to three years; (4) teachers in all types of schools should be professionally trained; (5) each state should establish a board of teacher education as a statutory body responsible for supervising standards of teacher preparation, granting certificates and professional degrees, and distributing such funds as may be made available for the more effective preparation of teachers; (6) teachers' colleges that come within the ambit of boards of teacher education should be developed to the point at which they can be granted autonomy; and (7) the staff of all teachers colleges should be recruited through open advertisement.

These recommendations heralded important new directions for teacher education in Australia. Prior to this time, individual states had developed their own education systems and had similarly been responsible for the funding involved in training their own teachers for such systems. The Australian Constitution, which was drawn up with the establishment of the Federation of the States in 1901, had in fact made it clear that the initiative in education belonged to the state. Gradual modifications of this proviso, however, enabled the Commonwealth to act on the Martin Committee's recommendation that Commonwealth funds be injected into teacher education within the states. This injection of nonstate government funds also promoted the autonomy of those teacher training institutions that had formerly been controlled by state education departments. The training of teachers in the universities in Australia had long been an activity independent of the various state education departments as Australian universities operated under their own autonomous governing councils. Teachers trained in nonuniversity institutions were now able to take courses developed by institutions that were not directly under the guidance and supervision of future employing authorities. The entry level for admission to such courses was now set at Year 12 rather than lower down in the secondary school, courses were extended from two to three years, and staff was recruited from the open market rather than from appointments made from within the respective state education systems.

The move to such autonomy was abetted by a further development proposed by the Martin Committee. In its recommendations relating to the expansion and future development of tertiary education in Australia, the committee had recommended that tertiary education be developed through three categories of institutions—universities, institutes or colleges, and boards of teacher education. The Australian government supported the notion that "advanced education" should be developed in new types of institutions and established the Australian

Commission on Advanced Education to supervise the development of such institutions. The Universities Commission was to continue its role in promoting the running of the university system. Teacher education rapidly became an important focus of activity for the "new" types of institutions, commonly referred to as colleges of advanced education.

This pattern continued until 1988 when the federal government released a white paper on higher education in Australia. This, in effect, ushered in a unified national system, with institutions being able to belong to it if they had student populations of over 2,000 and full Commonwealth funding only being granted to those who met this and certain other requirements. The result has been several mergers of previous colleges of advanced education either with other colleges or with universities; in addition, several of the larger colleges have become universities. Teacher education, both of a preservice and an in-service nature, is an accepted part of the educational profile of tertiary institutions within this unified system. This system marks the end of small, single-purpose institutions offering teacher education programs in Australia. From 1989, therefore, teacher education has been offered within institutions that are multipurpose and thus devoted to a wide range of disciplines and professional programs apart from teacher education.

## ISSUES AND PROBLEMS

### Issue 1: How Should Teacher Education Programs Be Structured?

As in other countries, opinion is divided in Australia on whether preservice teacher education should be offered as an undergraduate area of study. Currently, the various states utilize a large variety of approaches in the way they offer preservice teacher education for the some 75,000 students enrolled in Australian teacher education courses. The following list presents the range of programs available:

**Early childhood education:** three year undergraduate diploma; four-year undergraduate degree; one-year graduate diploma.

**Primary:** three-year undergraduate diploma; four-year undergraduate degree; one-year graduate diploma.

**Secondary:** three-year undergraduate diploma; four-year undergraduate degree; one-year graduate diploma.

**Technical and further education:** three-year undergraduate diploma; four-year undergraduate degree; one-year graduate diploma.

Many variations exist within these patterns. For example, in one state early childhood and primary preservice teacher education is offered on the basis of an initial three-year program, followed by a period of employment as a teacher and then the opportunity to return to study for a fourth year which leads to a bachelor of education award. Opportunities for further studies exist within all the above programs for teachers at an in-service teacher education level who wish to upgrade from a previous qualification. In recent years employers have moved from a basic employment requirement of a two-year teacher education program for early childhood and primary teachers to a three-year qualification, and several states have indicated that they will now move to a four-year requirement. As a consequence, institutions offering teacher education are placing a major emphasis on providing opportunities for teachers to upgrade qualifications. In addition to studying within the framework of programs described above, such teachers have also been given opportunities to specialize in particular areas of teaching through a variety of graduate and postgraduate diploma programs.

The pattern for secondary teachers is much the same, although a four-year preservice teacher education course is more usual than the three-year course plus teaching experience plus an in-service year model. Again, as in the case of early childhood and primary education, many teachers in Australian secondary schools are seeking to upgrade previous qualifications through studies at Australian higher education institutions. It is estimated that at present 27,000 Australian teachers have enrolled in teacher education courses, with many others also enrolled in nonteacher education awards.

At the early childhood and primary levels, an increase in the specific requirements stated by employers, such as those relating to the number of days for the practicum component and the courses that must be devoted to particular areas of teaching, appears to have strengthened the role of the concurrent undergraduate program approach. Emphasis on the grasp of content matter would seem to be directing secondary teacher education programs more toward the one-year graduate approach following an undergraduate program directed entirely to acquiring appropriate background in disciplines that will later serve as teaching specializations.

The issue on how preservice teacher education programs should be structured has generated much recent debate in Australia. In 1990 the latest Commonwealth government inquiry into teacher education (National Board of Employment, Education and Training, 1990) indicated a preference for an initial degree program in education of seven semesters, taken over a three-year period, followed by an appointment as an associate teacher in schools for two years. During this two-year period, associate teachers would undertake a two-year higher education course, while at the same time be guided and assisted by an experienced teacher during their teaching duties. For students who completed undergraduate degrees in areas other than education, a two-year graduate program, including at least one year as an associate teacher, would be available. These proposals have concerned teacher educators who see the initiative for preservice teacher education being assumed by employing authorities. Teacher organizations have also stated their concerns about this proposal, particularly in relation to the increased responsibilities that would be placed on teachers for training and supervising associate teachers. The added costs involved in locating more preservice teacher education within the school system may well be the final arbiter on how Australian preservice teacher education programs are structured. Of the issues at the forefront of debate in Australian teacher education, this question of the way teacher education programs will be structured is the one that is attracting most attention and divergence of viewpoints.

### Issue 2: How Should the Entrants to Teacher Education Programs Be Selected?

Entrance requirements to all Australian teacher education programs are set by the individual institutions, but certain characteristics are standard to all. For example, entry to both the preservice three-year diploma and four-year degree programs require the completion of secondary education (Year 12), with, in some cases, particular requirements for studies undertaken and passed at Year 12 also being defined. Students wishing to become secondary teachers in a particular curriculum area will usually have had to complete certain studies at a set level of achievement at Year 12 in such subject areas. Many institutions set a level of mathematics and English achievements at Year 12 for those students who wish to undertake early childhood or primary teacher education programs. However, in addition to school leavers, institutions admit many mature-age students to teacher education programs. Many of these will not have completed Year 12 studies in their previous educational background and are selected on the basis of specially devised, mature-age entry tests, interviews, and appropriate work experiences.

Several institutions are exploring student selection procedures in an attempt to ensure that all incoming student teachers possess the entrance requirements. An exemplar of such an approach is that being developed at an institution in the western suburbs of Melbourne (Toomey, 1989). In this institution a recruitment-selection process is being developed which involves the early identification of potential secondary science and mathematics teachers from students in local secondary schools and nurturing this interest to the point where such students pursue tertiary studies in mathematics and science and follow this up by a graduate diploma in education. In the case of potential early childhood and primary teachers, the institution is developing links with final-year students in local secondary schools that provide the students with information about teacher education courses. The application forms devised for these courses collect data from applicants on such matters as personal and academic background, schools attended, work experience, and reasons for wanting to pursue a career in teaching. Two testimonials are also collected: one that provides a rating on the applicants' suitability for teaching and a second report that links the applicants' mathematical abilities, capacity for independent work, and their written and oral abilities. Data from these application forms are then provided to interview panels that consist

of teacher educators and local teachers. Sessions are held with the members of
the interview panels to provide a briefing on the selection criteria adopted by
the institution. Such criteria include a demonstrated commitment to teaching in
the western suburbs of Melbourne; evidence of significant and relevant work
experience in the primary teaching field; sufficient scholastic components to
undertake a program; and perceived ability to become primary teachers. As an
interesting possible addition to this process, the institution is exploring a situation
where applicants will be asked to undertake a small simulated "teaching" task
as part of the selection process.

While this approach is a most comprehensive way to select students, many
other institutions are, to a lesser extent, developing procedures that will make
the selection process a much more critical element in the supply of teachers in
Australia.

Although these more comprehensive selection approaches receive widespread
recognition and acclaim, and may be quite laudable, the real issue centers on
the feasibility of such an approach to student selection. All higher education
institutions in Australia are experiencing problems securing adequate financial
resources. Selection of student intakes on the basis of secondary education scores
is a relatively resource-free process. Interviewing students, analyzing references,
and observing *in situ* performances are cost-intensive processes. Higher education
administrators are not able to meet the costs of such selection procedures. However, the advocates of such careful selection processes argue that they are cost
effective in the longer term in that course attrition rates are lowered and that
committed and able students make higher quality inputs to the teaching profession. At present the "resource guardians" hold sway.

### Issue 3: Is it Feasible to Establish National Standards for
### Teacher Registration?

Prior to the government's announcement in 1988 that there was to be a unified
system of higher education in Australia, awards (degrees), offered for the programs described earlier, fell into two categories. The first were those degrees
granted by universities which were made on behalf of the governing council of
the university itself and were not subjected to the scrutiny of an external agency.
In the second category, programs offered in the advanced education and technical
and further education sectors, the awards were accredited by the Australian
Council on Tertiary Awards (ACTA). This council was set up in January 1985
and was given the following functions: (1) to promote consistency throughout
Australia in the nomenclature used for tertiary awards and in the standards of
courses leading to those awards; (2) to encourage the development of consistent
relationships between courses and their associated awards; (3) to establish and
maintain liaison with the authorized bodies nominated by the state, Northern
Territory, and the Commonwealth ministers for education, and with other rel-

evant bodies; (4) to provide an information service at the national level in connection with the courses and awards registered; (5) to establish, maintain, and publish a National Register of Tertiary Awards; (6) to issue guidelines on the information to be contained in the Register, the nomenclature of awards and standards of courses for various awards, their registration and periodic registration, and the general conditions under which awards attaching to accredited courses may be included in the Register; and (7) to monitor adherence to these guidelines.

ACTA and its various state liaison bodies established external accrediting panels, usually consisting of academics from other tertiary institutions and representatives of employer groups and relevant professional organizations, to advise whether programs in the advanced education and technical and further education sectors met requirements for registration. Such panels were particularly asked to consider the general educational practices and standards of the institution(s) or system; the objectives of the particular course and the methods adopted to achieve these objectives; the admission requirements to the course; the duration of the course, having regard to entry requirements and course objectives; the breadth, depth, and balance in the course material involved and the intellectual effort required, as well as the procedures for approval of research projects where appropriate; the methods of assessment of student progress, including the use of external examiners for higher degrees; the relative emphasis on the teaching of skills in relation to the study of the discipline; any arrangements for practical training and experience as part of the course; the staff conducting the course, including numbers, professional qualifications and experience, educational expertise, and ability to serve the particular mode(s) of offering the course; and the accommodation and facilities including equipment, library, laboratories, workshops, and other instructional or research resources, as necessary for the particular course.

With the advent of the unified system in 1989, changes were made in the ways teacher education awards are approved. All tertiary institutions are now given the responsibility for developing procedures that will ensure that many of the aspects to which ACTA panels previously devoted attention will also be given attention in the unified system. The extent to which this may involve external groups is still evolving. However, it is of interest that the government white paper states as a requirement for institutions in the unified system "the review of curricula, staff development and teaching processes to ensure the relevance of courses to a broad range of client groups and to remove any elements of bias on grounds of income, race, culture or sex." Matched with this statement is the white paper's emphasis on performance indicators, with institutions being required to develop indicators that take into account "quality of teaching and curriculum design." In addition, in late December 1988 a report released by the Australian Vice-Chancellor's Committee and the Australian Committee of Directors and Principals in Advanced Education argued that performance reviews were essential for the proper conduct of higher education courses. Such statements indicate that in the coming years some form of scrutiny of awards provided in teacher education programs will likely emerge in Australia.

The relationship between the awards gained in tertiary institutions and the registration of teachers for employment purposes merits a brief mention here. The registration of teachers in Australia is the responsibility of individual employing authorities. Although such authorities and their registration boards, accept the awards gained at tertiary institutions, the required components expected to be a part of such awards vary from state to state. In fact, at a meeting of representatives from the registration boards in 1987, no general agreement could be reached on a standard set of requirements. Differences relate to such matters as curriculum content, number of days devoted to practice teaching, subjects studied in various disciplines, number of hours provided for specified curriculum areas, and so on. As a result of this meeting, a group consisting of representatives of several state authorities, from the Commonwealth's Council on Overseas Professional Qualifications (which provides advice to institutions and employers on the comparability of overseas qualifications with Australian qualifications) and ACTA, has been set up to determine whether a national standard qualification could be identified for future use.

The differing requirements from state to state for registration as teachers leads to much confusion. Institutions of higher education which offer teacher education programs within one state are constantly confronted with a range of requirements when establishing whether graduates from their programs will be eligible for employment in other areas in the country. Teachers who wish to move to other states often find they are not employable in such states. These two sources are placing pressure on employer groups to develop national requirements for teacher registration. Moves by the ministers of education to identify a national curriculum are bringing further pressure for change. The issue may be moving toward a resolution. For example, one state minister has declared that teachers registered in other states will be accepted for employment in that state beginning in 1991. This type of action might settle an issue that has hampered the portability of teaching qualifications in Australia.

### Issue 4: What Is a Desirable Balance for Teacher Education Programs Between Academic and Education Areas?

Although variations do exist from institution to institution, preservice teacher education programs in Australia fall into two main categories. The first takes the form of a three-year or four-year integrated pattern in which studies relating to academic or general studies in disciplines other than education, educational foundations studies, curriculum, and instruction studies, together with practice teaching in schools, are taken concurrently throughout the three-year or four-year duration of the degree or diploma. The second category consists of a one-year concentrated program in which studies in educational foundations, curriculum, and instruction, together with practice teaching in schools are provided. Within this category, commonly referred to as the "end-on" or graduate diploma approach, the academic or general studies component will have been taken previously in a separate or first degree course of studies.

*Academic Studies*

The general studies components of both approaches will generally have one of two major emphases. For the early childhood and primary specializations, student teachers will be encouraged to study at least one discipline through to third-year level, but then will be urged to broaden their studies to give them some background in such areas as art, music, and literature. For this reason, many institutions identify this section of their program as "Personal Development." It is not uncommon to find that certain "prescribed studies" are also identified within this strand; for example, many institutions now require their early childhood and primary students to undertake units in mathematics and computing.

The second emphasis in general studies will relate to secondary teacher education programs where students will be required to undertake studies through to third-year levels within the disciplines they have chosen as areas for their teaching specialization(s). In some states, students will also have to select certain units of study within the discipline areas which meet the requirements of employing authorities. For example, one state education department requires that its science teachers in lower secondary classes have completed studies in a specified number of units in each of biology, chemistry, and physics.

*Education Studies*

The educational foundations courses normally cover studies in philosophy, sociology, psychology, and curriculum theory either in integrated units of study or as separate units. In some institutions the educational foundation units have been further integrated by being linked with curriculum and instruction units. Other institutions have included in this strand of their program studies that present other perspectives on educational issues, such as those relating to multicultural education, the education of children with particular disabilities, and studies on gender and equity.

*Curriculum Studies*

The curriculum and instruction strand normally focuses on the teaching of the various curriculum areas. In early childhood and primary specializations, this will involve at least one unit of study in each of the primary school curriculum areas, with areas such as language arts and mathematics often having several units of study devoted to them over a three-or four-year course. For secondary specialization students, the focus will be on their particular teaching specialization area(s), and most students will be encouraged to take at least two such specializations.

*Practice Teaching*

The length of time given to practice teaching also varies from institution to institution. However, most three- and four-year programs fall within a range of eighty to one hundred days, while the graduate one-year programs fall within a range of forty to fifty days.

*A Core of Studies*

Several efforts have been made in Australia in recent years to identify in more specific details the requirements of a curriculum for teacher education. During the latter part of the 1970s and the early 1980s, this was attempted through a number of state and Commonwealth government inquiries. Such an example was the National Inquiry into Teacher Education and its subsequent report, popularly known as the Auchmuty Report, which detailed an impressive list of core studies that all teacher education programs in Australia should include (Auchmuty, 1980). This core was described in the report as consisting of subject disciplines and other dimensions of knowledge and experience; the organization of learning: curriculum design, and teaching methodology; human growth and development; theory of education: interdisciplinary, integrated, and related to the practice of teaching and learning; studies in contemporary culture: Australian society and its national and international settings, social trends, economics, politics, ideologies, and values; methods of inquiry and research; and practical experience: in classrooms and other community and work environments.

While this review and its report have served as a useful guide to those responsible for developing the curriculum of teacher education programs in the various tertiary institutions, it would not be accurate to state that the inquiry's findings have been followed up and become part of the Australian teacher education curriculum.

Similarly, other efforts to suggest what should be contained in a curriculum, such as that made by Turney and colleagues (1985) to develop a curriculum for the practicum, have also not been universally adopted. It is difficult to identify particular reasons for this outcome. Perhaps the best explanation offered is that teacher educators are so divided on what constitute the essential components of a teacher education curriculum that each program tends to reflect the prevailing wisdom of those involved in teaching the respective courses. This tends to make considerations of what components should be included within teacher education programs an ongoing issue within Australian teacher education. The balance tends to swing in favor of the most vocal proponents within a given program; if the "disciplines" advocates prevail, then these areas have a more important role in a given program. If the curriculum advocates are strong in another program, then this area is prominent within that program. This debate is ongoing.

Another approach currently being introduced in order to define the curriculum of teacher education may meet with more success in impacting on the curriculum for teacher education. This is being done through Commonwealth government reviews of the disciplines offered in tertiary education. A review of science and mathematics teacher education began in 1988, and a report was issued in October 1989. This report outlined ways in which the training of science and mathematics teachers should proceed within Australian tertiary institutions and made quite specific recommendations on the composition of the teacher education curriculum for science and mathematics. Institutions are being required to inform the Commonwealth government within a two-year period of how far they have progressed in implementing such recommendations. The issue here for teacher educators is what is to be omitted to make space for the new requirements.

## Issue 5: How Might Societal Needs Be Reflected Within Teacher Education Programs?

As discussed earlier, many inquiries have been conducted in recent years into how teacher education is conducted in Australia. In each instance, panels conducting these inquiries accepted detailed submissions from a wide range of community groups, thus providing a means whereby societal needs were identified and in turn communicated via the various inquiry reports to teacher educators.

As an example of the opportunity such inquiries have provided in Australia for community groups to convey their inputs into teacher education, an examination of the range of submissions received by the Queensland Board of Teacher Education's inquiry "Project 21: Teachers for the Twenty-First Century" is of interest (Watts, 1987).

A total of 483 submissions was received, containing inputs from classroom teachers, school principals, academics, parents, teachers unions and associations, educational consultants, subject teachers groups, and community organizations. Each section of the Project 21 report provides summaries of the views expressed in submissions and at public meetings. These summaries address issues such as the content of preservice teacher education, achieving quality in teaching, the continuing professional development of teachers, the recruitment and selection of teachers, and the future contexts of teaching. Inputs were made by individuals and groups presenting cases for the curriculum of teacher education to include attention to matters relating to multiculturalism, the education of Aboriginal people, the changed nature of family structures, female roles, the impact of technology, transition from school to work, and opportunities for equal participation in education for all members of a society.

In addition to the inquiries that have specifically addressed teacher education, community groups wishing to influence teacher education have had opportunities to do so through a range of inquiries that have addressed other issues. Such inquiries have called for public submissions on matters such as computer education (1983), achieving quality in education (1985), labor market roles (1985), education and the arts (1984), the teaching of English as a second language (1984), education for a multicultural society (1979), the education of girls (1984), special education (1984), and distance education (1986), to name but a few. Reports from these and many other inquiries and reviews have ensured that teacher educators in Australia have become alerted to societal needs as they develop the curricula and organization of teacher education programs.

This is one issue that is appropriately handled in most Australian teacher education programs. The major difficulties occur when program designers have to make decisions on how much or how little of a particular societal issue is included within a program, where such material is placed, and how the material is presented. Not all proponents of societal issues accept such decisions, and they keep teacher educators "on their toes" by pressuring for a greater emphasis to be given to their particular area.

### Issue 6: How Can the Articulation of Pre- and In-service Education Be Best Achieved?

The realization that the continuing education of teachers is of the utmost importance if quality education is to be achieved is now well established in Australia. A major thrust of the inquiries into teacher education which have been discussed in this chapter was to identify ways of ensuring the ongoing professional development of teachers once the preservice phase had been completed. Each of the reports issued by the state and Commonwealth inquiries devoted sections to this issue.

The National Inquiry (Auchmuty, 1980) recommended that all teachers in Australia be involved in at least five days of in-service education outside of school hours each year, that each teacher should be eligible for one term of full-time paid release after every seven years of service in order to follow an approved program of professional development, and that tertiary institutions should have their annual budget augmented by 5 percent each year in order to provide non-award courses for the teaching profession. A later inquiry made similar recommendations, and the most recent report on teacher education advocates that the equivalent of 2 percent of teacher salary budgets be devoted to in-service education. However, the economic climate has not permitted these recommendations to be implemented, and the funding now available for the continuing professional development of teachers is less than half of that available at the time of the National Inquiry.

Unfortunately, the decline in funding available for the continuing professional development of teachers has coincided with circumstances that have led to an unprecedented demand for such activities. The stability and immobility of a large percentage of the teaching workforce, changes in career paths for teachers resulting from lower numbers of teachers, the aging of the teaching service, fewer promotional opportunities, and pressure on teachers with two or three years of initial training to upgrade their qualifications—all have placed pressure on the availability of in-service education opportunities. This pressure has also been heightened by changes in school curriculum, advances in technology, societal changes, and flow-on pressures on schools which have caused teachers to make further demands on the provision of professional development opportunities.

The response of the Commonwealth government to this need in a time of economic restraints in public spending has been to develop means of identifying priority areas and to work with state governments and tertiary institutions in developing in-service education programs that would address such areas. In a recent report on teacher education (Hudson and Boomer, 1986), the Commonwealth government stated its criteria for such activity: professional development should be a high national priority, critical to improved educational outcomes for all students, and should be a shared responsibility among the Commonwealth, employing authorities, and the profession itself.

Matched with this Commonwealth input is that undertaken by the various state departments and employing authorities in the nongovernment sector, through the professional development bodies all state authorities have established. Through such bodies at both the Commonwealth and state levels, the clearest patterns of articulation of teacher education have in the past been achieved in Australia. However, these very agencies appear to have suffered most in the changed economic circumstances of education authorities. At both the national and state levels, the funding and size of professional development agencies have been drastically reduced; hence, their current impact on teacher education is much less than it was in the 1970s and early 1980s. The effects of this may well create the issues for teacher education in the 1990s as new curriculum areas are introduced, but the mechanisms no longer exist to offer extensive in-servicing of such new developments to teachers. This is one of the most critical challenges teacher educators in higher education must face as they consider what their involvement might be in stepping in to the vacuum.

As stated previously, 27,000 active teachers are currently enrolled in teacher education courses in Australian tertiary institutions—about one-third of the total teacher education enrollment. This provides another means of achieving articulation between the preservice and in-service sectors. Although institutions do not receive separate funding to provide such courses and teachers enroll in and pay for courses as do other tertiary students, it is evident that many of the courses offered within teacher education programs have been developed in order to provide appropriate courses for experienced teachers. In some states, institutions have entered into arrangements with employing authorities and teachers to make special provisions for in-service students. One example is in Tasmania where the Centre for Continuing Education provides an articulation between a variety of study options for teachers. The issue of the role of tertiary education institutions in in-service teacher education has been the subject of a recent government study (Johnson, 1988), once again indicating the importance placed on this activity in Australia.

A discussion of continuing professional development opportunities for teachers in Australia would not be complete without a mention of the recent growth of school-based professional development activities. Through funds supplied by

Commonwealth and state professional development agencies, as well as support from other groups, many schools now run their own professional development programs. Usually of short-term duration, addressing specific issues, and often led by an outside consultant, this type of professional development activity is now a well-entrenched feature of Australian in-service education. It should also be mentioned that most of the programs run as an induction for beginning teachers are also approached as a school-based activity in Australia. This avenue is providing much of the in-service education formerly offered through the Commonwealth and state-funded professional development centers. Teachers are now looking to have these types of activities credited toward award courses in higher education institutions. Agreement to do so is not always reached and represents a potential area of conflict if it is not handled in a sensitive way. Higher education authorities do not wish to offend teachers by downgrading school-based in-service courses. However, the integrity and standing of higher education awards must be maintained and protected.

### Issue 7: Is Research Changing the Directions of Teacher Education?

Interest in research into teacher education has intensified in Australia in the last two decades. This has been closely linked with the many inquiries into teacher education discussed earlier in this chapter. Each inquiry either commissioned or undertook its own research into a wide range of issues, thus providing the impetus for a number of key studies into such areas as the selection of students, the nature of the practicum, and the appropriateness of certain types of programs. This has been accompanied by an increased availability of funding for research, and opportunities to discuss and publicize findings. A carefully developed overview of such research has been recently supplied by R. Tisher (1987), who described the research under the categories of perceptions of teaching as a career, characteristics of teacher trainees, the nature and impact of preservice programs, skill (and other) components in preservice education, school experience: the supervisor and the practicum, beginning teachers: provisions, concerns and attitudes, and needs and provisions for in-service education.

In summarizing his review, Tisher concluded that the wide variety of research conducted in Australia in recent years has produced many perspectives on teacher education. He was not prepared to state, however, that the research had led to a well-established base of knowledge on which to develop teacher education programs and approaches. This is the dilemma now facing both researchers and research-granting bodies. Just what research is likely to impact on what occurs in teacher education programs?

Some evidence does indicate that previous research activity has impacted on practice. For example, research in such areas as microteaching, teaching in inner-city schools, and the development of skills for supervision of student teaching and the practicum has provided a sound knowledge base for many Australian teacher educators in terms of the development of a rationale for courses, the identification of program content, and the adoption of research-based teaching strategies. Perhaps there is hope that research is, in fact, influencing teacher education practice and that this will encourage funding bodies and researchers to help provide answers to the issues raised in earlier sections of this chapter.

## CONCLUSION

Several years ago an analysis was made of the major issues confronting teacher education in Australia in the early 1980s (Traill, 1982). The issues were: teacher supply and demand, and their impact on teacher education; the practicum and the relationships between teacher education programs and school systems; the continuing education of teachers; and what research affected teacher education. The Report of the Joint Review of Teacher Education (Hudson and Boomer, 1986) identified the issues as: how to adapt preservice teacher education programs as a result of changing circumstances and priorities in schools and society in general; the extent to which structural and administrative arrangements can adapt to new demands in preservice education; the length of preservice training; the length of the academic year for teacher education programs; and preparation to teach at both primary and secondary education levels.

The nature of the Queensland Board of Teacher Education's Project 21 report (Watts, 1987) indicated the major issues to be: the improvement of the outcomes of schooling; recruitment and selection of student teachers; the professional development of teachers, including induction and in-service programs; preservice teacher education, in particular the length and structure of programs, responsiveness of programs to change, content and goals, subject matter, the practicum, and clinical studies; the selection of teacher educators; research and development; reviews of teacher education programs; and heightened valuing of teacher education.

These statements reflect the continuing pressures being placed on teacher education in Australia. When placed within a scenario that involves decreased budgets for teacher education programs, governmental pressures to measure teacher education outcomes against a range of performance indicators, growing public interest in developing a national core curriculum and national assessment practices in the primary and secondary school systems, and the development of a unified system of higher education with the mergers and amalgamations that this implies, we can see that teacher education is entering a further critical stage that can be added to those of other eras as previously outlined. It would seem that government decisions will once again be playing a prominent role in setting the agenda for teacher education. The wisdom collected from the various inquiries that have been held into teacher education over the past decade or so may well be lost in the process.

## REFERENCES

Auchmuty, J. J. *Report of the National Inquiry in Teacher Education*. Canberra: Australian Government Printing Service, 1980.

Australian Commission on Advanced Education. *Teacher Education 1973–1975, Report of the Special Committee on Teacher Education*. Canberra: Australian Government Printing Service, 1973.

Hudson, H., and G. Boomer. *Improving Teacher Education, Report of the Joint Review of Teacher Education*. Canberra: Australian Government Printing Service, 1986.

Johnson, N. *The Role of Higher Education Institutions in Inservice Teacher Training*. Canberra: Australian Government Printing Service, 1988.

Karmel, P., Chairman. *Quality of Education in Australia. Report of the Quality of Education Review Committee*. Canberra: Australian Government Printing Service, 1985.

Martin, L. *The Report of the Committee on the Future of Tertiary Education in Australia*. Vols. 1, 2, and 3. Canberra: Australian Government Printing Service, 1965.

National Board of Employment, Education and Training. *Teacher Education in Australia*. Canberra: Australian Government Printing Service, 1990.

Tisher, R. "Research in Teacher Education in Australia." In K. Eltis, ed., *Australian Teacher Education in Review*. Adelaide: South Pacific Association for Teacher Education, 1987.

Toomey, R. *Producing Quality Teachers for Tomorrow's Australia*. Proceedings of the Annual Conference, Association of Directors of Teacher Education, Melbourne, January 1989.

Traill, R. D. "Major Issues in Teacher Education in Australia." In H. Leavitt and J. Fogle, eds., *Preparing for the Profession of Teaching*. Washington D.C.: International Council on Education for Teaching, 1982.

Turney, C., et al. *A New Basis for Teacher Education: The Practicum Curriculum*. Sydney: Sydniac Academic Press, 1985.

Watts, B. *Project 21: Teachers for the Twenty-First Century*. Brisbane: Queensland Board of Teacher Education, 1987.

# 3

# BRAZIL

## JOSÉ MARÍA COUTINHO

This chapter introduces the social, economic, and political context of Brazilian teacher education; provides a general overview of the Brazilian system for preparing teachers; and identifies and discusses contemporary issues surrounding teacher education in Brazil. These issues are (1) the need to develop a Brazilian teacher education model, (2) the lack of teacher participation in teacher education policy formation, (3) the lack of integration between the teaching of subject matter and pedagogy, (4) the need for higher quality of teacher education, (5) the need for higher quality of teacher continuing education, and (6) improvements in the working and life conditions of teachers.

## GENERAL BACKGROUND

### The Socio–Economic Context

Brazil is a society characterized by elitism; its social divisions are as great as any in the world. Traditionally, the Brazilian elites have made only minimal commitment to education for the masses. Education continues to consume less than 5 percent of the national budget and to be largely a privilege of the elite class. Consequently, it has been almost impossible to attract and train competent teachers, beyond those few highly trained from among the elites. During the past two decades, some signs of change have become evident, particularly because of the struggle of the teachers themselves and the demographic and economic growth that occurred during the military regime. There were 70 million inhabitants in 1960, which reached 90 million in 1970, 102 million in 1980, and 153 million in 1991. Through foreign investments and loans, Brazil's economy experienced a boom growth of more than 10 percent a year between 1968 and 1973. Subsequent to that period, however, an economic recession, with high inflation rates that at times reached more than 1,500 percent per year, has precipitated the national economy into stagflation and high unemployment.

At the present time Brazil is in a state of extreme economic difficulty. Some suggest it is on the brink of civil war, with urban and rural violence, murders, bank robberies, kidnappings, rapes, and lynchings frequent occurrences. Of the nation's 140 million people, 110 million are described as poor, 60 million of whom are classed as "miserables," of which 30 million are homeless street kids. There are more than 40 million illiterates, 15 million physically handi-capped, and 10 million school-aged youth outside the system.

### The Political Educational Context

Teacher education cannot be discussed outside the context of the political climate that has dominated Brazil for the past three decades. The military regime maintained an iron hand in politics from 1964 until 1985. This regime strength-ened the executive branch, with its succession of military presidents, and weak-ened the legislature. The national administration was characterized by such developments as the National Security Law, the National Intelligence Agency, military-police, establishment of political prisons, suppression of political rights, and banishments of activist students. Through all these unsettling events, teachers remained one of the most active voices for democracy and a liberal social condition, which meant that educational institutions were continually subjected to severe control and repression. Urban guerrilla activity, which started in 1969, was violently repressed and its leaders were assassinated and imprisoned. In the universities, departments of philosophy and sociology were closed. Comparative education and higher education programs were eliminated from curricula, and other teacher education courses were strangled. In their place came courses intended to indoctrinate a particular type of moral and civic education. Literacy programs were initiated which were intended to counteract the popular culture movements that drew their inspiration from Paulo Freire, known for his literacy and adult education programs for sensitizing the lower classes to their exploited state.

### THE EDUCATIONAL SYSTEM

In Brazil, the educational system parallels the extreme social divisions. The elites begin schooling in private institutions and remain there until they enter the university.

The masses enter the public schools, even if they are intellectually gifted, because few have the resources to pay for this schooling. The Brazilian gov-ernment has long supported a unified public educational program, having a minimum compulsory attendance provision of seven years. Structurally, the system begins with some state-supported and private kindergartens for four and five year olds. Prior to 1971, primary schools were five years in length, so young people completed them by the time they were eleven or twelve years of age. Admissions to secondary schools were based on a rigorous examination. The best students were tracked into the junior high school (*ginasio*), which was a four- or five-year program, after which students attended the senior high school (*colegio*) program for an additional three or four years. Those who did not qualify for this program, which was the majority of the students, were tracked out of schools altogether or into primary teacher education or vocational education. In 1971 it was decided to combine the primary school and the junior high school programs to create an eight-year elementary school. Under this arrangement, compulsory attendance was extended to eight years, and tracking would be deferred until the eight-year program was completed.

When the eight-year primary school was created, a program was instituted to give an additional year or more of training to those primary school teachers who intended to become subject matter specialists at the upper level of the elementary school. In addition, 284 new upper levels for primary schools (new *ginasios*) were created to serve as models for the new system. The curriculum of this school consisted of a core curriculum (communication and expression, social studies, and sciences) and specific studies (industrial arts, commerce, agriculture, technology, and home economics).

In spite of this positive structure, Brazilian education is characterized by a high dropout rate. Already by the second year of school, only 50 percent of the pupils remain in school. By the eighth grade only 20 percent remain, by the eleventh grade 10 percent remain, and only 5 percent are qualified to enter the university. This is not to say that progress has not been made. In the booming 1960s, there was a significant expansion of elementary education (79 percent), secondary (275 percent) and higher (356 percent) education. In spite of the economic conditions of the 1970s, growth continued, though at a much slower pace in elementary (39 percent), secondary (180 percent), and higher (204 percent) education. Most of this growth can be attributed to demographic growth (Paiva, 1985, pp. 2–4).

In spite of the official discourse about the value of education and teachers, in the past twenty-one years of military regime and the more recent democratic transition, the plight of teachers has deteriorated.

Low productivity of the educational system, low salaries for teachers, and unacceptable working conditions continue. The main reason for this situation is the government's decreased relative investment in education. For example, whereas 10 percent of the national budget was invested in education in 1967, only 6 percent was invested in 1983, and the figure now stands at approximately 5 percent. Brazil's various states and municipal governments are formally obliged to apply 25 percent of their budgets to education, but they typically apply only half of that obligation.

## THE SYSTEM OF TEACHER EDUCATION

### Beginnings of Teacher Education in Brazil

The Jesuits maintained a virtual monopoly of education and the training of teachers in Brazil for 210 years (1549–1759). The purpose of training was to educate a religious elite, devoted to the Christianization and Europeanization of the Indian and Portuguese-Brazilian children (Azevedor, 1964; Holanda, 1987).

Primary teachers were taught to impart the three R's, while at the secondary level, reserved for the elites, the *Ratio Studiorum*, an educational framework developed by the Jesuits, served as the pedagogical Bible. With the expulsion of the Jesuits in 1759, education fell into a vacuum and no teachers were trained to replace the Jesuits. In the absence of teachers, the king gave notary officers the charge of teaching reading, writing, and Christian doctrine, which marked the beginning of the tradition of the lay teacher in Brazil.

Throughout the nineteenth century, neither an integrated educational system nor a teacher preparation subsystem came into being. J. O. Azevedo (1964, p. 568) points out that "education in Brazil, throughout the nineteenth century had to continue unorganized, anarchical and desegregated." In spite of the 1824 Constitution, enacted after national independence in 1822, which proclaimed the creation of a national system of education, such a system did not materialize in the next one hundred years.

### The Lay Teachers

The existence of lay teachers is rooted in the origins of the Brazilian education system. Even after the first normal school graduates became active in 1837, lay teachers, those who have no formal teacher training, filled most of the teaching needs of the country. Such people were also recruited from among the liberal professions to occupy teaching positions in the secondary schools, but lay teachers are typically described as those whose maximum schooling was partial or full completion of the elementary school (Picanco, 1986, p. 9). Even as late as 1950, 48 percent of all Brazilian educators were lay teachers. This figure had decreased to 46 percent in 1960 and to 26 percent in 1985 (56 percent in rural areas). The decrease in the number of lay teachers during this time can be attributed to the growth of normal schools and colleges of philosophy, sciences, and letters, where teacher education takes place.

### Normal Schools

Normal schools trace their beginnings to Rio de Janeiro (1835), Bahia (1836), Ceara (1845), and São Paulo (1846), although some of these schools disappeared soon after they were established (Azevedo, 1964, p. 588). The return of the

Jesuits in 1842 as well as the arrival of American Protestants, whose private initiatives promoted the expansion of the secondary school system, reached a golden age between 1860 and 1890, having on one side, the Jesuit heritage of encyclopedism and American scholarship ideals on the other. The real development of normal schools began in 1880, when two schools, created in Rio de Janeiro in 1875 for the two sexes, were transformed into a single comprehensive institution, following a Massachusetts normal school model (Carnoy, 1974, p. 187). The typical training of the schools was two years beyond primary school. The normal school tradition lasted until 1971, when the Education Reform Law replaced them with several professionalized programs, according to their function.

Since 1990, plans have been to introduce primary teacher education programs into university training and to phase out the normal school, although the country cannot afford the cost of its new design. The normal school and lay teacher traditions will likely continue for a long time.

## The Secondary School Teacher Training System

Throughout most of Brazil's history, secondary teachers have been recruited mainly from among liberally educated professionals. Whatever teacher training they received was through self-instruction. It was not until 1937 that Brazil had its first formally trained secondary teachers. Based on the French professional model, colleges of philosophy, sciences, and letters worked closely with institutes of education at the university, so that future teachers could study at their specific content institutes and complement these programs with courses at the institutes of education.

Actually, this type of program developed rather quickly, considering that the first Brazilian university was created only in 1920 in Rio de Janeiro, followed by another in Minas Gerais in 1927 and São Paulo in 1934.

In the 1960s Brazil's fifteen universities came under heavy criticism for failing to keep pace with population growth and for not fulfilling their original mission of scientific investigation as well as cultural promotion and production. With the 1968 university reform, the Brazilian universities approached a North American model with universities divided into centers. Departments of education were usually located within the center for general studies.

Today, secondary teachers are graduated by the content institutes, where the conventional fields of study are located, but they complement their course of studies with courses at departments of education or pedagogic centers within the center of general studies.

## The Education of the University Professor

Unlike most countries of the world, Brazil has embarked on a novel program of training university professors. In the past, however, university faculty were usually drawn from those who possessed the necessary degree qualifications, preferably the master's degree or the doctorate. However, the overwhelming number of university personnel did not have such qualifications. As a part of the 1968 university reforms, a concerted effort was undertaken to raise the standard of Brazilian professors either abroad or at national centers. To prevent brain-drain, those who are sent abroad must commit themselves to teach at a Brazilian university for the same period spent at a foreign institution. Most professors actually take their training at a so-called national graduate department in a few privileged universities, where specialized extension courses and master's and doctorate degrees are offered.

Today, most university faculty hold a master's degree or a doctorate, which qualifies them for one of four ranks: auxiliary, assistant, associate, and full professorships. An associate professor must hold at least a master's degree, and a full professor must hold a doctorate.

## ISSUES AND PROBLEMS

Debates about teacher education in Brazil have a long and active history. For example, following the authoritarian Vargas regime (1930–1945), a national debate took place about the role of public versus private institutions, which led to the important National Education Law in 1961.

A major focus of attention was the claim that the teaching tradition should remain encyclopedic, intellectual, and authoritarian. Out of this debate emerged new directions for general education as well as the preparation of teachers who would contribute to a democratized Brazil. Unfortunately, the military regime, which came into power in 1964, closed off further open debate and imposed its own educational reforms in 1968 and 1971. The educational reform of 1971 was particularly vexing in that it tried to avoid criticisms leveled against the Brazilian educational tradition by emphasizing the professionalization aspects of education, as reflected in human capital theory and demands for sustained economic growth. The military regime relied on an economic development model for its reforms, which confused teachers and school clientele, who were also interested in development and in many other issues as well. In recent years a number of critical issues in teacher education have arisen, which remain unresolved, including the following:

### Issue 1: The Need to Develop a Brazilian Teacher
### Education Model

Experiences with Portuguese, British, French, and North American educational models have produced enormous dissatisfaction and confusion among teachers. In recent years Brazilian policymakers have been struggling to implement a new teacher training program that reflects Brazil's own cultural and social reality. An indigenous program is emerging, in large part, from a national debate between educators and subject matter specialists. This debate lasted more than twenty years, and has prompted teachers to take into their own hands the task of transforming education as an instrument of democratization and progress.

Even at the early stages of the military regime and its educational reforms, there was resistance to what has been described as cultural and scientific neo-colonialism, especially from inside the university walls. In other words, Brazil has imported academic models from the developed world, and has given little attention to their relevance to the Brazilian context. Unfortunately, the criticisms at that time were not directed toward the training of university professors and secondary school teachers. Rather, the major criticisms went to the training of so-called polyvalent teachers, who were a type of semiprofessional or para-professional for the upper level primary schools, rather than teachers, who had advanced specialized training in the various disciplines. The 1971 educational reforms mandated the establishment of an eight-year primary school and the establishment of 284 polyvalent upper level primary schools, which opened 240,000 new places for pupils and required the training of 23,400 new teachers (Berger, 1976, p. 280). The main criticism was that these new teachers were a kind of narrowly trained technician of teaching, which had been patterned after a model proposed by American consultants, who had advised the government in the 1960s.

The policies that regulated the training of these polyvalent teachers, issued in 1964 and 1966, stipulated that these teachers be trained in modified minimum curricula requiring only ten months' training for certification. The first such teachers to be trained, in the mid–1970s, were in social studies and the sciences, but much opposition was raised among existing teachers, who had to study four years at the universities to receive their credentials. They protested, in part, that these new polyvalent teachers were to receive twice the salaries of those with conventional credentials. The scientific community, such as the Brazilian Society for the Advancement of Science and the Brazilian Physics Society, also joined in protest, claiming that such teachers would be detrimental not only to education but also to science itself. In addition, the status and value of teachers themselves would deteriorate. The reaction to these policies was so great that the Ministry of Education was obligated to step back and successively postpone the mandatory implementation of the program.

Still another example of imported foreign systems into Brazil is reflected in the teacher education programs within the university structure and organization. During the early stages of the military regime, Brazilian universities adopted the credit and semester system, based on the University of Houston model in the United States. When we examine the way university teacher education is organized in Brazil today, we see that it is very similar to that in the United States. There will be foundations of education, administration and supervision, and counseling departments. There will be supervised student teaching. In addition, most of the instructors at this level will have advanced degrees, often from the United States, but also from England, Belgium, and France. These instructors tend to reinforce the foreign framework that they have learned.

Fortunately, since 1978, debates have reopened on the entire reformulation of teacher education courses that teachers would be subject to. The debates have centered on the kind of pedagogy that is appropriate to the Brazilian culture and reflective of Brazilian reality. These issues have not been resolved, and they continue to rage in the country's academic and professional circles.

### Issue 2: Lack of Teacher Participation in Teacher Education Policy

The laws of 1971, formulating teacher education policies, were top-down decrees that had come about without discussion with teachers themselves. The manner in which these decisions were made aroused skepticism and protests among the teachers, who saw the need to get personally involved in the transformation of education.

The military government's suppression of freedom of expression provoked national teacher distrust and precipitated an awakening among teachers that they were becoming an underclass. They saw themselves as recipients of a missionary-type zeal rather than being regarded as professionals. Their sense of discontent precipitated a national movement, somewhat similar to the nineteenth-century labor movement in Europe and the United States.

Even though a National Committee on the Preparation of Teachers was organized in Goiânia in 1980, which included teachers in discussions, teachers were becoming increasingly militant. Declaring that they were now a part of the working class of the country, they demanded a worker's struggle. For example, at the Fifteenth National Teachers Congress in 1982, promoted by the Brazilian Confederation of Teachers, teachers declared that they were now part of the general workers' struggle having labor status. This was the culmination of a process taking place in the late 1970s, when the teachers reorganized their associations under a more unionist basis, despite the fact that the government officially prohibited the organization of public servants, including teachers, into unions. For example, between 1980 and 1989 university professors organized six strikes in protest against the privatization efforts of public universities, with their 1.5 million students.

During the 1980s, however, the government once again became somewhat liberalized, and in 1988 the university, secondary, and primary teachers finally gained the constitutional right to unionize. Through this recognition several teacher organizations, including the Brazilian Society for the Advancement of Science, the National Association of History Teachers, and the Brazilian Association of Geographers, gained access to government agencies, with ensuing discussions with the Federal Educational Council and the Ministry of Education and Culture on teacher education.

The teachers' involvement with teacher education policy formation increased in the 1980s as innovative experiences in teacher education were initiated in universities in the states of Pernambuco, Minas Gerais, Rio Grande do Sul, Mato Grosso, and Rio de Janeiro. In 1981 alone, the Ministry of Education and Culture promoted seven seminars on reformulating training programs in education, where the content of teacher education courses was debated. In that same year, geography and history associations developed a series of seminars, which eventuated in the creation of the National Commission on Teacher Education. It soon published several documents on geography (1984), moral and civic education (1985), history (1986), and language (1986).

The emerging democratic shift of the Ministry of Education and Culture is evidenced by the fact that the higher education section of the ministry accepted the recommendations and suggestions formulated by the teachers' organizations at Campinas (São Paulo) in 1986. The debate continues, but new teacher education programs are emerging, with extensive input from the teachers and their organizations.

### Issue 3: Lack of Integration Between the Teaching of Subject Matter and Pedagogy

From the beginning of the current debates regarding the transformation of teacher education, there has been a general recognition that some integration must take place between the so-called content institutes, where the various fields of study exist, and the colleges of education. The task of integration is still to be accomplished. Several problems must be confronted, including the willingness of discipline people to work with teacher education personnel, in defining objectives for required licensing courses, in the options students have while working on their licenses, in the relationship between teaching and research at all units, and in the relationship between secondary and primary teacher preparation. The content institutes continue to undervalue those who are going into teaching, and there is a sense that courses not related to teaching are of higher quality and value.

The content institutes have been criticized for continuing to separate students in terms of their future objectives: teaching or research. Carvalho and Vianna (1988) point out the need for future teachers to have research experience, while studying at the university, and they suggest that "professionals must have research experience, epistemological knowledge of the specific content in order to know what to select to teach and to whom" (p. 144). There is also a growing awareness of the need to integrate the discipline's specific content with pedagogical content (curriculum, didactics, practice teaching, instructional technology, etc.). A national commission has been established to facilitate integrative efforts between content institutes and colleges of education at several universities.

A final point of integration is the coherence of university studies with the broader social reality where teachers operate. In other words, there must be a sociopolitical aspect of educational practice, which, according to N. Rodrigues (1985, p. 11) unfolds into preparation for three dimensions: political life, the world of work, and a comprehensive worldview. A number of suggestions are being offered to achieve such an end. One suggestion is that teacher education be based on a multidimensional educational process, including multidisciplinary teachers in all secondary and elementary schools, who are not only critical thinkers, but have professional competence and a political commitment as well.

## Issue 4: The Need for Higher Quality of Teacher Education

Even though Brazil has emphasized general culture and erudition since the time of the Jesuits, Brazilian education has had only a superficial preoccupation with teacher preparation. From the 1950s onward, however, politicians have stressed the importance of education, including teacher education. President Juscelino Kubitschek emphasized the practical and technical aspects of knowledge, the role of education in development, as well as the qualifications to work and produce. Then Presidents Jañio Quadros and João Goulart emphasized the raising of people's awareness or level of consciousness, although they did not minimize the technical aspects associated with general, civic, and political knowledge. Then, under the military regime (1964–1985), the quality of education became associated with the efficient development of human potential for work, the support of the regime, and self-realization as a worker-citizen, as defined in educational law. Today, quality of education is generally thought to include a strong political dimension, such as:

the pedagogical practice, developed inside the schools, capable of giving students from the popular social classes the instruments necessary to appropriate knowledge, in order to effectively have access to political participation processes of the country, in the struggle to overcome their marginalized condition in political decisions and in search for better life conditions (Ribeiro, 1989, p. 36; Chaui, 1982, p. 6).

The teacher's main struggle during the military regime was to oppose attempts to eliminate well-trained content specialists and to qualify teachers through short-duration courses for subject specialists and watered-down general programs for elementary school teachers. This struggle persists today. The normal schools, designated for the preparation of elementary school teachers, are actually often used as institutions that serve as production mills to give lower class girls a little cultivation and initiation into middle-class norms, so they can serve as house-keepers and home maidens for the wealthy. Their intent might be construed as something other than serving as rigorous educational institutions, but as finishing schools for the poor. As a consequence, more than half of those who graduate from normal schools do not even go into teaching. As the normal schools are phased out, it is hoped that all teachers of the future will come to have university training, so that the teacher variable will no longer contribute so strongly to the low productivity of the educational system.

Even at the best universities, however, the tendency is to consider teacher education as a minor function of education. This has led to the opening up of an array of private higher learning institutions, which offer short-duration programs of questionable quality that qualify teachers. Studies done in 1980s demonstrate that the deterioration of higher education, taking place in institutions having precarious administrative and teaching foundations, together with other factors, has contributed to the decline of the general quality of education. As stressed earlier, this criticism is especially directed to those programs for the new polyvalent teachers.

Currently, one of the most active ongoing debates in Brazil has arisen out of attempts to define programs that will produce teachers having sound intellectual and pedagogical substance, as well as the ability to deal with Brazil's socio-historical reality. This would translate into the creation of teachers who are politically active and who are capable of making education an instrument of liberation and bringing marginalized students into political participation and citizenship.

### Issue 5: The Need for Higher Quality of Teacher Continuing Education

Continuing education is a luxury to which very few teachers have access in Brazil. Burdened with a relatively low quality of life and the need to struggle for survival, teachers are unable to respond to official projects, which are usually publicized as being well planned and executed. The vast majority of teachers are unable to participate in any projects, because they are given no free time or resources to participate. Continuing education is available for those few heroic teachers who can afford to enroll. In spite of minimal or sporadic efforts by educational agencies such as universities, state ministries, and teacher associations, teachers feel deeply the need for further training.

Continuing education comes under varied labels. Courses and seminars are usually called in-service education, recycling training, or extension courses, when offered by universities. The nature of these courses and programs has long been dictated by the interests of the agencies or the instructors, rather than by the actual problems teachers are struggling to resolve. Celani (1988, p. 15), for example, criticizes traditional continuing education as limited, ill focused, and unrelated to the real experiences of teachers. In addition, these programs focus on specific projects rather than on shifts in attitudes, habits, and beliefs that may help teachers become more independent and resourceful in their work.

Several innovative efforts are being undertaken. One project taking place at a number of universities in English has involved teachers in the planning of in-service education, so that the teachers' interests are integrated into the work. Individuals at many universities are taking the initiative, without additional resources, to work directly with teachers in the field. One such project at the Espirito Santo State involves more than one thousand teachers per semester with the purpose of involving teachers as researchers in their own practice. A major difficulty is that these individual efforts fail to become part of the larger academic community, because so little communication takes place between institutions.

### Issue 6: Improving the Working and Life Conditions of Teachers

The crucial issue facing teacher education is always the urgent need to provide better working and life conditions for teachers. This issue may appear to be peripheral to teacher education itself, but one or two examples may clarify why it is central. In the first place, teacher candidates at the normal schools for elementary teaching rarely find teaching an attractive alternative. In fact, most of these teacher candidates are enrolled at the normal school because it provides a quick entrance to the job market after school in jobs such as clerical, house-keeping, and taking care of children in the homes of the wealthy. Consequently, the students are not anticipating teaching and do not attend to the kinds of skills needed by a teacher. They do not focus their energies on learning for teaching; rather, they concentrate on getting through and into the job market outside the school.

In the second place, it is common knowledge that the salaries of teachers are disastrously low. In 1986 the government determined that the minimal salary necessary for survival was Cr$3,793; the official minimum salary of teachers was Cr$804, or one-fourth that figure. At that time average salary of licensed secondary teachers was Cr$2,397 (Pereira and Nascimento, 1986, pp. 14–20). With the runaway inflation rate, the minimal salary necessary for survival in 1991 had spiraled to Cr$90,000, while the minimum salary for teachers stood at Cr$17,000. In other words, it had declined from one-fourth to one-fifth the salary deemed necessary for survival. The above figures are averages, but there are great regional disparities. The rural teacher is certainly the most marginalized. Rural salaries are so low that in the Northeast in 1983 a great number of teachers abandoned the classroom to work as menial laborers in an emergency government land reclamation project.

In the third place, the status of teachers is so low that most elementary teachers are ashamed to identify themselves as teachers. Unable to eat properly, live and dress adequately, receive proper medical care, and experience leisure, teachers are becoming increasingly hopeless about enhancing their lives. Most of those with talent are leaving the teaching profession and are randomly looking for better paid and higher status alternatives. Add to this condition the state's tendency to continue to treat teachers as objects of manipulation through authoritarian decrees and technobureaucratic logic, then one understands why teacher education is an unattractive option for most bright young people. Among the themes permeating the debate of educational issues today, democratization and the quality of education stand out. Teachers must be recognized as professionals and become increasingly involved in policymaking regarding their professional lives. Their standard of living must be elevated to one in which they can take pride. Otherwise, all other teacher education measures will be of little consequence.

## CONCLUSION

In this chapter we have touched on major issues surrounding Brazilian teacher education. The debates of the past two decades have centered heavily on the role of foreign educational models in Brazil, the role of teachers in policymaking, the manner in which subject fields can be integrated with pedagogical spheres, quality factors in teacher education including continuing education, and how to raise the working and general life conditions of teachers. Consensus has emerged from these debates in teacher organizations regarding the need to provide greater investments in education, to give greater value to teaching as a profession, and to move toward participative governance so that teachers have a greater voice. But teachers continue to face the low interest of elites in education in general, and the commitments of elites to the developed world.

Significantly, teachers have come to play a broker's role between the elites and the masses. Many of the best of the lower classes raise themselves through teacher education, and many in the small middle class remain as teachers of the elites. They are in touch with both worlds, and if solutions are found in Brazilian education, teachers have a central role to play.

## REFERENCES

Azevedo, J. O. *A Cultura Brasileira, Introducão ao Estudo da Cultura no Brasil.* São Paulo: Edições Melhoramentos, 1964.

Berger, M. *Educacão e Dependência.* Porto Alegre: DIFEL, 1976.

Carnoy, M. *Education as Cultural Imperialism.* New York: David McKay Co., 1974.

Carvalho, A.M.P. de, and D. M. Vianna. "A quem cabe a Licenciatura?" In *Ciência e Cultura.* Rio de Janeiro, No. 40 (2), (February 1988): 143–147.

Celani, M.A.A. "A Educação Continuada do Professor." In *Ciência e Cultura.* Rio de Janeiro, No. 40 (2) (February 1988): 158–163.

Chaui, M. de S. "O que é ser educador hoje?" Da arte à ciência: A Morte do Educador." In *O Educador: Vida e Morte.* Brasilia: Edições Graal Ltda., 1982, p. 53–70.

Holanda, S. B. *História Geral da Civilização Brasileira.* A Epoca Colonial, do Descobrimento à Expansão Territorial. São Paulo: Difel, 1987. Vol 1.

Paiva, V. "Perspectivas da Educação Brasileira." In INEP. *Em Aberto* ano 4, No. 25 (January/March, 1985): 1–8.

Pereira, J., and A. Nascimento. "Quanto ganha o professor brasileiro." In *Nova Escola.* São Paulo: Editora Abril, Ltda., Ano I, No. 7, (October 1986) 14–20.

Picanco, I.S. "Alguns elementos para discussão sobre o Professor Leigo no Ensino Brasileiro." In INEP. *Em Aberto.* Brasilia, ano 5, No. 32 (October-December 1986): 9–12.

Ribeiro, V.M.B. "A questâo da qualidade do ensino nos Planos Oficiais de Desenvolvimento da Educaçâo." In INEP. *Em Aberto*. Brasilia, ano 8, No. 44 (October-December 1989): 35–44.

Rodrigues, N. *Por uma Nova Escola*. São Paulo: Cortez & Editora, 1985.

# 4

# CANADA

## RUSSELL J. LESKIW AND VALERIE-DAWN RUDDELL GIRHINY

Education in Canada, including teacher education, is the responsibility of the ten provinces. While notable differences in education occur and problems unique to each province arise, the following ten issues and problems have defied easy resolution throughout much of Canada:

1. *Cycles of shortages and surpluses of teachers have occurred at fairly regular intervals across Canada. What strategies are required for the supply and demand of teachers to be consistently in approximate balance?* Shortages of teachers occur every seven to ten years, and they fall mostly in several subject or service area specializations. Occasionally, however, the shortages extend to the full range of teaching positions. Large surpluses can occur in the years between shortages, again in certain specializations or "across the board." This feast or famine in supply creates serious problems in the quality of service provided in the schools; furthermore, as a result, the status of teaching as a profession is brought into question.

Two highly specific features of this supply-demand problem have led to political and sociocultural as well as educational consequences.

2. *How can teachers best be prepared for schools in single-language, bilingual, and multiethnic communities?* Canada is officially a bilingual country, and instruction in both English and French languages is either required or desired in many schools. Moreover, a wide array of ethnic communities across Canada leads to demands for instruction in many other languages. The preparation of teachers who can speak and instruct in all these languages continues to be a major problem throughout Canada.

3. *How can teachers for children in First Nations (aboriginal) communities best be prepared in numbers sufficient to meet the demand?* First Nations (aboriginal) communities want teachers who are conversant with their languages

and other cultural attributes, but teacher education institutions across Canada are not graduating enough qualified teachers to meet this demand. In addition to their inadequate numbers, teachers may not be aware of the critical interrelationship between education and the cultural life of the First Nation communities.

4. *How can the whole educational community address the challenges of effecting improvements and preparing more teachers with relatively scarce resources?* The routing of funds to universities and the subsequent allocation to faculties of education has long been a point of contention among these faculties. Yet the faculties do not appear to have presented convincing arguments, nor have they received support from the professional education community. At the same time, additional demands are being placed on them, often without the accompanying increases in financial resources. What strategies need to be devised to address inequities in funding and in increasing professional support for the faculties?

5. *What mechanisms can best be used for coordinating demands by many groups for involvement in decisionmaking pertaining to teacher education?* The ministries of education, universities, school systems, professional associations of teachers, and vocal lay groups, all holding many differing views on teacher education, are clamoring for a voice in decisions pertaining to the preparation of teachers. What is the best way to involve these groups so that effective decision making can proceed expeditiously?

6. *Faculties of education should place the highest priority on preparing teachers. Yet the education community often questions whether faculties demonstrate this high commitment. What changes and what strategies are required to resolve the differences in expectations?* It has long been acknowledged that faculties of education are at the vortex of expectations between universities and the educational community. Universities demand a scholarly and research orientation, while school proponents desire a practice-oriented approach, including periodic return to teaching in the classroom. Satisfying both sets of demands—often held to be in conflict—has been very difficult. Can this impasse be resolved and, if so, how?

7. *Teacher trainers and teacher candidates are said to form an unhappy alliance at the university! Should the university retain full responsibility for the preparation of teachers?* Teacher candidates regularly express disillusionment with their preparation programs. Although some program and delivery reforms have lessened these concerns, the concerns are still there and, what is more, are vocally supported by practicing teachers and school administrators. What is the answer—a greater share of teacher education responsibility assumed by the schools? Or would this change merely transfer the site of the problems, the causes of which have not been addressed?

8. *What is the appropriate balance between theory and practice in teacher education programs?* Uncertainty over the type and extent of theoretical content in preparation programs and over its application to actual teaching is yet another facet of differing expectations held by different groups participating in decision

making about teacher education. Is there room for a blend of theory with practice? If so, what improvements can be achieved in effecting transferability of theory into practice by teachers? And should we expect a direct impact of this transfer on student learning?

9. *Advocates of research on teaching and on teacher education have had minimal success in presenting a convincing case in Canada. What is the real nature of their problem, what are the implications of the problem for teacher education, and how can these be addressed?* Most of the research in teacher education to which reference is made in Canada originates in the United States. Although nationalistic pride may explain some of the reticence in accepting this research, the real problems are more basic both in Canada and the United States. What are these problems and how important is it that they be addressed? And how can skeptical practitioners and an even more skeptical lay public and political constituency be made supportive?

10. *Educators have spoken about the importance of continuity in preservice, in-service, and continuing education of teachers. Yet progress in achieving this goal has been very slow. Why? How can progress be advanced? Are there ways to build in continuing adaptation by teachers to developing needs, roles, and technologies?* The advent of a new century in less than ten years has been used to dramatize the great changes that should occur, and much time has been spent theorizing about the specific responses required. Articulating the preparation that teachers already have with more immediate needs that arise as they carry out their teaching assignments now is not nearly as dramatic, but it is much more important. Furthermore, as new knowledge develops, teachers must become familiar with it. Yet teachers fulfill their assignments under such a variety of employment and school conditions that a systematic approach to addressing this problem has not been found.

The next section presents a number of factors in Canada which may affect the nature of solutions proposed and enacted. In a subsequent section the nine problems are described more fully, and a number of proposed solutions are considered. A final section is devoted to several concluding statements.


## GENERAL BACKGROUND

Enduring as well as changing characteristics of Canadian society exert both a deliberate and an indirect impact on teacher education across the country. Historic, economic, demographic, geographic, political, and sociocultural features necessitate varying responses to problems and issues as these contexts vary and interrelate. Descriptive features of Canadian education present their own peculiar challenge to teacher education. Full consideration of these societal and descriptive features is beyond the scope of this chapter. However, several of the more critically important features have been selected for discussion.

**Historic Factors**

Of the three levels of government in Canada—federal, provincial (state), and municipal (local)—only the provincial and municipal levels have formal jurisdiction over education. The federal government retains responsibility for the territories (areas not organized into provinces); furthermore, it shares the costs of postsecondary education, including teacher education, with the provinces. However, federal transfer payments are made to the provinces and not directly to the postsecondary institutions. Hence, any federal influence or coordination that might be exercised on any programs through funding is surrendered to the provinces.

Teacher education, as did the whole public education enterprise, historically assumed responsibility for integrating an increasing ethnic population into either the anglophone or the francophone society (Quebec). The influence of the ethnic community changed the assimilation process to one where attention in anglophone Canada was given to school instruction in some of these languages. In francophone Canada minority languages, including English, were viewed as likely contributing to the demise of French culture. Hence, schools played a different role—one of strengthening the French culture.

Of importance is the historical evolution of teacher education from the "normal" school common to many countries to its present status as an integral part of university programs. Although only one teachers' college now operates in Canada, representing an intermediate step in this evolutionary process, important vestiges of the normal-school period remain in the minds of former faculty members, teachers, and other school officials, politicians, and the general public. Several issues continue to be controversial because of the earlier, now romanticized, impressions of what teacher "training" was like. Entry qualifications, length of required preparation programs, focus on traditional pedagogical studies, minimal academic requirements for elementary teachers, demand for "practice"-oriented faculty members, and the low regard for research all exemplify the influence of the normal school on the planning and programming of teacher education today.

**Geographic and Demographic Factors**

As the largest country in the world geographically, Canada is marked by its vastness of territory and notable differences in topography; wide variations in climate regionally and seasonally; great diversity in natural resources and hence in the wealth of provinces; distinctively regional orientation; a population that is very small relative to the size of the country; unique settlement patterns by aboriginal and incoming peoples; and land features that facilitate north-south links (with the United States) by transportation and communication from all regions rather than east-west ties.

Of significance politically, socially, and economically is the aging of the population. Increasing percentages of the population are beyond the "middle" years of life and into retirement. Competition for services with younger citizens and school-age children, often expressed at election time, is a reality to which education agencies and institutions are slowly adapting. The demand for adult continuing education, for career retraining, and for training in retirement careers is adding a new challenge for education in general and teacher education specifically.

### Sociocultural Factors

First Nations peoples (aboriginals) and a diverse ethnic population in Canada present a rich cultural mix that only in recent years has been recognized and promoted widely. Expressed concerns for attending to the educational needs of the First Nations peoples as well as to needs created by official bilingual policies enacted by the federal government are foremost among the cultural issues requiring attention from teacher education institutions. Social changes in society— broken families, single-parent families, working parents and latchkey children, drug and alcohol problems—require awareness by teacher educators and teachers alike. These and other factors create unclear, competitive, and conflicting expectations of teachers by society. Often these expectations extend far beyond the traditional role of the school. When teachers do not satisfy the demands made by individuals and by articulate interest groups, severe strain and demoralizing criticism can take place. Perhaps the greatest challenge that teacher education faces is devising ways to prepare teachers for teaching in an uncertain world—and one of increasing complexity and diversity where the only certainty is change itself. Given that teaching itself is marked by uncertainty (and teacher candidates find this extremely frustrating), this challenge may be more than teacher education can resolve on its own.

### THE EDUCATIONAL SYSTEM

In 1989 there were 4,200 schools with an enrollment of forty-nine or fewer students and seventy-five with 2,000 or more—evidence of the wide variations in population density. The existence of so many schools with multigraded classrooms and of large elementary and secondary schools has obvious implications for teacher education: some teachers must be prepared for teaching all and some only several subject areas in the curriculum. Some will teach up to nine grades in one classroom, whereas others will teach only one or two subjects daily to a number of classes.

Pupil-teacher ratios have leveled off (at about 18:1), and so has school enrollment from declines in the early 1980s. Fairly static pupil-teacher ratios and school enrollments imply a consistent demand for teachers, provided that current attrition rates and school policies remain unchanged. In this respect, a significant development in recent years has been the pressure by teachers' organizations, through collective bargaining, to reduce pupil-teacher ratios and to receive more planning time. School boards and teachers, in their bargaining, tend to refer to research evidence or the lack of it pertaining to reduced ratios and their impact on student learning. Administration costs, the number of administrators and their salaries, have also entered the negotiations. All these demands, if met, will have a direct impact on the number of teachers required.

### School Organization

The grade system has been in use in all the provinces, although the organization of schools differs according to grades and levels. These differences in school organization, combined with other developments such as full or partial integration or continuous progress plans that eliminate grades, the existence of many schools of differing sizes and policies pertaining to subject specialization, and self-contained classrooms, all point to the need for teachers who can teach in a wide range of organizational patterns.

Schools in a number of provinces have been introduced to school-based management wherein they are heavily involved in planning and other decisions pertaining to school operation, including their own professional development. This change in the locus of decision making requires preparation of teachers in areas formerly reserved for administrators.

### Teacher Certification

Teacher certification is a responsibility of provincial departments of education in all provinces but one, British Columbia, where it has been assigned to a teachers' organization.

In most provinces some form of advisory council gives advice to the Minister of Education (the Ministry) on matters pertaining to teacher education, including certification. The range of certificates varies from province to province; provision for upgrading certificates must be made by universities for teachers from other provinces.

## THE SYSTEM OF TEACHER EDUCATION

Of the sixty-eight universities in Canada, thirty-eight offer teacher preparation programs. In some provinces, a portion of these programs may be taken at regional community colleges which become affiliated with the universities. Teacher education programs are of two basic types: (1) the integrated pattern in which professional and academic courses are taken simultaneously, and (2) the after-degree pattern in which the academic coursework is taken first. In this second pattern, one year of professional studies is normally completed to qualify for certification and two years for a B.Ed. degree. This one-year feature is one of the inconsistencies—an anachronism—surviving from the normal-school period, but with the added, underlying assumption that the more academic preparation a teacher receives, the less professional preparation is needed. The principle, common to most other professions, that the components of the professional phase are basic regardless of the length of academic studies, has long been advocated by faculties of education. It has not been accepted yet by governments, which provide the funding and grant teaching certificates. Regardless of patterns, across Canada, a gradual move is being made toward five years of teacher preparation.

Decentralization of teacher education programs is being advocated in several provinces, mostly because universities have generally not responded to regional needs and to numerous and frequent recommendations of school authorities. In these decentralized approaches, responsibilities for sectors of the teacher education programs have been assigned to regional community colleges. The first stage of this reassignment has involved collaborative arrangements between community colleges and existing universities. Precedent would seem to point to the likelihood that the collaborating colleges will in time press for and succeed in acquiring full independence in responsibility for teacher education. Such a change would markedly increase the number of teacher preparation institutions, with significant impact on quality control and financial allocation for programs. It would also have an impact on the nature of the programs and on the status of teaching as a profession.

## ISSUES AND PROBLEMS

### Issue 1: Cycles in the Supply and Demand of Teachers

Across Canada there are continuing difficulties in matching the supply with the demand for teachers. Until now, studies and surveys have been conducted in most provinces in order to project the need for teachers in the coming years. These studies have usually started with the current supply/demand data as the base and attempted to predict the situation in the coming years. These procedures have not resulted in decisions that have alleviated the shortages or oversupply of teachers. A number of provinces are instituting longitudinal studies that consider career patterns and choices, economic conditions, demographic factors, political policy impact, curricular requirements, nature of teacher preparation programs, mobility rates, and so on. Nevertheless, changes within any of these factors as well as their complex interrelationships may make more accurate forecasting, even within a single province, uncertain and unlikely.

The development of several political, economic, and social scenarios (proposing ''what if'' options) that are likely to prevail in the future appears to offer promise in applying the above factors more meaningfully. Thus, longitudinal (strategic) planning can utilize alternatives in interpreting and applying the data so as to match the scenario developed, leading to greater reliability of the projection techniques. The advent of sophisticated computer modeling makes it much easier to integrate scenarios, alternatives, and data. Policy formulation can then involve consideration of the best combination with circumstances that are most likely to result in a continuing supply of teachers. If such policy strategies are followed consistently, rather than just during periods of crisis, a resolution of the problems may be realized.

Of continuing concern has been the tendency at the political level to tinker with short-term approaches to resolve shortages of teachers. One of these approaches involves the use of graduates from academic programs who have little or no pedagogic preparation. Although this practice is not widespread at this time, anxiety arises from its introduction in Canada in at least one province and from its promotion at senior political levels across the United States. Continuing publicity of this and similar approaches in the U.S. media channels that reach a sizable portion of the Canadian public gives more substance to this anxiety. The educational community should move quickly in countering these inroads with information about policies proposed in Canada which are likely to be successful in addressing supply issues.

Seen historically, the issue of quality control has been inversely related to the supply and demand of teachers. When a surplus situation is at hand, requirements at the university and certification agency have become more demanding. Conversely, when shortages arise, exceptions to certification regulations and resorting to other expedient arrangements for licensing teachers come into evidence in departments of education. Furthermore, in this matter of supply and demand, when there is a surplus of teachers, such as that noted in the early 1980s, interest in longitudinal studies intended to address the surplus-shortage cycle diminishes.

### Issue 2: Preparing Teachers for Schools in Single-Language, Bilingual, and Multiethnic Communities

Federal government policies on bilingualism and multiculturalism, reinforced by financial grant transfers for facilitating implementation, have led to pressure on teacher education institutions to prepare teachers for many divergent assignments involving teaching in a variety of non-English languages. Since the population is sparsely distributed in most parts of the country, inequities have occurred in the application of these policies. Furthermore, higher costs have been incurred where policies have been implemented.

It may be that the current constitutional crisis, in which Quebec is seeking full sovereignty, may lead to a lessening in demand for French instruction outside Quebec. A concurrent trend away from instruction in other, non-English languages may also develop, an outgrowth of concerns that too much attention to bilingualism and multiculturalism has led to the disunity that characterizes Canada at this time. Only the passage of time will bring more insight into the language situation.

Should the present federal policies continue, universities might have to consider one or more options along the following lines:

1. recruiting candidates on the basis of a quota system to ensure that teachers with an adequate language base are available for the various demands of communities across Canada,

2. increasing cooperative arrangements with institutions—including some outside Canada—whose primary function is the preparation of graduates who speak one or more non-English languages fluently,

3. working directly with school systems and communities to facilitate formal learning of one or more non-English languages at an early age, thus providing universities with matriculants conversant in several languages,

4. relying on broad-based, collaborative efforts to emphasize the importance of satisfying needs by a growing minority student population to identify with teachers of similar cultural and linguistic backgrounds. Such efforts should involve commitment at all levels of society in both the public and private sectors.

### Issue 3: Preparing Teachers for Children in First Nations Communities

The most challenging facet of the teacher supply issue is the shortage of acculturated teachers for First Nations schools. Relatively few students of First Nations ancestry graduate from Canadian high schools with matriculation standing, and those who do, find a range of lucrative opportunities outside teaching to consider.

A number of universities—the University of British Columbia, the University of Saskatchewan, and Brandon University, for example—have undertaken programs specially designed to prepare teachers of First Nations children. One problem these institutions have encountered is the tendency of graduates of these programs either to select or migrate within a few years to urban settings, thereby again leaving schools in First Nations communities staffed by unacculturated teachers.

It would appear that here again, as in the case of meeting the demand for teachers from other ethnic minorities, a systematic, collaborative, committed, and long-range program should be instituted in each province to address needs appropriately.

### Issue 4: The Challenges of Effecting Improvements and Preparing More Teachers with Relatively Scarce Resources

The allocation of financial resources to institutions of higher learning and their distribution within these institutions have created complex sets of circumstances with which faculties of education must cope. Comparatively speaking, teacher education and education as a whole have fared well in Canada. More than $40 billion was invested in education in 1988 for an enrollment of 5.8 million students. Of this amount, $8.2 billion was invested at the university level for 500,000 students. Yet, people's expectations are high, as are the demands of a complex economy. The distribution and application of these financial resources have not reduced the relatively high levels of functional illiteracy and poverty in Canada. Within universities, allocations have not successfully addressed the needs of teacher education programs on a basis similar to that of other professional preparation programs. Admittedly, the demand for such large numbers of teachers, as compared to the demand for other professionals, would lead to a dramatic escalation in costs if a more equitable distribution of funds were attempted. Yet society and the university itself rarely acknowledge financial factors as possible causes when sharp criticism of teacher preparation programs arises.

Teacher education institutions are continually trying to cope with uncertain demands for teachers as a result of fluctuating student enrollments, varying economic conditions within and among provinces, differing political decisions affecting education and teacher education alike, variations in teacher retention and teacher retirement policies, and a host of other circumstances. Rarely is very much lead time given for faculties to respond to these demands in a rational manner.

Along with the need to develop formulas for more equitable distribution of funds to faculties of education, including, perhaps, further consideration of earmarked funding (a long-time nemesis of central university administrations), the issue of financial resources can have other significant ramifications for the teaching profession. Along with improved teacher education programs, higher salaries and better working conditions for teachers (which are the active goals of teachers' associations through collective bargaining) have created strong interest in teaching as a profession among both students entering university and those already involved in university studies in other specializations.

Economic policies advocated by federal and provincial governments have been directed to the attention of faculties of education in such widely varying areas as developing workforce needs, competitiveness with trading partners, reduction of functional illiteracy among adults, environmental and ecological issues, and the high incidence of at risk youth and adults.

With regard to the financial issues affecting teacher education, the following conditions require particular attention: the impact of federal political policies in the areas of bilingualism and multiculturalism; the presence or absence of bilateral agreements (reciprocity) in certification and the effect on teacher mobility; supply-demand for teachers in other provinces and regions; and the effect of geographical factors on teacher recruitment and retention.

The financial issue plays a critical role in teacher education in one other respect: the inadequacy of the support structure for idealized teacher education programs. In short, much knowledge is now available about desirable changes in teacher preparation and, despite much disagreement as to which of these might be implemented, many of these changes could be incorporated into ''lighthouse'' programs, if not into programs generally. But such changes as extension in the use of technology, interagency decision making, sequential field experiences, including internships and induction programs, appropriate supervisory and evaluative approaches, and incorporating research findings into teaching and teacher education are all expensive. Thus, teacher education programs have been traditionalized, and improvements have been largely stagnated by the popular view that teacher education should not cost more than academic programs in the arts and sciences. Admittedly, incidental improvements continue to be made, but most changes have been in the nature of "tinkering" with the arrangement and rearrangement of program sectors.

## Issue 5: Mechanisms for Coordinating Demands for Involvement in Decision Making Pertaining to Teacher Education

The presence of many stakeholder groups, that is, groups affected by and/or desiring an input into decision making, results in diverse views on most issues pertaining to teacher education. The most crucial of these issues is the knowledge base for teacher education. A brief review of the expectations by various stakeholder groups will illustrate the point.

*Levels of Government:* In addition to the many special interest groups, there are local and provincial levels of government (which occasionally also voice national imperatives from the federal level) - which seek attention to occupational skills, environmental education, literacy, redressing the *at risk* situation of many children and youth, and a host of other issues.

*Universities:* Universities may impose admission requirements, academic standards for programs (e.g., a liberal education focus), achievement and graduation standards requirements, and so on. The most obvious impact by the university as a whole upon the knowledge base, exerted mostly by academic departments in faculties of arts and sciences, is the offering of academic subject specializations to teacher education students and, subsequently through graduate schools, programs of graduate studies. Nearly 60 percent of the teacher education curriculum consists of courses from academic specializations.

*Faculties of Education:* These may at various times be advocates of reflection, personal biographies, effectiveness studies, and so forth, as major themes for the professional phase of the preparation program. They are also expected to be strong proponents of the professional phase itself and of its various components.

For most of the twentieth century educational psychology has dominated teacher education in the United States and Canada. Educational psychology was originally intended to lend academic respectability through scholarly and experimental studies, focusing heavily on measurement and statistical analysis. This emphasis has become a powerful tradition which has made it very difficult to introduce new emphases and different balances within programs.

*School Systems:* School authorities generally focus their interest in the knowledge base on practice-oriented activities (as opposed to theory and research). They affect and are involved in the knowledge base in numerous other ways: providing sites for field experiences, requesting various specializations and curriculum orientations, and requiring teachers for a variety of organizational patterns.

*Professional Associations:* Teachers' professional associations have been vocal proponents of teachers' rights, status, improved salaries and working conditions, and professional development. They have often come into conflict with provincial and national school trustees' (school board members) associations which represent the views of school boards and local taxpayers.

When planning and operating their teacher education programs, faculties of education have to negotiate among these stakeholder groups very carefully. Conflicting demands and expectations from these groups cannot always be accommodated, but most faculties have been able to balance the demands of practice-oriented groups such as school systems and their personnel on the one hand and academic, research-oriented forces at the university level on the other. In fact, they may have done so too successfully—they have been accused of playing off these two opposing emphases against each other for the purpose of maintaining full control of decision making in teacher education. While conflicting interests have made the decision-making task more demanding, there has also been much common ground. There is at least general agreement on the knowledge content of teacher education. The importance of subject specialization is unchallenged, although differences of opinion exist about the amount required at the elementary as opposed to the secondary level. Teacher candidates, however, having met university admission requirements first, continue to fulfill the required specialization criteria. To the extent that a university-wide liberal education focus is clearly enunciated, faculties of education, like other professional schools, encourage their graduates to become intelligent individuals and citizens. Yet there is an uneasy truce on other important matters—the length and nature of the professional component and, more recently, the decentralization of teacher education programs to community colleges. Currently, the college initiatives are under the rubric of universities, but pressure from college communities for independence of action and even for university status are already in evidence.

Some form of advisory council exists in most provinces, advising the Minister of Education on all matters pertaining to teacher education. Such councils usually have members from each of the groups listed above. The existence of advisory councils and of their operating procedures is a matter of expediency for provincial governments. These councils can be changed or discontinued (and have been) at any time. Furthermore, the individual stakeholder groups may have their own agendas and priorities, or they may pay scant attention to teacher education. Faculties and ministries of education may be unimpressed with the need for advisory councils and shared decision making. They may prefer to "wheel and deal" on their own and thus be in a better position to influence the course of decision making directly. In addition, the operations of the councils can easily become heavily politicized and thus be inefficient in terms of expediting decision making and retaining flexibility in considering needed changes. Finally, the delicate role of a chairperson in assisting interagency collaboration, mostly unrecognized, can spell the difference between the effectiveness and the failure of the council.

Difficult as reaching agreement may appear, diversity of views may in fact contribute to unity through diversity—programming that meets needs through a variety of options.

### Issue 6: Changes and Strategies Needed to Resolve the Differences in Expectations Between Faculties of Education and the Education Community

It should be assumed that members of faculties of education are qualified by virtue of advanced graduate study, scholarly activity and competent instructional performance, knowledge of school curricula, school teaching experience, and continuing contact with the schools. Thus, they should acknowledge and perform the three basic functions of faculties of education: prepare teachers, add to knowledge about teaching and learning, and assist in disseminating this knowledge to school practitioners.

A balance should be sought in the type of qualifications of faculty members and their involvement in the faculty's functions. The university's full commitment and support to such faculty efforts are crucial (for its reward structure must recognize the equal importance of research, scholarship, and instruction) both on campus and in professional upgrading and continuing education. The importance of this statement cannot be overestimated, for despite extensive lip service it is most often disregarded. Furthermore, the sacredness of research as a major criterion (despite written and verbal claims to the contrary) in the reward system leaves little doubt in the minds of faculty members that ''publish or perish'' is in fact the criterion that must guide them. It seems to matter little that only a small percentage of university faculty members do and have in fact been engaged in meaningful research and that the majority have misused their time and society's resources pursuing ends of doubtful value. A possible resolution to the benefit of the university, faculty member, and school system lies in the separate recognition of research and scholarship in the university reward system.

Since optimizing intellectual capacity and expanding and extending knowledge are among the several crucial goals of a university, it should be acknowledged that all university faculty must be aware of the research, the developing knowledge, and the experimentation in their specializations. This is equally true of all phases of professional teacher preparation, including the field experience component. They must also assume responsibility for evaluating, synthesizing, analyzing, and interpreting this knowledge in terms of their assignments as faculty members. In these ways faculty members will satisfy the scholarship criterion. The expansion of knowledge horizons through the infusion of new knowledge is a research function carried on by a small percentage of faculty members who may or may not carry university teaching responsibilities.

Recognition of scholarship as a criterion would enable faculty members to perform important functions recognized within school systems rather than giving lip-service to them as is now claimed. Admittedly, numbers of faculty members are disinterested in undergraduate teacher education and are consistently searching for opportunities to disengage themselves from such responsibilities—and hence from school-based components. They would prefer to confine their involvement to such activities as are given to them on campus—hopefully at the graduate level.

It might also be useful to view the total impact of teacher education on the development of the individual candidate, on the candidate's eventual growth into a practicing professional, and on the candidate's role as a member of a professional association. In this instance, the concept of spheres of influence can be applied wherein faculties and school systems will agree on spheres where each will have preeminence, where responsibility will be shared, and where lesser roles will be taken.

An additional conflict that occurs in most faculties of education pertains to the degree and the subsequent impact of differing loyalties by faculty members to their respective fields of study. These fall within three categories. In the first category are faculty members in specializations who take on the characteristics of their parent disciplines in the arts and sciences. In the second category are members engaged in pedagogical fields such as curriculum who tend to consider themselves more as members of a professional school. In the third category are members whose major responsibility lies in the field experience component and who tend to reflect the expectations and practices of their peers in the schools. Unfortunately, there is a clear pecking order with attached gradations of status moving downward toward the third category. On the average, those members in the last two categories are more likely to view themselves as arms of the teaching profession, whereas those in the first category tend to consider themselves to be in closer association with their parent academic disciplines (though not necessarily with the acceptance and approval of these disciplines). They then choose to stay aloof from the teaching profession and from much of what goes on in teacher education.

These features of "faculty culture" pose difficulties in program planning and implementation. They also exert a strong impact on the type of reward system that operates in the faculties of education.

### Issue 7: The University's Ambiguous Role in Preparing Teachers

Teacher candidates may acknowledge that the university has a significant role in their preparation; yet many will claim that it has not performed this role to their satisfaction. On their first exposure to field experiences they learn that teachers and administrators feel much the same way.

The prime reason for severe criticism of pedagogical courses is the matter of transferability of knowledge from college courses to practice in the classroom.

Many faculties leave the matter of transfer to individual candidates. Despite the heavy emphasis on field experiences in many programs, this transfer has not been facilitated. Neither faculty nor school supervisors have ''led'' the teacher candidate toward integrating both academic and pedagogical knowledge into the teacher's instructional plan. The key questions in this kind of integration have often gone unasked—and thus unsolved. How does the *teacher* decide what practices to use? How are these practices actually used? How can previous knowledge help the teacher in deciding and acting? What events that teachers see as useful can be utilized to help teachers understand classroom situations and then to carry this understanding into their teaching?

School systems continue to view practical experiences as the most important part of teacher education. They believe that the major function of teacher education is to prepare teachers to work effectively under authentic classroom conditions. Herein is their Achilles heel; system administrators develop their own perceptions and devices for deciding what makes effective teaching. These devices primarily assist the administrators in being accountable to their employers and to the public for what goes on in the classroom. Unfortunately, these external accountability criteria rarely capture the essence of the teacher's perception of the internal classroom situation.

Teacher education programs have been planned largely by university-based faculty members. Such external influence as has been exerted on this planning has come from the certification policies enacted at provincial political levels. Insofar as faculty members are the most likely to be familiar with the required theory, research, experimentation, and the totality of the conditions of practice, this approach can be justified. Where it falls considerably short of desired procedure is in its focus; the approach shows little evidence of acknowledging the crucial centrality of the teaching act in the classrooms.

Some key questions in this centrality of teaching are: What is teaching? What is it that the teacher really does in teaching? How does the teacher make decisions about what to do in teaching? Under what conditions can a teacher best make these decisions? Under what conditions will these decisions lead to the best teaching by the teacher? Focus on these key questions should also drastically alter the evaluation approaches utilized by university supervisors in student teaching—and consequently by school supervisors who are usually required to complete university-prescribed evaluation forms. Supervisors will seek answers to specific questions from the teaching observed (which will have been discussed in advance with the teaching candidate) and utilize devices that collect information about the questions in enough detail to lead to a meaningful conference with the teacher candidate following the teaching assignment. Teacher and supervisor will then ascertain the extent to which the teacher candidate has accomplished the objectives (and in so doing has provided answers to the questions). It is hoped that gone from use will be the various forms of rating scales, demeaning as these are to teaching and to the teacher candidate.

This is not to say that related issues such as characteristics of teaching, appropriate teaching behavior, developmental characteristics of students, and teacher effectiveness have not been addressed. They have, and often at great length. But, again, teacher candidates appear not to have internalized the inquiry features necessary for addressing these key questions as they are teaching. There is insufficient evidence that it is the teacher who has been "empowered" as the key decision maker and not some individual(s) external to the teaching process.

### Issue 8: Continuing Differences over the Appropriate Balance Between Theory and Practice in Teacher Education Programs

The debate about the relationship between theory and practice continues, despite the superficiality of the issue. Rigid stances by proponents of either view lead to much defensive posturing by both sectors. Faculty members continue to seek ways to escape field responsibilities, often citing "new research about field experiences," "the need to perform more important work," or "a new scholarly orientation that denies or minimizes the place of field experience" in teacher education. Practitioners, whether at government or the school's administrative or instructional levels, tend to hold scholarly activities suspect. This is a tragic circumstance in both instances and one that requires changing if schools are to become centers of inquiry about teaching and learning.

There is much emerging knowledge in many fields of teaching: teaching practices and their effects, subject and pedagogical knowledge needed to teach students, how teachers actually carry out curriculum plans and teaching practices in the classroom, how teachers translate knowledge into action, and so on. Of course, effective ways must be found to disseminate this new knowledge among classroom teachers, but suspicion about "so much theory" and "that's research" must be addressed first.

### Issue 9: The Disputed Value of Research on Teaching and Teacher Education

The need for teacher education is widely accepted. Also accepted are liberal education, subject specialization, field experience, and professional preparation as components of teacher education. Moreover, there has been little outcry in Canada about any specific feature of these components. But it is also because of faith: there has been little substantiation of any decision made through organized research initiative.

Research in teacher education has not been a high priority in Canada, and at present little research is being done. The writer's interviews in a number of teacher education faculties revealed an absence of policies and initiatives pertaining to faculty-wide research. Any research underway is mostly in the area of field experiences and is limited to the collection and analysis of data.

Because individual faculty members are left to their own initiatives in pursuing research activities, it is not surprising that such research or scholarly work as is being done is confined to the teaching specialty of the faculty member. Con-comitantly, few faculty members carry program-wide assignments in teacher education. Only those with administrative or supervisory responsibility see the entire teacher education effort—and they usually have neither the time nor the energy left to devote to research. Individuals outside the university who have macro interests in teacher education have difficulty obtaining financial support from funding agencies that have been geared to supporting university-sponsored research.

Yet another problem with research is that much of it has been preoccupied with causality and quantification and has relied mostly on statistics as the basic language of analysis and theory construction. Since only limited research is being done in Canada, much of the above research comes from the United States. In both Canada and the United States, reaction from scholars and practitioners has been negative because of the inadequacy and inappropriateness of much of this research. More usable research should focus on what teachers know and do and on the kinds of decisions they make as they teach. Such research will obviously use a different range of methodologies that is more in keeping with field orientation.

## Issue 10: Continuity in Preservice, In-service, and Continuing Education of Teachers

The idea that teacher education should be viewed as a continuum—preservice, in-service, and continuing education—is based on the premise of career-long learning in both academic and professional fields. Much new knowledge is being accumulated in the professional fields which constitutes the preservice phase. Obviously, this knowledge has to be acquired through in-service and continuing education (formal and informal) by practicing teachers. Many teacher roles and responsibilities form the substance of preservice programs; knowledge of these programs will require upgrading. In addition, new roles will have to be learned and assumed, for example, member of a staff, member of a teachers' organi-zation, member of a school council (school-based management), and member of one or more professional organizations.

New teaching assignments that may require new knowledge and orientation frequently occur during a teacher's career. It is highly significant that these requirements portray a developmental rather than a deficit approach to in-service education. Furthermore, most of these developments may require collaborative relationships among universities, departments of education, school systems, teachers' associations, professional organizations, community groups, and, in-creasingly, the private sector. Orientation to the collaborative approach as a strategy, quite apart from the content, will be required; few people have expertise in interagency collaboration.

The contributions of preservice, in-service, and continuing education within the continuum might be specifically delineated, and responsibility for each move carefully designated.

The in-service area is an area in which much uncertainty and even confusion reigns. Quite apart from the involvement of numerous stakeholders and agencies, issues of purpose, incentives, process, setting, timing, delivery, evaluation, and rewards need to be resolved.

Although much literature exists in the field of in-service education, formal study after the fashion of preservice preparation should be undertaken to reach a far higher degree of consensus and to attempt greater recognition of the essential need for in-service as a normal counterpart of preservice education.

## CONCLUSION

Many issues pertaining to teacher education are receiving attention in Canada; we could easily add to the list of those discussed in this chapter. The appropriate use of technology in all facets of preservice and the extension of its use to in-service programs is one such example. The progress made by teaching toward professional status, the desirability of continuing such progress, and the implications of these deliberations for teacher education are complex questions in the minds of many educators. More specific areas such as evaluation of teacher education programs and program accountability, greater integration of program sectors, and induction programs are under greater or lesser consideration, depending on time and region.

Concentration on the problems being experienced or debated may create the erroneous impression that nothing is right about teacher education in Canada. This is not the case, and we certainly do not intend to give such an impression in this chapter. Many positive developments should be acknowledged: for example, the widespreasd recognition of the uniqueness of each individual's abilities, learning styles, and pace of development; the importance of the active involvement of students in a wide range of individual and group situations, including problem solving; applying the use of multiple resources, including computer and interactive technological devices; encouraging creative and critical thinking; attention to important societal issues such as environment and ecology, multiculturalism, globalism, sex equity, child abuse, and literacy and many others, including those mentioned in various sections of this chapter.

It would appear that enough proposals have been presented that could resolve many of the problems in teacher education, thus restoring hope, excitement, and challenge to the field. Many of these proposals do not require much fanfare or the commitment of extensive additional funding, the exceptions being the issues in financing and researching teacher education. The chief stumbling block is the absence of the political will to act so as to ensure continued and systematic development. Instead, the actions taken may be piecemeal and attention-seeking—and even these occur only infrequently.

# REFERENCES

Beyer, Landon, et al. *Preparing Teachers as Professionals: The Role of Educational Studies and Other Liberal Disciplines.* New York: Teachers College, Columbia University, 1989.

Bolin, Frances. *Teacher Renewal: Professional Issues and Personal Choices.* New York: Teachers College, Columbia University, 1987.

Christensen, J., and Linda Tofel. "Teacher Education in the 1990's: Looking Ahead While Learning from the Past." *Action in Teacher Education.* Reston, Va.: Association of Teacher Educators, 1990.

Corrigan, Dean, and Martin Haberman. "The Content of Teacher Education," *Handbook of Research on Teacher Education.* New York: MacMillan Publishing Co., 1990.

Grimmett, Peter, and Gaalen L. Ericksen, eds. *Reflection in Teacher Education.* Vancouver, B.C.: Pacific Educational Press, University of British Columbia, 1988.

Leskiw, Russell. "A Case Study of Teacher Education in Canada." Unpublished paper presented to the International Council on Education for Teaching (ICET) joint Unesco/ICET project on Teacher Education. Washington, D.C.: The Council, 1989.

Leskiw, Russell, ed. *Teacher Preparation in British Columbia.* A report to the Minister of Education, Science and Technology by the Joint Board of Teacher Education. Victoria, B.C.: The Board, 1981.

Ontario Ministry of Education and Ministry of Colleges and Universities. *Final Report of the Teacher Education Steering Committee.* Toronto: September 1988.

Wideen, Marvin F., and Patricia Holborn. "Research in Canadian Teacher Education: Promises and Problems." *Canadian Journal of Education* 11, no. 4 (1986): 557–583.

# 5

# CHINA

## MAE CHU CHANG AND LYNN PAINE

China's teacher education stands at an important turning point.[1] For teacher education to change in ways that support the nation's development plans, four major policy issues must be addressed:

1. Clarifying goals for teacher education.
2. Resolving mismatches in the structure of teacher education.
3. Strengthening the content of teacher education programs, which are narrow, outdated, and disconnected from professional practice.
4. Improving conditions of teaching that have turned people away from teaching and teacher education.

This chapter examines each of these policy challenges and their interconnections.

### GENERAL BACKGROUND

China, as the second largest country in the world and the world's most populous nation, operates on a scale that many non-Chinese cannot fathom. It comprises significant diversity, and it is poor, considered by the World Bank as a low-income developing country. Together these characteristics stand as starting points to understanding the severity and complexity of educational problems and the difficulty involved in implementing change.

China occupies 9.6 million square kilometers, which makes it larger than the United States and only slightly smaller than Canada. At its northern border (shared with the USSR, Mongolia, and North Korea), it experiences harsh winters, while its southern regions, bordering on Vietnam, Burma, and Laos, are tropical and semitropical. In its west and southwest (bordering Afghanistan, Pakistan, India, Nepal, Sikkim, and Bhutan) stand some of the world's highest mountains and large desert area, while its eastern regions include green country crisscrossed by rivers, lakes, and canals. Despite its huge land mass, the country is crowded. Only about half of China's land is arable, and over 90 percent of its 1.13 billion population lives in the eastern half of the country. China's unique history of four thousand years of continuous civilization and intense population density has put heavy burdens on what has remained predominantly an agrarian society.

Certainly there is great variation within the country. The range of topography and climate has produced distinct economic regions, each with long histories and varying degrees of contact with the cosmopolitan world. While the sorghum farmers of northeast China, rice growers in the south, and nomadic sheepherders in the west all live off the land, their lives, living standards, and the educational experiences of their children may differ greatly. Urban-rural distinctions are also significant. With underdeveloped systems of transportation and communication and decades of sharply contrasting access to material and cultural goods, the roughly 80 percent of the population that has remained in the countryside has led lives very different from the 20 percent in the cities. Despite national curricula and unified exams for promotion to higher education, children and youth in rural and urban China traditionally and even today differ in their exposure to the world, the range of their horizons, and the options available to them in and after leaving school. Finally, despite a standard national language, a common written language, and thousands of years of national cultural tradition, China has great cultural variety, supported in part by natural and economic regional differences and maintained by a host of distinct dialects that are linguistically different and fifty-five major ethnic minority groups (who constitute 6 percent of the population). In considering teacher education in China we should note that, while the various forms of diversity described above are important for understanding the Chinese *experience* (including many educational experiences), education as an enterprise is organized by national policies of a centralized educational system. However, implementation of the policies differ enormously from province to province, depending on the resource constraints in each province.

By the mid and late 1800s China's imperial tradition was unable to compete with the more modern, aggressive capitalist countries vying internationally for raw materials and markets. Although the western powers never formally colonized the country, China, after its defeat in the Opium Wars, suffered decades of economic, political, and social humiliation at the hands of Westerners and the Japanese. Claiming territorial rights over rich parcels of China's land, these countries in the late nineteenth and early twentieth centuries made inroads culturally as well, particularly among urban Chinese. The longstanding Confucian approach to education, an elite education that stressed literacy and moral cultivation, was challenged by reformers who often supported their proposals with examples from other countries. Reformers called for the establishment of modern, mass education, with schools to be more technical, science oriented, and practical. Although Western missionaries and Chinese reformist intellectuals sympathetic to or conversant in U.S., Japanese, and German practices never had total success in implementing such a national system of education, their influence is part of China's educational history. More recently, as a new communist state was formed in 1949, Soviet educational practices were transposed to Chinese schools and universities. Vestiges of these early Confucian, Western reformist, and Soviet influences are all layered in China's schools and teaching.

The challenge for leaders of the People's Republic of China has been to find a way to feed, house, and educate its enormous population in ways that borrow useful knowledge from other countries while building a socialist modernization that is uniquely Chinese. Complicating this difficult challenge, of course, has been the fact that national construction of an infrastructure has had to occur even though the country is relatively poor. This makes every policy decision difficult. After the death of Mao Zedong, however, and by the late 1970s, China's leaders committed themselves to modernization and national development. Yet the mass social and political protests in Beijing and elsewhere in 1989 and the military and political crackdown that followed poignantly hint at the difficulty China has long faced and confronts even more directly in this modernization era of walking the delicate line of entering an increasingly integrated world system while maintaining national unity, integrity, and strength.

Teachers are at the center of China's hopes for constructing a new society. Yet, in many ways, teachers are caught by centuries-long conservative traditions and the background that shapes their country. Their education and, in particular, its reform, illustrates the challenge China faces at the close of the twentieth century.

## THE SYSTEM OF TEACHER EDUCATION

With a decade of economic reform, the government's commitment to modernization, the introduction of compulsory education, and China's increasing participation in the international arena, the education system in the last decade of the twentieth century is being challenged to keep pace with new knowledge flooding into China as well as changes in thinking and lifestyles brought about by reforms. The schools, teachers, and hence teacher education are under great pressure to change. The establishment of a compulsory education law in 1986 and the subsequent campaign for popularizing nine years of schooling challenge educators to extend schooling to larger numbers of children and youth than ever before. A major policy reform of 1985, the Resolution on the Reform of the Education System (hereafter referred to as the Education Decision), further complicates the educators' charge by calling for greater differentiation in curricula and types of schooling.[2] Finally, from education, scientific and technological, and political circles have come calls for teachers to introduce innovations that stress the active participation of students and the development of students' independent and creative thinking, which are considered the foundations for social and technological transformation.

To respond to this expanded and revised mission, teacher education stands at the crossroads of change. The dominant practices of the past have become the focus of criticism internal and external to teacher education. The teacher education curriculum, for example, exemplifies the traditional text-driven conception of teaching. The normal university curriculum defines teaching as the transmission of subject matter knowledge. Teachers are typically trained in one discipline only; cross-disciplinary or interdisciplinary thinking often associated with problem solving or creative thinking is not encouraged. Attention to students as learners is ignored.

Compounding the problems of teacher education are issues of recruitment to and retention in teaching. As China has moved from a centrally planned economy to a mixed economy with planning as well as market mechanisms, alternative career opportunities have opened up. Furthermore, the contract responsibility system in the agricultural sector and the bonus programs in industry have allowed most state workers to increase their incomes. Conditions of service in the teaching profession, including career ladders, promotion criteria, and evaluation procedures, relative to other occupations, are not adequate to attract the best people to the profession. Some teacher training institutions have had to lower their standards of admission to fill up places in the incoming classes. In an attempt to reverse these trends, China's State Education Commission (SEdC) is reviewing its policies and practices with regard to teacher education and conditions of service.

With teacher education facing challenges and policy dilemmas, who is involved in identifying the issues and considering alternatives? Preservice, inservice, and on-service teacher education occurs in a range of structurally distinct institutions, all under the authority, ultimately, of the State Education Commission.[3] In the next section we describe the current system under the SEdC's authority as background to understanding the policy debates and challenges facing the SEdC, provincial and local education authorities, and teacher educators.

## The Current System of Teacher Education

Teacher education is conducted at three levels, with normal universities at the apex of the system. Primary teachers are trained in secondary normal schools which provide three- and four-year programs that enroll lower secondary school graduates; lower secondary school teachers are trained in normal colleges that provide two- and three-year postsecondary programs; and upper secondary teachers as well as faculty members of all the above teacher training institutions and the Institutes of Education (which carry out much of the in-service and on-service work) are trained in normal universities. Graduates of normal universities sometimes become key administrators in provincial and local education bureaus. Provincial and municipal institutes of education are assisted in in-service teacher education work through local-level teacher refresher schools, a teacher education television system, correspondence programs, a national teacher corps, and school-based in-service. Although the State Education Commission prescribes the curriculum, textbooks, guidelines for buildings, facilities, teacher–student ratio, dormitory space per student and so on, the financing for teacher education comes from the reporting agencies of the respective institutions. Thus, except for the few normal universities, financing for about 3,600 teacher education institutions comes mainly from county, prefecture, and sometimes provincial governments. Although a uniform set of guidelines governs similar institutions across the country, tremendous variations actually exist, for not all local governments have the resources to provide facilities that meet the state guidelines.

In 1990 there were 3,632 teacher training institutions in the country with an enrollment of 2.1 million trainees. Although this is probably the largest teacher training system in the world, it barely meets the demand of a massive school system. Chinese schools enroll approximately 132 million primary, 41 million lower secondary, and 8 million upper secondary school students, representing gross enrollment ratios of 107, 52, and 16 percent, respectively. At the primary education level the problem is the quality of teachers, while at the secondary level both quantitative and qualitative problems exist.

Because of the state's population control program, the demand for primary teachers is expected to decrease from 5.4 million in 1987 to 5.0 million in 1990 and remain relatively stable thereafter. With the annual addition of graduates from primary teacher training schools, there is already a surplus of teachers in primary education. At the same time, owing to the life tenure of the teachers, the current 2.1 million unqualified primary teachers who lack the required education credentials cannot be replaced.

Demand for new and qualified teachers at the lower secondary level is great, however, given the mandate to provide compulsory education through nine years. In order to achieve universal basic education at the lower secondary level, the number of teachers would have to increase from 2.2 million in 1985 to 3.1 million in the year 2000. Of those 2.2 million, about 1.6 million are unqualified (i.e., lacking the appropriate education credentials). In an interview, an SEdC official said that 1989 estimates for qualified teachers showed that 71 percent of elementary, 43 percent of senior high, and only 41 percent of junior high teachers met degree requirements.

Qualifications in terms of degrees is only part of the problem; in additions, many teachers are unqualified in that they are not capable of teaching the state-mandated curriculum. The need for qualified teachers was identified as a policy problem in the 1985 Education Decision, with the target set that "in five or a bit more years, the vast majority of teachers should be capable of carrying out teaching work." According to 1985 statistics, 2.4 million practicing teachers did not meet basic standards and needed inservice education. Given the enormity of the task, the first goal is to help people obtain the ability to teach and then attend to satisfying degree and formal preparation requirements.

The combination of this national context and these educational factors has produced policy issues in teacher education that have a special urgency. There is a need to change the kind of teaching being done in schools today, but what that change should look like, how teachers are best prepared for it, how institutional programs should be arranged to support this sort of reform, and how good teachers can be recruited to and encouraged to remain in teaching are all matters that have generated much discussion and, in some cases, prolonged debate. We explore these issues below.

## ISSUES AND PROBLEMS

### Issue 1: Clarifying the Goals of Teacher Education—Visions of Teaching and Learning

Policy issues in teacher education in China, as in other countries, depend largely on policy debates in the schools. What kind of teacher education system should be developed depends on what kind of teacher, for what kind of school, is the goal. Critics of China's teacher education system blame it for a tradition of separation from the real world and the realities of schools. But by the mid–1980s teacher education institutions and the policies that shape them could not ignore important changes in society and the concomitant changes in elementary and secondary education.

The question of goals and purposes has long plagued China's teacher education. In fact, in the post–Mao years, the mission and value of teacher education became the focus of the hottest debate and the topic of the greatest amount of teacher education research. From an analysis of one hundred articles on teacher education published after 1978 (often considered the true beginning of the post–Mao period), it was found that nearly 50 percent of them addressed the purpose and value of teacher education. Defining the mission of teacher education appears to be a persistent policy dilemma. The issue of whether teacher education veers too much toward either its academic function or its professional function, which was widely discussed before the Cultural Revolution or after it in the late 1970s, remains central to policy debates in the 1990s.[4]

Reforms aimed at improving the quality of education by emphasizing the need to meet the challenge of the twenty-first century and a new technological era heightened demands on teacher preparation. Since the beginning of the post–Mao period, many have called for a transformation of teaching and a new kind of learning in school. A statement Deng Xiaoping made in 1983 at a Beijing school epitomized this concern and goal: "Education should face modernization, the world, and the future." Since then educators, policymakers, and teacher education researchers have discussed the implications of such a goal. Advocates claim that teachers need new knowledge and skills if they are to teach for the future. A common theme in these discussions of teaching innovation is the stress on active learning, with the teacher as a guide rather than as the centerpiece. Teaching, proponents argue, should put more emphasis on problem solving, creativity, and independent thinking. SEdC Vice-Commissioner He Dongchang typified this approach in his identification of the intellectual goals of education: ''we should not only train students to have a command of certain advanced cultural and scientific knowledge, but also pay enough attention to helping them develop, from early childhood, the ability to live and think independently and to foster their enterprising spirit and initiative.''

The state's response to the 1989 democracy protests dramatizes the complexity of this issue and the difficulty of defining the degree to which active participation should be encouraged in school and society. But even in the wake of political repression against protestors, the state remains officially committed to changing traditional teaching methods in favor of innovative instruction and considering the challenge of education in the twenty-first century.

The pressure for more teachers with professional preparation, more preparation in a range of new fields, and skills and knowledge for teaching in new ways places heavy burdens on schools and teachers, which today are organized to produce conventional text- and test-driven teaching and learning. The difficulties implicit in the challenge to change is clear if we consider the dominant school practices.

A teacher in the typical Chinese classroom faces at least forty-five to fifty students, lined in rows at wooden tables or desks, often jammed with student texts and reference materials.[5] The teacher, who is most often a man and probably has less than the desired number of years or kind of training expected for a teacher of that age group of learners, has forty-five minutes to work with the students on any one day. The time is carefully orchestrated, from the greeting at the start of the period to a formal class dismissal. In between these two events, the teacher will do the majority of talking. The period's lesson will focus on the text (over which the teacher has no power of selection), and students will be called on to answer questions about that text. The teacher is likely to review, introduce new material from the text, and ask very structured questions about it or organize students in drill and practice for thirty-five of the class's forty-five minutes. The teacher may roam around the classroom during this time, but students remain in their rows, the only movement coming as individual students stand to respond to questions. The remaining ten minutes of the period may entail students involved in a teacher-guided discussion, practicing techniques or approaches introduced in the text, or reading or re-reading passages pointed out by the teacher. There will be very little off-task talk or activity. On-task activity initiated by students, such as student-initiated discussion or questions, except in the final activity of the period, will be rare. So is attention to differences among students. Instead, most classrooms spend most of their time in teacher-directed, whole-group activity. Although today many teachers are working hard to change this style and in some cases are engaged in serious experimentation, this de-

scription of teacher-centered instruction organized around transmission of knowledge that is text-based characterizes prevalent practices at both elementary and
secondary school.[6]

To change this teaching, and to do it at a time when the contexts of schools—
their curricula, their clients, and the system within which they work—are themselves undergoing rapid change, presents real dilemmas for teacher education.
What should the goal of teacher education be? What sort of teacher should be
produced by teacher education programs? These questions persist, despite decades of discussion.

### Issue 2: Structure of Teacher Education

The problem of defining what good teaching is and consequently of stating
teacher education's objective is both expressed in and highlighted by the structures that house teacher education, their irrational overlap, and the content of
their work. Although the government has reiterated the need for teacher education
to be responsive to basic education, its reform and innovation, the structures
and content of teacher education in fact often represent a poor match with the
needs of tomorrow's basic education. The curriculum is more geared toward an
elitist education to prepare students for higher education.

"The government has repeatedly emphasized that the guiding principles of
teacher education should be effective implementation of a nine-year compulsory
education program and the improvement of basic education (elementary and
secondary education) in the new era of technology.''[7] The state has also "re-
affirmed the importance of political and ideological education to assure the overall
goal of teacher education, i.e., to cultivate cultured persons as teachers with
lofty ideals, high morality, strong discipline, and a sense of mission as educators—'the engineers of the human soul' and 'the gardeners of the nation's
flowers.' ''[8] But practice does not always follow policy, as some schools consistently focus away from basic education and on elite schooling; many pay only
lip-service to the moral development of teachers; and many prepare teachers for
the conventional teaching of today, rather than for tomorrow's schools.

Consider first the structural dimension. Formally, a clear division of labor
exists among the several kinds of programs that educate teachers: teacher training
schools prepare elementary teachers; teacher training colleges prepare junior high
school teachers; teacher training universities educate senior high teachers; and
education institutes conduct in-service education. In practice, however, several
factors in the organizational environment work against this rational allocation
of tasks.

Shortages of teachers at each level, particularly in secondary schooling, make
schools willing and even eager to accept teacher preparation graduates for a level
of schooling higher than that for which they were prepared. Hence, for example,
not infrequently normal school graduates, though officially educated in preparation for elementary school teaching, are assigned to junior high rather than to

elementary posts, and until very recently normal university graduates often ended up teaching at the postsecondary rather than the secondary level. Graduates themselves tend to welcome the mismatch between their training and their assignment since in doing so they attain a higher status position than they would otherwise. But despite any individual satisfaction, the result of a poor match between training and posting is a muddying of institutional purpose, further complicating a teacher education program's question, "What kind of teacher should be trained?"

The current structure of teacher education, with separate institutions for each level of education and for pre- and in-service education, cannot respond to the changing teacher supply and demand. Even though the primary school-age population is shrinking and a teacher surplus is already evident at the primary level, 85 percent of teacher training institutions (covering 65 percent of total enrollments) are geared solely to the training of primary teachers. At the same time, only 9 percent of the teacher training institutions have the mission of training lower secondary teachers, despite the fact that teacher shortages are the most severe at this level. However, the county-run "normal schools," which prepare primary teachers, cannot be converted to train secondary teachers, since this function belongs to prefecture and provincial governments. The same problem applies to in-service teacher training institutions, whose main purpose is to provide "unqualified teachers" with appropriate education credentials. According to World Bank projections, in advanced provinces (about 50 percent of the provinces) this problem would be resolved by 1995, while the other provinces would take about two decades to train all the unqualified teachers. What would happen to the in-service teacher training institutions in those provinces without any unqualified teachers? Thus, the structure of teacher education has become a supply-driven system contributing to the imbalances in the teaching force. In the final analysis, what is so distinctive about each level of education and about pre- and in-service education that separate institutions have to be established for each?

The other organizational factor comes from horizontal links to teacher education rather than vertical integration within it. Given the organizational climate within which these schools exist, teacher training institutions, especially the normal universities, compete with and even emulate peer nonteacher training institutions. Many critics point to the tendency of normal colleges and universities to "copy the comprehensive university," thereby emphasizing academic preparation at the expense of professional training. While the looking towards comprehensive universities has been officially repudiated, proponents wanting to "aim at secondary schools" complain that too many people still equate quality with academic elitism. Critics have decried the tendency for normal colleges to emulate comprehensive universities, for normal schools and colleges to try "blindly" to upgrade their status (by becoming colleges or universities), and for in-service institutes to emulate full-time normal universities.[9]

Teacher education is distinguished from other education by the teacher training character or the special characteristic of teacher training. This distinction has been the focus of much policy discussion. Is there a distinctively normal aspect of teacher education? Interview and documentary research in the early and mid–1980s found that there was a difference of opinion over whether or not this aspect exists. Most people interviewed asserted that there was some special characteristic unique to teacher education, but did not appear to be in general agreement on the nature of that character. As one teacher educator interviewed said, the post–Mao period has been a time of groping to figure out what the characteristic is.[10]

The debate on the special character of teacher education raised questions about the appropriateness of separate teacher education programs. This tradition of housing teacher education in monotechnic or specialized institutions has produced what one Chinese researcher called a system characterized by "going it alone" and "closed doorism." As a result, the teacher education system cannot make use of superior facilities and intellectual resources outside the system . . . , thus hindering the development of teacher education itself. In addition, this arrangement cannot meet the demand for teachers. For example, at a normal college education work conference held in 1987, an SEdC official claimed that over the period of the seventh Five-Year Plan elementary schools would need 1.1 million new teachers, whereas teacher training schools would only be able to supply 900,000. Of the 900,000 new junior high teachers that would be needed during that period, teacher training colleges could train only 500,000. And teacher training universities could train only 270,000 to 280,000 new teachers, even though senior high schools would need to add 300,000 to their teaching ranks. In other words, existing structures for teacher education were estimated as falling 620,000 teachers short of supplying the newly trained teachers demanded.

A partial solution, in addition to enlarging and strengthening existing teacher education programs, involves expanding the types of institutions engaged in preparing teachers. Consequently, comprehensive universities and other kinds of institutions are now beginning to shoulder some of this training burden. In 1990 the SEdC reported 490,000 students in teacher training colleges and universities but 530,000 students overall enrolled in teacher education programs. The presence of 40,000 prospective teachers being trained outside of stand alone teacher education institutions indicates that education policymakers have already reached some consensus on the need to expand the range of settings used to train teachers in order to meet demand. Less amenable to quick resolution is what such a decision means about the desirable balance between types of institutions. Similarly unresolved are questions about the necessity to maintain teacher training colleges and universities as separate institutions in light of the participation of diversified (i.e., not monotechnic) institutions in the preparation of teachers. The persistent difficulty in defining the distinctive mission and nature of teacher education expresses itself in these discussions about structure.

## Issue 3: The Content of Teacher Education

Apart from but related to dilemmas regarding the institutional structure of teacher education and the structure of the teacher education system is the problem of what teacher education should contain. It is the content, as expressed in the curriculum of preservice teacher education, that has been the focus of the greatest dissatisfaction and debate.[11]

An example of this debate is found in the question of specialization. What are the appropriate specialties in a teacher education program? Early and strong Soviet influence on Chinese higher education produced a highly specialized approach to academic majors. How well does this serve the needs of teachers, who need to be able to think in multi-, inter-, or cross-disciplinary ways? Today SEdC officials describe the structure of specialization as not well matched. Analysts point to a need to adjust specialization to fit changes in school curricula. The problem becomes an important policy issue, particularly for rural teacher preparation (which, in terms of people involved, constitutes the largest amount of teacher education activity), since rural schools, often smaller and less well staffed than urban schools, may expect a teacher to teach more than one field or subject.

The content of a specialization, like the curriculum of teacher education more generally, varies with the level of institution. Yet, because of historical, cultural, and political factors affecting the conceptualization of teaching and the influence of foreign (especially Soviet) models of curriculum planning, certain patterns in the curriculum run across all levels. Programs are geared toward developing knowledge and skills in four areas: "political and professional dedication . . . a sound and rich knowledge in the subjects they teach . . . a good understanding of pedagogical principles as well as the ability to apply them in teaching . . . and the ability to analyze and discuss educational problems.[12]

These goals are enacted through a curriculum in each level of preservice teacher education which organizes courses and experiences in the categories of general knowledge, knowledge of the subject(s) to be taught in school, educational theory and practice, and political education. These are not equally attended to, however, for subject matter knowledge tends to dominate. In general, students take a heavy course load that gives them a highly scheduled program of study, many classes each week, few opportunities for practice or independent study, and infrequent choice of electives. This arrangement itself is reproductive of a knowledge-transmission model of teaching which places the learner in a passive role.

Certainly, there are variations to this general theme, with program type and amount of local experimentation chiefly accounting for the differences. Yet the general pattern can be seen if we consider the different teacher education curricular arrangements in teacher training schools, colleges, and universities.

Programs in teacher training schools—both three- and four-year types—include courses in what are seen as basic subjects (such as mathematics and language); general knowledge (such as geography, history, or public hygiene); music, physical education, and art; and professional training (in pedagogy, psychology, and teaching materials and methods). Time is also allocated to productive labor. Although the curriculum of these preservice programs for elementary teachers is broader than that for future secondary school teachers, preparation in school subjects predominates, much as it does in the other levels of teacher education. Records of formal programs suggest that approximately 56 percent of a student's time in the program is devoted to coursework in school subjects, and mathematics and language study alone account for 39 percent of a student's course hours. Time in methods courses, pedagogy and psychology, and student teaching and other practical courses is very constricted, given the number of other courses students must take. In the curriculum introduced in 1980, for four-year teacher training schools, pedagogy and psychology accounted for only about 6 percent of the curriculum, while methods coursework in math and language represented another 4.8 percent.[13] And while eight weeks of student teaching are required in the three-year program and ten weeks in the four-year program, field research in 1990 found that schools often lack resources and facilities, and may be forced to opt for only a four-week experience in a student's three-year program.

These tendencies toward subject matter specialization, the minor role given professional education courses, and the limited occasions for professional practice are even more evident in the programs of the two- and three-year (associates of arts—A.A.) teacher training colleges and the four-year (bachelor of arts—B.A.) teacher training universities. In 1989 there were 260 tertiary-level teacher education institutions, 78 of which granted the B.A and 182 the equivalent of the A.A. degree. The 532,000 students enrolled in teacher education specialize from the start. They enter their program as students in a major that corresponds to the secondary curriculum (except in a few programs in such departments as education or library science). Specific proportions vary with the major and the institution, but on average for much of the 1980s work in the student's major typically represented between 60 and 70 percent (for the B.A.) or 75 percent (for the A.A.) of a student's program. General education (including politics, foreign languages, and physical education) accounted for approximately 25 percent (in the B.A. and the three-year A.A.) and 15 percent (for the two-year A.A.), and professional education coursework (generally, pedagogy, psychology, and subject-specific methods) occupied only about 5 percent of the total for a B.A. student's hours and 8.9 to 11.9 percent of an A.A. student's hours. Just as formal coursework in education is proportionately limited, so too are opportunities for professional practice (or field experiences), with the A.A. students having four to six weeks and the B.A. six to eight weeks of student teaching. For teacher training universities, this educational practice represents only 4 percent of credits or course hours.

These figures and percentages represent the formal curriculum of teacher education. What occurs in practice and hence in the hidden curriculum that is expressed reinforces the ideas implicit in the formal program structure: that teachers are first and foremost responsible for transmitting subject matter knowledge. The conveying of this message—both the message and its form, as represented in the formal and hidden curricula and the pedagogy of teacher education—has been under sustained and increasing criticism for much of the post–Mao era.

Criticism, especially since the 1985 Education Decision, has focused on certain major themes, regardless of whether the critic represents the SEdC, teacher education institutions, or educational research. Reforms, it is argued, need to occur in accordance with and to strengthen teacher education's relationship to the development of basic education. The areas necessary for change are wide ranging: curriculum structure, teaching content and requirements, teaching measures and styles all need significant reform. Many argue that an important part of that reform involves clarifying and highlighting the special characteristic of teacher education. One prominent aspect of teacher education's distinctive quality means stressing the "basics": curriculum reform in teacher education must pay primary attention to teaching foundation courses, improving their instructional quality, and appropriately broadening the types of foundation courses offered.

Reform also requires greater cross-fertilization between the humanities and the sciences. More interdisciplinary work, applied courses, and applied skills and knowledge should be developed. Critics advocate reducing the overemphasis on knowledge (to the neglect of skills and dispositions), and the overspecialization and heavy orientation of most contemporary programs toward subject matter. Accompanying these goals, since 1986 the SEdC has urged the reduction of courses, simplification of instructional content, and strict control of instructional hours as a way of increasing opportunities for students to study on their own and develop independent thinking skills and creativity. The narrow preparation that is the result of a curriculum that consists of at least 80 percent required courses should be changed by introducing a greater role for electives and opportunities for broadening the knowledge base of future teachers'. Finally, the pedagogy of teacher education is seen as outdated and in need of reform.

Although the state has endorsed curriculum reform that would reduce narrow subject matter preparation, two other areas of special concern to critics are the political/moral curriculum and professional education preparation. Finding the proper balance between technical (subject matter) and political preparation has long been a challenge for teacher education in China. Interviews with SEdC officials in 1990 revealed continued (in fact, heightened) attention to this area, as one official listed political thinking and moral education as one of the three major issues that need to be solved in the normal school curriculum. Teachers play a moral role through their job of educating the whole person. Thus, teaching is conceptualized as a vocation that demands ideals, political rectitude, professional dedication, and personal sacrifice. Finding ways to develop this commitment through the curriculum is a concern of policymakers.

Perhaps more than any single component of the curriculum, the professional education courses and experiences have been targeted for change. An SEdC official wrote that the education curriculum is not sufficiently emphasized, has empty theories devoid of content, is unfocused and disconnected, has outdated methods and techniques, too few course hours and lacks necessary investment. Even though many teacher education institutions have made reforms in their education coursework, this component still occupies a very small role; it represents only about 5 percent of the future secondary teacher's courses (in contrast to the 15 percent it occupied in the 1950s). Critics claim that the education core is further weakened by its separation from schools and hence its inability to keep up with the development of precollegiate education. SEdC interviews in 1990 revealed internal criticism of the core's content and teaching, particularly the traditional pedagogy course, which has witnessed little change in recent years.

SEdC work at all levels of teacher education institutions, as well as teacher education research, has encouraged more connection to school realities and more opportunities to develop pedagogical skills. The findings of one research project, which surveyed secondary schools' evaluations of Nanjing Teachers University graduates' teaching, illustrates the need for change. Areas related to pedagogical skills and knowledge, particularly the ability to solve real problems and the educational reform situation (described as reflecting mastery of educational knowledge), received the weakest evaluations. Common responses to these problems are recommendations to strengthen the practical experiences of teacher education students. Seen as traditionally weak, student teaching has been analyzed as needing improvement in its administration, placement, content, time, methods, supervision, and financial support.

The agenda for curriculum change is apparently great. Whereas defining a vision of the mission and goals of teacher education has proven problematic over the years, discussions about reforming the structure and content of teacher education gained momentum in the post–Mao era. At this point there appears to be a consensus about the proper targets for criticism: structures of teacher education that are hard pressed to meet the demand for teachers, a frequent mismatch between level of preparation and subsequent teaching assignment, and curricula that are bound by institutional histories and conceptualizations of teaching that leave new teachers poorly prepared to meet the challenges of a basic education system undergoing rapid transformation. Given this far-reaching critique of the present curricular structures, actual solutions and reforms are slow and complex. The complexity of teacher education reform is exacerbated by issues related to the conditions of teaching and teaching's associated problems of recruitment and retention.

### Issue 4: Teaching Conditions and the Impact on Recruitment

Both the need to reform teacher education and the problems of its reforms are directly affected by the conditions and position of teaching. In China, a history of extreme shifts in the political treatment of teachers—including years of criticism and abuse during the Cultural Revolution—combined with a tradition of relatively few economic rewards for the profession has severely affected the career appeal of teaching.

Soon after the end of the 1966–1976 Cultural Revolution era, the negative impact of that period's political persecution of teachers was recognized as a major policy problem requiring attention. Since the late 1970s, the party and state have increasingly championed the situation of teachers, initially stressing ways to improve their social and political status and eventually introducing measures to ameliorate their economic position. This strategy grew out of the awareness, as suggested by General Secretary of the Party and former Premier Li Peng, that gradually raising the social position and economic treatment of elementary and secondary teachers to attract outstanding personnel to teaching is a basic measure for stabilizing and improving the teaching force. Most noteworthy among a number of reforms are the establishment of a national Teachers' Day to honor the profession and its members, campaigns to increase the number of teachers admitted to the Chinese Communist party, and a variety of wage increases and wage structure reforms, including a 1987 decision to issue a 10 percent across-the-board salary increase for all precollegiate teachers.[14] The increases did not keep up with inflation, however, and overall the changes have had limited impact on teacher education's ability to recruit and select the best candidates for teaching.

In the early aftermath of the Cultural Revolution, teacher education, especially teacher training colleges and universities, had little appeal for outstanding students. Typically, the academically most capable students have not chosen to go into teaching, moving instead into elite academic senior high schools or, at the postsecondary level, into comprehensive or engineering colleges and universities. In contrast, teacher education institutions have tended to appeal to candidates who needed some way to stay in school, a guarantee of an "iron rice bowl" (job security), or an inexpensive option for further education. Interview and survey research has found that large numbers of students who end up in teacher education institutions do so as a second (or even last) resort. For example, studies at two teacher education institutions found that 24 percent and 38.6 percent, respectively, of the students surveyed had not listed teacher education as their first choice during their participation in the national higher education entrance examination. Teacher education's appeal was simply that it offered these students admissions when other more desirable types of schools did not. The guarantee of a job assignment for a teacher training school graduate (in contrast to the fate of graduates from ordinary comprehensive secondary schools) and for graduates of teacher training colleges and universities also holds some attraction for some students, as does the fact that teacher education has traditionally provided a special stipend to its students.

The result is a cohort of students entering teacher education either academically weaker or professionally less committed than policymakers and teacher educators would like. In response, the reforms of the early 1980s aimed at drawing better students into teaching. These efforts included encouraging greater publicity of teacher education programs and giving teacher education institutions preference in selecting their students. Ordinary teacher training universities were allowed to participate with and even precede ''key'' (or elite) universities in selecting students for the unified national entrance examination. Yet because admissions reflect the matching of student and university preferences and because few students identify teacher education institutions as their first choice, teacher training programs still failed to draw and admit the top students.

In light of that experience, more recently the SEdC approved early admissions for teacher education institutions, as well as the maintenance of a stipend system, despite its elimination in much of higher education. These incentives were intended to appeal to capable students who would be attracted by the security of money or an opportunity for early admission (and the chance to compete later in the regular admission cycle, if the early attempt proved unsuccessful). SEdC, provincial, and teacher education institution officials reported in interviews that these measures were effective but limited, still failing to attract the strongest students.

The widespread implementation of a fixed destination program illustrates one more reform that has had positive effects within limits. In that program, rural students are recruited and allowed to be admitted to teacher education with lower than the required test scores under the condition that they must return to their rural area to teach. This program is very successful in serving the need of supplying teachers to otherwise hard-to-fill rural posts. Yet by doing this through partial lowering of admissions cutoff scores, the reform also fails to bring the academically most talented students to teaching.

All these reforms have had some usefulness. Still, recruitment difficulties remain a serious problem. Although news accounts note the successes of some teacher education institutions (such as in Tianjin and Beijing) which have many candidates seeking admission as their first preference, these stories fail to point out that the sought-after programs tend to be urban teacher education institutions whose graduates are guaranteed placement in nearby urban schools. In fact, more representative of the challenges facing teacher education, especially in preparing junior and senior high teachers, are reports from provincial institutions such as those in Hubei and Jiangsu, where programs have not even been able to fill their quota of students. As an extreme example of the problems teacher training institutions face, consider the provincial teacher training college that had planned to admit 147 students but had only one list it as their choice.

What partial successes there are in recruiting generate their own problems, especially as teacher education programs are filled with students who have little interest in or commitment to teaching. A 1989 Shansi study found that 71.4 percent of students surveyed said they had entered teacher education to achieve other goals and 57.9 percent were not willing to become teachers. The serious challenges raised by the philosophical, structural and curricular problems discussed earlier in this chapter are exacerbated by students unwilling to study teacher education and disdainful of teaching.

Accompanying the recruitment difficulties that teacher education programs face is the problem they have in supplying their graduates to teaching. Two aspects of this problem have been discussed already: the inability of specialized institutions of teacher education to keep pace with the demand for teachers, especially at the junior high level and in certain subject areas, and the mismatch created as teacher education graduates go to teach at levels of schooling for which they are unprepared. But there is a third type of supply problem: the wastage of graduates who never enter teaching.

Given many students' lack of intrinsic interest in teaching, it is not surprising that many graduates of teacher education programs, particularly those from colleges and universities, have tried to avoid being posted to teaching. Teacher training institutions offer their students the guarantee of work upon graduation, with the placement assignment for the student made through prefectural, provincial, and/or national labor plans. But not all graduates get assigned teacher positions in education or at the level they are prepared for. In fact, in the mid–1980s SEdC Vice-Commissioner Liu Bin claimed there was an actual decline in the proportion of teacher college graduates going to secondary school teaching. Positions in expanding higher education programs, government bureaus, research institutes, and business all drew graduates away from the jobs for which they had been prepared. The wastage was particularly acute at the elite, nationally SEdC-administered teacher training universities. One such institution, Northeast Teachers University, until 1988 had only about 30 percent of its preservice secondary teaching students posted to secondary teaching. Even at the provincially or county-administered nonelite institutions, allocation patterns were problematic. A Hebei Provincial Education Commission's analysis of the labor trends of five years of graduates (1984–1988) from its province's two ordinary teacher training universities, eleven teacher training colleges, and thirty teacher training schools found that one-third of the B.A. teacher education graduates, one-half of the A.A. teacher training graduates, and one-third of the teacher training school graduates had not been assigned to senior, junior, or elementary teaching, respectively. That is, their assignments did not correspond to the teacher education plan for preparing and allocating teachers.

Thus, it is little wonder that, in addition to calling for reform of teacher education admissions, policymakers have urged job assignments for teacher education graduates that keep graduates within the education sector and at the appropriate level of schooling. Policy in recent years has severely restricted the ability of noneducation units to hire teacher education graduates, the early 1980s shortage of college-educated government officials and college teachers has been reduced, and the state has made repeated calls to improve the efficient allocation of trained teachers. More curricular and extracurricular time devoted to strengthening students' professional commitment has also taken place. These developments have produced noticeable improvements since 1988. In a 1990 interview, for example, an SEdC official reported that at twenty-one provincially administered key teacher training universities, 77 percent of the graduates had gone

to secondary school teaching and "almost all" the teacher training college graduates had entered teaching. Nevertheless, school-level interviews at rural junior
high schools in 1990 still found many recent teacher training school graduates
being inappropriately assigned to teach junior high.

In short, clear gains have been made in both admissions to and allocation
from teacher education. The size of the demand, however, coupled with enough
recent evidence of low material rewards from teaching (which in 1987 ranked
eleventh of twelve occupations in average income), limit the extent to which
current reforms can succeed.

## CONCLUSION

Society and schools are changing in ways that put new and complex demands
on teacher education. Teacher education has been searching for a revised mission
and a new vision of the kind of teacher it should produce. Its structural problems
require nothing less than a rethinking of the entire higher education system. Its
contents need far-reaching readjustment to fit this contemporary vision. Yet it
also needs ways to recruit and allocate talented people to teaching, and the
possibilities for attracting this talent are severely restricted by factors outside the
control of teacher education, particularly the conditions of teaching as a profession. These four policy areas—visions, structure, curricular content, and recruitment—are thorny ones, with long histories that reflect political and
demographic pressures. Their resolution is made all the more complex by the
way they affect each other. Teacher education is at a crossroads for policymakers;
they need to debate and decide on alternatives, making hard choices, including
sacrifices, in order to establish a new direction for teacher education to meet
China's ambitious educational, social, and technological goals.

## NOTES

1. Research for this chapter was supported by grants from the Committee for Scholarly
Communication with the People's Republic of China (CSCPRC) and Michigan State
University. The views expressed are those of the authors only and do not in any way
reflect those of CSCPRC, Michigan State University, or the World Bank.

2. For an English text of the reform decision, see "Reform of China's Educational
Structure: Decision of the Communist Party of China (CPC) Central Committee (May
1985)" (Beijing: Foreign Language Press, 1985), pp. 1–12. For discussion of the reforms,
see, for example, Zhou Nanzhao, "Historical Contexts of Educational Reform in Present
Day China," *Interchange* 19, nos. 3/4 (Fall/Winter 1988): 8–18; Keith Lewin and Xu
Hui, "Rethinking Revolution: Reflections on China's 1985 Educational Reforms," *Comparative Education* 25, no. 1 (1989): 7–17; Ronald F. Price, "The Politics of Contemporary Educational Reform in China," in Edgar Gumbert, ed., *Making the Future: Politics
and Educational Reform in the United States, England, the Soviet Union, China, and
Cuba* (Atlanta: Georgia State University, Center for Cross-Cultural Education, 1988),
pp. 99–114.

3. Teacher training schools, while guided in their basic principles by the State Education Commission, are administered directly by provinces, prefectures, or county bureaus of education. Teacher training colleges in their administration are similarly guided by policies set by the SEdC but administered by the provinces. Teacher training universities include six that are administered directly by the SEdC, while the rest receive guidelines from the SEdC but are administered provincially.

4. Lynn Paine, "Teacher Education in the People's Republic of China," in Edgar Gumbert, ed., *Fit to Teach: Teacher Education in International Perspective* (Atlanta: Georgia State University, Center for Cross-Cultural Education, 1990), pp. 127–156.

5. Rural elementary schools often have smaller class sizes, although 1990 field research found school consolidation underway which was aiming to produce class sizes of about forty to forty-five.

6. Lynn Webster Paine, "The Teacher as Virtuoso: A Chinese Model for Teaching," *Teachers College Record* 92, no. 1 (Fall 1990): 49–81.

7. Lin Bing and Yang Zhiling, "Innovations and New Initiatives in Teacher Education in the People's Republic of China: A Summary Report" (Beijing: Beijing Normal University, 1989), p. 15.

8. Ibid.

9. "Liu Bin Tongzhi," p. 131; He, "Wei Jainshe," p. 46; Yu Qinglian, "The Strategic Position and Prospects of Teachers' Education," *Canadian and International Education* 16, no. 1 (1987): 114–122.

10. Lynn Webster Paine, "Reform and Balance in Chinese Teacher Education," Ph.D. diss., Stanford University, 1985.

11. In discussions of in-service teacher education, content debates have been far fewer than have discussions of expanding and improving delivery systems.

12. Billie L.C. Lo, "Teacher Education in the Eighties," in Ruth Hayhoe, ed. *Contemporary Chinese Education* (Armonk, N.Y.: M. E. Sharpe, 1984), pp. 162–163.

13. Wang Congfang, "Pre-Service and In-Service Teacher Education in China," *Canadian and International Education* 16, no. 1 (1987): 160.

14. Department of Basic Education, State Education Commission, *Basic Education of China* (Beijing: People's Education Press, 1989), pp. 109–110; Lynn Paine, "Reforming Teachers: The Organization, Reproduction, and Transformation of Teaching," in Irving Epstein, ed., *Chinese Education: Problems, Policies and Prospects* (New York: Garland Publishing, forthcoming).

# 6

# EGYPT

## TAHER RAZIK AND DIAA EL-DIN A. ZAHER

Egypt has historically been the key planner and executor of economic and social behavior in the Middle East and the Islamic world. For seven thousand years, Egyptian educational institutes have been centers of knowledge, instruction, and civilization. Al Azhar University, established in A.D. 739, is one of the oldest universities in the world. Its faculties still continue the strong tradition of preparing scholars in a wide variety of disciplines. Many Al Azhar graduates have assumed strategic economic, political, and academic leadership positions throughout the Mideast. The forces of history have shaped Egyptian education at all levels since the nation has long held a pivotal role in the development and politics of the Middle East. During the nineteenth century, Egypt was victimized by colonial powers from Europe and the Ottoman Empire, which resulted in the imposition of non-Egyptian models of schooling. However, by the 1920s Egypt had regained its freedom and the consequent right to develop its own national plans for education.

During the first half of the twentieth century, Egyptian schools were only moderately developed. Education for the elite continued as it had during the colonial period. The revolutionary change in Egypt's educational system arrived with the rise of the leader Gamal Abdel-Nasser in July 1952. Nasser initiated national reform and development plans that resulted in the expansion of Egyptian public education and the strengthening of university programs. Education was designed to include strong concern for teaching Islamic values as well as the sciences and humanities. Nasser, whose ambition was to develop the Arab world beyond Egypt, encouraged teacher education for the entire region. The exportation of teachers became a key part of Egypt's diplomatic relations with other Arab nations.

This brief historical account provides some initial background for the following discussion. It serves to preface the content of this chapter, reviews the societal factors influencing teacher education, describes the Egyptian educational system and the nation's current teacher preparation programs, and, most importantly, explains the issues and problems impinging on Egyptian teacher education today. These include:

1. Inadequate support of in-service education.
2. Lack of sufficient emphasis on pedagogy.
3. Overcoming the stereotype of the teacher as lecturer.
4. Inadequate curriculum for preparing teachers for basic education.
5. Deficient and uncoordinated policy research.
6. Dearth of good candidates for teaching.
7. Unfulfilled professional potential of the Teachers Syndicate.
8. Undermining effect of private tutoring.

## GENERAL BACKGROUND

Population, economic, political, social, and cultural factors have all played an integral part in shaping the Egyptian societal context which has subsequently affected teacher education.

### Population Factors

The population factor has held utmost importance for Egyptian educational planners during the past forty years. Population increased rapidly during the 1970s: elementary school children numbered 3,676,000 in 1970 and 4,548,058 in 1979. Similar increases were observed at all school levels. This dramatic increase has resulted in an extreme demand for the development of new schools and the preparation of an adequate supply of teachers. Currently, 91 percent of all school-aged children are enrolled in schools, according to government reports. However, when the 91 percent figure is adjusted for school dropouts and students repeating grades, the enrollment figure is reduced to 84 percent. Fewer female than male students are enrolled. The current illiteracy rate is higher for women than for men. Historically, many girls have dropped out of school at the end of their basic compulsory program either to work or to marry. A new law prohibiting girls from marrying prior to age sixteen has begun slowly to affect the female dropout rate. However, evidence still indicates that many women are illiterate. This fact is affecting the population increase; the average Egyptian woman has six children. This is an alarming condition to educational planners who see a dramatic increase in the population, an increase in female illiteracy, and an increase in the demand for schools during the 1990s.

The population explosion has created several problems for Egypt. Educational institutes and the government have not been able to meet the exploding demand for school facilities adequately. Classes are now held in many nonschool buildings; class sizes are large, and schools operate on double- and triple-schedule shifts each day.

## Economic Factors

The rapid increase in population affects all the other features of the societal context, particularly the *economic* factors. Historically, Egypt's economy has been based on the development and use of the nation's natural resources. Agriculture dominated the economy during the colonial period and continued to be Egypt's major source of income in the first several decades of the twentieth century. Efforts at industrialization, development of oil revenues, tourism, Suez Canal income, and Egyptian expatriates working in various Arab countries, particularly the Arab Gulf States, helped to diversify the Egyptian economy from 1960 to the present. However, political conflict and the consequent need for military defense systems weakened efforts to build an industrialized economy. As of 1989, the World Bank defined Egypt as a lower-middle income country where the per capita income was U.S. $660.00. Currently, agriculture accounts for 22 percent of the gross national product (GNP), transport and communication accounts for 42 percent of GNP, manufacturing, mining, and construction 24 percent, and the remainder of the GNP is generated through a variety of service industries (World Bank, 1989). In order to secure the necessary workforce for the expanding economy, which is straining owing to the population explosion, the government passed a law in 1984 guaranteeing well-paying jobs in Egypt to graduates of university and technical institutions.

The current overall unemployment rate is very high: 15 percent. The rate for women is an astounding 40 percent in many regions. This is largely because Egypt has not recovered from the economic recession that followed its military defeat in 1967. In addition, constant political crises in the Middle East have slowed down the government's organized efforts for societal development.

In spite of the hardships confronting the Egyptian economy, the government has strongly supported education. The government has consistently committed funds to planning for schools which will prepare students for a rapidly changing society and workplace.

The current labor market is congested, however. This is a sign that the schools are not adjusted to adequately produce a balanced workforce. The result of government educational policies has been an imbalance in preparing students for a diverse economy. Therefore, many graduates of the educational system, except those in the specialized areas of medicine, engineering, and education, are unemployed in spite of the 1984 guaranteed-job law.

Several attempts have been made to coordinate education with development plans in order to decrease unemployment and stabilize the economy. In 1963 the government formed a permanent committee to study the needs of the work-

force, and in 1976 a National Council for Manpower and Training was created
to coordinate personnel and educational planning.

### Political Factors

Political factors have also strongly influenced Egyptian education. Many modernization attempts in the early and mid-twentieth century included governmental
plans to improve the overall standard of education as a means of securing democracy. In 1956 the Egyptian Constitution included the guarantee of free education for all. Gradually, confusion over the nature of the political state began to
affect this free education guarantee. From 1959 on, the concept of the *economic
state* dominated the worldview of the governing class; private ownership evolved
into a public ownership system. Education was designed as a tool to promote that
change; technical schools, a reliance on social production, and the development
of human resources became the groundwork of the educational plans. In the 1960s
the political focus was on the nation as a *social state*; the government tried to unite
the Arab States in this philosophy. Therefore, during these years, schools were
directed to instruct strong Islamic values and democratic ideals. The 1970s and
1980s had different orientations altogether. In the 1970s the concept of the *institutional state* led to raising the overall status of education. For example, the government organized its services and development programs through bureaucratic
departments/ministries. The Egyptian Ministry of Education institutionalized education through policies that improved schooling at all levels. In the 1980s fuller
democratization of the nation occurred; citizens were given greater roles in decision making, and education was supported as a vehicle for assuring the democracy's stability. As a result, programs were changed to include courses promoting
responsible citizenship and the exercise of Islamic values.

All this clearly reveals that education has been affected by the political climate
in Egypt. Since 1952 specifically, the political system has been in a state of
transformation and experimentation. The result in education has been a confusing
set of policies designed to address the changing political and economic conditions. The role of governmental bureaucracies has increased considerably during
the past forty years as Egypt has attempted to modernize. Often, this created a
conflict of interest which has fragmented development plans in education. Different interest groups dominated the presidential cabinet at different times since
the 1950s. As a result, some long-range educational plans were never realized
owing to political unrest and lack of consistent funding.

### Social and Cultural Factors

Egypt's social and cultural characteristics are closely related to its political
and economic conditions. This has been especially true in the past forty years
when a large working class emerged to alter the society that had been previously
defined by sharp class differences. Education became a means for the poorer

classes to aspire to a better social and economic status. The strong autocratic government, rooted in the Islamic tradition of the protective father, sometimes conflicted with the democratization efforts in schools. Nevertheless, during this period the number of schools increased, and the technical schools were more widely developed in an attempt to address the spiralling social demand for education.

In the 1960s Egypt relied on its strong alliance with the Soviet Union. During this time the Egyptian leaders attempted to use socialist ideology as a guide for economic, social, cultural, and educational development. The USSR, in hopes of building a strong alliance with such an influential nation in the Middle East, provided top-rate Egyptian students with scholarships for doctoral studies both in Russia and in Eastern Bloc communist nations. Egyptian scholars had previously studied exclusively in specialized doctoral programs in the elite universities of the United States, England, and France. By the 1970s, however, the Egyptian-Russian ties were crumbling. Scholars once again returned to the universities of Western Europe and the United States to pursue doctorates; this reflected the overall pro-democracy change in the government's orientation. Internal and external political changes have caused Egypt to strengthen its alliance with the United States during the past two decades. An open door policy and a one-party political system have helped end some confusion in government policy. The social result of the open door has been a diversification of the labor force and the influx of Western consumerism. This latter trend has eroded some of the traditional Egyptian respect allotted to human service professions. As the upper and middle classes strive to increase their individual wealth and status in Western terms, they have begun to develop condescending attitudes toward manual and low technical work, the very types of work that currently supply large sums of capital in the GNP. Unfortunately, this development, together with constant political crises within the Mideast, has created a variety of social problems which the nation cannot address effectively.

The effect of these changes on education is obvious. Technical education is sought by fewer students, even though the market demand for technical workers is increasing. Academic and theoretical education is attracting more students, who expect the government to deliver on its guarantee of jobs. Conflict in the higher education community centers around the debate about the importance of practical versus theoretical education at all levels.

The changing role of women is an important factor in Egyptian education. A primary Islamic tenet is to instruct all people; however, in the past, women in Egypt have had only limited accessibility to education. Since the 1950s, however, attitudes toward women's access to schools and the workplace have been moderately liberalized. This change is seen most dramatically in the decrease in female illiteracy, which had been reduced from 95 percent in 1927 to 62 percent in 1986. (The 1986 illiteracy rate for males was 38 percent.)

Only 10 percent of women in Egypt, however, are gainfully employed, and the majority of these are in education. Most working women have completed the secondary school program and have taken courses beyond this level. Nearly twice as many women in the workforce have university degrees than do men. Field studies indicate that women are entering the workforce both through their new access to, and success in, education, and the increase in their family income at a time of rapidly increasing inflation.

During the past twenty-five years women have attended school in higher numbers. This change, combined with a change in attitudes to support women entering professions, has also affected the quality of the teaching population. Although women still assume more primary teaching positions, the demand for teachers at all levels and the supply of well-educated women has increased the number of women teaching in secondary, technical, and university levels. The opening of management-level jobs in the private sector, industry, commerce, agriculture, and government has drawn some women away from pursuing teaching owing to teaching's lower socioeconomic status. Currently, there are no special incentives for women to enter teaching. However, the fact that they are available candidates because of their status in the draft for mandatory service in the military or in community service makes them a prime pool of future teachers. The overall effects of women populating the teacher workforce will not be known for some time. Teacher preparation courses have not centered on women's issues in the past; this may become an important policy issue in the future in any Islamic society.

Collectively, all these factors influence the Egyptian society and the emergence of educational plans for both the general citizenry and, more specifically, for teachers. Egyptian teacher preparation must be designed with consideration of all these factors if the schools are to be agents of positive social development.

## THE EDUCATIONAL SYSTEM

Free education for every Egyptian citizen is a guaranteed constitutional right. The government supervises the educational system, which has undergone several changes. The system described here is the present Egyptian system. It functions on the premise of continually providing free education to all. The high rate of illiteracy, 49 percent, seems to be an irony in light of the design of the system. However, many students, eventually counted as illiterates, drop out of school at an early age in order to work for family support. In addition, many students drop out and enter the large ranks of unskilled laborers who easily find self-supporting jobs throughout the Arab-speaking world.

Basic education, which is compulsory, is provided in a two-cycle, eight-year period. The first five years are the primary education cycle. Students may attend nongovernment private schools or religious schools for this cycle (5 percent of the population does attend these schools), or they may attend government schools. The primary schools enroll 60 percent of the total school population for all levels of schooling in Egypt. Approximately 45 percent of these primary students are girls; the majority of primary teachers are women.

The second cycle of three years of compulsory education occurs in preparatory schools. These schools account for 20 percent of the total Egyptian school enrollment. By law, the two stages of compulsory basic education are to provide opportunities to develop individual abilities and to learn values, manners, academic content, and practical skills. The overall goal at this level is to prepare youths to be productive members of their communities. The curriculum at this level centers around environmental, social, economic, and health topics that are relevant to youths' lives. Specific courses are also offered in religion, languages, communication, and basic skills. In the preparatory stage, topics from vocational and professional occupations are also introduced. These include agriculture, industry, commerce, and home economics.

The basic compulsory eight-year cycle is followed by the secondary education cycle, which is divided into two sections: general secondary education and technical secondary education. In order to be admitted to the general secondary level, students must successfully complete the final exam, given nationally at the end of the preparatory stage. The general secondary stage lasts three years; the first two years are comprised of general studies followed by a third year of some type of specialized study. Successful completion of the national test at the end of the third year results in the students' achievement of a general secondary certificate which, when combined with a strong academic record, can be used as an entry ticket to higher education. Since educational opportunities vary by region and faculty, many students engage private tutors during their third year of secondary school in order to prepare for the national test. Access to private tutors is an essential tool in passing the national exam. The national exam is a nightmare for every parent and student. The exam is extremely difficult and covers all content areas through the secondary curriculum. Students are ranked for possible college application on the basis of their exam scores. Currently, more parents want their children to have the opportunity to pursue higher education. They see higher education as a gateway to higher income and social status. Since the universities cannot accommodate all secondary level graduates, the national exam has become the procedure for assessing higher education applicants. Poor scores on the national exam remand students to application to technical institutes. Therefore, private tutoring has become a lucrative second job for teachers. Many double their official schoolday salaries by tutoring an additional eight hours each day. Parents of poor and middle-class children actually construct family budgets regularly to include a tutor's salary for their children in all levels of school. The Ministry of Education has repeatedly defeated efforts to change the national exam.

Technical secondary education is important in Egypt because it is the main source of providing manpower in the diversifying economy. Approximately 67 percent of secondary students enroll in this technical program. Only 1 percent of these students will ever advance to university study. The curriculum in the technical schools is supervised by the government upon the advice of committees representing commerce, industry, and agriculture. This curriculum includes courses that provide students with knowledge and skills required in practical work situations as well as a basic academic core of courses. At present the labor market cannot absorb all graduates of the technical schools; many remain un-employed for four to six years after graduation.

In addition to the primary and secondary stages, pre-primary kindergartens and nursery schools have been developed. These schools, dating back to the turn of the twentieth century, have long traditions of providing activities through which young children can learn sound values of religion, social cooperation, and physical well-being. In 1977 a presidential decree bolstered the development of these schools through the establishment of a National Committee on the Welfare of Children. This committee has initiated special support for pre-primary education through social and university programs.

An Islamic education system exists as a parallel to the government-sponsored system described above. This system, also known as the Al-Azhar system, has gone through a number of changes since the 1950s. Currently, the system is characterized by a four-year primary stage, a three-year preparatory stage, and a four-year secondary stage. The curriculum in the Islamic education system consists of the normal curriculum taught in the general schools in addition to the Koran and Islamic sciences. There is an increased demand for these Islamic schools since their graduates are automatically accepted into Egypt's Al-Azhar University and since there is a renewed desire for religious education. The Islamic schools have significant enrollment; girls and boys attend separate schools.

Finally, there are two other types of schools in Egypt today: special education schools and private village schools. Special education schools are government-sponsored schools serving the gifted and talented, the mentally retarded, and the physically handicapped. Private village schools are a carryover from colonial nineteenth-century Egypt. These schools are attached to mosques and offer schooling with tuition fees.

## THE SYSTEM OF TEACHER EDUCATION

Teachers are prepared in different ways to teach in classrooms at various levels in the Egyptian system. Pre-primary grade teachers have traditionally been women with little formal university training. During recent years programs with some semblance to Western early childhood education programs have emerged in Egyptian university schools of education. Teacher candidates for pre-primary education are now encouraged to choose an area of early childhood studies as a specialization in their university studies. Such areas are media, children's theater/library, early child psychology, children's literature, and museum study. In addition, candidates study courses in normal child development, development of disabled children, and development of the gifted and talented.

Primary school teachers are graduates of all-women post-primary teacher train-ing institutes. After completing preparatory school, these teachers enroll in a five-year teacher training institute and then begin their teaching careers. During

the past decade more primary teachers have enrolled in university teacher preparation courses. As a part of the national initiatives to reform education, students
studying to become teachers are asked to study with the new university faculties
dedicated to primary school specialization. Teachers who have not attended the
university programs are offered ongoing access to university courses as a means
of continuing their professional development.

Preparatory and secondary teachers are educated by one of the twenty-two
university faculties throughout Egypt which comprise the nation's schools of
education. In addition, technical institutes offer teacher candidates specialized
courses in skill areas.

The university faculties of education provide two distinct preparation programs: integrated preparation and continuing preparation. Students enrolled in
the integrated teacher preparation course are required to take two years of education and academic core courses. These include principles of education and
psychology, principles of teaching, social and historical foundations of education,
and basic culture courses. If students successfully pass an exam at the end of
the second year, they can advance to Years 3 and 4 of the program. In these
latter years they must successfully complete courses in methodology, educational
psychology and technology, educational philosophy, comparative education, curriculum, and social psychology, as well as specialized and cultural courses. In
addition, teacher candidates perform student teaching in preparatory school during their third year and in secondary school in their fourth year. Upon completion
of the four-year program, a student is qualified for a bachelor of arts degree in
one of the following specialized areas: Arabic and Islamic studies, English,
French, German, history, geography, philosophy, or sociology; or a bachelor
of science degree in one of the following specialized areas: mathematics, chemistry, physics, natural history, commercial education, agricultural education, and
basic education.

The Continuing Teacher Preparation course is aimed at educating graduates
of noneducation faculties to become teachers. These candidates enroll in education courses full time for one year or part time for two years. These courses
parallel those offered in the first two years of an education degree. Successful
completion of these courses results in earning a general diploma in education
and an appointment as a preparatory school teacher. Graduates of both this general
diploma program and the Integrated program may apply to take postgraduate
studies in education if they have achieved good grades in their coursework.

Recently, university faculties have noted an increase in the quality of the
students. The increasing number of students taking the national exam has increased the quality of the overall pool of applicants in higher education. Programs
have become more competitive because of the greater social demand for schooling. In addition, candidates realize that good university grades yield money
allowances, and successful completion of the degree allows them both to teach
in schools and to earn extra money through private tutoring for the national
exams. Furthermore, education is in high demand throughout the Arab nations,

and Egyptian-educated teachers can easily work as expatriates in these other nations, especially in the Arab Gulf States and African countries.

Technical school teachers are now trained in special institutes. Previously, these teachers were trained in a few technical institutes that were later coopted by university faculties of engineering. In 1988 the National Council for Education and Educational Research and Technology recommended new methods for training technical teachers.

## ISSUES AND PROBLEMS

As indicated at the beginning of this chapter, several issues and problems are affecting the preparation of teachers in Egypt today. Here we will discuss the specific nature of these problems.

### Issue 1: Inadequate Support of In-Service Education

In-service training has become the major approach for improving the professional development of teachers and, consequently, improving the quality of their classroom performance. Tremendous social, scientific, and technological changes have caused teachers to assume many roles in Egyptian schools: master teacher, teacher aide, educational technologist, programmer, manager, and guidance counselor. The Ministry of Education has a long history of offering some support for the concept of ongoing, in-service education. Since the 1950's several in-service training centers have been established throughout Egypt. These centers have worked in collaboration with other Arab and African educators and with educators from Europe and the United States in order to train teachers specifically in foreign languages and modern mathematics.

In spite of a 1974 presidential decree to establish training institutes, the policy of in-service training in education has met with varied success. The General Administration for Training and the Training Departments of Educational Directorates form a sometimes cumbersome bureaucracy. The objectives of both offices are ideal: to improve teaching at all levels. However, in the absence of consistent funding and human resources, the actual implementation of sequential, effective in-service education does not always occur. Most of the government-sponsored institutes are now designed to provide courses through which teachers can become supervisors.

Perhaps the most influential in-service training available occurs through the contributions of centers for training, housed in university faculties of education. Many of these centers provide academic courses, seminars, workshops, professional libraries, and language laboratories to practicing teachers. Some of these centers are funded by the universities, some through United States Agency for International Development (USAID) and others through other foreign nations and universities. While these in-service courses are offered, aside from the incentive of moving up a job grade to the level of supervisor, teachers have no tangible incentives to attend. Since a majority of the current corps of teachers spend their nonschool time tutoring for increased income, they do not often volunteer to attend in-service programs held in after-school sessions.

In 1988 the Ministry of Education realized that a more carefully planned in-service program was needed in order to meet the practical needs of teachers. In-service programs are now offered on innovative methodologies in an attempt to make both pedagogy and curriculum content more relevant to students' lives. These programs cover such topics as microteaching, distant education, case studies, and teaching simulation. Microteaching seminars provide teachers with an opportunity to practice lessons and activities and to receive evaluation and critical feedback from peers and scholars. In sessions devoted to distant training, teachers are given an opportunity to practice using electronic teleconferencing as a strategy for broadening students' exposure to curriculum content. Case studies of actual Egyptian classroom problems are also used in in-service study groups as a means of providing reflective practice exercises. Finally, some in-service instructors use teaching simulations as a way of introducing teachers to a sequence of new methods and activities.

An overall criticism of Egyptian schools has been that the curriculum is irrelevant to students. Thus, the recent in-service opportunities are designed to help teachers develop their own methodology and curriculum content, in order to engage students in the learning process. Unfortunately, there are no national or district, ongoing in-service projects developed by teachers for teachers. Such a continuum of projects would require a major commitment of funds and human resources on the part of the Ministry of Education.

## Issue 2: Lack of Emphasis on Pedagogy

The passage of the Basic Education Law which mandated compulsory basic education has created a need for twelve thousand new teachers annually. The supply of teachers for basic education is critical to prevent constant overcrowding of classrooms. Many teachers assuming basic education positions have not received preparation in pedagogy. Their background has included subject area courses and coursework to teach classes in basic literacy. Teachers at the secondary levels have bachelor's degrees plus a year of study in a university's school of education. However, few of these two cohorts of teachers have studied any methodology. Since they are products of schools, teacher training institutes, and universities where the lecture is the primary mode of teaching, they do not easily adapt to the role of the teacher-as-guide or instructional manager. These latter roles are stipulated in the national curricula which has been built on a systems model. Therefore, many teachers in the active ranks need in-service education in diverse methodologies that can be used in instruction.

The need for in-service education in pedagogy mirrors the need for similar courses in teacher training institutes and universities. The teacher training institutes have a curriculum that is the equivalent of the secondary school curriculum. Professional education courses do not begin before the final years. University-level courses are superficial. The content of the basic and secondary curricula, however, requires that the teacher have a varied repertoire of skills. The goals of both curricula range from providing coursework for basic literacy to developing higher level thinking skills. Therefore, in the absence of varied pedagogical courses at the preparation stage, in-service courses need to be provided. The ministry recognizes that retention of youths in the basic education program will rely on teachers' methods and course content being relevant. Currently, however, the in-service programs are hampered because the department that handles in-service activities is isolated from the other ministry departments responsible for qualitative change.

In the 1980's two university studies highlighted the specific in-service and preservice competencies that would optimally become required for teachers. These competencies included the ability to provide varied learning activities, to maintain classroom management, to use varied materials, to develop student participation, to promote a positive social climate, to coordinate cross-curriculum learning, and to teach problem-solving and critical thinking. The need for in-service education in these areas is further compounded by the lack of clear uniform implementation of the basic and secondary education programs.

## Issue 3: Overcoming the Stereotype of the Teacher as Lecturer

Another problem emerging in Egyptian teacher education is the prevalence of the archaic image of the teacher as solely an information giver. Whereas the Ministry of Education is promoting a dynamic curriculum rooted in the view of learning as an activity, the teacher is still, for the most part, being trained to lecture. The new curriculum requires that teachers view themselves and be treated as facilitators of learning. This requires not only new technical skills on the part of the teacher, but significant changes in institutional and societal attitudes as well. As yet teacher preparation does not include courses that alter this perception. Therefore, there is a need to identify the attributes that a teacher needs to possess in the basic and secondary classrooms. Egyptian educational researchers suggest that the role of an instructional manager as an assessor of student performance, a provider of learning activities, and a monitor of the effects of a given educational technology is more appropriate to today's Egyptian classroom. Operationally, this change in role/image will occur only if teachers are taught content *and* skills in formulating objectives, diagnosing learner readiness, prescribing appropriate experiences, developing curriculum resources, and evaluating performance.

This suggestion is not new to most of the Western world, nor is it new to scholars and teachers in Egypt. The problem is manifold; there is an acute need for teachers at all levels, there are limited financial resources to support teacher preparation and in-service education, and the introduction and implementation of basic education has been somewhat chaotic throughout the nation. Compounded with these factors is the reality that candidates entering the teaching ranks in Egypt are not those who have the strongest academic background or highest scores of the national exam. On the contrary, the teachers are secondary school graduates or those university graduates who have not been accepted in more prestigious academic disciplines, for example, medicine and engineering. All these factors affect who becomes a teacher and how they perceive their role in Egyptian classrooms.

## Issue 4: Inadequate Curriculum for Preparing Teachers for Basic Education

The lack of standardized coursework at the basic education level has caused another problem for Egyptian teacher educators. Although a standard curriculum exists, task analysis for the purpose of training teachers has not occurred systematically. Therefore, many teachers have no real-world experience of what teaching a given unit or subject requires in terms of engaging students in learning. As a result, many teachers resort to using methods of rote learning which have been used in national programs to eradicate illiteracy. Without provisions for overall accountability, teachers are left to work independently. Scholars providing plans to remedy this problem suggest that accountability could serve as a catalyst for improving the teachers' performance. However, they also suggest that teachers must be taught what accountability involves: for example, measures of teacher competency, student performance, and measures of skills and utilization of knowledge. This accountability awareness, of course, would need to be enhanced by an ongoing program of related in-service and preservice programs. In the latter programs, sequences of coursework would necessarily be revamped to include specific courses in instructional analysis, curriculum content, and student teaching. Each of these courses with a standard focus on the basic education program would help to standardize the quality of the program and to promote a shared language and collegiality among program teachers.

## Issue 5: Deficient and Uncoordinated Policy Research

The lack of research components in Egyptian teacher education programs is hampering the achievement of the national educational mission. The Ministry of Education's mandates sometimes reflect a lack of understanding of schools and the slowness of institutional change in a rapidly changing society. Some research has occurred, including field studies aimed at describing the quality of the preparation programs and teacher performance. However, the politicized teachers syndicate and the resiliency of the Ministry of Education have promoted traditional teacher education programs and ignored some research. Research has revealed that many teachers in the field are unqualified and cannot gain access to the in-service courses at teacher centers because of an unequal geographic distribution of the centers. External consultants have suggested that the Ministry of Education involve its teachers in the process of researching their own system of teaching and studying it as a means of informing designers of teacher education systems. However, there are no systematic channels of communication where such research or information may be reported back into the preparation programs.

Egyptian scientific educational research was originally modeled on American pragmatic causal models. Research was designed according to statistical models and focused on answering questions relative to the effects of student and environmental characteristics on rates of learning. Most research has occurred in isolated sectors of schools of education housed in Egypt's main universities. The Egyptian research has largely resulted in teacher education programs characterized by study of psychology, environmental factors, cultural values, experiential education, and the Egyptianization of the Stanford Binet IQ test.

Other initiatives in educational research have occurred sporadically in Egyptian universities in an effort to inform the practice of teaching. Since the 1940s universities have sponsored research projects within master's and doctorate programs that have been aimed at increasing effective planning in the areas of educational economics, adult education, special education, and educational administration. In 1955 the government's General Administration of Technical Research and Projects was established in the Ministry of Education. By 1972 this became a permanent committee, the National Council for Educational Research. Ideally, both university and ministry-sponsored research could help to develop a better system for educating Egypt's teachers. Since the sponsored research has been centered on Egyptian educational needs and settings, it could inform a more effective teacher preparation process. However, the Ministry of Education has shown little leadership in supporting the implementation of research results. The ministry serves political, not academic, concerns, and, therefore, the Council for Research has suffered for a lack of money and personnel. Without central leadership from the ministry, the university and government research has not been coordinated to inform national policy. This absence of coordination has also been a factor in Egypt's weak links to research-driven planning strategies that are used by regional and international development agencies that are attempting to improve teaching throughout the Mideast.

Since 1987, educational reforms have resulted in several attempts to strengthen research and practical implementation. In 1990 a National Center for Educational Evaluation and Tests was formed in collaboration with a newly formed Central Administration for Educational Planning. Currently, a program sponsored by the U.S. Agency for International Development is being implemented to coordinate research activities from all Egyptian agencies involved in educational planning; teacher education is just one small part of this study.

### Issue 6: Dearth of Good Candidates for Teaching

As mentioned above, many candidates entering education are not stellar; this fact must be qualified, however. In a nation with a 49 percent illiteracy level, all those students who achieve a university degree or secondary certificate are members of the educated cohort. Nevertheless, like many of its neighboring nations, Egypt faces a shortage of skilled personnel. Preservice teachers willingly work as expatriates in neighboring countries as opposed to assuming Egyptian teaching jobs with lower salaries. Some of the best students, who are most able to handle content and develop a diverse repertoire of skills, are therefore lost to Egyptian education programs.

Supply and demand concepts applied to the teacher workforce in Egypt involve both quality and quantity issues. In the mid–1970s quantity was a major problem; the nation had a shortage of twenty thousand teachers and, therefore, was forced to recruit some candidates who were less qualified than previously employed teachers. The government also recruited teachers by offering the General Diploma Program to college graduates who were not education majors. In order to meet the acute shortage of technical school teachers, university graduates in technical fields who did not achieve good grades were required to become teachers instead of applying for more financially lucrative jobs. Egypt continues to provide a supply of expatriate teachers to other Arab countries as a means of maintaining diplomatic ties in the region. This creates a domestic shortage of teachers since many teachers work in other countries that pay higher salaries than Egypt.

Generally, the teaching profession has been deteriorating in spite of increasing competition for university seats. The best students are first assigned to the other professional schools at the university since graduation from those schools assures high-paying jobs in Egypt and other Arab nations. As a result of low standards, extreme demand, and a lack of economic incentives, teachers have lower socioeconomic status than other professionals. Increased Western consumerism has created a popular demand for consumer goods. Since teachers' salaries alone do not allow for high consumerism, they choose to tutor for extra wages. This is tantamount to being forced into a second job in order to compete with other Egyptian professionals. Until 1981, there was no standard method of qualifying teachers or standardizing their preparation. In 1981 the Ministry of Education recommended that primary teachers be unilaterally enrolled in an ongoing education program sponsored by a university faculty of education. The courses are given after school hours and are a part of a university degree program. Teachers attend the courses even if they don't intend to apply to a degree program. Gradually, the Ministry of Education hopes to close the five-year post-primary teacher training institutes where primary teachers previously attended. University-based continuing education and expanded degree programs will replace the institutes. The aim of this change is both to provide a more solid academic preparation of teachers and to standardize teacher preparation at the primary level.

### Issue 7: The Unfulfilled Professional Potential of the Teachers' Syndicate

The Teachers' Syndicate is the largest syndicate of teachers with the largest financial resources in Egypt and the Arab world. Currently, the syndicate has five hundred thousand members. It could be an extremely influential lobby to promote teacher professionalism, the service of the national education goals, the improvement of teacher education, and the general national development. Today, however, the syndicate excludes national causes from its agenda and devotes its efforts to securing the social and economic status of its members. Some scholars believe that this is a result of the government's policy to exclude the syndicate from participating in the design of national educational policies. Nor is the syndicate invited to participate in any decisions made by educational councils working to advise the development of technical training institutes or the Egyptian Parliament education committee. Egyptian educators agree that the syndicate's power and its members' insights gleaned from the grass-roots levels of schooling are being wasted owing to internal and external political pressures.

The external factors are connected with the government guardianship that has been imposed on the syndicate since it was formed. The syndicate has been traditionally directed by a member of the government's Ministry of Education who does not represent the ideas or values of the rank-and-file teachers. There-fore, the syndicate leadership is a puppet to the official ministry policy which is not always congruent with the teachers' policy desires. It appears that after the revolution of the 1950s political blocs were abolished, so that organized workers in any field would not strike or organize opposition to the government. The government considers the syndicate to be a gift of the revolution to teachers and demands its ongoing loyalty in return. To that end, government intelligence personnel are assigned to keep an eye on syndicate meetings and activities.

Internally, the syndicate is weak, since the teaching profession is traditionally conservative and the socioeconomic status of teachers is decreasing in the chang-ing economy. A review of the syndicate's activities indicates that priority is always given to promotion and increasing pension allowances. None of its agen-das suggests in any way that it promotes reform of teacher education. In addition, the syndicate serves as a means of social control of the profession. A minority now dictates a loyalist policy and controls arbitration for special allowances. It is reasonable to conclude that the syndicate is not a strong force in shaping improvements in teacher preparation. The syndicate's greatest effect in this area is negative. It protects the roles of teachers as tutors and political loyalists and, therein, renders static a very dynamic profession. All teachers belong to the syndicate; many of its critics believe that it could be the key force in catalyzing the reform of Egyptian education and Egyptian teacher education. However, given its members' current economic concerns the syndicate accepts its com-placent political role.

## Issue 8: The Undermining Effect of Private Tutoring

As noted earlier, through private tutoring for the national exams teachers have historically earned supplementary income and students have reinforced their school lessons to prepare for the exams. However, as the educational reformers of the 1980s attempted to strengthen the Egyptian school system at all levels, they began to see the popularity of tutoring as a serious problem that could undermine the system. Students have begun to disregard ministry-designed curricula and replace it with tutor-recommended materials and lessons that have been successfully used as exam preparation tools. In 1983 the Ministry of Education announced that private tutoring was a burden to parents who were paying monthly salaries for private teachers as well as paying high taxes supporting the government schools.

Private tutoring is a response to the inequality of educational opportunity in Egypt. Good teachers and facilities are most often found in upper class neighborhoods. In the absence of a standard teacher preparation program, evaluation of teachers and programs is at best arbitrary. Citizens who want their children to have the best chance at national exams take advantage of the low pay/status of teachers and hire them as private tutors. Most citizens accept this arrangement as a means of having some control over their children's education.

In terms of teacher preparation, private tutoring's popularity is a challenge to program designers. Reformers are attempting to improve the overall quality of teacher preparation in order to strengthen the system enough so that private tutoring is not needed. By lengthening the school day hours and upgrading teacher pay and by providing in-service training for teachers, the reformers are hoping that students will begin to be fully prepared for national exams during their official schooling. However, teachers sometimes see private tutoring as a more important part of their workday than their official classroom duties. Since very little regulation of classroom teaching or curriculum occurs, teachers are not systematically encouraged to attend in-service programs or to upgrade their methods and curriculum. Consequently, private tutoring takes precedence in many teachers' lives over in-service activities or school committee work because of the increased income it provides.

## CONCLUSION

Egypt's rapidly growing population, its geopolitical importance in the Mideast, its diversifying economy, and its constant involvement in Mideast conflicts are all factors that determine the nation's internal and external policies. There is no more crucial need internally than the need for the continued development of a strong education system at all levels. The preparation of teachers is an essential part of this development and the development of the Arab world. With an ample supply of qualified teachers, the economy would have a chance to stabilize and Egypt would enjoy the defense of a literate population. These are only ideals, however.

Several fundamental problems plague Egyptian education as a whole and teacher education specifically. The fluctuating economy, changing social classes, and political ambivalence influence all aspects of education. Lack of strong leadership both in the Ministry of Education and the Teachers' Syndicate has thwarted efforts to coordinate research and planning to strengthen the teaching profession. The absence of consistent funding for in-service programs and for formative and summative evaluations of education allows a random set of teacher qualifications to continue. At the same time, tight political control of the teaching profession and low salaries have hurt efforts to mobilize teachers toward establishing high standards for their profession. The weakness of the Teachers' Syndicate and the lack of coordinated university efforts have contributed to poorly defined criteria for effective teaching.

If education in general is to be strengthened in Egypt, it must be strengthened from within through the professional activities of well-prepared teachers. This will mean that the Ministry of Education and all high-level educators must coordinate their efforts to create and implement policies that promote university-based teacher preparation, research on specific educational issues, incentives for improving the teacher's social status, ongoing in-service education of teachers in the areas of effective methods and the use of technological knowledge bases, and syndicate involvement in nonpoliticized professional policymaking. In addition, these planners will need to tap the nation's greatest resource: its people and, specifically, women as candidates for the teaching profession.

## REFERENCES

Academy for Educational Development, Inc. *Basic Education: An Assessment, Curriculum and Teacher Education*. Washington, D.C.: Prepared for the Ministry of Education of the Arab Republic of Egypt, 1984.

Central Organization for Planning and Management. "Policies of Education and Training and the Labour Market in the Arab Republic of Egypt." A working paper submitted to Regional Seminar on Education and Training and the Labour Market in the Arab World, Cairo, January 23–25, 1990, pp. 11–12.

Cochran, J. *Education in Egypt*. London: Cross Helm Publishers, 1986.

Kandeel, Amany. *Education Policies in the Nile Valley, Somalia & Dijbanti*. Amman, Jordan: Arab Thought Forum 1989, p. 14.

Komber, Mahmond. "Teachers' Syndicate, Between Criticism and Contesting." *Cairo Educational Journal* 28 (1976): 45–50.

National Center for Educational Research and Development. "Developing the Policies for Teachers In-Service Training Plans, In Light of Experience of U.S.A. & England: Comparative study." Cairo: NCFERD, 1990, pp. 24–64.

Razik, Taher. *Systems Approach to Teacher Training and Curriculum Development: The Case of Developing Countries*. Paris: Unesco, International Institute for Educational Planning, 1972.

Souror, F. *Reform of the Educational System of Egypt*. Cairo: Ministry of Education, 1989.

World Bank. *World Development Report*. New York: Oxford University Press, 1989.

Zaher, Diaa El-Din. "How the Arab Intelligentsia Think About Education Future." Amman, Jordan: Arab Thought Forum, 1991.

# 7

# ENGLAND AND WALES

## HARRY JUDGE

The issues touching on teacher education in England and Wales have much in common with those in other countries. This chapter maintains that those issues have changed fundamentally over time (and for that reason a historical approach is adopted here) and that they can be effectively analyzed in terms of the content, location, and control of teacher education. Issues of *content* relate to the balance within teacher education between academic and professional concerns; issues of *location* relate to the articulation between teacher education and higher education; and issues of *control* relate to the power of the state and other agencies in determining the nature of teacher education itself.

## THE SYSTEM OF TEACHER EDUCATION

In England and Wales (Scotland and Northern Ireland have their own peculiarities) teacher education and training reflect the tensions and contradictions that invariably lie at the heart of educational policy. In these two countries, as indeed in so many others, much can be learned about national attitudes toward education by observing national habits in teacher training. In France, for example, those attitudes and habits are dominated by a characteristic republican virtue and by the concept of teacher as *fonctionnaire*, inadequately translated as "civil servant." In the United States, by contrast, the training of teachers reflects an open and generous view of education and of universal rights of access to it and a doctrine of the lay control of teachers and their work. For such reasons, the aspiration of American (and British) teachers toward professional status finds no parallel in France.[1]

The crucial and most difficult task involved in teacher education is to generate a supply of teachers that will match—in quality, quantity, and type—the needs of the schools. Such a matching is particularly difficult and, from an analytical point of view, especially interesting, at a time of rapid change in the ideologies and practices of schooling. Recent developments in Britain have been marked by a profound, and some would argue revolutionary and irreversible, change in the relationship of the national government to public schooling. Through the Education Act of 1988 and the cluster of reforms associated with it, the national government has redefined its own responsibilities for control of the national system. Previously, the conventional wisdom had been that the central government provided many of the resources for education and set broad national goals, but that detailed control of the curriculum and of teachers lay with elected local authorities and such professional leaders as head teachers and Her Majesty's inspectors. Unsurprisingly, that conventional wisdom—based on a somewhat specialized definition of ''partnership''—also dominated the untidy world of teacher education. Changes in policy toward schools, whether or not explicit, found their analogues in changes toward policies in teacher education. Those latter changes, however, often lagged years or even decades behind those affecting the elementary and secondary schools. These considerations lend a special interest to the case study of teacher education.

Throughout the 1980s central government in Britain adopted a consistent set of policies toward education at all levels. A national curriculum was adopted, to be reinforced by the testing of all pupils at defined ages. Within such a framework, greater autonomy is now conceded to schools and a larger freedom of choice of schools to parents of pupils. For the first time (albeit with the significant exceptions noted below), the government is defining and monitoring the content of courses of teacher training in an effort to ensure at once the elevation and the uniformity of standards within courses of teacher preparation. Such shifts of emphasis reflect a governmental and popular concern with efficiency, in the preparation of teachers as in the delivery of public education to the populace. Efficiency, as a theme, has dominated debates on teacher education since 1970; at earlier stages the dominant and successive themes were elitist and, in the heady reforms after World War II, comprehensive. These key terms—*elitist, comprehensive, efficient*—are, of course, no more than serviceable but imperfect labels for complicated and sometimes contradictory attitudes and developments. In any case the interplay among them is more important than any neat set of chronological successions. But they do help to identify broad and successive changes. In the first (elitist) phase teacher training was conceptualized, as in so many countries and until quite recently in some, within two exclusive categories. The mainstream of teacher training was marked by a functional and intellectually unambitious view of the enterprise: the state and voluntary bodies supported by it should produce competent teachers of the basic skills to the children of the masses. On the other hand, a university-based education (sometimes supplemented by a very modest injection of strictly professional preparation) would form the teachers for the upper and middle classes as well as the abler and carefully selected children of the working classes.

The comprehensive phase, anticipated in the 1920s and enjoying its full flowering in the 1960s, was dominated by different views—imperfectly articulated and applied—of schooling, teaching, and (as a consequence) of teacher training. The formal decline of selection of pupils at the age of eleven into separate types of secondary school was accompanied by an effort to provide similar patterns of training for teachers of all types, and to associate that training with universities and the awarding of degrees. The rigidities of the two-track system were softened. Debates on schooling as on teacher training were dominated by issues of equity, parity, and access. This comprehensive phase has now evolved, not without jolts and discontinuities, into a period already characterized as being determined by the values of efficiency.

In each of the three phases three distinct themes have recurred and interacted with one another. These themes, to be pursued across the three historical phases, are here labeled *content, location,* and *control.* Issues of content concern primarily what it is that is taught to students in teacher education, and in particular the balance between academic studies and practical or professional work. Issues of location concern, of course, the relationship of teacher education to the mainstream of higher education (epitomized by the university) and to the so-called lower schools. Issues of control in their turn relate to the powers and responsibilities of central government, of the religious and voluntary bodies as the historic providers of much of teacher education, and of local governments as the principal employers of teachers and providers (but only until 1990) of most of the nonuniversity institutions of teacher education. The themes resonate through all three historical phases. The argument of the rest of the chapter may therefore be introduced by a simple grid showing historical themes in teacher education:

| | ELITIST | COMPREHENSIVE | EFFICIENT |
|---|---|---|---|
| Content | | | |
| Location | | | |
| Control | | | |

## ISSUES AND PROBLEMS

### Issue 1: Problems Emanating from the Elitist Phase

Teacher education in England and Wales is a product of history rather than of logic, although much has been achieved in the past twenty years to give it more shape and coherence. Although as a consequence it is now more of a system than ever before, it is still marked by curious inherited divisions, both between curricular patterns of teacher education (and underlying ideologies) and between types of institution. These divisions were created in the nineteenth century and can only be understood in that historical context. They are not without analogies elsewhere in Europe, but they stand in marked contrast to the present situation in the United States. They are rooted in patterns of schooling, and specifically in the sharp distinction throughout the last century and well into this between on the one hand public elementary education and on the other secondary education provided only for a privileged minority. Serious and vocational teacher education was for a long time confined to the preparation of teachers for those public elementary schools.[2]

Until 1870 those schools were provided exclusively by voluntary religious bodies, albeit with a growing measure of support and intervention from the state. Many of the teachers in them were in no sense qualified or licensed, but both the providers of the schools and the state as the source of finance had an obvious interest in raising the standards of teaching. This was attempted by an array of measures, including financial incentives for teachers who chose to seek certification, and the control of that process of certification by public examinations and by the monitoring functions of Her Majesty's inspectors (HMI). Throughout the second half of the century the main source of teachers was the pool of student teachers, who in return for modest payments and some free tuition worked as apprentices to more experienced practitioners. Such teacher training as existed was therefore undertaken for the most part within the culture of the elementary schools themselves, and for the majority that was for long generally deemed to be sufficient.

For a minority of the more able and determined, postschool training was provided through one- or two-year courses in the handful of training colleges that the religious bodies had provided for their own teachers, again with varying measures of state support justifying government intervention in their management. By midcentury a score of such colleges existed. Those student teachers who did not secure scholarships to them could nevertheless continue to teach as uncertificated teachers or submit themselves, without having attended a training college, to the national examination provided by the government as the one gate to certificated status. These colleges owed much to Scottish and continental examples, and became both more significant and (given their monopoly) more anomalous after the introduction to England and Wales in 1870 of secular public elementary schools, under the control of elected school boards.[3] With the important exception noted below, there was no secular alternative to these denominational colleges, which depended for their survival both on financial support from the government and on a supply of students from the pool of student teachers. By 1900 there was only one certificated teacher for each 75 pupils, and only one trained teacher (that is, who had attended a college) for each 128 pupils. Moreover, the student teachers themselves provided a significant direct contribution to the workforce: of 139.818 teachers in service in elementary schools in 1902, 30.785 were student teachers.

From the beginning of this century, local public education authorities were encouraged to build their own training colleges, although only a score of such institutions had been established before 1914. Public and political pressures on an untidy system became stronger, and opposition to the student teacher system more articulate. The minimum age for school admission was raised, and the roots of teacher training in the elementary school weakened. Scholarships were provided for prospective teachers willing to stay on in secondary schools, and teacher education took a further step toward what was later to be defined as higher education. By 1914 most of the student teachers had disappeared, and most prospective teachers began their professional training after leaving secondary school (or its equivalent) and in one of the colleges. Those colleges, while not neglecting vocational concerns, were often marked by a strong academic bias in their curriculum, and many students in them sought to combine their regular program with contemporaneous study in university courses. The public authorities generally resisted this tendency, for example, by withdrawing recognition from colleges which allowed students to combine a two- or three-year course with work for a university degree. But it was long before attendance at a college, and subsequent success in an examination, became a necessary condition for employment as a teacher: as late as 1926 there was one uncertificated teacher for three that were certificated, and in many rural areas the numbers were equal.

The training of elementary teachers was therefore an important item on the policy agenda: not until very much later was that true for secondary school teachers. Even after the spread of public secondary schools in the early years of this century, possession of a university degree was thought to be a sufficient guarantee of competence as a teacher. Indeed, such legal provisions survived into the 1970s, and the attitudes underlying them even longer than that. The universities became involved in the business of teacher training almost by accident. In the late nineteenth century all the training colleges were religious establishments, and this monopoly was offensive to many. Therefore, several universities gladly accepted the government's invitation to establish what were known as day training colleges, to provide a secular alternative to the conventional residential colleges for elementary teachers: sixteen such colleges existed at the turn of the century. Their contribution to the training of elementary teachers represented nearly one-quarter of the total provision. Some of them quietly developed secondary departments, which in time responded to the general view among the associations of secondary teachers that the appropriate pattern of education and training for their members should be a bachelor's degree followed by a one-year university-based professional course. Early in this century this became the norm for those graduates who attached importance to any kind of formal training. The average annual number in this category for the whole country in the years before World War I was only 200, and of these 160 were women. In 1938 only 60 percent of the male graduates teaching in secondary schools had received this or any other kind of formal training. Even in the 1960s, and until such training was made compulsory, nearly half of all the graduates going into teaching received no kind of training.

The universities therefore became the home of a particular kind of teacher training, possibly well adapted to the particular needs of secondary schools, and—partly because they successfully insisted on a four-year course as a minimum if both a degree and professional training were to be achieved—they were distanced from the larger but less prestigious business of preparing elementary school teachers. The training colleges outside the universities became the home of the two-year course, combining (often uneasily) academic and professional work. Teacher training gradually became the normal requirement for elementary school teachers, but not for their secondary cousins. Management of the training colleges, now separated from the structures of elementary and secondary schooling but still distanced from the universities in higher education, was exercised by the local education and denominational authorities. Central government exercised tight control over the logistics and curriculum and examinations of the colleges; the universities depended on it for recognition, but thereafter (strengthened by the voluntary nature of the training provided) enjoyed a considerable measure of autonomy, conferring, for example, their own diplomas as alternatives to the state certification examination. Between the two world wars a largely symbolic attempt was made to draw the two separate sectors a little closer together by establishing joint boards to conduct the examinations for teacher candidates in the colleges, and so limit the influence of government on the content of courses. But at the end of the elitist phase (marked roughly by the passing of the great Education Act of 1944), a very sharp dichotomy had been established between voluntary training within the universities for the academic secondary schools and an effectively compulsory one within the colleges for the elementary sector. These divisions still have geological importance, and the comments on content, location, and control made in this chapter can now be incorporated in the grid displayed previously.

## Issue 2: Problems Emanating from the Comprehensive Phase

There are two reasons for attaching the convenient label of *comprehensive* to the second major phase in the development of British teacher education (from 1944 to 1972). As it has already been argued, the key to understanding the purposes and structure of teacher education—and not in Britain alone—lies in the relationship between the schools and the activities of teacher education itself. During the years under review the structure of British schooling changed dramatically: first, by the introduction after 1944 of universal secondary education, albeit of a bipartite variety and, second, by the acceleration during the 1960s toward the introduction of the comprehensive secondary school designed to incorporate the academic and general secondary schools that had preceded it.[4] The symmetrical relationship between a dual system of teacher education and a dual system of schooling was destroyed, but the necessary adjustments to teacher education were made only slowly and painfully. Meanwhile, the national system was becoming more comprehensive in yet another sense as efforts were redoubled to bring the untidy business of teacher education firmly and unambiguously within the mainstream of higher education.

Major changes were outlined in the year of the 1944 act: from an early date, only *qualified teachers* (the new technical term) were to be employed, and qualification would depend (except, still, for university graduates) on attending an approved course of training. The gates seemed to be closing on an emerging profession. A new relationship was attempted between the universities and the colleges through regional forms of organization which assumed responsibility (not always exercised with firmness and imagination) for the procedures leading to qualified teacher status, for the courses of study in the colleges, and for examinations. In principle, the central government had yielded a great deal of its historic control. Even in practice the system became a great deal more liberal and decentralized than it had been (or was again to become). The legal minimum school-leaving age was raised twice in these years and, along with the successful demands for smaller classes, contributed to an impressive increase in the number of teacher training places and of institutions (as well as of their size and effectiveness). The output from the colleges in 1939 had been six thousand; by the early 1970s, when the peak was reached, it was forty thousand. Even so, the length of the course had been extended from two to three years at the beginning of the 1960s, and by the end of that decade some 10 percent of all students were completing a fourth year in order to qualify for the newly introduced degree of bachelor of education (the B.Ed.).

The colleges therefore came to resemble more closely other establishments of higher education. Not only were their courses of study more academically serious, but also there was a marked shift toward laicization: this shift had taken place rapidly after 1944. In 1939 there had been sixty-three voluntary (mostly denominational) colleges and only twenty-eight maintained by the local education authorities; by 1951 the voluntary category had shrunk to fifty-six, while the local mushroomed to 76. They were shortly to acquire a greater measure of responsibility for their own affairs through the reconstitution of governing bodies and the representation on them of faculty members. The universities themselves preserved their interest in the one-year course of training for graduates, which was not made compulsory until the early 1970s (and even then with significant loopholes).

These years were also marked by expansion and diversification within higher education as a whole. University teacher training related only to the academic grammar and independent schools and had existed comfortably alongside, albeit at a considerable distance from, teacher training in the colleges designed to meet the needs of a separate elementary school system. But, already in the 1960s, the universities had ceased to be the only nationally recognized establishments of higher education. Alongside them, with government encouragement, the thirty polytechnics had grown indistinguishable in many ways from the universities, though subject (as they will now no longer be) to control by local government.[5] A straightforward marriage between universities and colleges of education was ardently desired by many reformers but had not proved possible to achieve: too many issues of power, prestige, and finance were involved. But a higher education "family," which now included polytechnics and some colleges of higher education alongside the older universities, would need to clarify its relationship with a training college system marked by increasing ambiguities of purpose and status. That status had itself been subtly modified in the mid–1960s by a simple and inexpensive change of title from training college to college of education.[6]

The James Committee, appointed by Margaret Thatcher in 1971 when she was secretary of state for education and science, therefore faced a rich crop of problems and questions. Changes in the school system meant that the machinery of training was now badly out of line with it: teachers could no longer be professionally classified as being concerned only with younger or less academically talented pupils, or vice versa. The college of education system had come to maturity, in terms of size and the length of the courses offered. But its relationship to higher education as a whole remained uncertain and uncomfortable. Moreover, the startling growth of the past decade had inevitably raised problems of quality and stability. Perhaps most serious of all, the quest for academic respectability—associated in part with the lengthening of the course, and more directly with the B.Ed. degree—was believed to have generated a neglect of professional concerns and an insensitivity to the real needs of schools and of prospective classroom teachers. In terms reminiscent of the early 1900s, it was objected that the colleges were unduly preoccupied with conventional university standards of subject mastery and scholarship. To make things worse, it was stated that the professional study of education had itself been etherealized. These years marked the heyday of the study of the four disciplines of education: sociology, psychology, philosophy, and history.

Many of these anxieties were doubtless misplaced or exaggerated, but the structural problems underlying the polemic were real enough. The solutions proposed by the James Committee were not formally adopted, but they had no small influence on the evolution of the present arrangements. The solutions were integrated by an effort to dignify and clarify the term *professional*. For that reason the strongest emphasis was placed on the professional development of the teacher in service through a range of educational and training activities. The formal distinction between concurrent (as in the colleges) and consecutive (as in the universities) forms of teacher education was rejected as unhelpful. All prospective teachers should first complete a well-planned phase of personal higher education (the so-called first cycle) before proceeding to a second and sharply professional cycle of teacher preparation, sited partly within higher education and partly in the setting of real schools. The degree to be awarded after these two stages was to be a B.A. (Ed.) and was conceived as being a degree in teaching rather than in a subject called education. The intention in many of these details was to imply a flattering analogy with the professional and practical education offered (or so it is still fashionable to suppose) in medicine. The colleges' dependent relationship on the universities was to be terminated and in effect a third sector of higher education was created, based in large measure on the existing colleges, many of which would wish to diversify their programs of study. The committee was skeptical of the advantages of teachers being educated in relative isolation from the rest of their contemporaries.[7]

The 1972 Report conveniently marks the transition from the *comprehensive* to the *efficient* phase. The phase it concluded was marked, in terms of the explanatory grid, by a shift in content toward academic values and purposes, against which there was then a strong reaction. As for location, attempts to incorporate the colleges within the university sector were unsuccessful, but the growth of higher education itself opened up new possibilities for the future. As for control, central government preserved tight management of the funding and logistics of the system, while relinquishing much of the professional and academic responsibility for it. These very themes were to be given a new importance, and in some ways new definitions, in the succeeding (that is, contemporary) phase which has been dominated by an unexpectedly abrupt decline in the number of places required for teacher training. That decline, coupled with the government's new and vigorous determination to reassert control of the values as well as the mechanics of the system, explains much in the present British pattern.[8]

## Issue 3: Problems Emanating from the Efficient Phase

The mid–1970s mark a watershed in the history of education in Britain. The Labour prime minister's speech at Oxford in October 1976 was widely and correctly perceived as a forceful attempt to break away from many of the conventions of the past. Standards were not high enough; the basics were being neglected; the educating professions had not been sensitive to public and parental anxieties; the needs of industry had been neglected; central government had not given a decisive lead; and a great debate was needed. In spite of the contemporary disclaimers, it was clear that government proposed to intervene much more directly in the design and delivery of the school curriculum. The momentum in that direction was accelerated by the Conservative victory in the general election of 1979 and was consolidated in the elections of 1983 and (even more clearly) 1987. There were, of course, profoundly important shifts of emphasis as a result of these Conservative victories—notably in the attack on the powers of local education authorities, the new powers to be given to parents as consumers, and the accompanying stress on privatization. However, in the corridors of power there is now a well-established consensus that more intervention is required, at least in the short term, to restore the educational system to a healthy state. A much more overt interest in the business of teacher education was therefore to be expected.

The pervading pessimism of the early 1970s was generated in part by the worldwide economic crisis caused by the rise in oil prices and in part by the simple facts of demographic decline. Consistent declines in the birthrate, in Britain as elsewhere, placed the system under great strain since contraction is nearly always more painful than expansion, even if the expansion is inadequately funded. The effects on the recently expanded world of teacher education were only too obvious. Government, which had financed that expansion, now found itself with wide and unchallenged powers in slimming down the provision, and used those administrative powers to produce significant changes in shape as well as in scale. In 1972, outside the universities which were sheltered from the storms that were about to break, there were 130,407 students in teacher training. In 1978 there were 36,000 and, although since then modest adjustments have been made, the effects of that shock will be permanent. It is not simply a question of less of the same. The college of education system has effectively disappeared, and only a handful of such single-purpose institutions survive. The separate regional and national organization of those colleges has been abolished. Many were brusquely closed; others were absorbed as going concerns by polytechnics or, in a few cases, universities; many more diversified their programs of study in order to include a wider range of work for degrees and similar qualifications. These changes were part of a redrawing of the map of higher education, more than half of which is now conducted outside the universities.

The planning opportunity has been taken to redress the balance of the contributions made by the universities, on the one hand, and by the colleges of education (where they survived) on the other, the polytechnics into which some were absorbed, and the colleges of higher education (which some became)— here referred to as a group, and for convenience, as "the colleges." In this sense the colleges (now the polytechnic and college sector in cumbersome official parlance) were until recently oddly referred to as "the public sector" in order to distinguish them from the universities which, though also publicly funded, have conventionally been regarded as enjoying a considerable measure of autonomy. In the early 1970s, when enrollments were, of course, highest, teacher education was provided in 27 universities and 180 colleges. By 1983, when most of the surgery had been accomplished, it was provided in only 56 colleges— and 27 universities! Within the colleges, the last admissions to the three-year certificate course were in 1979, and all teacher candidates in those colleges now proceed to the B.Ed. degree. More surprising perhaps has been the marked shift within the colleges from the concurrent to the consecutive mode—from the B.Ed. to the one-year postgraduate course. This shift, from the longer to the shorter courses of the type advocated by the James Committee, has further tilted the university/colleges balance toward the former. It has also had the effect, intended or not, of ensuring that the universities continue to concentrate, albeit not exclusively, on the secondary schools, whereas most prospective primary (that is, elementary) school teachers are trained in the colleges, which nevertheless make a substantial contribution to the staffing needs of the secondary schools. In a curious and incomplete sense, the much sharper divisions of the nineteenth century still influence the shape of the system.

These features of present British teacher education can be illustrated by the figures for admission to courses of teacher education in September 1987. The total university share of admissions is 32 percent, contrasted with a tiny 4.4 percent in 1972. Nevertheless, 48 percent of secondary teachers are trained outside the universities. The universities, to the tune of 78 percent of their total admissions, are predominantly concerned with teachers for the secondary schools. Fifty-four percent of all students are on the one-year graduate, consecutive, course. These changes, taken cumulatively, are of great force: a much higher proportion than ever before of future teachers are being trained in the universities, and a much higher proportion in courses where the focus, at least in principle, is on professional preparation rather than academic study. Here, then, are marked changes in the readings on the explanatory grid for the two themes of *content* and *location*.

But the current *efficient* phase of teacher education differs even more profoundly from its immediate predecessor. In the 1960s government placed most of the expansion of teacher education outside the universities, although it may be doubted whether in the circumstances of that decade any real alternative was open to it. But, unlike government in the *elitist* phase in its relationship to the college sector, it purposefully abstained from seeking to direct the nature of the courses provided: this was the business of universities, the regional organizations grouped around universities, or the colleges themselves. This is why 1976 represents a watershed in the British educational polity, for no government that cares publicly about the school curriculum can be indifferent to the curriculum of those establishments that produce teachers for them.[9] Nevertheless, few observers in, say, 1979 anticipated the lengths to which a British government would go in asserting, or in some sense reasserting, its right to control such matters. The secretary of state for education and science, who has the undoubted legal authority to confer or deny the status of qualified teacher, has ruled that access to that status shall normally be through courses of preparation approved by him. That approval is secured only if a number of conditions, or criteria, is satisfied and it is conferred or denied on the recommendation of a Council for the Accreditation of Teacher Education, the members of which he appoints. Universities, unlike the colleges, have been exempt from the visits of Her Majesty's inspectors, although they have always been free to invite such visits. That position has not been altered legally. But the Council (CATE) can make a recommendation only if it has access to a report written by the inspectors; every university in England and Wales offering courses of teacher training has now received such a visit. It is not yet clear whether CATE, when it has reported on all university and college courses, will continue to exist.

What the criteria make clear is that government has strong views about the proper nature of teacher training. There is firm and unsurprising emphasis, which at present is of particular importance for students for the B.Ed., on the importance of academic subject studies. Some have publicly regretted that this emphasis is not in the best interests of prospective primary school teachers: in that sense, the debate on content is far from dead. Equally marked is the concern with pedagogy, a word, if not a concept, that had ceased to be used very much in the 1960s. Those who teach teachers should themselves have had recent experience of teaching; teaching practice must be extensive and well organized; experienced teachers must themselves be involved in the selection of students for courses and in the preparation of them. Similarly, students must be introduced to the importance of multicultural education and of pupils who have special educational needs, and must have a good understanding of the social context in which they are to work. All this represents an overt and principled attempt to give teacher education, of whatever type and wherever located, a sharp professional and practical focus.[10] What has been devalued, in colleges and universities alike, is the study of educational disciplines in the styles that had become orthodox in many establishments. The political and demographic changes of the late 1970s and the 1980s have produced many of the intended effects of the James Report: a second cycle (though not in those terms) for the majority of intending teachers, and a sharp emphasis on the professional imperatives of that cycle. Moreover, the segregated colleges of education have all but disappeared, and the distinction between university and college has substantially diminished. Although the primary/secondary distinction is, of course, still important, it no longer corresponds either to a simple difference of location or to variation in the type, graduate or not, of program. University and college are engaged in fundamentally similar work and are unambiguously subject to the same controls.

Nevertheless, some critical questions obtrude. In the efficient phase, the question of content has been decisively resolved: for all prospective teachers the stress is to be on knowledge of basic subject matter (mathematics, a foreign language, or whatever) and on professional pedagogy: ''abstract theory'' has been beaten on the head. This clarity has been achieved by government control, exercised not only on the colleges (as previously in the elitist phase), but also on the universities. The issue of location has been redefined, with a growing similarity of program structure (the consecutive mode), a much larger share of the market for the universities, and a softening of the historic distinction between the university and the college sectors. Under the Education Act of 1988, the two sectors will be similarly managed, with the removal of all colleges (including, of course, the polytechnics) from local authority control and the creation of twin funding councils at the national level, designed to apply government policies.[11] One critical question therefore relates to the rationality of any continuing distinction between provision by the universities and the rest of teacher education. It is simplistic to suppose that the universities will automatically preserve some inherent commitment to teacher education based on research. Indeed, the requirements of the new criteria (including a significantly longer teaching year) make it more difficult than ever before to pay serious attention to scholarly as distinct from vocational responsibilities.

## CONCLUSION

The dilemmas faced by England and Wales may well oblige the institutions, and not just the universities, to devise new patterns of teacher education in which the legitimate demands of utility are integrated with an open and inquiring approach to the tasks of teaching and the roles of the teacher: the internship scheme at Oxford University, developed in close association with a group of schools, is, of course, one example of such an effort.[12] Such efforts are more readily deployed within the consecutive pattern of graduate teacher training, protected from the competitive internal pressures of the B.Ed., within which the objectives of a subject-based academic education and of professional preparation can be reconciled only with difficulty. In any case, there now seems to be no clear rationale for the B.Ed. as a concurrent form of training, with its historical origins in the old training college model operating within a very different universe of secondary and higher education. Students themselves seem likely to prefer forms of higher education which allow them to defer final choices of career and to acquire bachelor degrees that have wider currency than the single-purpose B.Ed.

For such reasons, postgraduate teacher training is likely to become the dominant form of teacher education in Great Britain in the twenty-first century. Developed forms of the internship may well become the preferred model of such training. But this pair of probabilities raises paradoxes and dangers. There is an unpleasant possibility that the stress on school-based teacher training will be misinterpreted and distorted. In particular, the critical and autonomous role of the university may be threatened by being eliminated. If the stress on practical competence is excessive or exclusive, it may be falsely assumed that the schools themselves or the employers can take the whole of the responsibility for teacher training. Nothing could be more destructive of the dignity or the independence of the teaching profession, on which a healthy and critical democracy depends. By challenging the arid monopoly of a theory-based university, internship deploys the language of partnership. But partnership is reciprocal, and without a major part for university or college teacher education will become, as it was a century ago, unimaginative, docile, and repetitive. In 1988 the government decided to introduce a scheme under which some prospective teachers of mature years would be recruited to the schools and given by their employers modest on-the-job training in which universities and colleges might play little or no part. In 1990 it initiated a pilot scheme, of potentially wider scope, under which prospective teachers would be given a two-year period of combined employment and training during which responsibility for their preparation would be shared by their employers and, less substantially, the training institutions. This latter scheme is much closer to the spirit of internship and, indeed, to a two-year pattern of teacher preparation for which the James Report argued (and which I was happy to advocate some years ago).[13] Much will depend on the contribution to be made by universities and others and on the freedom allowed to them to behave with reaoned autonomy.

The Education Reform Act of 1988 has changed much in the British educational landscape, and probably more dramatically than any previous measure.[14] In particular, it has changed the relationships between government and other elected agencies and between schools and teacher education. It is the same central government that now regulates what must be taught and in what amounts that has the parallel responsibility for demonstrating that a sufficient supply of appropriately trained teachers is delivered in order to meet those legal requirements. If government order decrees that more mathematics and science and foreign languages are now to be taught, then government must deliver the necessary teachers. In the past such a responsibility has been weaker and more dispersed, and the relationship between teachers and curriculum has been more flexible. The pressures on government to intervene powerfully in the mechanisms that control the supply of teachers through higher education will be irresistible. And those pressures will come to bear most oppressively in the mid–1990s when for demographic reasons the conventional supply of teachers will be most at risk and the school population rising.

Already we see plain signs of pressure on teachers and on their sense of worth and professional style. They have lost and not yet had restored their rights of participation in the processes by which salaries and conditions of service are determined. Acts and regulations now determine in unprecedented ways the details of what is to be taught. Appraisal and the techniques of human resource management erode traditional, and not always erroneous, ways of thinking and feeling about teaching as a way of life. Such factors are likely to discourage the intelligent and well-motivated men and women who are needed in the schools from committing themselves to teaching or from undertaking rigorous courses of professional preparation, if easy means of access to the responsibilities of a teacher are proffered. In such times, it is all the more important that teacher education should be confident, soundly based in established and autonomous institutions able to resist successive changes of political mood, and yet rooted in the real world of schools and the pupils they educate.

## NOTES

Appreciation is expressed to the editor and to Georgia State University for their willingness to allow much of the material in this chapter to be taken from the author's chapter in Edgar B. Gumbert, ed., *Fit to Teach: Teacher Education in International Perspective* (Atlanta: Center for Cross-cultural Education, Georgia State University, 1990).

1. See, for the United States, Jonas F. Soltis, ed., *Reforming Teacher Education* (New York: Teachers College Press, 1987). For several other countries, see Gumbert, ed., *Fit to Teach*. For the comments on the case of France, see Harry Judge, "Cross-National Perceptions of Teachers," *Comparative Education Review* 32, no. 2 (1988): 143–158.

2. Much of the information used in the following paragraphs is taken from H. C. Dent, *The Training of Teachers in England and Wales, 1800–1975* (London: Hodder and Stoughton, 1975) and P.H.J.H. Gosden, *The Evolution of a Profession* (Oxford: Basil Blackwell, 1972).

3. Marjorie Cruickshank, *History of the Training of Teachers in Scotland* (London: University of London Press, 1970).

4. Harry Judge, *A Generation of Schooling: English Secondary Schools since 1944* (Oxford and New York: Oxford University Press, 1984).

5. Tony Becher, ed., *British Higher Education* (London: Allen and Unwin, 1987).

6. William Taylor, "Robbins and the education of teachers," *Oxford Review of Education* 14, no. 1 (1988): 49–58.

7. *Teacher Education and Training: A Report by a Committee of Enquiry Appointed by the Secretary of State for Education and Science, under the Chairmanship of Lord James of Rusholme* (London: Her Majesty's Stationery Office, 1972).

8. Harry Judge, "From Quantity to Quality: Teacher Education in Britain," in Thomas J. Lasley, ed., *Issues in Teacher Education* (Washington, D.C.: American Association of Colleges of Teacher Education, 1986), vol. 2, pp. 55–64.

9. *Teaching Quality: Presented to Parliament by Command of Her Majesty, March 1983* (London: Her Majesty's Stationery Office, 1983).

10. *Initial Teacher Training: Approval of Courses, Circular 3/84* (London: Department of Education and Science, 1984).

11. *Higher Education: Meeting the Challenge: Presented to Parliament by Command of Her Majesty, April 1987* (London: Her Majesty's Stationery Office, 1987).

12. Peter Benton, ed., *The Internship Scheme* (London: Gulbenkian Foundation, in press).

13. *Qualified Teacher Status: Consultation Document* (London: Department of Education and Science, 1988). Letter from Department of Education and Science to Chief Education Officers and others, "Articled Teacher Pilot Scheme," June 27, 1989. Harry Judge, "Degrees of Certainty," *Times Educational Supplement* 3 (March 1981).

14. On the new act, see Stuart Maclure, *Education Reformed: A Guide to the Education Reform Act, 1988* (London: Hodder and Stoughton, 1988).

# 8

# GERMANY

## CHRISTA HÄNDLE

In the process of German unification two different systems of teacher education, each contrary in central aspects, must be integrated and coordinated. This chapter presents a study that describes the main differences in teacher education in the two parts of Germany; compares the reform issues that evolved from reform projects of teacher education in the 1970s in West Germany with the traditions in East Germany; describes possible changes in teacher education in the new federal states; outlines conditions in the social context that determine these developments in unified Germany; and deals with future possibilities.

## THE SYSTEM OF TEACHER EDUCATION

### Teacher Training Institutions: Separation Versus Integration of Training

In East Germany, teachers have been trained at three institutions. The education of primary school teachers (grades 1–4) was offered at a technical school level at Institutes for Teacher Education. Certified teachers (grades 5–12) were educated at both teachers' colleges and universities. However, a vertical component characterized this system: certain majors or double majors were offered at either institution. Although this approach was favorable to the integration and participation of students in the departments, it also meant limited choices and fewer opportunities for students to change majors. These teachers were trained for small, dual-track schools (grades 1–10) and additional selective high schools (grades 11–12) leading to the college entrance examination (*abitur*).

In West Germany during periods of teacher shortages and educational reforms in the 1970s, the status of teacher education and the profession improved. Preparation for all teaching professions shifted to universities and other institutions of higher education. Colleges for teachers who were preparing for the lower status schools in the school system hierarchy (elementary: grades 1–4; main school: grades 5–9; intermediate: grades 5–10) were integrated into the university. At the same time, the full-day comprehensive school system could not be introduced. Comprehensive schools were added to the three half-day school types existing at the secondary level (*Gymnasium*, *Realschule*, *Hauptschule*).

### Single- Versus Double-Phase Training

In East Germany as in other European nations, there was no second phase of teacher training outside of the university. Teaching practice was integrated into the studies. Initiation into the profession took place during a one-year internship during the fifth year of study. It was supervised by staff at the teacher training institutions, although owing to long distances between the schools and the teacher training institutions, this was not very intensive. Thus, the cooperating teachers, who often obtained additional training, were of crucial importance for the introduction of the beginner.

Teachers in West Germany have had to pass a second phase of teacher education under the control of the school administration, lasting two years. They are required to teach or observe twelve lessons a week at school and to take part in one general seminar and two others for subject matter. During this phase they get some payment. This educational requirement is much more fixed than that at the university, and there is little choice of seminars or teaching staff. After teachers have passed a second state examination, they may apply for a permanent position in the school system.

The second training phase developed during the nineteenth century specifically for teachers in the selective high schools, because during their university studies they were not sufficently trained for their jobs. It was required for all teachers in West Germany by the early 1980s.

### Admission and Certification: Regulation Versus Freedom

Admission to teacher education in East Germany was planned in response to the demand for teachers in the school system. The Institutes for Teacher Education, where teachers for grades 1 to 4 in East Germany were trained, recruited graduates from the ten-grade comprehensive schools. Applicants for teacher education were recommended by their schools. Admission depended not only on the applicants' political loyalty, but also on their practical competence as shown in pedagogic clubs and tasks, for example, tutoring pupils and working with children in summer holiday camps.

Teachers for grades 5 to 12 had to pass a selective form (grades 1–12) of the public school system in order to gain admission into the university system. They were admitted to colleges of teacher education and to universities according to the centrally defined demand for teachers of various subjects. They had to pass the courses in the prescribed time and were certain to get jobs afterward. Most of them were married and had children when entering teaching, thereby improving their chances of obtaining an apartment.

West Germany has historically allowed much more freedom of admission in teacher education. After thirteen years of selective schooling and passing of the *abitur*, students may enroll in institutions and subjects of their own choice, without restrictions. After a minimum study time of three and a half or five years, students must pass a first state examination. Subsequently, they apply for a second phase of teacher education and must pass a second state examination. Permanent appointments depend on the grades they receive.

Completion of the first and second state examinations does not guarantee anyone a job as a teacher in West Germany, and there have been recurring cycles of shortage and surplus of teachers since the nineteenth century. In times of teacher scarcity, changes were made in training programs to facilitate a speedy recovery from the problem. Among these changes were widespread recruiting, shorter supplementary educational programs, more integrated and practice-oriented studies, educational reforms, and improvements in status. During periods of teacher surplus and unemployment, however, admission regulations turned restrictive, study requirements and examination standards were raised, and there were fewer initiatives toward reform. The severe fluctuations in teacher demand have meant that during periods of teacher unemployment, capacities have been reduced and the qualified staff has moved to other fields (Schmidt and Schulz, 1990).

## Curriculum: Homogeneity Versus Heterogeneity

In East Germany different subjects were concentrated at different universities or teacher training colleges in order to permit greater differentiation and better coordination of courses of study. The curriculum was centrally prescribed and lasted five years for secondary teachers at universities and teacher training colleges and three years for elementary school teachers. Methods courses and practical experiences were integrated. In fixed seminar groups, all prospective teachers attended the same sequence of courses. If the students did not pass them, they had to leave. The percentage of dropouts was rather low owing to a low student-teacher ratio and significant student support by means of scholarships and rooms in dormitories.

Today teacher education in West Germany is strongly subject-oriented, but there are significant differences among federal states. Because of the strong tradition of freedom of choice in both teaching and learning at institutions of higher education in West Germany, there are few coordinated programs for teacher training. For students, this leads to massive difficulties in coordinating and integrating courses (Händle and Nitsch, 1991). There are high dropout rates in teacher education, especially during times of teacher unemployment.

### In-Service Education: Mandatory Versus Voluntary

In East Germany in-service education was compulsory. There were inspectors, advisers, and regional centers for in-service education, which offered supervision, lectures, and courses. Among teacher education staff, usually many school teachers had additional qualifications and degrees.

In East Germany state institutions are also responsible for the third training phase of in-service education. This is not a mandatory phase of teacher education in West Germany. Participants obtain a reduced teaching load but receive no additional pay for their participation. Practicing teachers are experiencing more difficulty acquiring additional degrees and joining the university staff.

## REFORM ISSUES

Integration in East German teacher education was centrally administered and also supported through the homogeneous style of living and strong social controls in the small institutions, departments, and units of higher education. The opposite is true for the West German states, where teacher training is not integrated because of the states' heterogeneous concepts and lifestyles, and the freedom of teaching and study at the universities, which have become mass institutions. During the educational reforms of the 1970s, the main issue in West Germany had been to achieve better integration in various areas of teacher education (Händle, 1989). Many programs were set up aiming at more integration. Many of them were discontinued in the late 1970s as unemployment of teachers grew.

One issue that has been discussed as a result of the German unification process is whether the relatively unintegrated teacher education in the West should be imitated in the eastern federal states, or whether the eastern traditions of shorter studies and more integrated programs should be kept, while admitting more freedom of choice and differentiation of courses.

### Institutional Integration

West German teacher education was widely integrated into the universities during the 1970s. Now the new federal states are quickly catching up. Teacher education for elementary school (grades 1–4) is being upgraded by means of integrating institutes for teacher education with teachers' colleges and universities. In addition, many colleges for teachers have been incorporated into universities since the unification. This could cause potential difficulties, if problems inherent in the western university system are perpetuated in the eastern system. Integration of teacher education at the university level brought about greater equality among teachers with respect to status, but it was also accompanied by weaker practical orientation and curricular integration. Institutional integration has led to more in-depth study of subjects, while attenuating professional orientation of teacher education (Rosenbusch et al., 1988).

Setting priorities in scientific, subject-oriented teacher education is especially problematic for the teaching profession in primary, intermediate, and special schools for the handicapped, because of the specific social and pedagogical demands in these schools. After the integration at universities, the quality of teacher education in West Germany has not yet been tested in the schools, since it was only introduced to all levels during the 1980s, when few teachers were being hired. The discrepancy between pedagogical and social problems in schools, and the preparation for such problems in teacher education, could gain significance throughout the 1990s, as replacements in schools grow, and universities continue to lack a job-oriented approach to the social and pedagogical tasks, which are part of the teaching job.

The possibilities of offering integrated studies with special traits, which would be an attractive on-the-job market, are especially good for the new federal states of Germany. It remains to be seen whether, and to what extent, these opportunities will be realized, or whether the problems of western organizational forms and procedures will simply be copied.

## Integration of Professional Studies

The second training phase has been widely criticized in documentary and research studies in West Germany. Set up in the nineteenth century, it was designed to compensate for the secondary school teachers' lack of practical training during their university studies. In adopting this educational form for all teachers, their status has improved, but not their professional qualification. The mere existence of such a second training phase restricts professional aims at the university. It leads to an institutionalized discontinuity in personnel and curriculum, thus causing orientation and qualification problems for the students. Substantial dropout rates have been one of the outcomes. This additional two-year second training phase has also led to an increase in length of study, which means that teachers' potential starting dates are unnecessarily postponed.

Despite lack of evidence supporting the claims that teachers in an outside-university second training phase in West Germany are better qualified, this system was established in the 1980s. Because single-phase teacher education under the auspices of universities was the regular form in East Germany, it might be possible to maintain this organizational structure there, especially in terms of prospective European integration and attempts at mutual recognition of degrees. Unions and professional organizations have supported the further development of a single-phase teacher education. Nevertheless, in the current phase of teacher unemployment, restrictive adaptation and recognition policies have been on the agenda. Such issues were in part regulated by the central government of East Germany, which was in power until October 1990. This regulation was neither debated nor approved in Parliament or in its Commission on Education. It now seems that the new eastern states will not use their cultural and educational autonomy to maintain their universities' responsibility for teacher education. It is also an open question whether studies of single-phase teacher training will be possible.

### Curriculum Integration

The West German reforms of the 1970s entailed integrated studies and projects that were offered at different stages during the course of study. They were introduced mainly during the entrance phase and integrated with practical experiences during the first phase, for example, in student teaching. This trend was phased out during the 1980s. Today, cooperative approaches, offering integrated programs, are usually based on individual initiatives and do not receive much institutional support. Thus, currently they are offered only by, and for, limited groups. West German universities give greater support to research efforts than to efforts in teaching and practical professional training (Bayer et al., 1982; Gakenbiehl, 1975). Owing to the strong traditions of freedom of teaching and study at German universities, state attempts have largely failed to structure the curricula in teacher education more strongly through examination requirements and commissions on study reform.

Whereas in West Germany beginning teachers have often been inadequately prepared, a prescribed sequence of courses and a strong practical training did exist in teacher education in East Germany. It remains to be seen how much coordination and cooperation will be achieved if there is more freedom in designing curricula and course content.

### Integration of Pre- and In-Service Education and School Development

In West Germany seminars offered by the school administration during the second training phase have a gatekeeping function for entrance into the job market. They separate the universities from the confrontation with the tasks and problems in schools. Therefore, universities and schools have become isolated, especially with regard to in-service education of teachers and school development. A ten-year experiment at the University of Oldenburg tested single-phase study programs. In this experiment, integration was supported through a new teaching staff of "contact teachers." These were practicing teachers, working in the projects of teacher training at the university ten hours a week, thus combining engagement in teacher education with further qualification, while staying involved in their schools and implementing reforms there.

In-service education for practicing teachers was widely supported in East Germany and was offered in regional pedagogical centers, at research schools, in graduate studies, and in research projects at universities. However, such continuing education was strongly regulated and monitored. In the future it could become more open, liberal, pluralistic, and democratic.

## POSSIBLE SCENARIOS FOR THE DEVELOPMENT OF
## TEACHER EDUCATION IN THE NEW STATES

Descriptions and problem analyses of the issues of integration in various areas have shown that different systems of teacher education in East and West have their advantages and disadvantages. Each section could learn from the other.

There are various ways of developing teacher education in the process of unification. Within the range of inner changes in existing institutions, or by a mere adoption of the West German regulations and institutions of teacher education, reforms may occur. Here are three possible scenarios. The first one emanated from reform concepts discussed during the first half of 1990; the second developed during the second half of that year; and the third one has emerged since the beginning of 1991.

### The First Reform Scenario

Developing teacher training within existing institutions, while upgrading and connecting them with institutions for teacher education at the university level, would have distinct advantages. Integration of the two phases of teacher education, curricular integration, and the integration of pre- and in-service education mutually support each other. However, introducing an institutionally separate dual-phase educational program makes it more difficult. Greater equality for the education of teachers for different schools could be achieved without unifying the institutions and programs. Smaller training units from different traditions facilitate distinction and pluralization, as well as internal agreement and integration. Emphasis could be placed on curricular reforms and the support of initiative and autonomy. Ideological change should not be regulated but should come from participants themselves, who utilize the newly won opportunity to acquire information freely.

Especially because of its ideological control and regimentation, the school system of the former German Democratic Republic has been delegitimized. But this system also encompassed structures that were in line with European standards as well as with reform concepts in the Federal Republic of Germany: for example, comprehensive schools, full day care for children up to the fourth grade, and afternoon programs for the later grades, single-phase teacher education, and compulsory in-service training. These programs have been considered a good basis for developing teacher education and schools.

Despite problems of control and regulation within this system, teachers in East Germany had broader responsibilities for education and teaching. They experienced lasting social relationships in public education and a good deal of informal cooperation. Greater freedom and democracy within the framework of existing institutions can support school development, and strengthen professional involvement, as well as the qualification of teachers. A single-phase teacher education would have the advantage of reducing study time as well as costs involved in teacher education. On the other hand, reorganization and destruction of prevailing institutions could bring about insecurity, thus weakening the teaching staff's involvement and cooperation in tackling current problems.

### The Second Reform Scenario

The attention the new eastern states have paid to the recognition of their certification in 1990 gave the appearance that a compromise had been effected to set up a formal, two-phase teacher education and to include two state examinations, while giving universities responsibility for introducing new teachers into the job, this was the case until now in East Germany. It appeared to be especially appropriate since universities could guarantee more openness and freedom of choice than the school administration, especially in East Germany. Qualitative superiority of such programs was expected to be achieved by having practicing teachers participate in the education of students of universities for some years. Joint teacher-professor commissions could choose this staff.

A project approach was expected to support curricular integration. Connections between preservice and continuing education of teachers at universities were meant to stimulate reforms and improvements in teacher education and in schools. Such programs promised to facilitate an exchange of ideas and experiences between East and West.

The West German states were expected to gain from the introduction of a formal two-phase program to be integrated into universities. Such models were to be tested and compared in East and West. Formal university-based, two-phase teacher education in West Germany meant that existing second-phase institutions would have to be integrated into universities. Such changes in the old states could be based on the interests of the staff in some of these institutions.

### The Third Reform Scenario

At the beginning of 1991, pressure to take action on unification meant that the educational system of West Germany would become the model for the new East German states, despite the better fit of the established system with respect to international standards. Independent development within the East German educational system was stopped at the end of 1990, when many educational departments and institutions were closed down, and their employees dismissed. Just as in Berlin, where the specifics of the eastern educational system could not survive the uniting of the two cities, other East German states were taking over personnel, regulations, and structures from the old western states of the Federal Republic.

As a result of East Germany's weak democratic traditions, bureaucratic regulations and control appear more effective now than they have been in the old West German states. Thus, the disadvantages of a two-phase teacher education program, for example, the "reality shock" when teachers enter their jobs, could become an even more serious problem.

Lack of job-oriented training in the current social crisis of large-scale unemployment and growing competition could cause educational and teaching problems in East German schools to mount. An integrated pedagogical and social background in teaching would be even more crucial than before.

## GENERAL BACKGROUND

Since the borders have opened, integration of the new states into the federation has been achieved mainly on an administrative and bureaucratic level, in terms of carrying over personnel from the old regime.

The notion prevails that a Western standard of living can best be reached through assimilation and nearly complete adoption of the West Germany economic, political, and educational system. There seems to be little or no time for comparative analyses of the two educational systems. Everyday problems in securing employment and accomplishing the tasks of everyday life have top priority in East Germany during this period of social and political restructuring. Dismissals, or fear of political disciplinary measures, have created a situation in which West German regulations and institutions have readily been adopted.

The East German states that were reestablished after the borders opened formally enjoy full cultural autonomy. Even so, there are strong educational policy pressures toward adopting the West German school system and forms of teacher education. The deadlines for adapting East German teacher training by the fall of 1991 were too close for much independent development (Händle and Nitsch, 1981).

Depending on political party majority, different options for reorganizing the educational system emerge. The educational policy of the conservative Christian Democratic Union (CDU), which has won the vote and dominates the government in all new eastern states except Brandenburg, has targeted its policy at reestablishing the half-day, three-tiered secondary school system (Hauptschule, Realschule, Gymnasium), with noticeable differentiations within the teaching profession. The Social Democratic party (SPD) favors inner reforms and is striving to maintain full-day comprehensive schools, as well as one-phase teacher training programs.

During the period of educational reform in West Germany, everyone agreed that changes should not be introduced by centrally administered planning policy. Instead, changes would have to be discussed with experts and with those participating in the development of novel models. New models would have to be carefully developed and evaluated through research projects. Up to now, even after the change of government in West Germany, the existing educational framework has been basically retained. Although some aspects have been "frozen," none was completely abolished. This is currently not the case in the new states of East Germany. At the moment, it remains unclear as to what extent the traditions in teacher training in East Germany will survive unification.

Limitations in range of experience and the availability of information in East Germany did not facilitate development or implementation of their own traditions. Unfamiliar with the practices and the cultural sovereignty of the states of West Germany, the people in the East did not know that a wide spectrum of educational practices and institutions was in operation. East Germans are now familiarizing themselves with the fact that different options can be formulated and achieved. Until now, the East Germans have had the experience that individual initiative was possible only to a limited extent within the framework of decisions made from above. The new eastern states lack experience in articulating interests and finding and implementing new alternatives. Traditional authoritarian government control and regulation, prevalent in both parts of Germany, seems to be stricter in the school system of the new East German states, because the public there is not yet accustomed to opposition, participation, and defense of their traditions.

Throughout the current process of unification, progressive reform groups in West Germany have hesitated to give advice or cooperation, hoping that change would gain its own momentum. On the other hand, conservative advocates who are in a position to export existing West German laws and regulations have succeeded in moving quickly into decision-making roles. This has been reinforced by the fact that conservative parties now govern most of the new federal states.

Various conflicts have developed regarding teacher education. A matching of teachers' salaries will only be implemented gradually, while teaching load and teacher-student ratios increase in the new states. Primary school teachers in the East receive lower salaries and have been required to gain further qualification through supplementary training programs, in order to obtain a status equal to that of their primary school colleagues in the West. Students of education are losing previously guaranteed dormitory places as well as jobs. The switch from a comprehensive socialist school to a four-track Western system (primary plus four types of secondary school) in general is adding instability and discontinuity. Female teachers are experiencing greater difficulty, since public child-care programs are being cut. However, such conflicts and financial restrictions could in the long run strengthen and upgrade traditions of integration in East Germany's teacher education.

Teacher education in Germany is also influenced by division of labor between the family and public education. A traditional division of labor still prevails in West Germany, where the upbringing of children is still, to a high degree, the task of the family. There are not enough programs for preschool-age children, and there are few full-day schools. A three-track school system and the double-phase teacher training programs, with an emphasis on scientific knowledge, subject matter, and comparative neglect of education for social and personal development, all fit into this division of labor. The western schools emphasize cognitive and subject matter learning while leaving the responsibility for personal development and social relationships to the family and other organizations. Therefore, success in the traditional West German educational system can only be partially attributed to that system, since it only functions with much assistance from the family, mainly the mothers, each afternoon.

The very division of labor between family and school explains why educational reformists' concepts of open instruction, better social learning, and personal development have not been successfully expanded in educational institutions in West Germany. Half-day schools have little time for such practices. In addition, high-prestige schools, the selective high schools (Gymnasien) which are usually half-day schools, set norms, forcing full-day schools, mostly comprehensive reform schools, to adopt similar policies. Thus, these schools make it more difficult to set other educational goals or even to accept them as equivalent. Contrary to the public ideals of social learning and social integration in West Germany, subject-oriented and achievement-oriented learning has become most important in norms and organization of all types of schools, even in that of the comprehensive schools.

West German scientific approaches and lesson-oriented teaching since the 1970s have also become more important in teacher education than other qualities such as class reponsibility, leisure activities, and school life. The second training phase, as a critical phase of professional socialization, conveys in its hidden curriculum an orientation toward high standards in "model lessons" and subject matter learning. It thereby neglects learner participation and individual pupil's needs in daily school life.

The traditional division of labor between school and family in West Germany causes disadvantages for working mothers. Mothers who are also teachers are responsible for their own children in the afternoon, competing against other mothers who are just housewives. However, in West Germany teachers with young children may have worktime reduction and extended leave (with guaranteed reemployment). This enables them, through various initiatives and working groups, to advance their personal qualifications for teaching in the course of caring for their own children. The specific social competence they are gaining in this way, however, is not central for their professional tasks in West German schools. There female teachers bring their additional social competence, mainly on a compensatory basis, into the school system.

Teacher training and the educational system in East Germany have a broader responsibility for growing generations. Afternoon care for children from grades 1 through 4 was offered, and diverse activities such as afternoon and vacation programs were available, also for the later grades. By formally including professional teachers and students in these care programs, they could informally enhance their qualifications beyond those needed in lessons. Despite (or even because of) the extensive responsibilities allocated to public education and training, teacher education had a low status in East Germany. Most of the teachers have been women. Cognitive and scientific learning were given top priority in the lessons. Social training and personal development remained secondary and were dealt with rather informally, and had lesser priority during afternoon hours.

Financial restrictions, as well as the growing unemployment of women in East Germany, who are being expected to dispense unpaid education to the rising generation, have fostered the reintroduction of a half-day school system in East Germany, with priority on subject matter in schools and teacher education.

## CONCLUSION

In both parts of Germany, integration of subject and social learning, as well as personal development, has been achieved neither in teacher education nor in the school system. At present, this has been insufficiently achieved in East Germany within the framework of integrated, unified, but one-sided and doctrinal pedagogical concepts and institutions. One of the main challenges for teacher training in the 1990s will be to maintain and integrate the best of both traditions: the broad responsibility of teachers and the school system for the rising generation, as it was established in East Germany, in combination with the diversity and freedom of choice that is typical for teacher education and the school system in West Germany. Eventually, a better balance of social learning, personal development, and subject matter studies can be achieved in East and West.

Independent development of teacher education in the new German states can only gain from the prospective European integration. An orientation toward other European countries supports curricular reform issues in the existing organizational framework.

A perspective of maintenance and further development of university responsibility for the entire education of teachers goes beyond current teacher training in the old states of West Germany. In this respect, exchange and cooperation of teacher training institutions between European nations could be of help.

Regarding European integration, the uniqueness of the West German two-phase system of teacher education poses problems. While European Community resolutions foresee European-wide recognition of four-year university degrees and professional experience as equivalent, West German educational authorities are calling for additional training programs in state-run institutions as a hiring requirement for non-German personnel. This would reinforce a national mechanism of state control and selection.

Fear of nonacceptance of degrees, administrative dominance, and power politics in the new states in East Germany imply that prospects of a single-phase training program are dim. Rather, the West German two-phase teacher education appears to be the dominating educational model. But adoption of the old framework can secure mobility only to a limited extent. In times of teacher unemployment, the western states prefer to hire in-state candidates and graduates of their own institutions. During periods of open positions for teachers, however, teachers with diverse backgrounds are usually hired. Reforms are becoming increasingly important; the teacher shortage in the 1990s, the growing problems in schools, and the widening gap between professional qualification and the real tasks and problems that teachers have to manage in schools. Teachers from East German states have a good chance to sell themselves on the West German job market as well if integrated structures can be kept and developed there. Until now, well-educated personnel from East Germany have been successfully integrated into the West German job market.

On the basis of their tradition of competence in Eastern European languages as well as their geographical location, the new East German states could easily cooperate with teacher training programs in Eastern European countries. This would provide opportunities for exchange and communication of various cultural traditions in Germany, within the scope of the cultural autonomy of the states of the federation. In relation to Eastern and Western European nations, Germany has a unique opportunity to maintain and develop the best of different traditions.

## REFERENCES

Bayer, Manfred et al. ed. *Alternativen in der Lehrerausbildung*. Reinbek: Rowohlt, 1982, S. 213–220.

Gukenbiehl, Hermann E. *Tendenzen zur Verwissenschaftlichung der Lehrerausbildung*. Weinheim: Beltz, 1975.

Händle, Christa. *Lehrerausbildung*. In Deiter Lenzen, ed. *Pädagogische Grundbegriffe*. Reinbek: Rowohlt, 1989, S. 938–955.

Händle, Christa. *Lehrerbildung und Berufspraxis*. Weinheim: Beltz, 1972.

Händle, Christa, and Wolfgang Nitsch, ed. *Integrierte Lehrerausbildung bleibt aktuell*. Materialien zur deutsch-deutschen Reformdikussion. Oldenburg: Zentrum für pädagogische Berfuspraxios, 1991.

Händle, Christa, and Wolfgang Nitsch. *Steuerung des Lehrerstudiums*. Hamburg: AHD, 1981.

Rosenbusch, Heinz, et al. *Schulreif?* Frankfurt: Lang, 1988.

Schmidt, Gerlind, and Dieter Schulz. "Zur Situation des Lehrers in beiden deutschen Staaten." In *Bildung und Erziehung* 43 (1990): H. 1.

# 9

## ISRAEL

### MIRIAM BEN-PERETZ AND YUVAL DROR

This chapter deals with two critical issues in teacher education: how to prepare teachers to deal with the multicultural and conflict-laden society of Israel; and how to resolve the tensions between academic and pedagogic orientations in programs to prepare teachers.

### GENERAL BACKGROUND

Israel is a multicultural and conflict-ridden society. The state of Israel was founded in 1948 after the United Nations confirmed the partition of Palestine. Jews had started to return to their ancient homeland in the last quarter of the nineteenth century in order to escape ongoing persecution in the Diaspora and to reestablish their national and cultural identity. During World War II almost a third of the Jewish people were killed in the Holocaust. Survivors and refugees from German concentration camps, as well as immigrants from North Africa and the Middle East, poured into the newly established state, forming a veritable patchwork of languages and cultures amidst the Arab population. Jews from different backgrounds revived their ancient language, Hebrew, and formed a vibrant democracy. The country developed modern agricultural science and technology, while attempting to focus on the main issue of achieving peace. Education has always played a major role in this endeavor.

The ethnic, religious, and cultural heterogeneity was the source of continuous external and internal conflict and unrest. During its brief existence, Israel has suffered from five wars and has never known a day of tranquility. The main political issues confronting Israel are peace with its neighbors, a solution to the Palestinian problem, and the abolishment of inequalities. The peace agreement with Egypt signed in 1978 has become a ray of hope for the future of the region. At present about 18 percent of the Israeli population are minority groups—

Moslem Arabs, Christian Arabs, and Druze. The Jewish population is composed of two main sections: Ashkenazy Jews, of European and American ancestry, and Sepharadi Jews, of North African and Middle Eastern origin. Ideologically, Jews are also divided according to their identification with religious movements in Judaism. This division leads to two subsystems in the centralist educational organization of Israel: state schools and state religious schools. Another, an ultraorthodox system, though funded by the state, is not under the supervision of the Ministry of Education and Culture. In the Arab sector most schools are administered by the ministry, although some are private religious schools. State schools serve students from a variety of cultural backgrounds; the heterogeneous composition of the school requires special attention in teacher education programs. The Arab minority in Israel raises the crucial issue of peaceful coexistence in a common state. Different ethnic and religious groups may prefer separate schools for their children. Separation may lead to further alienation, exacerbating the need to deal with the educational implications of Israel's ethnic and religious mosaic through teacher education.

## THE SYSTEM OF TEACHER EDUCATION

How is it possible to deal with Israeli heterogeneity in teacher education programs? Examining this issue in its historical context, we find that an ideological shift has occurred since 1948, the year the state of Israel was established. Three main dilemmas can be identified in this process. The first is the dilemma between the desire to form one nation out of immigrants of many origins and the acceptance of the legitimacy of their cultural pluralism. Another dilemma concerns the separation between different educational streams that existed in Israel, namely, the general stream, the labor-oriented stream, and the religious stream. The general stream attempted to create a common school for all sectors of society, while the labor-oriented stream was based on socialist ideology, and the religious catered to the needs of the orthodox community. The dilemma was between unification of these streams in the name of common values shared by all, and their continued separation in the name of ideological diversity. The third dilemma pertains to the nature of the Arab educational system. Should it be a separate entity, responding to the national and religious aspirations of the Arab minority in Israel, or should it be integrated with the general school system?

These dilemmas and the eventual policy decisions had structural and conceptual implications for teacher education in Israel. During the first twenty years of Israel's existence as a state, the reigning and accepted policy was clearly oriented toward a melting pot ideology. Whereas before the establishment of the state of Israel, the different educational streams were part of the system, an attempt was made to abolish the streams in 1953. This attempt was never completely successful. Although the labor-oriented stream was amalgamated with the general stream, the Jewish religious stream and the Arab, Moslem, or Christian schools continued to constitute separate systems under state supervision.

Teacher education colleges were also divided ideologically and were affiliated with the various educational streams. This differentiation persisted, though some of the labor-oriented colleges were integrated with a general college when they were geographically close to each other. The teacher education colleges of the Kibbutz movement have always kept their unique orientation and their commitment to the utopian ideology of the Kibbutz.

What were some of the unique characteristics of the different institutions of teacher education? Although the general colleges emphasized liberal and professional pedagogical principles with a strong commitment to the creation of a shared cultural basis, the labor colleges celebrated the values of the labor movement, socialism, cooperation, mutual responsibility, and equity. Religious colleges stressed religious studies, and strict observance of religious laws and customs.

The integration ideology that was dominant in the 1950s and 1960s found its most powerful and challenging expression in the school reform of 1963 which changed the structure of the educational system in Israel. Instead of the existing structure of eight years of elementary school plus four years of secondary school, a three-level system was created. The new system consisted of a six-year elementary school, a three-year junior high school, and a three-year senior high school. A junior high school was introduced in order (1) to integrate children of different ethnic and socioeconomic sectors of society in a joint heterogeneous school setting, and (2) to raise the level of academic achievement and to close the gap between children of different backgrounds.

This reform necessitated major curricular changes and an adjustment of teacher education programs. In the former system, teachers of the first through eighth grades of the elementary school were graduates of teacher education colleges without an academic degree. After the reform, the seventh and eighth grade became part of the junior high school, and teachers were expected to have a B.A. or comparable degree.

In the beginning, special in-service programs for elementary teachers were set up in order to upgrade their subject matter knowledge and to prepare them for teaching in the new junior high school. Later, the teacher education system responded to the new demand for teachers with academic degrees by transforming some of the existing teacher education colleges into institutions that granted the B.Ed. degree, preparing teachers for junior high school and for elementary schools. The issue of academization of teacher education programs will be dealt with in greater depth in subsequent sections of this chapter.

## Location of Teacher Education in Israel

Teacher education in Israel today is carried out in two main locations:

1. Colleges of teacher education which educate teachers for grades K–6 and 7–9, the junior high school. Teacher education for the junior high school level is also carried

out in universities. There are different streams of teacher education colleges: general colleges, vocational colleges (such as physical education colleges), religious colleges, and colleges of the Kibbutz movement. Colleges accept students after high school. Their programs last two to three years and include subject matter studies: foundation disciplines of education, such as psychology; method courses; and the practicum. Some teacher education colleges in Israel grant the B.Ed. degree, after four years of study.

2. Departments of teacher education in universities educate teachers for junior and senior high schools. Students are usually accepted in their third year of studies toward a B.A. degree in the various disciplines. Studies in the departments of teacher education usually last two years and include foundation disciplines, method courses, and the practicum. Graduating students receive a teaching certificate which is acknowledged by the Ministry of Education. Departments of teacher education at universities may offer a variety of programs, beyond the usual format of two years of study. There are one-year programs for postgraduate students and three-year programs leading to a B.A. in teaching. Different programs may focus on special subjects, such as art or technology, or prepare teachers for specific target populations, such as adults or students in special education. Special programs also exist which prepare teachers for alternative school forms, such as open schools. The predominant age of the student teachers is twenty-two or more years.

### Teacher Education in Military Service

The Israeli army runs an educational system for soldiers. The teachers in this system are mainly young women soldiers, straight out of high school, who volunteer for this work and who are placed in a special three-month course. The army handles three different areas of teacher education.

- Preparation of teachers of soldiers who have not completed elementary schools. These male and female soldiers come mainly from a low socioeconomic environment, lack basic academic skills, and have little motivation for serving in the army and for studying. The army provides them with a second educational chance.

- Preparation of teachers for new immigrants in the army who study Hebrew and local culture.

- Preparation of teachers for teaching in regular schools in small and distant rural communities and development towns that lack teachers. This is one of the societal obligations which the Israeli military accepted upon its formation.

Army-trained teachers volunteer for this special mode of military service. They are mainly young women who have some experience of working with youth groups and who are highly motivated for a meaningful army service. Soldier-teachers receive special ten-week training in the army for their future role as teachers and participate regularly in in-service courses throughout their service. Soldier-teachers who teach in development towns and rural communities receive longer basic training for their role and continue to study regularly through in-service courses in teacher education colleges. During their military service, they may accumulate the equivalent of two full years of studies out of the four years needed to fulfill the requirements of a B.Ed. degree.

The preparatory courses are similar to regular teacher education programs, with an additional focus on the specific needs of the intended target populations. The military preparatory courses for teachers are under the jurisdiction of the education branch of the army, but they are mostly staffed by the faculty members of universities and teacher education colleges who fulfill their reserve duties in this way.

Soldier-teachers who teach in rural areas are supervised by the military, as well as by the Ministry of Education and Culture. Most of the soldier-teachers do not continue to work as teachers upon leaving the army. Many turn, however, to academic studies in the various domains of human services such as psychology and social work.

## Teacher Education in the Kibbutz

The Kibbutz movement in Israel was founded in 1910 in Degania, near the Lake of Galilee, by a handful of utopian idealists. Today, about eighty years later, the movement encompasses 126,000 members in 270 Kibbutz settlements—about 3 percent of the population of Israel. From focusing solely on agriculture, the Kibbutz has become involved in industry. About 23 percent of Kibbutz members work in industry and provide 8 percent of Israeli industrial production. The Kibbutz movement also produces 40 percent of all the agricultural yield of Israel.

The goals of the Kibbutz movement have always combined Zionism and socialism, emphasizing democratic and egalitarian communal life and reliance on one's own labor. All resources, property, and funds belong to the commune; there is no private property. Kibbutz members contribute their work for the welfare of their commune which supplies all their needs—lodging, food, education, cultural activities, and medical care. The Kibbutz has always striven to create a new and different social order.

In spite of many changes in the everyday lifestyle of the Kibbutz, for instance, moving the children of the Kibbutz from common sleeping quarters to sleeping with the family, the Kibbutz movement has proven its long-term existence. The successful establishment of socialist communes may be traced back to the strength of the ideological commitment of their members, to the principle of mutual responsibility of all communes, and to the power of adaptation to a changing society.

A close relationship between educator and student is a basic principle of Kibbutz education. Informal relations between teachers, administrators, and students are part of the school culture and act as an example of what can exist in the future schools in which students will teach. The students are treated as real partners, including representation on disciplinary committees, taking part in decision making about general policy, and evaluating their teachers through formal and nonformal feedback processes.

The ideological message of the education colleges of the Kibbutz is clear and attracts pupils, especially teachers who agree with the social and educational ideology of the institution. Still, about half the teachers and students are not Kibbutz members.

The principle of ideological education is very important. Every student has to study two courses: one on Kibbutz and the other on Kibbutz education. There are special frameworks for ideological subjects as additions (and sometimes alternatives) to regular studies. In these frameworks the students encounter different nondoctrinaire and personal approaches to moral education with the emphasis on values clarification and the just community.

There is permanent contact between the education departments of the Kibbutz movements and the Kibbutz schools. Students visit elementary and secondary Kibbutz schools, teach in them, and carry out personal and research projects.

### Retaining Novice Teachers

At present six colleges out of twenty-eight grant the B.Ed. degree. According to the census of 1988, 12,679 students were enrolled in the twenty-eight colleges. About 2,400 students participate each year in the teacher education programs in Israeli universities. The percentage of graduates of colleges and universities who are absorbed into the school system is between 45 and 60 percent. Significant numbers of novice teachers drop out of school. Attempts are made to raise the number of graduates who join the educational system and to lower the number of dropouts.

The danger of dropping out of the profession seems to be greatest during the first years of teaching when novice teachers may be overwhelmed by the manifold difficulties and problems of life in classrooms. Therefore, the Ministry of Education and Culture is at present funding various experimental programs of teacher induction into schools. The main common feature of these programs, which are run by colleges of teacher education and departments of teacher education at universities, is that faculty members at these institutions continue to keep close professional contact with the novice teachers during their first year of teaching.

### ISSUES AND PROBLEMS

Two critical issues will be treated in the following parts of this chapter: (1) The issue of teacher education in the multicultural and conflict-ridden society of Israel, in terms of the conflicting goals of diversity and unity; and (2) the issue of conceptual and structural reform of teacher education, as reflecting the perceived dichotomy between "the child" and "the curriculum" (Dewey, 1902), and its accompanying tensions.

## Issue 1: Diversity and Unity

The Israeli school reform of 1963 changed the structure of the educational system through the introduction of the comprehensive junior high school. The main goals of this reform concern the issue of social and academic integration of different sectors of Israeli society. These structural changes were accompanied by certain curricular modifications in the teacher education programs. Student teachers were expected to learn about cultural differences and to acquire appropriate teaching skills for coping with heterogeneous classes. It became apparent that the adopted measures were insufficient and that teachers graduating from teacher education colleges, or from departments of teacher education at universities, lacked the necessary theoretical and practical knowledge base for dealing with heterogeneous classes in the newly formed junior high school. The ideological shift in the Israeli society toward cultural pluralism, which became more and more powerful in the 1970s and 1980s, caused new curricular changes in the educational system and was accompanied by another change in teacher education programs.

### From Melting Pot to Multiculturalism

The emerging orientation toward multiculturalism and the new emphasis on cultural divergency were influenced by the rising political power of "oriental" (Sephardi) Jews, especially those whose origins were in Morocco. One of the policy outcomes related to this turnabout from a melting pot orientation to multiculturalism was the development of innovative curricula that focused on the unique features of different ethnic cultures (Moroccan, Yemenite, Bedouin, and so on) which make up the societal mosaic of Israel. The response to the new ideology in teacher education programs was very slow. In 1979 a special committee set up to investigate the educational reform in Israel published its findings. The report stressed the fact that most teachers who were transferred to the newly formed junior high school lacked the necessary skills to teach heterogeneous classes. The report blamed teacher education programs for the insufficient preparation of teachers to cope with the changes in the school system and with the need to implement the policy of multiculturalism in schools. Since the beginning of the 1980s, teacher education colleges and departments of teacher education in universities have attempted to adapt their curriculum to these needs. Thus, we may find that about 20 percent of the curriculum of teacher education at the Hebrew University in Jerusalem in 1986 was devoted to teaching in heterogeneous classes, and dealt with issues of multiculturalism, such as Jewish-Arab coexistence (Lamm, 1986). At the University of Haifa all students studying to become teachers are required to participate in special courses on multicultur-

alism, to join workshops on teaching in heterogeneous classes, and to take part
in study groups on the educational aspects of Jewish-Arab coexistence.

### Coexistence in Teacher Education Programs

Jewish-Arab coexistence in Israel, though linked to the Palestinian-Israeli
conflict, is treated as separate from the issues of armed disputes between Israel
and its neighboring Arab states. The Jewish-Arab conflict has been accompanied
by bloodshed, agony, and despair. Yet, until a peace settlement is achieved,
attempts have to be made to counteract alienation and violence. The many
educational projects dealing with the coexistence issue stress the democratic
character of Israel and the need to create modes of life that enable all citizens
of Israel to live together in a multicultural society. The basis for achieving this
goal is mutual acceptance of the different national identities and cultures in
Israel. Special programs have been developed for Israeli schools. For example,
a textbook called *The Arab Citizens of Israel* is part of the curriculum in civics
in all Israeli high schools.

Another set of curriculum materials, called *Israel: A Multicultural Society*, is
structured around the personal stories of individuals and families who belong to
different religious, ethnic, and social groups. In-service and preservice education
programs attempt to prepare teachers to deal with these issues in their classrooms.
At the University of Haifa, where about 20 percent of students are Arab, Jewish
and Arab students interact daily, study together, and enter into disputes with
each other, transcending stereotypical divisions. Moreover, at the Department
of Teacher Education at the University of Haifa, pairs of student teachers, an
Arab and a Jew, work together at preparing and implementing materials dealing
with the issue of coexistence for use in classrooms.

The following are examples of treating the crucial theme of coexistence in
teacher education programs.

The educational program for kindergarten teachers at the David Yellin Teacher
Education College emphasizes several concepts such as stereotypes, minority/
majority relations, and coexistence. The main goal is to raise the awareness of
children that Israeli society is composed of Jews and Arabs. Teachers are ac-
quainted with a variety of teaching aids: films; stories; pictures; games; and so
on.

The program of Kerem Colege, which trains teachers for elementary and junior
high schools, deals with the following concepts: rights of the individual, freedom
of speech, equality, and minority/majority relations. The program is based on
political science, history, and Jewish philosophy. Its aim is to provide student
teachers with an appropriate knowledge base for dealing with issues of democracy
and coexistence in their future classrooms.

As stated above, the Jewish-Arab coexistence project is a central component
in the teacher education program of the University of Haifa. In the workshops
students discuss their personal experiences and general societal issues pertaining
to Jewish-Arab relationships. Peer teaching of specially prepared curriculum

materials provides opportunities for reflecting on the problems of teaching about democracy and coexistence.

The involvement of students in this project grew over the years, and participation is high. Students often continue their discussions after the meetings. Changes in students' perception of the possibility of coexistence have been noted.

### Multicultural Education: Jews and Arabs

The ideological shift from a melting pot ideology to multiculturalism affected the education of the Arab sector through a change in the curriculum and through modifications of teacher education programs. In 1977 the minister of education and culture ruled that state education in the Arab sector would be based on Arab cultural values, would serve the advancement of Arab identity, and would emphasize the common interests of all Israeli citizens. After that decision, state curricula were divided into three types: (1) curricula in English, mathematics, the sciences, and so on, which were identical for the Jewish and Arab sector; (2) curricula that were adapted to the specific needs and requirements of each sector, such as curricula in history, emphasizing the historical background of each ethnic group; and (3) curricula that were developed differentially for each sector, such as Arab language and literature, Hebrew language and literature, and religious studies.

Arab educators are actively involved in developing curriculum materials according to these new guidelines. Arab and Jewish educators contribute jointly to many educational programs and projects that are implemented by the Ministry of Education and Culture, as well as by other organizations, which aim at fostering peaceful coexistence between Jews and Arabs in the state of Israel.

How did the new ideology affect teacher education programs? The unity/diversity dilemma regarding the nature of Arab education in Israel, mentioned above, has been settled in favor of diversity as far as the elementary and junior high schools are concerned. Arab elementary school teachers are educated in Arab teacher education colleges. These enjoy the same autonomy as Jewish orthodox teacher education colleges or the colleges of the Kibbutz movement. Arab teachers for junior, and especially senior, high school levels are educated jointly with their Jewish peers in departments of teacher education in universities. Special programs have been planned in response to the needs of the Arab sector for the elementary level, where most of the teaching in these programs is carried out in Arabic. In the Beit Berl Teacher Education College, for instance, the special program for Arab educators (1989) emphasizes the following goals for students:

• Knowledge of the educational system in the Arab sector.
• Knowledge in subject matter areas.
• Knowledge of the Arabic language, culture, history, and religion.
• Knowledge of Arab society and commitment to peaceful coexistence between Jews and Arabs in Israel.

• Mastery of teaching strategies that are congruent with the needs and requirement of the Arab community.

• Promotion of awareness of the conflicts that accompany the transition of a traditional society to a Westernized way of life without losing its values and its identity.

These goals are served by the curriculum of the special programs that emphasize areas of studies such as Islam, Arab literature, changes in Arab society, and other relevant topics.

Teacher education in special domains, for instance, physical education, is shared by Jews and Arabs in the same teacher education college. Teacher education for junior, and especially for senior, high schools takes place in departments of teacher education in universities in which Jewish and Arab students participate in the same programs with few adaptations to the cultural uniqueness of each ethnic group. The participation in joint classes itself is perceived as contributory to mutual acceptance and tolerance.

In view of the rising national feeling of Israeli Arabs, the issues of multiculturalism and peaceful coexistence are of cardinal importance and warrant indepth considerations by Jewish and Arab educators, especially those concerned with educating future teachers.

### The Language Issue in a Multicultural Society

Among the issues that concern any multicultural society is that of language. The problem is how to serve unity through a common language while preserving the heritage languages of each societal group.

Israel has two official languages, Hebrew and Arabic. Members of the Arab minority usually speak fluent Arabic, whereas relatively few Jews speak Arabic. In most cases, Arab teachers teach Hebrew and Hebrew literature in Arab schools, after receiving appropriate training in colleges or universities. The curriculum materials tend to be outdated and unmotivating to Arab students. Lately, attempts have been made to update the curriculum. The curriculum of schools in the Jewish sector includes the teaching of Arabic, but not enough time is allocated to this important topic. As a result, the Ministry of Education and Culture has initiated a new policy whereby Arabic will be taught in the Jewish sector from the first grade of elementary school, thus turning Israel into a truly bilingual society. This new policy requires the training of large numbers of teachers and the preparation of special curriculum materials.

Immigrants to Israel learn Hebrew in special immersion programs. Special inservice teacher education programs prepare teachers for this function. At present, immigration from the Soviet Union poses new problems for the educational system as well as for teacher education programs. Many of the new immigrants lack basic knowledge about Israel and have to be absorbed into a social structure with which they are not familiar. Special summer programs are planned for students from the Soviet Union, and these programs require special teacher training.

About 5 percent of the Soviet immigrants are teachers, and others tend to turn to teaching. Special in-service programs in colleges of teacher education have been set up to prepare them for the professional aspects of teaching in Israel. On the other hand, Israeli teachers are called upon to familiarize themselves with the culture and special needs of the new immigrants.

## Issue 2: Academization Versus Humanization in Teacher Education Programs

The terms *academization* and *humanization* are taken from a memorandum by E. Jaffe (1974), the then director of the Department of Teacher Education in the Ministry of Education and Culture. By academization Jaffe meant focusing on knowledge of subject matter, on the one hand, and on the in-depth study of foundation disciplines, such as psychology, on the other. Humanization, as used in Jaffe's memorandum, referred to a paidocentric or child-centered approach in education, in which teaching and teacher education centered on the learner, specifically his or her characteristics and needs. Jaffe claimed that both academization and humanization have to be integrated into teacher education programs.

Jaffe's differentiation between academization and humanization is closely linked to a later typology of teacher education programs. Lomsky-Feder and Cahana (1988), analyzed the image of teachers in Israeli society and identified different types of teacher education based on two criteria: (1) emphasis on pedagogy (humanization) versus emphasis on subjects (academization), and (2) teacher education as an open versus a closed process. A rigid type of academic teacher education is characterized by a closed process of professionalization, which focuses on knowledge of subject matter and maximizes directives and control. Pedagogical open teacher education focuses on liberal education, as well as on pedagogy, and leaves room for student teachers to engage in trial-and-error experimentation in teaching. Such a clear dichotomy does not exist in reality, but teacher education in Israel has tried to balance those two orientations. The following pages will deal with the tension between academization and humanization and its expression in teacher education in Israel from a historical perspective.

### The Issue in Historical Perspective

At the beginning of the twentieth century Israel had few teacher education institutions. Most of the teachers in these colleges were from Germany and Austria and had brought with them the humanistic tradition of the German teacher education seminar. Pedagogy and method courses were linked with subject matter areas and the practicum, as opposed to university-type specialization and separation between study of the disciplines and study of pedagogy and methods.

This linkage of disciplines, pedagogy, and teaching methods represents the "simultaneous" order of topics in teacher education, which characterizes the

humanistic approach. Special emphasis was given to practical experiences; sometimes up to 70 percent of the student teachers' time was devoted to the practicum.
Student teachers started their teacher training after twelve years of regular schooling, and not after several years of university-level studies of the disciplines. The
curriculum of teacher education during that period did not differentiate between
teachers of different subject areas. The aim was to educate an unspecialized
teacher, who would be able to teach all subjects at the elementary school level.
The general teacher was expected to focus on the emotional well-being of his
or her students and to function as an educator interested in the whole child, and
not just in that child's academic achievement.

Over the years, elements of academization became significant in teacher education programs. One of the first steps in this direction was the extension of
years of study in teacher education institutes from two to three years after
completion of high school studies. Separate programs for teachers of humanities
and of sciences were introduced slowly. The major thrust for academization was
linked to the establishment of departments of teacher education in universities,
the first one at the Hebrew University in Jerusalem in 1936. Several causes
combined to bring about this development. In the 1930s refugees from Nazi
Germany came to the country, creating a need for more secondary education
institutions. A shortage of high school teachers existed, and at that time there
were no appropriate teacher education programs for that level. On the other hand,
the refugees became a source of personnel for secondary teaching. The Hebrew
University has granted master's degrees since 1931, but the graduates have lacked
pedagogical knowledge. The then existing teacher education institutions provided
a general liberal education combined with pedagogical training, but this mode
of teacher education was not deemed appropriate for secondary education. Thus,
the time was ripe for the start of a Department of Teacher Education at the
Hebrew University with a strong American orientation—a view of education as
a field of academic study extending beyond the practical aspects of teacher
training.

In the years 1936–1939 three divisions were founded in the new department:
pedagogy, educational psychology, and foundations of education. In 1952 the
department was transformed into the School of Education and was authorized
to grant the B.A., M.A. and Ph.D. degrees in education, as well as diplomas
of high school teacher education. When other universities were founded in Israel,
they followed the same mode.

The mode of teacher education at universities was, and is, primarily sequential.
After two years of subject matter studies, students start a two-year program at
the Department of Teacher Education. During the first of these two years they
finish their B.A. studies. The second year is devoted to studying toward a teaching
certificate in the discipline/s they have majored in. The emphasis on prerequisite
knowledge in the disciplines they are going to teach is a characteristic of the
academization of teacher education. This mode of professionalization is close
to the orientation of the Holmes group in the United States (1986) and to the

proposals of the Carnegie Forum on Education (Task Force, 1986). The academization of teacher education did not express itself only in greater emphasis on subject matter knowledge and in the growing differentiation between teacher education for different subject areas. Other dimensions of academization are also significant.

Student teachers in colleges of teacher education spend most of their training in a "class" of students with whom they share most of their courses and practical experiences. The teaching methods are similar to those in high school. In a sense their training experiences are analogous to their school experiences. Because of the manifold duties of teachers in Israel, which include the role of "educator" who is responsible for the social and personal development of his or her students, such a mode of teacher education is perceived as highly appropriate.

On the other hand, in university departments of teacher education, student teachers do not form a cohesive group. They study in a variety of university departments, according to their choice of subject matter, and in various courses in education. Students are closer to the academic mode that stresses the creation of knowledge and not solely its dissemination. Thus, they are further removed from the "humanistic" aspect of teacher education. In Israel the Ministry of Education views this situation as an obstacle for teacher education, especially teacher education for kindergarten and elementary schools. University departments do not train teachers for these age groups, although they would like to do so. The tension between teacher education colleges and university departments for teacher education continues to this day. It is a reflection of the tension between academization and humanization in teacher education programs. A special commission that was set up to enforce the academization of colleges as far back as 1962 decided that the university ethos was not suitable for the necessary integration of subject matter knowledge and social needs. This committee recognized the central position of humanization in teacher education programs. The process of academization of teacher education colleges was suspended for some time, and the proposed linkage to universities was not realized. This situation changed dramatically in the late 1970s and 1980s.

The Israeli school reform, mentioned in the previous section, caused a growing demand for teachers who possessed academic qualifications. The tide toward academization could not be stemmed. In 1971 another commission ruled that colleges should attain academic status leading to a B.Ed. degree. This commission tried to integrate the academic and the humanistic approach by stressing the importance of the social and personal aspects of the teacher-student interaction, but it soon became clear that academization was the main goal. The official policy of the Ministry of Education and Culture is to reduce the number of teacher education colleges and to upgrade their professional and academic status. In the 1980s the number of teacher education colleges was reduced, and six academic colleges, granting B.Ed. degrees were established under the supervision of the Israeli Council of Higher Education.

In these academic colleges, entrance requirements were raised, the curriculum focused on subject matter studies and specialization, and faculty and students were encouraged to participate in educational research activities. Academization had won.

At the same time teacher education colleges opted for academization, and departments of teacher education at the universities tried to integrate social concerns into their programs, balancing academization with humanization. Thus, we find in the Department of Teacher Education at the University of Haifa a special program for social education. Such programs focus on nonformal education and on extracurricular activities. The theoretical basis for these programs is oriented toward issues of value education, interpersonal communication, political education, and the like. Participants are required to be involved in individual and group projects in schools that focus on personal problems of students or on general societal issues.

**Efforts at Reconciliation**

Because of the persistent tension between colleges of teacher education and departments of teacher education at universities, efforts have been made to reach some mode of cooperation through the establishment of a Joint Steering Committee. One of the first steps in the process of coordination and cooperation was the foundation of a joint journal of teacher education: *The Road to Teaching*. This journal provide readers with theoretical and empirical insights into the process of teacher education. Its target audience are teacher educators and researchers in issues of teacher education.

The Joint Steering Committee examines the relationships between the different institutions of teacher education in Israel. Thus, for instance, it attempted to clarify the options of graduates of colleges to continue their studies at the universities. Cooperation in research between faculty members at both types of institutions is another area of common interest. The joint committee is an attempt to serve as a bridge between the different educational orientations that are still characteristic of each institution and to alleviate some of the mutual distrust between them.

**CONCLUSION**

Teacher education programs in Israel reflect the basic goals and structures of the Israeli educational system. Whereas in some cultures, social and religious issues, as well as value education, are in the domains of family and church, responsibility for these issues in Israel is part of the ethos of schools. Teachers are always expected to ''educate'' their students, and not to limit themselves to the teaching of skills or subject matter knowledge. These expectations shape the curriculum of teacher education programs, which include important components of informal education, as was demonstrated above. This basic orientation blurs the sharp distinction between academic and humanistic teacher education. The overarching goal of education and of teacher education in Israel is to integrate the academic and the humanistic approaches (Gal, 1985).

The special function of teacher education as serving societal integration has caused a strong emphasis on appropriate teaching strategies for heterogeneous classes, based on individualized or on cooperative learning modes (Adar, 1981).

On the other hand, after the ideological shift toward multiculturalism, teacher education programs show a growing awareness of ethnicity and diversity. Ideological and religious streams keep their unique features. It is important to note, however, that in ideologically oriented colleges, such as the Kibbutz Teacher Education College (Oranim), about 50 percent of student teachers are not Kibbutz members.

External influences played a major role in the development of teacher education in Israel. Until the 1960s the main impact was Central European. Over the years, North American educational approaches became more dominant and shaped the school structure, as evident by the establishment of the junior high schools, and its consequent impact on teacher education programs. Student teachers, especially those studying at departments of teacher education in university, read English or translated American educational literature. Terms like *objectives*, *structure of knowledge*, and *discovery learning* have become part of their professional language. An interesting issue for further inquiry would be to investigate how the growth of a common knowledge base in learning to teach, shared by teacher education programs in different countries, would change the nature of teaching in these countries.

## REFERENCES

Adar, L., ed. *Teaching in Heterogeneous Classes*. A Report of a Joint U.S.A.-Israeli Seminar. Jerusalem: Hebrew University Publications, 1981.

Amir, B. "Report of the Public Committee for Investigating the Reform in the Educational System of Israel." Jerusalem: Ministry of Education and Culture, 1979 (in Hebrew).

Dewey, John. *The Child and the Curriculum*. Chicago: University of Chicago Press, 1902.

Gal, M. "Informal Education in Israel. Random Events or Intentional Systems Fulfilling Social and Educational Functions." In W. Ackerman et al., eds., *Education in an Emerging Society: The Israeli System*, pp. 601–666, Tel Aviv, Jerusalem: Kibbutz Meuchad Press and Van-Lear Institute, 1985 (in Hebrew).

Holmes Group Report. *Tomorrow's Teachers*. East Lansing, Mich.: Holmes Group, Michigan State University, 1986.

Jaffe, E. *Academization and Humanization in Teacher Education, Jerusalem*. Jerusalem: Ministry of Education and Culture, 1947 (in Hebrew).

Lamm, Z. "Teacher Education in Israel: The Present Situation." *European Journal of Teacher Education* 9, no. 3 (1988): 233–245.

Lomsky-Feeder, E., and R. Cahana. *The Image of Teachers in the Israeli Society*. Jerusalem: School of Education, Hebrew University, 1988 (in Hebrew).

Report of the Commission for Investigating Problems and Issues Concerning Teacher
    Education Colleges. Jerusalem: Ministry of Education and Culture, 1971 (in
    Hebrew).
Task Force on Teaching as a Profession. *A Nation Prepared: Teachers for the 21st
    Century*. Washington, D.C.: Carnegie Forum on Education, 1986.

# 10

# JAPAN

## MANABU SATO

During the 1980s teacher education in Japan, as in many other nations, became one of the most critical areas of educational reform. Faced with a school crisis characterized by vandalism and student apathy, many citizens have directed their attention to teachers and their education. Quality control of teacher education has become a nationwide concern among parents, students, educational administrators, university researchers, economists, and politicians.

It is ironic that the Japanese people are despairing of their schools and are critical of their teachers at the very time that Japanese schools are receiving the highest praise in foreign countries. Throughout the 1980s, educators, economists, and politicians around the world expressed a tremendous amount of admiration for Japanese education. It is said that each airplane landing at Narita Tokyo International Airport transports at least one foreign researcher or journalist to observe a school. While this may be an exaggeration, it is true that the more Japanese schooling has been praised by foreign observers, the more Japanese teachers, students, and parents have been puzzled and worried over a sense of impending school crisis.

Recent teacher education reform has taken place in the context of complicated social issues emanating from a rapidly industrialized society under the bureaucratic political system. We must therefore examine the issues of teacher education in social, cultural, and historical perspective.

Two issues are basic to the reform of teacher education in Japan. The first concerns ways of establishing the role of the teacher as an autonomous professional in response to growing hostility and apathy among students, pressured by an overregulated and demanding system of education. The second issue refers to the adequacy of teaching standards raised through specifying detailed requirements for preservice education and the in-service training system introduced in the recent educational reform.

## GENERAL BACKGROUND

### Negative Views of Japanese Education

In the 1980s foreign researchers and journalists all over the world described Japan as a paradise where school education promoted incredibly high levels of achievement. (In this context we should remember that Marco Polo reported Japan as a golden land about seven hundred years ago.) The Japanese themselves, however, sadly concluded that their school system had been seriously wounded.

Positive evaluations of Japanese education focus only on a narrow range of factors. Many point to the high level of achievement test scores or the low illiteracy rate (only 0.7 percent). Without question these factors have contributed to the rapid economic development in Japan.

These factors alone, however, are insufficient grounds for asserting the excellence of Japanese school education. A high level of literacy had already been attained before the modern school system was established in 1872. A high level of achievement test scores is also a matter of course. Japan's homogeneous race, language, and culture have resulted in a centralized educational system, a uniform curriculum, and high standards of educational efficiency. Japanese students attend the school 240 days per year, one-third more days than U.S. students. In addition, they learn a narrow subject matter, which is easily assessed by means of achievement tests under the pressure of the hard competition of the entrance examination.

In recent years, foreign journals have given some attention to the negative side of Japanese education. They mention rote learning, a lack of creative thinking, entrance examination pressure, the heavy stresses placed on teachers and students with so much content to be learned, the bullying of children, and so on. These are similar to what the Japanese people themselves have said in the last decade.

These negative evaluations of Japanese education are but another aspect of the same phenomenon that produces the positive evaluations: both are the result of the centralized, efficient, educational system and the national standardized curriculum. Under this system, the principle of equality has functioned to promote uniformity, and the principle of educational freedom has been transformed into free competition on entrance examinations. This centralized, efficient educational system reflects the bureaucratic and industrial nature of Japanese society. It is the key to understanding both the positive and the negative assessments of Japanese education.

## THE EDUCATIONAL SYSTEM

In the 1980s educational reform and teacher education reform were designed to resolve the educational crisis derived from too rapid industrialization under the bureaucratic, uniform educational system. In the early days of the decade, a public increasingly aware of a school crisis proposed these reforms.

The first symptom of this school crisis appeared as school violence broke out in 1980. This spread particularly in junior high schools throughout the country year after year. After the wave of school violence had subsided, student apathy took its place. The newspapers, journals, and television news have reported increased numbers of dropouts, autistic children, juvenile delinquents, students with a psychological hatred of schooling, bullying children, teacher burnout and their corporal punishment.

The school crisis affects both teachers and students and is a result of the complicated problems that have accumulated during the past three decades: the pressure of entrance examinations, too much concern with school efficiency, and other social and cultural problems stemming from rapid industrialization. In fact, the changes in schools have been drastic. The percentage of the appropriate age group enrolled at each school level has increased rapidly—senior high schools from 52 percent in 1955 to 94 percent in 1985, and universities and colleges from 9 percent in 1955 to 32 percent in 1985. The explosion of school enrollment has intensified competition. As a result, all senior high schools, colleges, and universities have been differentiated into a hierarchy of test scores on entrance examinations. In addition, *Juku*—informal lessons to supplement school work after school—has spread all over the country. According to a Ministry of Education survey, the *Juku* attendance rate of ninth grade students was 47 percent in 1985.

Bureaucratic management has spread in pursuit of educational efficiency since the national curriculum was enacted in 1958. Teaching has become textbook-oriented and teacher-centered, and students have been forced into passive rote learning. The number of teacher-proof packages of subject matter developed on the authority of the national curriculum has grown. Thus, the centralized bureaucratic school system, which is seen to promote high standards of test scores, forms a dominant structure of Japanese education.

Outside of the school, social, economic, and cultural changes are prevalent. The majority of the employed population was listed as farmer in the 1950s, industrial worker in the 1960s to 1970s, and businessman in the 1980s. Gross national product (GNP) in 1986 was 450 percent of that in 1970. Rapid industrialization and economic development were accompanied by serious byproducts, such as a meritocracy characterized by extreme competition in school entrance examinations, environmental health hazards affecting children, as well as an ideology of industrialism in which the principle of efficiency dominates curriculum, teaching, and school management.

The school crisis in the 1980s was an outcome of these drastic changes both inside and outside of the schools. However, politicians, economists, and journalists have simply asserted that all of Japan's school troubles have resulted from incompetent and unenthusiastic teachers, without inquiring into the many factors of the crisis and without reflecting on their own responsibilities. Newspapers and television have reported the decline of teaching competence and condemned teachers for their lack of accountability. Teachers have become scapegoats.

The Japan Teachers' Union has lost power and the ability to influence policy because of the decrease of membership from 86 percent of total teachers in 1958 to 49 percent in 1987. In addition, the union lost cohesion when it split into a right and left wing in 1989. Thus, the education and teacher education reform movements in the 1980s were dominantly implemented with a top-down approach without much input from teachers.

In 1984 the national government set up the National Council on Educational Reform as an ad hoc advisory committee to the prime minister. It offered a wide range of recommendations to reconstruct the educational system, making it more effective and flexible in order to keep up with internationalized society and information age. Upon receiving the recommendations, the cabinet set forth a paper on policy guidelines for the implementation of educational reform in 1987, which included the following seven key items: lifelong learning, moral education, flexible control of higher education, cooperative research by universities and private sectors, internationalization of education, introduction of special financial arrangements, and an advisory organization for educational reform. Subsequently, teacher education was reformed in accordance with these seven key items.

## THE SYSTEM OF TEACHER EDUCATION

In 1987 the Ministry of Education organized an educational personnel training council that recommended the revised minimum requirements for teacher certification. In the next year, the Educational Personnel Certificate Law regulating the preservice curriculum in detail was revised. In addition, a new in-service training system for beginning teachers was put into place, and in 1989 teacher in-service programs were reorganized.

The revised Educational Personnel Certificate Law regulates a tripartite certificate system by introducing a master's degree certificate and the requirement of increased and restrictive course credits for preservice programs. The master's degree certificate will change the basic structure of teacher education because for forty years Japanese teachers have been prepared mainly through the four-year course at universities. Obviously the revised regulation of teacher certificate reflects several aspects of the compromises made by the Ministry of Education in advancing educational reform. First, the ministry ignored the universities' concern for flexibility in constructing the preservice curriculum, restricting it in more rigid detail. Consequently, it became too difficult for the universities to develop other than the standard curriculum in each institution.

Second, the revised certificate insufficiently required higher standards for teaching. For example, the ministry could not abolish the second class certificate (two-year preservice course) because of the strong pressure from the junior colleges. In the advanced class certificate, the act allowed the substitution of three years of teaching experience for nine credits of university graduate courses because of the lack of scholarship funds to support many teachers attending universities. This provision tends to debase the new master's degree for teachers.

Third, despite the new policies of improving teachers' practical competence in preservice education, the new requirements introduced only a few new courses, in counseling, extracurricular activities, and teaching technology. The revision neglected one of the most critical issues of the preservice curriculum: how to prolong the extremely short term of student teaching (two weeks for the high school teacher certificate and four weeks for the elementary teacher certificate). The Ministry of Education could introduce only a one-week orientation course for student teachers at university without prolonging the term of student teaching itself. This was due to the opposition of university scholars who emphasize the value of liberal arts in preparing teachers. It was also opposed by school principals because only one-fourth of all student teachers enter the teaching profession. Meanwhile, in 1989 the Ministry of Education launched a step-by-step in-service education program for beginning teachers in every type of school in accordance with the new policy for lifelong education.

The in-service training system for beginning teachers is composed of two parts: apprenticeship training in a school (about seventy days a year) and lecture courses in teacher training centers (about thirty-five days a year). Both use traditional training styles. In apprenticeship training, the first-year teachers are mentored by a retired teacher or a veteran in the school in order to master teaching skills. At the teacher training centers, lecture courses are offered in subject matter fields, teaching techniques, and educational goals.

These are the recent trends in teacher education reform in Japan. Certain questions remain. Will the top-down reform improve the great variety of teachers' efforts to resolve the school crisis? Will these reforms make the teaching profession more attractive? These issues must be examined.

## ISSUES AND PROBLEMS

### Issue 1: The Teacher as Professional

In order to clarify the social status and role of Japanese teachers, it is useful to rethink the definition of a teaching profession from a historical point of view. The definition is indeed an unavoidable problem because it became a major controversial issue after teachers were released from the role of national servants in the postwar educational reform. For instance, the Japan Teachers' Union and the Ministry of Education have controverted the definition and polarized it as teacher-as-worker versus teacher-as-exploited-servant for forty years. However, both definitions neglect the complexity of teaching and the professional autonomy of teachers. If we recognize the complex situation where teachers encounter professional problems and solve them, it is inevitable to rethink the concept of teacher beyond the polarity of teacher-as-worker versus teacher-as-exploited-servant.

The concept of teacher in Japan is very complicated. The Japanese use three terms for teacher: *sensei*, *kyouin*, and *kyoushi*. The first term, *sensei*, means a person whom all people should look up to. In this sense, not only teachers but also politicians, doctors, professors, novelists, and artists are usually called *sensei*. This is the most conventional and traditional concept of the three. The second term, *kyouin*, is rather a legal term. It sounds bureaucratic. All the laws, official regulations, and formal documents are written with this term. It is an institutionalized concept that defines teachers as public servants. The third term, *kyoushi*, is closest to the concept of teacher in English, because it implies teacher as professional, although its meaning has gradually been enlarged to connote the first and the second terms. These three terms are used interchangeably in the Japanese context, reflecting the complexity in the social status and professional roles of Japanese teachers.

The concept of teacher as a professional does not yet exist solidly in Japan. Under the national curriculum that regulates educational content in detail, teachers do not have as much autonomous freedom and responsibility as do other professionals. They are regarded not so much as professionals but as public servants or technicians who can devote themselves to predetermined tasks. In a survey of 3,987 elementary and secondary teachers in Mie Prefecture in 1981, about 90 percent taught mainly by the textbooks checked by the Ministry of Education. During the past three decades this tendency has grown as a result of the centralized, efficient system of school administration and the pressure of parents and students under the entrance examination system.

*Public Servant or Professional: A Historical Background*

The basic concept of the teaching profession is deeply rooted in a historical background of Japanese teachers. In prewar days, teachers were educated at normal schools and were regarded as national servants. The nation determined the aims and contents of education rigidly and teachers had to conform, while they were respected by people only as sacred, devoted, and virtuous persons. The teacher's status as national servant was not changed. Nevertheless, the progressive educators declared their professional autonomy in the 1920s. The growing militarism in the 1930s defeated their innovative movement.

Postwar educational reform enabled teachers to extricate themselves from the status of national servant. The report of the United States Education Commission to Japan in 1946 recommended that teachers liberate themselves from militaristic nationalism and bureaucratic authoritarianism and that they retain academic freedom and professional autonomy. In the same year, the Education Reform Committee recommended that teacher preservice education be placed within the universities. All teacher preservice programs have been offered at universities since the Law for Licensing Educational Personnel was promulgated in 1949.

The social status of teachers was transformed from that of national servant to public servant. The Law Concerning Special Regulations for Educational Public Service Personnel enacted in 1949 took into account the teacher's special role. It prescribed the same regulations as for other public servants. The Law Concerning Salaries of Personnel enacted in 1953 differentiated the salary system from other public servants.

Meanwhile, the progressive education era, 1947–1955, was the most vital one for teachers in the history of Japanese education. Child-centered education was a symbol of democratic society in the postwar age, and Dewey's philosophy was the bible of almost every teacher. The curriculum development movement, in which numerous teachers passionately participated, spread all over the country as the revitalization of the heritage of progressive education in the 1920s. Indeed, the national survey of the National Institute for Educational Research in 1951 indicated that over 80 percent of teachers participated in developing their own school curricula and that about 85 percent of the schools adopted the unit teaching method in social studies and in science teaching based on the doctrine of child-centeredness. The movement led to professional autonomy, and teachers organized innumerable voluntary study groups both inside and outside of the schools. The Japan Teachers' Union, established in 1947, also enhanced teachers' autonomy by promoting voluntary studies. The union held annual study meetings for teachers at national, prefectural, and local levels, in which teachers developed their professional culture by sharing their practical experience and principles with each other.

The professionalization of teachers was aborted by revitalized bureaucratic policies beginning in the mid–1950s. Teacher freedom and autonomy were gradually restricted. First, teachers' political activities were prohibited by the Law Concerning Provisional Measures for Securing Political Neutrality of Education in Compulsory Schools and the revised Special Regulations for Educational Public Service Personnel in 1954. Second, the teacher's professional autonomy was also restricted. The national curriculum was announced in 1958, and the check system of textbooks was implemented. Since then, teachers have been obliged to be obedient to the national curriculum which has been revised about every ten years. The textbooks, checked by the Ministry of Education, have become uniform. Even though teachers' salaries have been improved by governors, they were given in exchange for restricting their professional freedom and autonomy. Thus, the centralized, efficient system of education has established the concept of teacher as a public servant.

*Constraints on Professional Autonomy*

In the past three decades, teachers could not break out of the public's perception of teachers as public servants. Although the Japan Teachers' Union employed the slogan of teacher-as-worker, teacher-as-laborer, or teacher-as-proletariat, its efforts could only achieve improvement of teachers' salaries and several working conditions, instead of helping to recapture professional freedom and autonomy.

Indeed, since 1971, the salaries of Japanese teachers have been better than those of other nations. The average annual salary of the beginning elementary school teachers is only a little below the starting salary of assistant professors of national universities. Despite the fact that the salaries of business have gone up as a result of the recent economic development, the teaching profession is still attractive to many adolescents. It is attractive for women because they are treated on a par with men and because they are given eight paid weeks of maternity leave and one unpaid year of child-care leave. Therefore, the number of applicants for teaching has not decreased during the past ten years despite the worsening school crisis.

Despite improvements in salary, teachers as public servants must endure many constraints under the centralized efficient system of education—for example, too detailed prescriptions of national curriculum, too much content to be taught, too much uniformity in textbooks checked by the Ministry of Education, too many school hours and days (students: over a thousand lesson hours, 240 days per year; teaching load of about 19 lessons for the elementary school, and about 15 lessons for the secondary school, per week); too many students in a classroom (at most 45, average number of pupils per class: 31.5 for elementary school, 38.1 for lower secondary school, in 1987); too much standardization of time allotment (45 minutes per lesson in elementary schools and 50 minutes per lesson in secondary schools); and too many trivial jobs added to teaching responsibilities. What is more, teachers have become heavily burdened in coping with the pressures applied by parents and students under the entrance examination system and increasing student delinquency and apathy. In recent years, teachers have become isolated from one another because there is little time for interaction.

This brief description of the historical background of teachers' social status indicates that the teachers in Japan are regarded primarily as public servants, who are obliged to devote themselves to the tasks confined within a bureaucratic system.

## The Informal Professional Culture of Japanese Teachers

Beyond the formal confines of teacher as public servant, the heritage of the professional, informal culture, which originated in the progressive education movements in the 1920s and the late 1940s, is still being handed down. It remains active in informal in-service enterprises. For example, almost all elementary schools hold in-house case study workshops based on classroom observation three to ten times a year. In junior or senior high schools these usually occur one to three times annually. Innumerable teachers record their practices to reflect on them; many others write case books or reports in their journals.

In addition, numerous voluntary study groups that adopt case methods have been organized. The nationwide teacher groups have formed nearly two hundred summer workshops. According to a survey of 3,987 teachers in 1981, over half of them had been active in some voluntary study groups, excluding the study groups organized by the teachers' union and by school boards. One-fifth of the teachers were active in them at that time. These informal study groups of teachers in-service have played very important roles in guaranteeing the high quality of teaching and in opening the pathway to teachers' autonomous professional culture within the bureaucratic school system and its traditional culture.

In fact, some say that excellent teachers in Japan have grown primarily by means of informal voluntary study networks or in-service training in their schools. The progressive education movements in the 1920s and the late 1940s nurtured a great number of excellent teachers. But these elder teachers retired ten to thirty years ago. The demographic composition of the school teachers has been renewed completely. Ten years from now, the teaching force will be occupied by the teachers who have been educated only in the bureaucratic, efficient schools. Informal functions to develop the teaching profession have become weak, and their priority for young teachers has diminished year by year. Instead, the formal functions of the teacher in-service training system have been strengthened.

### Issue 2: The Teacher as Technician in In-service Programs

In the past two decades, teacher education has expanded its domain from preservice education to in-service education. In other words, teacher education is now regarded as lifelong education. Teacher in-service education is offered at many institutions. There are both formal and informal agencies and programs for teacher in-service education. The formal resources comprise (1) Ministry of Education, National Education Center: intensive in-service training courses for principals, vice-principals, and experienced teachers; (2) prefectural educational boards and local teacher training centers: in-service training lecture courses for teachers and study meetings of each subject; and (3) Universities: master's degree courses for teachers in-service and workshops. The informal resources comprise (1) the teachers' union: national and local annual study meetings; (2) voluntary study groups: case study monthly meetings and journals; (3) schools: in-house study workshops based on classroom observation; and (4) self-study: reflective report of teacher's own teaching.

Formal teacher in-service programs are implemented mainly at local teacher training centers in the mode of lecture courses, whereas informal teacher in-service programs are conducted at schools and in informal study groups in the mode of case studies on teaching. Each style corresponds to two different models of teacher role, that is, the technician training model and the professional development model.

Formal teacher in-service programs have expanded mainly since 1960. About two hundred teacher training centers were founded in the 1960s and 1970s. About thirty universities set up the master's course for teachers in-service in the 1970s and 1980s. Many kinds of teacher training programs, teaching technology, scientific research on teaching, and teacher-proof packages of subject matter were developed in the 1970s. The in-service training system for beginning teachers was set up in 1989.

These advances allow the Ministry of Education and prefectural educational boards to prepare many in-service programs and to systematize them. In addition, since the 1960s the Ministry of Education and local educational boards have enlarged certain designated research and development schools. By means of this system, teachers' practice and research have been confined not only by the national curriculum but also by the designated R&D school system. In recent years, the National Institute for Educational Research has gathered at least four thousand research papers written by teachers per year, many of which are printed at the designated R&D schools.

The formal in-service programs are characterized as the technician training model, because they have several features: (1) emphasis on the prescribed knowledge, techniques, skills, and attitudes; (2) pursuit of universal efficiency and standardization; (3) disregard of individual practical problem; and (4) restriction of teacher autonomy and freedom. The model is still dominant in Japanese teacher in-service education.

It has been asserted that in Japan teachers should cover broad fields of theoretical knowledge offered by university researchers and a large number of specific skills and attitudes taught in lecture courses at teacher training centers of school boards. Each prefectural teacher training center offers nearly a thousand lecture courses for teachers every year. Including small lecture courses at the city or local centers, over ten thousand courses may be given for teachers in-service, nationwide, in a year. In this system, the main places for teachers' growth are outside their classrooms. Their practice is treated as an application of prescribed theories and techniques. Their growth is regarded as technical expertise.

### The Central Locus of Teachers' Professional Growth

Many teachers have claimed that the theoretical knowledge taught at universities and the teaching techniques transmitted at teacher training centers are not useful to improving their own teaching. Many point out that the best way to improve teaching is by reflecting on their own teaching and that the most effective advisers are their colleagues at school.

In a 1982 study conducted by the Japanese Society for the Study of Education (1985), 422 beginning teachers were asked to name two persons who, in their judgment, had been most helpful to them in learning how to teach. In other words, who had been the most effective advisers? The overwhelming majority (61 percent) of beginning teachers named elder teachers as their best source of advice on teaching. Next in importance were head teachers of the same grade and colleagues of the same age, named by approximately one-third of respondents. In descending order of importance but at significantly lower levels were department heads, college friends, principals, university professors, and supervisors. The differences in response between males and females were insignificant, as were differences between elementary school and secondary school teachers.

In another study conducted in 1981 in Mie Prefecture (Kamiyama et al., 1983),

3,987 teachers were asked to name the most effective factor in developing their teaching competence. The four most frequently mentioned sources of help were: advice from colleagues, school in-house workshops, learning from students, and excellent books and case reports. There was little difference between the selections of teachers of different grade levels with one exception. Elementary school teachers overwhelmingly cited school in-house workshops as proving most useful to them. Other factors were selected much less frequently: voluntary study groups, advice from principal, school board teacher training center, and advice from parents.

The above data strongly suggest that the central locus for teachers' professional growth ought to be their own school and that the functions of many in-service opportunities should be reorganized to form a structure of concentric circles centering on each teacher's own teaching.

The above findings also suggest that informal in-service resources are effective in developing teachers' professional culture in Japan. The richness of these informal in-service opportunities is just the keystone that might guarantee high-quality Japanese education. Excellent teachers who grow in the informal study networks play very important roles in encouraging teachers' practical study in the schools beyond the bureaucratic educational system.

*Conflicting Modes of Teacher In-service Education*

In informal in-service teacher education as in other professional fields, the dominant mode is the case study method. Teachers report on their own cases with narrative documentation or with videotape recording of their teaching. The cases are diagnosed, illuminated, and criticized from multiple points of view by attendant teachers. Through reflecting and deliberation, teachers share their personal practical knowledge with each other and develop alternative approaches. This approach is characterized as the practice-critique-development approach as contrasted with the research-development-diffusion approach in formal in-service programs. The informal teacher in-service programs epitomize the professional development model based on the case study method or practice-critique-development approach.

It is important that two streams of in-service education, the technician training model and the professional development model, confront each other in the Japanese context. The Ministry of Education has strengthened the dominant status of the technician training model by requiring apprenticeship and lecture course programs for beginning teachers and by expanding in-service training programs for experienced teachers. In contrast to this formal trend, the informal forces of teachers' self or mutual development opportunities have diminished along with the retirement of innovative, experienced teachers, a change of generation.

With the growing problems of trying to teach disaffected, hostile, and bored students, it is likely that greater emphasis on the professional in-service model will be necessary.

## CONCLUSION

As mentioned above, Japanese teacher education reforms in the 1980s were a result of three conflicting reform forces based on three different models of the teaching profession: the traditional teacher as public servant model, the conservative teacher as technician model, and the progressive teacher as professional model.

The roles of teacher as public servant and teacher as technician are deeply rooted in the centralized, efficient educational system in Japan and its school culture. The teacher as public servant is based on the principle of self-devotion to public service, which well meets the needs of a bureaucratic administration system. The teacher as technician derives from the principle of teaching efficiency, which is well matched to the needs of parents and students under the pressure of entrance examinations, as well as to the needs of economic efficiency in the industrialized society.

In contrast, the teacher as professional corresponds with another prototype of teacher. The teacher as professional is founded on the principle of teacher's autonomy and wisdom, which is consistent with a democratic society, intellectual freedom, and cognition of individual differences.

Indeed, Japanese teachers have endeavored to cultivate their own professional culture in their schools and in their informal study groups for many years. If Japanese education ought to be admired, its excellence should be recognized as the rich products of the informal professional culture that innovative teachers have built since the early days of this century. And if Japanese education is considered to be at risk, its crisis should be defined in terms of the gradual diminution of the informal professional culture of teachers. Instead, the roles of teacher as public servant and teacher as technician have penetrated the schools under the top-down teacher education reform.

Teachers are, of course, essential elements in promoting excellence of education. In the case of Japanese teachers, their excellence derives from the professional wisdom cultivated by informal teacher in-service efforts. A way to empower their professional wisdom and autonomy in Japan may be in establishing more solidly the concept of teacher as professional and in executing experiments in teacher in-service education based on the professional development model. Standing opposed to the top-down formal teacher training system, grass-roots approaches to reform teacher in-service education are partly embodied in the following efforts.

First, many schools strengthen the function of in-house case study workshops in pursuit of becoming clinical centers for teachers of the neighboring schools. Although these clinical schools are not too powerful because the case method of teaching is not sophisticated, these schools could become the most effective agencies in which teachers establish their professional autonomy.

Second, many voluntary study groups develop case studies on teaching and publish a large number of case journals and books. Teachers' journals that carry teaching cases not only provide teachers with significant information but also form the teachers' professional networks. Their activities and journals are still important means of cultivating teachers' professionalism.

Third, several universities offer workshops on case methods through advancing teacher researcher collaboration. Unfortunately, educational research at the universities and teaching practice at the schools have been separated in the Japanese context. In addition, the recent specialization of educational research and the complexity of the school crisis widen the gulf between university researchers and school teachers. But university-school collaboration is a fitting vehicle by which teachers make their professional culture more intellectual. Many teachers' colleges have established practical research centers for students and experienced teachers which promise to be the location of collaborative research for university researchers, students, and teachers.

Fourth, several teacher training centers adopt case methods in in-service programs by collaborating with educational researchers.

These experimental efforts are still constrained by the dominant bureaucratic system of teacher in-service education. Nevertheless, these are the starting points from which to establish the solid professional culture beyond the role of teacher as public servant and teacher as technician.

## REFERENCES

Cummings, William. *Education and Equality in Japan*. Princeton, N.J.: Princeton University Press, 1980.

Cummings, William, et al., eds. *Educational Policies in Crisis*. New York: Praeger, 1986.

Japanese Society for the Study of Education, Research Committee on Educational System. *Kyoushi Kyouiku no Kadai [Issues of Teacher Education]*. Tokyo: Meiji Tosho, 1985.

Kamiyama, M., H. Sakamoto, K. Imazu, H. Sato, and M. Sato. Kyoushoku nitaisuru Kyoushi no Taido [Teachers' attitudes to their profession]. *Mie University Educational Research Bulletin* 34 (1983).

Ministry of Education, Science and Culture. *Education in Japan: A Graphic Presentation*. Tokyo: Gyousei Publishers, 1989.

Ministry of Education, Science and Culture. *Outline of Education in Japan*. Tokyo: Unesco Asian Culture Center, 1989.

Ministry of Education, Science and Culture. *Japan's Modern Education System: A History of the First Hundred Years*. Tokyo: Ministry of Education, Science and Culture, 1980.

Rohlen, Thomas. *Japan's High Schools*. Berkeley: University of California Press, 1983.

Sato, Manabu. "Research on Teaching and In-service Education: An Experiment to Empower Wisdom of Teachers." Paper presented at the Second Annual Meeting at Honolulu of the Japan/U.S. Teacher Education Consortium. American Association of Colleges for Teacher Education, 1989.

Sato, M., K. Akita, and N. Iwakawa. "Practical Thinking Styles of Teachers: A Comparative Study of Expert and Novice Thought Processes and Its Implications for

Rethinking Teacher Education in Japan.'' Paper presented at the Third Annual Meeting at Tokyo of the Japan/U.S. Teacher Education Consortium, American Association of Colleges for Teacher Education, 1990.

Sato, Nancy. ''Japanese Education Where It Counts: In the Classroom.'' Paper presented at the Third Annual Meeting at Tokyo of the Japan/U.S. Teacher Education Consortium, American Association of Colleges for Teacher Education, 1990.

Stevenson, H., H. Azuma, and K. Hakuta, eds. *Child Development and Education in Japan*. New York: W. H. Freeman and Co., 1986.

U.S. Department of Education. *Japanese Education Today*. Washington, D.C.: U.S. Government Printing Office, 1987.

White, Merry. *The Japanese Educational Challenge: A Commitment to Children*. New York: Macmillan, 1987.

# 11

## MALAWI

### J. B. KUTHEMBA MWALE

Many key issues in teacher education remain unresolved in Malawi. One of the most basic is disagreement over the old, long-standing dogma that teachers are born and not made. Related to this still-debated issue are a number of others; (1) how to promote a policy of in-service upgrading of teachers, (2) how to improve the quality of teacher candidates, (3) how to deal with the uneasy relationship between teacher education and the universities, and finally (4) how to promote the kind of research that would be useful in formulating educational policy.

### GENERAL BACKGROUND

Malawi is an independent sovereign state lying in the eastern, Central African region. It is bordered to the north and northwest by the Republic of Tanzania, to the east, south, and southwest by Mozambique, and to the west by Zambia. Its size is 118,428 square kilometers, of which one-fifth is covered by water. The country has magnificent scenery, a fresh-water lake, fine national parks, and almost year-round sunshine. It is a land-locked country whose length is 900 kilometers. It was called Nyasaland Protectorate during the British colonial era.

The population of Malawi is nearly 9 million, increasing at an annual rate of 3 percent. More than 90 percent of the population lives in the rural area. The country has three distinct religious groups—Christianity, Islam, and traditional African religions—and three main ethnic groups—Malawian Africans who form the largest single group; Asians, mostly from India, Pakistan, and Sri Lanka; and others from Europe, Great Britain, Canada, the United States, and Australia.

Malawi's main industries are agriculturally based, and they include the growing and processing of tobacco, cotton, tea, sugar, maize, rice, ground nuts, and, to a lesser extent, coffee, soya beans, and cashew nuts. Fishing on Lake Malawi is developing very rapidly for export. The official language of business is English while the national language is Chichewa, spoken by more than 85 percent of the population. Among Malawi's trading partners are Great Britain, Japan, Canada, the United States, South Africa, Germany, Australia, and India.

## THE EDUCATIONAL SYSTEM

The system of formal education includes an eight-year primary cycle that enrolls children at the age of six or seven. Those who pass a selection examination at the end of the eighth year enter the four-year secondary level. National examinations are given at the end of the second and fourth years. Those who do very well on the fourth-year examination are selected for university programs. Those who are not selected may choose to enter primary teacher education colleges, technical colleges, and other vocational institutions. There is also a distance education college that offers courses from the primary to the secondary level as well as for the Primary Teacher Education Upgrading Certificate.

Nonformal education is offered by a different ministry and concentrates on adult literacy, functional literacy, training for new roles, and education for social and national development. In 1966, two years after Malawi's independence from Britain, the population was about 4 million. Of these, only 10 percent were literate. Today, twenty-five years later, the percentage of illiterates remains pretty much the same, despite the government's attempts to expand formal education. School enrollment increased from about 368,000 in 1964 to 1,203,000 in 1989, but illiteracy still remains alarmingly high. The high dropout rate, which fluctuates between 25 percent in Grade 5 to 15 percent in other grades, contributes to the illiteracy problem. In addition, at Grade 8 there is an alarming repetition rate of over 40 percent.

Illiteracy is concentrated in the rural areas, and it is estimated that 100,000 persons are being added to the illiteracy pool every year owing to school dropouts. More than half are females. This trend is not likely to change without a special national effort. It is expected that when the two ministries involved with education, the Ministry of Education and the Ministry of Culture and Community Services, jointly attack the situation, a change for the better may occur.

## THE SYSTEM OF TEACHER EDUCATION

The history of teacher education in Malawi falls into three distinct periods: the missionary period, 1870–1929; the colonial era, 1929–1964; and the independent era, 1964 to the present. Each period had its own peculiar activities, goals, practices, policies, and problems.

The Western Christian missionaries launched education activities in the mid–1870s. Their aim was to establish schools for converts to learn reading and writing in the vernacular and simple arithmetic. The objective of such formal education was the ability to read the Bible, teach, and preach the word of God to fellow natives. The university's Mission to Central Africa (the result of David Livingston's appeal to British universities to help in opening up Central Africa) and the Scottish missionaries were mostly evangelists with some knowledge of artisan trades. In their school curriculum they included technical subjects such as bricklaying and carpentry. However, the Catholic missionaries, though also evangelists, tended to emphasize the three R's and much pulpit preaching. The Dutch Reformed Church missionaries came from South Africa, having just been defeated by the British in war. Hating the British, they concentrated on the Bible and other activities, refraining from introducing serious academic content. It seems that each missionary group sent personnel according to its own conception of the mission to be accomplished. However, government and private individuals publicly acknowledge that missionaries made a great positive contribution and laid a solid foundation for further education and religion in Malawi.

Since these missionaries were not educators, they did not develop an appropriate common curriculum for their schools and the little they taught differed from one missionary organization to the other. After realizing that their schools needed qualified teachers with appropriate instructional skills and techniques, the missionaries established teacher training colleges, each with its own curriculum and emphasis. Hence, no coordination, cooperation, and common evaluation of the program and the products' standards took place.

Some colleges emphasized teaching methods and religious instruction; others emphasized academic content and practical skills such as carpentry, bricklaying, woodwork, and agriculture; and still others stressed evangelism and pulpit preaching. This difference in emphasis was reflected in both the teachers produced and the pupils who graduated from schools manned by those teachers.

The curriculum which each missionary establishment developed was consistent with their conception of their mission and what it had set out to achieve. However, the products of such curriculum were to serve a single government or group of people. The government tended to employ some of the graduates of mission schools as clerks, messengers, tax collectors, and police. It was discovered that graduates from certain mission schools were better educated than those from other schools. In addition, some spoke better English than others—hence the need for a common curriculum.

The missionaries attempted to develop a common curriculum, design similar teacher education programs, and devise common evaluation instruments for teacher education. Such attempts were unsuccessful until 1926 when the colonial government, as a coordinating body, established a government Department of Education to run and control formal education in the country.

The problems facing teacher education in the missionary era included lack of a common curriculum, lack of an integrated system of formal education, poor standards, and lack of educational planning, supervision, and evaluation. These continued to plague the system of education in the colonial era.

In this period, teacher education began to develop as an integral part of the formal education system. Following from the Commission of Inquiry on African Education in the country, an American team of teacher educators established a Jeans Teachers College for educating primary school teachers in 1929. A coherent curriculum for teacher education was developed. A successful attempt was made to address the teacher education problems and issues inherited from the missionary era.

Consistent with formal Western education practices, school supervisors were appointed, common evaluation measurements were established, and criteria for standardizing teacher education standards were put in place. By 1933 the colonial government officially recognized the teachers' certificate examinations. Candidates who passed that examination became officially recognized as primary school teachers.

The quality of these teachers was rather poor largely because of the primary school system itself, from which the teachers came. Most of the teacher trainers were unqualified for the job they did. Most, if not all, college teachers were missionary personnel, competent in evangelism, pulpit preaching, and Bible knowledge as well as in some crafts and trades, but not in teacher education.

The standards could not be raised unless the structural level of teacher candidates was improved. Hence, a team of experts was asked to study the possibility of establishing secondary education in the country. A Commission of Inquiry was formed in 1936 to recommend raising entry qualifications to teacher education colleges. This recommendation was carried out after secondary school education was established in 1940, and by 1949 cohorts of higher calibre students began to enter teachers' colleges. They were academically and physically mature and very ready for professional training as teachers.

By the eve of independence in 1964, teacher education still had problems of standards, inadequate numbers of appropriately qualified persons, both in the field and colleges, and problems of planning for teacher education. The issue of standards had been remedied. Some student-teachers, particularly at Domasi Government Teachers College, had full secondary school certificates.

The independent period inherited a number of problems, issues, controversies, and criticisms from the two earlier periods. In essence, the new era had to reformulate the educational policy in general and teacher education policy in particular. It had to plan for education, determine the goals and aims of education in the country, and review the school and college curriculum to suit the new aspirations.

## ISSUES AND PROBLEMS

By independence day, teacher education in Malawi had to contend with lack of official policy in teacher education, and lack of planning, supervision, research, and focus. It also inherited the popular controversy that teachers are born, not made; hence, there was no reason to spend money on teacher education.

In an attempt to solve these problems or improve the situation, the new nation

developed a policy of expanding the teacher education facilities: physical structures, personnel, and materials. It established a teacher education section at the
ministry headquarters responsible for administering, supervising, and evaluating
teacher education programs and products. It voted more money for teacher
education, contrary to the popular view that teachers are born, not made, and
that there was no justification for spending money on teacher training. However,
there was still an issue regarding the absence of planning and research in teacher
education. As a result, programs and curriculum changes were made without
justification, for there were no research data to support any proposed changes
in the programs or in the curriculum.

Since independence, some policy initiatives have not borne fruit. If anything,
they have pushed the system back to square one or forced it into making a U-
turn. For example, there was a policy to phase out some teachers' colleges in
favor of a few large ones. However, the policy was changed, and new ones were
constructed to take the place of those phased out.

## Issue 1: In-service Upgrading of Teachers

Soon after independence, Malawi discovered that it could not educate its people
formally through the face-to-face method but needed a college of distance education to supplement the efforts of the formal school. The problem was (and
still is) that more primary school leavers are qualified for secondary level education, but there were, and still are, fewer places for everybody. Thus, the need
to establish the College of Distance Education arose. The college is under the
Ministry of Education and Culture and is run by civil servants. Students enroll
through the district education officers dotted throughout the country. Because
the Malawian population has a great desire and need for higher education student
motivation is very high, substantiated by a high success rate in examinations.
The future of the College of Distance Education is very bright, and the university
will soon join it by offering university courses via distance means.

With regard to academic and professional standards, the official policy of the
independent government was to encourage teachers to use and benefit from the
newly established College of Distance Education to upgrade themselves. Some
good programs were put in place for teachers to take and upgrade themselves
from teacher Grade 4 to Grade 3 and from Grade 3 to Grade 2 and so on.

The policy helped raise the level of teacher quality, knowledge, and professional skills. However, the policy was abandoned in favor of promoting teachers
through mere interviews. As a result of the new policy, many unqualified teachers, especially of Grade 4 and some of Grade 3, were promoted to Grade 1,
which goes with a professional responsibility of headship at the primary school
level.

Professionally, this policy has discouraged teachers of lower qualifications
from studying to upgrade themselves. They tend to sit and wait for a chance to
receive upgrading on a "silver platter." In an attempt to justify this policy, it

was said that it intended to phase out all lowly qualified teachers' grades. This policy has negatively affected the standards of education and administration in the primary schools.

## Issue 2: Improving the Low Quality of Teacher Candidates

The shortage of quality teachers at every level of the educational system is another problem that has plagued the system. At the eve of independence there were very few schools at both primary and secondary levels. After independence many schools, particularly primary schools, sprang up like mushrooms under the self-help project system. The secondary sector also increased through the deliberate policy of building at least a secondary school in each district.

Following this unprecedented increase in schools was the severe shortage of appropriately qualified teachers. The government's policy was to send better primary school teachers to teach at the secondary school level and recruit unqualified teachers to teach at the primary level. After draining away all better teachers from primary to secondary, the policy was directed at the rest of primary schools. They were sent to secondary teacher education colleges to train and obtain education that would equip them for secondary school teaching.

This policy has caused a severe decline in academic and professional standards, particularly in primary schools. Professionally, we believe that the primary school child should be taught by the best teacher possible. As a foundation for all education, there was a great need to see that the primary school teachers were the best the country could have. If the child starts poorly and badly in school, it is believed that the whole education of that child is chaotic and the child himself is disappointed, frustrated, and disinterested.

Twenty years after independence, teacher education in Malawi is experiencing both old and new problems and controversies. The shortage of appropriately qualified teachers remains, as do the controversies of whether or not teacher education lecturers should be specifically trained; whether practice teaching is necessary in teacher education programs; whether there should be any teacher education at all; and whether school experience is necessary for a student teacher.

The shortage of appropriately qualified teachers in the country at both primary and secondary levels is very much pronounced. The government realizes that the shortage of teachers negatively affects academic standards in schools and results in poor graduates. Hence, the government has entered into loan schemes to secure funds in order to produce enough teachers.

Both the primary and secondary level teacher education colleges receive teacher candidates from the secondary education level. In most cases, particularly those going to the primary teacher education colleges, they are of poor calibre in that they are those left after the best are selected for other avenues. Hence, many start off on a wrong footing with poor motivation to teach.

Some of these candidates do not complete the program. They leave as soon as there is something better that they can go to. Those who manage to complete the program, particularly in the secondary teacher education colleges, end up going elsewhere. This state of affairs perpetuates the shortage. In an attempt to address this shortage, the Ministry of Education and Culture has decided that all unqualified teachers in the primary sector should receive one year of teacher education courses to become fully fledged teachers. In addition, a three-year distance teacher education project has been launched to train teachers, partly by distance and partly face to face. Both programs are running side by side in primary teacher education colleges.

## Issue 3: The Uneasy Relationship Between Teacher Education and University

At secondary teacher education colleges, the issues and controversies are rather different. There are issues or controversies such as the question of practice teaching for student teachers; whether a general degree plus a postgraduate certificate in education should replace the traditional four- or five-year B.Ed. and whether or not teacher education lecturers need special training for their job.

Teacher education programs that take place in the university context and environment are usually resisted. Universities are not seen as places for teacher education. Since most university lecturers and professors have academic qualifications, they teach and their university students pass examinations. They do not see why there should be teacher education at all. It does not occur to them that teaching in schools and lecturing at tertiary education levels are two different things. From their background, the university lecturers see no need to expose student teachers to real-life school experiences. They do not see the need or value of professional courses or pedagogy because they did not go through it and they think it is not necessary. It is the same mentality that questions the value of practice teaching for student teachers.

Most university professors propose the abolition of pedagogy. Students would be educated through the general degree route, at the end of which they would be given basic knowledge and skills in teaching. Such an arrangement does not take into account that teaching, like medicine, is a profession. One has to acquire appropriate attitudes, relevant skills, and techniques for the profession and appropriate values shared by the professionals in the trade. These can only be acquired slowly as students learn and practice the profession.

Through a lack of understanding, colleagues do not see the need to establish special programs for producing teacher educators for the country's teacher education colleges. Most of them believe that anyone with a degree, particularly a Ph.D., can train school teachers. Most faculties of education or schools of education that operate within the university premises or confines find it extremely difficult to get their professional views accepted by their colleagues in other faculties. As a consequence, education courses or programs are unpopular in many universities, and their faculties are taken less seriously by their colleagues.

In an attempt to remedy the situation, certain proposals have been put forward, for example, to teach student teachers separately from their colleagues in the other disciplines. This proposal has been criticized on the basis that the student teachers can end up being less academically prepared. The other option, of teaching them as mixed groups with their colleagues in other disciplines, is opposed by those who claim that there will be no time for practice teaching. For if the student teachers go on to practice teaching their colleagues will not wait for them but will proceed with the more content.

These issues and controversies are still being debated, and nobody has yet proposed a viable solution acceptable to both professionals and other academics. However, the products of the current teacher education programs may suffer pedagogically since not enough time is given to the study and practice of pedagogical skills.

### Issue 4: Promoting Useful Research

Educational research is a forgotten subject in most developing countries, and Malawi is no exception. Since the establishment of the Department of Education in 1926, there has been no substantial or deliberate policy to engage a researcher or do educational research to support policy initiatives. Decisions have always been made either from intuition or trial and error. After learning from experience that western educational studies should not be used uncritically, attempts were made in the late 1970s to establish a research unit/section within the Ministry of Education and Culture. The section did not go far because of the problem of transfers. All the section personnel were civil servants who were subject to transfers to the general service. Hence, there was no continuity. During the period 1979–1982, the author was appointed national researcher to lead and guide educational researchers in a special project. After the project, the situation returned to square one.

At present, however, the University of Malawi has established the Center for Educational Research and Training with financial assistance from a World Bank loan. Such a center will be responsible for conducting educational research in the country and training educational researchers for Malawi.

We look at the future with great confidence and hope that educational policy and decisions will be made or influenced by valid research findings.

### REFERENCES

Banda, Kelvin N. *Brief History of Education in Malawi*. Blantyre: Dzuka Publishing Co., 1982.

Bishop, G. D. *Alternative Strategies for Education*. London: Macmillan, 1989.

Brewer, J. P. "Notes on Maravi Origin and Migration." *African Studies* 9 (1950): 32–34.

Greenland, J. *Inservice Teacher Education in Anglophone Africa*. London: Macmillan, 1983.

Herskovits, M. J. "The Culture Area of Africa." *African Journal* 111 No. 1 (1930): 72–73.

Hodgson, A.G.O. "Notes on the Chewa and Ngoni of Dowa District of Nyasaland Protectorate." *Royal Anthropological Institute of Great Britain and Ireland Journal* 63 (1923).

Marwick, M. G. "Notes on Some Chewa Rituals." *African Studies* 27, no. 1 (1968).

Ministry of Education and Culture. *Education Statistics 1988*. Lilongwe, Malawi, 1989.

Ministry of Education and Culture. *Education Service Review*. Blantyre: Price Waterhouse Report, 1985.

Ministry of Education and Culture. *National Education Plan 1985–1995*. Lilongwe, Malawi: 1985.

Nthara, Y. *History of Chewa People*. Lusaka, Northern Rhodesia: Publication Bureau, 1965.

Price, T. "More about Maravi." *African Studies* 11 (1952): 75–79.

Tew, M. *People of Lake Nyasa Region*. London: Oxford University Press, 1950.

# 12

# MALAYSIA

## A. LOURDUSAMY AND SOK KHIM TAN

As in most countries, teacher education in Malaysia faces a number of problems. This country study examines three such problems: the lack of continuous professional development of teachers, the lack of relevant research helpful to the development of teacher education, and the declining status of teachers in the country.

Malaysia places great emphasis on preservice teacher education. The programs offered are directed toward developing basic teaching skills for teacher certification, so that trained teachers can enter the profession and obtain tenure. Having obtained the certificate of education/diploma in education, teachers in general seldom endeavor to improve themselves professionally.

At the same time, teacher education programs in Malaysia need further development. Most of the teacher education curricula in developing countries are based on principles and theories developed in the Western world. There is an acute lack of research for theory development which could be used in teacher education in developing countries like Malaysia. In addition to these problems, the status of teachers appears to be declining. At the time of independence and during the early developmental period of Malaysian history, when there were very few industrial activities, teaching was a sought-after profession. With the advent of industrial development in the last decade, teaching no longer enjoys its favorable status among young people. They are attracted to other more challenging, often more prestigious and better paying opportunities available in the industrial and service sectors. As a result, teacher education programs do not necessarily attract the best candidates and the profession in turn suffers in image.

## GENERAL BACKGROUND

Malaysia consists of peninsular Malaysia at the tip of mainland Southeast Asia, while the states of Sabah and Sarawak are on the island of Borneo located in the South China Sea. Peninsular Malaysia, known as Malaya, attained independence from British rule in August 1957. In 1963 Sabah and Sarawak joined Malaya to form Malaysia. Malaysia is a parliamentary democracy with a constitutional monarch ruling the nation.

The population of the country is approximately 17 million comprising Malays, Chinese, Indians, Ibans, Kadazans, and other races. In peninsular Malaysia the population consists mainly of the Malays, the Chinese, and the Indians, while in Sabah and Sarawak the population is dominated by Ibans, Kadazans, and Chinese.

Bahasa Malaysia (the Malay language) is the national language, whereas the languages of the other races and English are maintained and developed within the national education system. In general, the different races in the country use their mother tongues in the family and social setting, but for all interracial and official communication the national language is extensively used. English is the second language in Malaysia. It is taught from Grade 1 to university level in the national education system. It is widely spoken and used in the commercial sector.

Islam, Christianity, Hinduism, Buddhism, and Taoism are the main religions in Malaysia, with Islam having the status of the official state religion. The Malaysian Constitution guarantees freedom of worship. The Malays are Muslims, whereas most of the Chinese are either Buddhists or Taoists. The Indians are mainly Hindus, and the Ibans and Kadazans are primarily Christians or Muslims. Hence, a visitor to Malaysia will see many mosques, temples, and churches throughout the country.

The Malaysian economy is robust. At present the leading economic sector in the country is manufacturing, followed by agriculture and mining. The leading export-oriented manufactured products are electrical and electronic products, textiles, and wearing apparel as well as rubber-based products. In the primary commodity production sector, Malaysia is the world's largest exporter of palm oil, natural rubber, and tropical timber and a leading world exporter of cocoa beans and pepper. Malaysia is also one of the leading exporters of tin and steel.

## THE EDUCATIONAL SYSTEM

Education has its roots in pre-independence Malaysia where each community was left on its own to provide education to its young. With independence, Malaysia inherited a pluralistic system of education. That is, primary school education was offered in four languages, namely, English, Malay, Chinese, and Tamil, and secondary education was available in the English and Chinese medium. Instead of perpetuating the anomalies inherent in a plural system of education, the then newly elected government recognized the role education can play in national integration. It set up a committee (Razak Committee) to recommend ways of uniting, through education, the different ethnic groups to form a united nation. This led to the establishment of the national education system with a common syllabus that used Malay and English as the main medium of instruction but allowed the existence of Chinese and Tamil schools within the national system at the primary school level. It also led to the reorganization of the teaching profession and to the establishment of a unified teaching service to cater to the needs of the different types of national schools. Thus, the national education system of independent Malaysia was born.

Further changes were made. Free primary education was introduced, and the school-leaving age was raised to fifteen years. With that began the quantitative expansion of education in Malaysia. Every child of school-going age was assured a place in the primary school. The aim was to educate people to man the growing economy of developing Malaysia.

Another major educational change took place in 1970. English was phased out as a medium of instruction in secondary schools. This phasing-out process continued at the secondary level up to 1980 and was carried into the tertiary level progressively. Today, Malay is the only medium of instruction at the secondary and tertiary level, while Malay, Chinese, and Tamil are still used in primary schools.

In 1979 further changes were introduced in the national education system. The new changes were concerned with making education relevant and effective to meet national needs and aspirations. Much emphasis is now placed on providing greater accessibility to education and training and on developing a curriculum suitable to the Malaysian context. In 1983 a new primary school curriculum was introduced. This curriculum emphasized the overall development of the child and the acquisition of the basic skills of reading, writing, and arithmetic. The year 1988 saw the first stage in the implementation of an integrated secondary school curriculum. This was another move toward implementing the standard of education, with emphasis on the development of the emotional, spiritual, intellectual, and physical aspect of each individual child in an integrated manner. Unlike the earlier curriculum, the new one does not overemphasize the preparation of students for higher education by undue stress on academic orientation but gives more attention to imparting values and skills that shape students into citizens with patriotism and high moral values. This phase marks the beginning of the qualitative improvement in the different aspects of education such as curriculum, support services, and teacher education.

## THE SYSTEM OF TEACHER EDUCATION

The development of education in any country has far-reaching implications for teacher education since the effectiveness of any education system is dependent on the effectiveness of the delivery system. The development of teacher education in Malaysia parallels the development of the education system in the country.

Before independence there was a separate system of producing teachers for the vernacular schools and the English-medium schools. In the beginning, teachers for the Chinese and Tamil were recruited directly from China and British India, respectively, whereas the teachers for the Malay schools were recruited from those who had experience teaching the Quranic classes in the villages. In 1878 a Malay College was opened in Singapore to train Malay teachers. In 1900 a new college was opened in Malacca, followed by another in Matang, Perak, in 1913. All these colleges were closed with the opening of a centralized college at Tanjung Malim, Perak, in 1922 for the preparation of male Malay teachers. The expansion of Malay girls' education created a demand for trained Malay female teachers. In 1935 a Malay Women's Training College was opened in Malacca. About the same time the Chinese and Indians, realizing the need to inculcate a Malayan outlook in their schools as well as to meet the growing demands for trained teachers, set up training centers in major towns to train teachers locally.

The English-medium schools, on the other hand, drew their supply of teachers from the Christian missionaries who came to Malaysia with the British. The shortage of teachers in these schools led the Woolley Committee in 1870 to recommend that a system of teacher training be provided to overcome the problem. In 1905 a training program known as the Normal Class Training was opened in Kuala Lumpur. In this program the trainee teachers attended weekend courses. The response was encouraging, and this led to the setting up of a two-year normal training program in Penang in 1907 to provide training for prospective English-medium teachers. However, the acute shortage of secondary school teachers followed the increase in the school-going population during the decade after World War II. This led to the establishment of two teacher training colleges in England: in Kirby in 1951 and in Brinsford Lodge in 1955. The reliance on the two colleges abroad to train teachers for the secondary schools was made necessary by the difficulties of recruiting teaching staff who would be prepared to come out from Britain to Malaysia for an extended period. These difficulties were due mainly to the dangers to life created by the communist insurrection during the post–World War II period. This temporary measure, adopted to meet immediate demands for secondary school teachers created by postwar conditions, accelerated the expansion of education and proved a great success. The operation of these two colleges ceased in 1964 with the establishment of five colleges in Penang and Kuala Lumpur.

The implementation of free primary education in 1962 brought about a marked increase in the enrollment of primary schools. The extension of universal education from six to nine years, in 1965, saw more pupils entering secondary schools. These changes in the education system posed a strain on the existing training facilities and the supply of teachers. Five residential teacher training colleges were established in 1964 in Penang and Kuala Lumpur, and a sixth was opened in 1966 in Johor Bharu. Besides these residential colleges, regional centers were opened in the different parts of the country. These centers offered a two-year "sandwich" course. The student teachers attended weekend lectures at these centers and did part-time teaching in schools around the centers. They were required to follow the syllabus of the full-time residential colleges and take the same common examinations.

One striking result of the implementation of the reorganized program of teacher training was the marked reduction of untrained teachers from over 80 percent in 1956 to less than 40 percent in 1966. The 1969 education review committee recommended an integrated teacher training program in which all students at the teachers' college level were trained to teach at the upper primary level and then could elect to specialize in the lower primary or lower secondary level. This program was implemented in 1973. In 1981 a three-year teacher training program was implemented, with greater attention being focused on quality. Since 1985 the duration was reduced to two and a half years except for the program for trade courses which remains a three-year program. At present there are twenty-eight teacher training colleges throughout the country. During the early period of independence there was only one university in the country, the University of Malaya; it was established in 1959 at Kuala Lumpur and became responsible for training secondary school graduates. The rapid expansion of education in Malaysia necessitated the establishment of a number of universities. At present there are seven universities in the country with five of them offering various programs in teacher education.

## Issue 1: The Lack of Continuing Professional Development of Teachers

In general, the teacher education program at both the college and university levels consists of three main components: academic, education theory, and practical. In the academic component the would-be teachers are required to gain knowledge in one or two school subjects that they plan to teach in schools. At the university, they take courses leading to a degree in science or humanities. The theoretical component generally consists of the foundation courses in education—philosophy, history, sociology, and psychology; methods courses for the teaching of various school subjects; and supporting courses like classroom measurement and evaluation, educational technology, counseling, and management. The practical component consists of teaching practice in schools for a period of between twelve and sixteen weeks.

The very nature and content of the preservice teacher education programs at both the teacher training college and university levels clearly show that they are geared to prepare would-be teachers with sufficient knowledge of content matter in the subject they intend to teach. At the same time they are designed to equip them with some basic pedagogical and management skills—the mechanics of the profession. However, a teacher in the present day-classrooms encounters a multitude of difficult issues and problems.

The deputy education director of teacher education recently pointed out (*The New Strait Times*, September 30, 1990) that some teachers feel so intimidated by bright children in their schools that they can find no other recourse but to seek transfer to a less challenging environment or adopt authoritarian and dogmatic teaching styles. They find that they cannot cope with the complexities before them. The editor of the newspaper commentary wrote that teacher education was not just a two and a half or three-year program in which young trainees can be equipped with all the necessary skills to teach. It takes much more to be able to stand before a class and impart knowledge in a creative, convincing, and interesting manner.

Another survey found that teachers worried about a number of problems they encountered in the classroom such as difficulty in controlling the students, as well as the students' negative attitudes, lack of interest in studies, passiveness, and failure to understand the lessons taught. These problems made it difficult for teachers to carry on their work, and it affected their feeling of satisfaction. One of the coping strategies some teachers resort to is to behave in an "I don't care" manner.

In a recent survey carried out in Malaysia involving 2,423 teachers with an average of ten years of service (Paul, 1973), 30 percent of the teachers surveyed had never attended in-service courses of any kind and another 25 percent had attended only one in-service course during the previous three years of their teaching careers.

The three in-service courses most frequently attended by the teachers are the courses on implementation of new curriculum, teaching of the national language, and courses in the teaching of English. Most of the teachers who reported attending in-service courses did so in 1980–1987 during the implementation of the new primary school curriculum.

With regard to the teachers' own professional development, only 21 percent of the teachers reported being a member of a professional association. Of these, nearly 55 percent belong to a teachers' union rather than a professional association. However, 78 percent of the teachers surveyed reported reading materials related to their profession. Among those reading relevant books, 50 percent read only one to two books per year.

Though at the preservice level, student teachers are exposed to principles, theories, and problem-solving techniques related to issues and problems in the classroom. However, they remain only at the knowledge level. Training in the analysis, synthesis, and application of principles and theories in the solving of classroom problems is inadequate at this level owing generally to lack of time and insufficient classroom experience. Hence, the need has arisen for a well-organized in-service professional program in the educational system and for continuing self-development of teachers.

In the Malaysian context, once the trained teachers, whether from the universities or from the training colleges, are employed in the national education system, their further professional development becomes the responsibility of the Ministry of Education and the teachers themselves. This aspect of the development of teachers is handled by two divisions in the Ministry of Education, namely, the School Division and the Curriculum Development Division, by means of in-service programs in collaboration with the state education departments, teacher training colleges, and universities.

There are three types of in-service programs:

1. Enrichment programs to raise and update the level of expertise and knowledge of teachers, school administrators, and key personnel by means of full-time short courses for three to six months.

2. Familiarization programs to orient and update teachers' knowledge and competencies related to demands in the new curriculum implemented in the school system. These are generally conducted as seminars and workshops. Recently, in-house training packages have been developed to familiarize teachers with the contents and approaches introduced in the new integrated school curriculum.

3. Specialization programs to train personnel in special education such as remedial education, audiovisual education, guidance and counseling, physical and health education, and education of the handicapped. These are generally full-time one-year courses in colleges or universities.

In the Malaysian scene the bulk of the in-service programs are of the second type and help teachers effectively implement new curricula in the school system and utilize materials produced for the new curricula. This type of in-service program is usually conducted during weekends and/or during the school vacations. An elaborate network has been established throughout the country to run these programs. The programs are decentralized and conducted in school facilities. The key personnel from each state are given briefings at the national level, and they in turn run the courses at the district and school level. Recently, the head teachers have been involved in the supervision of in-service activities in their schools.

The participation of teachers in enrichment and specialization programs is very limited, however. Few establishments within the Ministry of Education structure conduct such programs. As such, these types of in-service programs are conducted only when the need arises as a result of some policy change. Only selected teachers participate in such programs. This type of situation has resulted in a belief among Malaysian teachers that going through a preservice education program trains a person to be a teacher throughout life and that there is no need for any further self-development to be proficient and innovative in the education system.

Teachers have some apathy toward professional development. If this attitude is left unchecked, it can bring about the deterioration of education quality in the country. Realizing the need for a professional development institute, the Ministry of Education set up the Ministry of Education Staff Training Institute (MESTI) which is now known as the Institute Aminuddin Baki at Genting Highland. Organized in 1979, it was especially created to update the knowledge and skill of school administrators. Since then, the role of the institution has been widened to provide courses for the professional development of teachers in general. Presently, the institute is conducting courses for the upgrading of teachers in the newly implemented, two-tier salary system. It is generally agreed that the institute's role in upgrading teachers' professional skills should be extended. In this respect the colleges and universities could also play an important role by designing and offering short courses for teachers in continuing education programs. At present the universities offer only master's programs and in-service bachelor of education programs for employed teachers.

## Issue 2: Lack of Relevant Research on Teacher Education

Teacher education in Malaysia needs the support of educational research to develop models that are relevant to its schools and culture and to meet its needs. It is estimated that 768 research studies have been carried out in the field of education (Paul, 1973). These include academic theses as well as papers and other published works and commissioned projects that constitute large-scale studies commissioned by the Ministry of Education. These studies are often carried out by teams of researchers either from the local universities or from the ministry. The kind of research needed by teacher education, however, is still lacking. Two kinds of research are needed in the area of teacher training programs. First, research must be done in the area of cognitive development of Malaysian children—how these children are learning in schools, and what their learning styles and levels of cognitive development are. Findings from these studies would be used to develop models of effective teaching for the country. The second research area is more directly related to teacher education itself. What kinds of programs are effective with Malaysian teachers?

To date, few studies have been carried out on the cognitive development of Malaysian children. A study conducted in 1988 (Unesco) estimated that 20 percent of the research carried out was focused on students, while another 16 percent dealt with curriculum and instruction. But the Southeast Asian Bibliographic and Abstracting Services, which represents one of the comprehensive listings of research in Southeast Asia, reports only one study that looked into the study of the general cognitive development of students. Although a few studies touched on cognitive levels of students as related to learning specific materials in the curriculum, they did not focus on the learning styles or processes in the classroom or the cognitive development of the students per se. Most studies of students involved personality profiles, achievement, preference, and perceptions or attitudes toward different methods of teaching, curriculum, and even textbooks. A few studies have also centered on strategies of learning such as the use of videotapes and self-instructional materials, inductive/deductive approaches in teaching, comparison of guided discovery and expository didactic methods of teaching, training in concept attainment skills, and cognitive preferences of students. Many of these studies involve perceptions rather than a study of what actually happens in the classroom, or with the students.

Because these studies are isolated and discrete in widely different subject areas and populations, they do not provide a comprehensive guide to educators for developing teacher education programs that are more suitable to the entire country. As was observed twelve years ago, these research studies have arisen from the interest of individuals rather than from the needs of institutions and educational systems for research to guide their policy and activities (Awang et al., 1978). Their singularity has resulted in fragmentation of information. Thus they do not provide complete information for effective and widespread modeling.

A bibliographic search of educational research studies listed in the Southeast Asian Bibliographic and Abstracting Services revealed that fifty studies related to teacher education have been carried out. Almost all these studies were conducted between 1970 and 1988, and they were either master's or doctoral theses. The search turned up no commissioned studies. The topics covered by these fifty studies differed widely and can be broadly divided into five areas of concern: studies of teacher education programs (19), characteristics of teachers (13), specific methods of training teachers (6), assessment of abilities or proficiency in specific areas of student teachers (3), and research concerning teacher training institutions such as its administration, role, or policies on teacher education (9). The nineteen studies concerning teacher education programs are mainly curriculum studies that involve analysis of curriculum content, development of curriculum, or comparative studies of the programs. Seven of the studies are concerned with teachers or student teachers' perceptions of the training programs they have gone through. These studies mostly use the survey questionnaire as a means of obtaining teachers' or student teachers' perceptions. Another popular area of study is teacher characteristics which includes teacher profiles, job satisfaction, and attitudes. The thirteen studies in this area are wide ranging. Some studies compare personality patterns of student teachers in training colleges and the university and the characteristics of effective experienced teachers or student teachers. Thus, although these studies can be grouped broadly into five categories, a wide range of topics are covered and they are again fragmentary. They may provide limited and an ad hoc kind of improvement in the individual teacher education programs, but the knowledge they impart is not comprehensive enough to effect major changes or development in teacher education. In addition, the studies in both areas are self-contained research in that they are not part of a larger program or thrust of research in a local institution. Furthermore, the sample size of these studies is usually too small to make their finding generalizable. Lacking in the area of teacher education are studies on identifying models for effective teaching. Support for such studies is needed even at the expense of research in the more basic areas of student learning.

Of the fifty studies on teacher education, half were studies carried out to satisfy the degree requirements of foreign universities. In total, about 87 percent of the doctoral and 23 percent of the master's studies were carried out to satisfy foreign degree requirements. From these studies Avalos and Haddad (1981) concluded that research problems and findings have been imported from the Western countries to the local scene. The studies carried out as degree requirements for local universities seem to reflect studies carried out in foreign universities. There is a need to investigate the extent to which research findings generated elsewhere are valid in the local culture and environment. How do Malaysian students learn? How are teachers coping?

How are Malaysian students and teachers meeting educational aims? This question remains unanswered. Little is known through research of what happens in the Malaysian classroom. Only an estimated three studies have actually involved classroom observation rather than the use of questionnaires or tests. Without such first-hand knowledge, it is difficult to envisage what is needed for a teacher education program. Recent attempts have been made to study the implementation of the new primary school curriculum, but much still needs to be done. One of the main purposes of these studies is to provide training in research procedures for the doctoral candidate. At the moment, they account for most of the research that is carried out in the country. Thus, they could be used both to train new researchers and to meet the larger need of generating Malaysian-developed teacher education models to satisfy local needs. What is needed is the identification of Malaysian research priorities and the encouragement of both local researchers and those satisfying foreign degree requirements to work in these areas.

### Issue 3: The Declining Status of Teachers

Many different aspects make up a profession's status in the community, such as income, quality of training, and qualifications, as well as the expectations of the public. In 1982 the Ministry of Education surveyed the public's perceptions of teachers. The survey was conducted in conjunction with a workshop on developing a philosophy of teacher education in Malaysia. The survey sample consisted of 1,348 people drawn from leaders, various occupational groups, parents, school personnel, students, and youths. Two kinds of perceptions were asked: what they perceived to be the actual situation, and what they thought should be the ideal situation.

The population was asked a direct question on the status or social prestige of being a teacher. When asked how much social status/prestige teachers have, 55 percent of the sample thought that the status of primary school teachers was "average," whereas 71 percent thought ideally it should be "high." In the case of secondary school teachers, 37 percent believed that the status was "average," while, ideally, 82 percent said that it should be above average and high. In terms of *income*, 48 percent of respondents felt that teachers' income was only average, but 59 percent of respondents felt that it should be high. Considering teachers as *models of proper behavior*, 60 percent and 52 percent of the sample thought that teachers at primary and secondary schools, respectively, were "very much" the models of proper behavior, while 84 and 85 percent, respectively, of the sample felt that teachers ideally should be the models of proper behavior. In terms of teacher preparation, 61 and 62 percent of the sample thought that primary and secondary school teachers were adequately prepared, but 34 and 33 percent thought that teachers in these two levels were not adequately prepared. Finally, when asked to select five professions that were most important to society, teachers of all three levels were ranked second, behind only doctors.

Clearly, income, which is often related to the prestige of a profession, does not account for this high ranking. It is expected that teaching, which is part of the civil service in Malaysia, cannot command incomes that will match those of the private commercial sector. Undoubtedly, the social standing, moral aspects, and professionalism of teachers, especially in their preparation, explain the status of teachers. The results of the survey showed that teachers' status with the general public is not as high as it could be.

With regard to professionalism, teacher status has not fared well. Some do not consider teaching a profession. First, in Malaysia teaching is often regarded as "only a half-day job" because school facilities are used for different students in morning or afternoon sessions. Teaching is often viewed as an occupation and not a career. In fact, there is a saying, "if you want work of fairly good renumeration and yet have time to spend with your family, go into teaching." The implication is that the job is neither mentally nor time demanding. Many women enter teaching. At the undergraduate level, in teacher education courses, women consistently outnumber men. A 1986 Ministry of Education survey revealed that at the primary school level, women teachers outnumbered men by 50,529 to 47,532. At the secondary level, however, the numbers favored the men, but by only a small margin—29,834 men to 28,389 women. In the case of untrained teachers, women outnumbered men two to one for both primary and secondary levels. Teaching is the only profession in Malaysia that has almost equal numbers of men and women.

Among professional people, teaching is not generally viewed as a profession, the chief reason being that anyone with content qualifications is viewed as qualified to teach, albeit as a temporary teacher. This is practiced in the schools as a stopgap measure. Figures available for 1986 showed that untrained teachers make up 15 percent of primary school teachers. In secondary schools the problem is negligible, for only 3 percent of the teachers are not trained. But the problem is not merely one of trained and untrained teachers. In a recent study, it was found that 45, 43, and 28 percent of those who taught the national language, science, and geography, respectively, were not specialized in these subject matter areas. However, some teachers of chemistry, Malay literature, and biology also were not teaching in their areas of specialization (Paul, 1973). Thus, there is the problem of matching the training of teachers to the subjects they are teaching. One aspect that has contributed to teaching as a respected occupation, if not profession, has been that the teacher is the one who has knowledge of the subject matter. The mismatch of teachers and subjects weakens this perception of teachers.

Recently, this professional aspect of teaching was further damaged by the creation of a new category of teachers. Graduates in other fields with a good command of English had been given a nine-month course in the teaching of English and had been posted as English teachers to schools. These teachers have degrees in such fields as engineering, accounting, and the social sciences. The ability to produce proficient English teachers from this category has been seriously questioned (*New Strait Times*, July 10, 1990). The teachers are placed in the graduate teacher category as permanent staff. Thus, another category of teachers has been created—those having knowledge of specific subject matter but lacking general professional training. Such actions again raise the question of who is qualified to teach, and they certainly tarnish the professionalism of the teaching profession.

The changing role of the school and teachers since the nation gained independence has contributed greatly to the declining status of teachers. In the early days of the education system, the perceived role of the school had been considered vocational and utilitarian and not concerned with promoting a genuine culture (Wong and Ee, 1971). Transmission of values and codes of conduct has been the responsibility of the extended family. Today, schools are expected to inculcate values and conduct in addition to fulfilling their vocational responsibilities. They are trying hard, but they are poor substitutes for the extended family. Teachers, who have essentially received no training for such roles, find it hard to meet expectations. The rapid expansion of the school system since independence and the extension of free schooling to nine years have produced an explosive demand for teachers. This has resulted in many stopgap measures, and naturally a greater intake means that the system is less selective.

Nonetheless, the Ministry of Education has taken several encouraging steps aimed at improving the standard of teaching in schools. The trend is toward having only university graduate teachers in all secondary schools. Only non-graduate teachers can teach in the primary schools. In addition, the ministry has sponsored a large number of in-service teachers in obtaining bachelor's and master's degrees in education, with the aim of improving teaching standards. But the issue of *control* of who enters the profession remains a problem and critically affects the status of professionalism.

## CONCLUSION

Teachers and teacher educators in the present-day Malaysian context are facing many challenges. Society may be asking the schools to undertake goals they cannot achieve. A serious issue to be resolved is what schools can reasonably accomplish and how this can be made the subject of professional responsibility.

Two possible directions of development should be an increased effort in the research area and in the designing of appropriate in-service programs. These two areas represent the means by which the quality of teaching can be improved substantially. With respect to in-service programs, courses have to be designed to help teachers benefit from their experiences in the classroom rather than programs whose content is exclusively focused on new curriculum content and general approaches. In the area of research, Malaysian models of effective and continuous teacher preparation must be developed, firmly based on the variables involved in teaching the Malaysian child.

Teacher status is a problem that cannot be directly solved. It has many facets. But the teacher's proficiency and effectiveness in the classroom based on Malaysian-tested and -designed models of teaching and teacher education are two elements directly tied to enhanced professionalism.

## REFERENCES

Avalos, B. and W. Haddad. *A Review of Teacher Effectiveness Research in Africa, India, Latin America, Middle East, Malaysia, Philippines, and Thailand: Synthesis of Results*. Ottawa: International Development Research Council, TS23s, 1981.

Awang, Had Salleh, et al. *A Critical Review of Research in Malaysia on Effectiveness of Teachers*. Kuala Lumpur: University of Malaya, 1978.

Ball, Stephen J., and Ivor F. Goodson, eds. *Teachers' Lives and Careers*. London: Falmer Press, 1985.

Gopinathan, S., and H. D. Nielsen. *Educational Research Environments in Southeast Asia*. Singapore: Chopmen Publishers, 1988.

Maznah, Ismail, et al. "The Relationship Between Teacher Qualities and Teacher Effectiveness." Unpublished report, Ministry of Education, Malaysia, 1989.

Ministry of Education. *Educational Statistics of Malaysia 1986*. Kuala Lumpur: Educational Planning and Research Division, Ministry of Education, 1986.

Ministry of Education. *The Philosophy of Teacher Education in Malaysia: Report of the National Workshop and Survey*. Kuala Lumpur: Teacher Education Division, Ministry of Education, Malaysia, 1982.

Paul, Chang. *Educational Development in a Plural Society*. Singapore: Academic Publications, 1973.

Unesco. *Professional Development of Educational Personnel*. Bangkok: Unesco, 1985.

Wong, F.H.K., and T. H. Ee. *Education in Malaysia*. Kuala Lumpur: Heinemann, 1971.

# 13

# NIGERIA

## OLUSOLA AVOSEH

Nigeria has been independent for about thirty years, but the teething problems of growth are very much in evidence. Political instability, economic underdevelopment, and social inequities die hard. These are some of the side effects of the colonial experience, which was the attempt to evolve a nation-state from the diverse ethnic groups that were at various stages of political and economic development before colonialism. However, the general argument attributing the establishment of larger political units out of previously separate groups and communities to colonialism has been called into question. This process had gone on in the past, as evidenced by the Old Oyo Kingdom to the south and the Fulani Emirate to the north. The colonial experience should be regarded as a catalyst speeding up the process rather than as a cause of the process.

The most important fundamental change was the emergence of three economic subsectors: modern, transitional, and traditional. The modern sector makes a demand on high-level school-produced skills, whereas the transitional subsector is characterized by small-scale business and industries, and self-employment. The traditional sector is rural-based and characterized mainly by a subsistence economy. This economic situation, it was argued, was the consequence of colonialism which brought the Third World countries into the capitalistic economic system as a satellite, supplying raw materials for the British (and now largely Western) industries while consuming its finished products.

Since obtaining independence in 1960, the state has undergone some changes in order to modify the colonial character of most activities. At first, the state gradually assumed control of these activities, but currently the private sector is taking greater precedence because it can better organize some activities. Even when the state has shed many of its activities, it is discovered that the state's responsibilities have not significantly diminished. Public servants and private entrepreneurs are demanding education that will make them more specialized and professionalized in their various fields.

Thus, the long-standing belief in the role of education in mediating change by providing the knowledge, skills, and attitudes relevant in the changing circumstances has been reinforced. It is thought that teachers, if properly prepared, hold the key to the solution of development problems. This belief has influenced the attention given to teacher education in Nigeria since the government published the report of the task force set up to study postsecondary and higher education (Federal Ministry of Education, 1960).

The term *teacher education* as used in this chapter denotes strategies for teacher preparation which may be undertaken in institutions established for such a purpose as well as for noncollege-based preparations for upgrading unqualified and underqualified teachers. This broad approach is a product of the evolution of teacher education in Nigeria and the rapid expansion of education at all levels. The demands made for a large supply of qualified teachers necessitated the adoption of alternative strategies to allow teacher education to keep pace with the school population explosion as well as to meet the objectives of public policies.

Public policies are informed by political, economic, and social conditions. They give rise to structural changes and curricular innovations and thus constitute the framework within which teacher education issues can be discussed. In this Nigerian country study, a number of teacher education issues and problems have become important over time.

1. How to streamline all preservice and in-service teacher education programs.

2. How to increase the professional status of teaching through the establishment of a teachers' council.

3. How to attract abler students by raising the level of difficulty of teacher education programs.

4. How to meet the special needs of schools by providing an optimal mix of teacher education programs.

5. How to reduce teacher education costs by adopting alternative teacher preparation strategies such as long-distance teaching.

6. How to prepare teachers to write their own textbooks and produce their own instructional materials.

Before discussing these issues and problems, we will examine certain characteristics of the Nigerian society, specifically, the social context within which teacher education evolved; the relationship of school reform to teacher education; and the organizational arrangements for formulating and implementing teacher education policies.

## GENERAL BACKGROUND

In the not too distant past, Nigeria was often referred to as a *geographical expression*. This phrase was used to summarize the fundamental differences of culture and social organization among the various groups, each with its own language or dialect and at various levels of development, before the present boundaries were drawn. Different parts were brought under colonial rule at different times. For example, while Lagos and the coastal area were administered as part of Gold Coast (now Ghana), the Niger Delta area was administered by the Royal Niger Company, a firm granted a charter for that purpose by the British government. The conquest of the north was well underway. It was only in 1914 that Nigeria became an entity as a result of the amalgamation of northern and southern Nigeria brought about by Lord Lugard.

Most of the coastal regions around Lagos (on the littoral), Warri, Port Harcourt, and Calabar, spread across the Niger Delta, have had considerable contact with trading firms. Thus, they have had some exposure to European customs and patterns of behavior.

In 1842 British missionaries arrived, entering through Badagry, on the coast and west of Lagos. They came in small numbers and represented different denominations, principally the Church Missionary Society and the Wesleyan Society (Methodist). Their journey to the hinterland was delayed because of the war between the Egba and the Dahomey peoples. The Egba people had their capital in Abeokuta, a city about 60 miles north of Lagos, whereas the Dahomeans came from an area that is now the modern Republic of Benin. This delay led to the use of Badagry as a transit camp, and in 1845 the first elementary school referred to as "the nursery of the infant church" was established. Later the Church Missionary Society missionaries built schools in Lagos, Abeokuta, and Ibadan.

Because of the small number of missionaries, the difficulty of the African terrain, and the problem of safety, missionary effort was restricted to the coastal areas and a few miles inland from the coast. It is noteworthy that missionary activities were given a boost by the African members, particularly Samuel Ajayi Crowther, the slave boy who later became a bishop. He was taken into slavery from a Yoruba town, Oshogun. His effort in translating the Bible into Yoruba, one of the three main Nigerian Languages, remains one of the outstanding efforts of the missionaries at that time since new converts could be taught to read the Bible in their own language.

The main purpose of missionary activities was to evangelize; consequently, missionary schools were established to fulfill limited objectives. Resources were inadequate to provide educational services to an increasingly large area brought under British rule. Besides, the small number of missionary volunteers made it compelling that Nigerians be trained to assist in the effort to bring the people to a level of literacy that would facilitate their ability to read the Bible.

## THE SYSTEM OF TEACHER EDUCATION

When missionary schools were established, no formal training was given to teachers. Most of those employed to teach received informal instructions in the missionaries' homes. Candidates were selected for the promise they showed as leaders, for their intelligence, and for the zeal with which they embraced the word of God. Since they were expected to serve both as catechists and teachers, moral training and the ability to preach and evangelize were emphasized. After 1880 when government grants were made to voluntary agencies and teachers were expected to sit for examinations under a West Coast inspectorate, these teacher-catechists were found inadequate in pedagogical skills. Many teachers managed eventually to meet professional standards largely by self-effort, that is, through self-learning.

Toward the end of the nineteenth century, missionary bodies began to make pioneering efforts in formal teacher education, mainly in their areas of missionary activities. These efforts were directed at the education of primary school teachers.

The approach to the preparation of preservice teachers was haphazard. Different types of programs were initiated in response to needs as they arose. There was no well-formulated teacher education policy. During the first half of the twentieth century there was a proliferation of teacher training colleges under private or parochial proprietorship referred to as voluntary agencies. As the school system expanded, the demand for teachers was met by creating a four-year and, much later, a two-year program. The two-year program served as a halfway house in the training program of elementary school teachers. This was the way teacher education evolved in Nigeria (see Table 1).

Table 1 illustrates the variety of programs available for the preparation of primary school teachers, which may have accounted for the confusion in teacher education for this category of teachers. The designations of the certificates for the first three grades of teachers have been changing over the years. The Grade III teachers' certificate was first awarded as the elementary teachers' certificate, whereas the Grade II teachers' certificate was first designated as the higher elementary teachers' certificate. The Grade IIA teachers were designated as pivotal teachers perhaps because they could teach either in the primary or lower secondary schools. The teacher training colleges that offer these programs are being phased out. The last category on the table, the Nigeria certificate of education, will eventually become the minimum qualification for entry into teaching.

Despite the establishment of a secondary school in Lagos by the Church Missionary Society as early as 1895, there was no institution for the preparation of secondary school teachers until 1934. In that year, Yaba Higher College in Lagos was established to produce middle-level professionals—doctors, pharmacists, surveyors, and science teachers.

A large number of secondary school teachers in this early period were those who had received training as primary school teachers but had studied hard for

**Table 1**
**Teacher Training Patterns in Nigeria for Primary Schools**

| Grade | Primary Schooling (Years) | Secondary Schooling (Years) | Teacher Education (Years) | Total in Years | Remarks |
|---|---|---|---|---|---|
| III | 8 | – | 2 | 10 | This category has now been phased out. |
| II | 8 | – | 4 | 12 | |
| | 6 | – | 5 | 11 | Now phased out. |
| | 6 | 3 | 3 | 12 | |
| | 6 | 5 | 2 | 13 | For unsuccessful Secondary School Graduates. |
| | 6 | 5 | 1 | 12 | For Successful Secondary School Graduates. |
| IIA | 8 | 6 | 2 | 16 | Special Grade II Teachers can teach at the lower level of Sunday School. |
| Associate-ship Cert-ficate in Education (A.C.E.) | 8(6) | – | 5 | 13 | The last year of teacher education is spent in the University as in-service training after a minimum of five years' experience. |
| Nigeria Certificate in Education (Primary Education Specializa-tion) | 6 | 5 | 3 | 14 | The 3 years of teacher education is spent in a College of Education. |

university admission in Britain or Sierra Leone. It was here that for a long time since 1876 the only university in West Africa had been established. Before 1960, there were few secondary schools; many teachers obtained university degrees without a high school education by dint of hard work, after training for primary school teaching. Such teachers, after obtaining bachelors' degrees, were employed to teach in the secondary school. However, when the first university in Nigeria was founded in Ibadan as a college affiliated with the University of London and awarding the external degrees of the London institution, a one-year post-graduate diploma program was mounted to give one-year professional training to university graduates. Correspondingly, a two-year associateship diploma in education program was devised for nondegree holders as a two-year postsecondary school or post–teachers' Grade II qualification. In addition to a high school or teachers' college qualification, applicants were required to obtain two advanced-level pass of the London University general certificate in education.

During the early postindependence years and as a consequence of the implementation of the recommendations of the Task Force on Education (Federal Ministry of Education, 1960), a three-year college of education emerged for the preparation of teachers for the junior secondary school. Similarly, faculties of education were established to prepare teachers for the senior secondary school by offering combined honors degrees in education and one or two teaching subjects. At this stage it is important to examine how these changes are related to what schools do.

## School Reforms and Teacher Education

Reforms in teacher education often arise from conditions of schooling that are the consequences of social, economic, and political needs, which in turn influence educational policies. Public statements in Nigeria often point to a direct linkage between the development of society and economic growth, which, viewed from the perspective of educational planning, is seen in quantitative terms.

In Nigeria's thirty years of independence, the expansion of education at all levels has been impressive. In 1960 3 million pupils were in all-primary schools, but by 1975 primary school enrollment had exceeded 6 million and by 1985 it had reached 15 million.

The secondary school enrollment growth was no less impressive—from a paltry 135,400 students in all the country's secondary schools in 1960 to about 400,000 in 1975 and 3 million in 1985. Statistics show, however, that the growth in school population has not been matched by the growth in teacher supply. Hence, one of the cardinal objectives of teacher education would be to meet this need. The growth in school enrollment is a consequence of the policy of universal primary education implemented in 1976 and the "Free-Education-at-All-Levels" policy implemented by the civilian administrations of five southwestern states from 1980 to 1984.

The National Policy on Education of 1977 (revised in 1981) set out the goals of educational reforms. These were derived from the goals set in development plans, namely, the creation of a new society that is egalitarian, democratic, and characterized by full opportunities. The document prescribes structural changes and curricular reforms that would help the Nigerians attain the society they want.

The curricular reform adopted in the Nigerian National Policy on Education emphasizes the sciences, Nigerian languages, and technical and vocational subjects. The policy is to change the orientation of the school clientele from theoretical to practical subjects, inculcate the dignity of labor, and discourage interest in white-collar jobs only.

These changes—quantitative, structural, and curricular—have tremendous implications for teacher education. For example, the six-year secondary school that has replaced the five-year type makes a greater demand on the secondary school teacher than ever before. The objective of primary education has been expanded.

It is not enough to inculcate literacy and numeracy but also to lay a sound basis for scientific and reflective thinking. Thus, teachers need an intellectual and professional background that will make them cope with the demands that these reforms make on them.

## Organizational Arrangement for the Formulation and Implementation of Teacher Education Policies

The inherited laissez-faire approach of the colonial administration to teacher education disappeared in the 1970s when the state governments and the federal government assumed responsibility for education at all levels, except pre-primary. By the mid–1960s, three colleges of education (initially styled advanced teachers' colleges) were put in place: one each in eastern, western, and northern Nigeria and established in Lagos by 1973. In 1977 there were seven such colleges, but in 1990 the number had increased to fifty-three. The principal task of the colleges is to develop high standard teacher education programs in middle-level colleges although the federal government has now approved seven of these colleges to develop programs up to the degree level. There are also specialized colleges of education which offer either only technical and business education or special education programs. The latter prepare teachers of the handicapped and the gifted children.

A National Curriculum Conference held in 1969 (Adarelegbe, 1969) recognized that the quality of the education system depended on the quality and adequacy of its teachers; there was a need to improve the teacher's quality of life; there was a need to eliminate the confusion in teacher education; and changes in teacher education could not ignore conditions or problems of schooling that were consequences of public policies.

The report of this conference formed the basis of the first National Policy on Education published in 1977 with a section devoted to teacher education. Ideas about teacher education were crystallized, and the main objectives of teacher education were identified: (1) to produce highly motivated, conscientious, and efficient classroom teachers for all levels of the educational system; (2) to encourage the spirit of inquiry and creativity in teachers; (3) to help teachers fit into the social life of the community and society at large and to enhance their commitment to national objectives; and (4) to enhance teachers' commitment to the teaching profession.

The federal government has set up committees for initiating, formulating, and implementing policies on teacher education. An example is the Joint Consultative Committee on Education which recommends policies on all aspects of education. The committee discusses proposals from subcommittees and makes recommendations to the National Council on Education, which is the highest national policymaking body on education. It is presided over by the minister of education, and the states are represented by their commissioners for education who are usually accompanied by a strong team of officials.

In 1989 the federal government set up the National Commission for Colleges of Education (NCCE) for the purpose of accrediting teacher education programs and monitoring standards in colleges of education. The NCCE has taken steps to establish national minimum standards and has concluded arrangements for visiting colleges of education for the purpose of accrediting their programs. Since there are no private colleges of education, it is expected that public funds will be allocated to upgrade the facilities in these colleges in ways that are unprecedented. This is already happening in universities through the accreditation programs of the National Universities Commission.

## ISSUES AND PROBLEMS

### Issue 1: How to Streamline All Preservice and In-service Teacher Education Programs

The analysis of the evolution of teacher education programs revealed that different kinds of programs were developed to meet specific needs. Some were short-term solutions such as the two-year elementary teachers' certificate program for the lower elementary school and a two-year associateship diploma in education offered at the university for serving teachers who have passed two teaching subjects at the advanced level of the general certificate of education. There was also a wide range of admission requirements for primary school teachers. Such measures have brought into teaching several categories of qualified and underqualified teachers and have adversely affected the image of the teaching profession. The streamlining of teacher education programs especially at nonuniversity institutions will presumably reduce the number of categories of teachers. This will make the monitoring of standards less cumbersome.

This issue also touches on the disparity between the status of the primary school teachers vis-à-vis that of the secondary school teachers. The proliferation of the short-term teacher education programs has affected primary school teachers more than their counterparts in the secondary school. Whereas secondary school teachers are expected to be university or college of education graduates, primary school teachers are almost never college graduates. The lower status of primary school teachers is reinforced by the variety of low entry qualifications accepted for their training programs. They also receive an inferior education. Thus characterized by inferior education, primary school teachers are paid lower salaries and have lower prestige in the community than secondary school teachers. Primary school teaching is generally looked on as a dead end. This situation creates a social and academic distance between primary and secondary school teachers on the one hand and teachers generally and their counterparts in other subsectors of the economy on the other.

By the end of 1988 the federal government had put in place a National Primary Education Commission to coordinate primary education activities throughout the country. The states have correspondingly set up primary school management boards with responsibilities for the administration and supervision of primary education within each state. This arrangement ensured that primary schools were adequately staffed, that teachers' salaries were regularly paid, and that adequate facilities were provided. The long-run result should be a high standard of primary education. Nigerians were dismayed when the federal government promulgated a decree that abolished this institutional arrangement, which offered hope for a qualitative primary education. The new decree transfers responsibilities for primary education to the local governments. The statutory financial allocation to local governments will be paid directly to them by the federal government. Since the changes have just been made, it would be presumptive to assess the success of the dominance of local government in primary education matters.

As a followup to the implementation of the primary education improvement program, each college of education is expected to establish a school of primary education studies as an academic/professional unit. The National Commission for Colleges of Education has set up a committee of experts to harmonize all programs on primary education studies. Simultaneously with this development is the gradual but steady phasing out of Grade II teachers' colleges. Thus, it is expected that within the decade of the 1990s the minimum qualification for entry into teaching at any level of the education system will be the Nigeria certificate in education (NCE).

## Issue 2: How to Increase the Professional Status of Teaching

Closely associated with the issue discussed above is that of a coordinating body for teacher education and teachers' matters generally. Examples of the legal, medical, and engineering professions, to mention a few, keep the discussion of this issue alive. It is generally assumed that setting up a National Teachers' Council will enhance the improvement in the quality of teacher education and the condition of service for teachers. This is also assumed to be a step in the process of professionalizing teaching in Nigeria. The council will, among other things, be responsible for the accreditation of all teaching programs, thus ensuring that minimum standards are attained, maintained, and improved upon.

If teacher education is henceforth offered only at the colleges of education and the universities whose coordinating bodies (National Commission for Colleges of Education and National Universities Commission, respectively) are autonomous, the National Teachers' Council will provide a point of articulation for teacher education at both levels.

Another role for the council is the registration of teachers and the initiation of policies on teacher education. Registration of teachers by a superordinate body will ensure that those entering into teaching are well prepared for their jobs. It is recognized that a Teachers' Council may not eliminate unqualified teachers completely from the school system unless the economy improves substantially. However, it will mean that unqualified staff will not be registered as teachers unless they obtain the minimum entry qualification into the profession. There is

a law that requires that minimum standards be established for every level of
education. In teacher education, the National Commission for Colleges of Education and the National Universities Commission have established what these
standards should be for the preparation of nongraduate and graduate teachers,
respectively. The minimum standards relate to (1) the total credit hours required
for graduation; (2) the compulsory courses that must be offered; (3) the ratio of
academic to professional courses that must be offered; and (4) the quality of
teachers that must teach these courses in terms of their qualifications and years
of experience.

The minimum standards constitute the bottom line below which no program
of teacher education must sink and above which every program should rise.
Every tertiary institution is subject to visits by appropriate accreditation panels
for the purpose of monitoring academic and professional standards. Graduates
from any teacher education program so accredited will be eligible for registration.
Although accreditation procedures have begun, the Teachers' Council has not
yet been established, so this issue remains unsolved. This issue is receiving the
attention of the federal government authorities.

### Issue 3: How to Attract Abler Students

Teacher education has not enjoyed parity of esteem with programs that lead
to other professions, such as law, medicine, engineering, and accountancy.
Colleges of education admission requirements are not as rigorous as those of the
university and the polytechnics. Even in universities where minimum admission
requirements are the same across faculties, the faculty of education attracts
undergraduates in the lowest 10 percent or, at best, bright students who have
failed to secure admission into other faculties. Such students have no commitment
to teaching when they finish their program.

In a more recent reform of university curricula, the years of university education leading to the professions have been increased by one year. For engineering
and law programs, an undergraduate will spend five years instead of four, whereas
medical students will spend six years instead of five. But the years of university
education have not been increased for teacher education. Apart from agriculture,
education is the largest industry in the country to date. The future of the nation's
children and the level of social development depend in part on what schools do.
It is believed that teacher education should attract the best brains available. In
some colleges, one-year remedial programs are offered to weak students in
subjects such as French, the sciences, and mathematics, to correct their deficiencies and so improve admission intake into those courses.

Teacher education has not attracted students of high ability because of the
low esteem teaching has among other professions. This observation is validated
by a survey carried out at the Lagos State University where 50 percent from a
sample of one thousand students of education sought admission into the faculty

of education because they were rejected by their preferred faculties, while 36 percent did not want to go into teaching after the completion of their programs.

There are two possibilities for improving this situation: one concerns changing the image of teaching, and the other is the possibility of establishing a pedagogic university for the education industry.

The whole business of training the personnel required in the education industry which has been known to absorb as much as 40 to 50 percent of public revenue is in need of revitalization. About 90 percent of public recurrent revenue for education goes to pay teachers' salaries and allowances. However, teachers compare their salaries and conditions of service with those of their counterparts in other sectors of the economy. With the education industry expanding very rapidly, federal and state governments are hard put to pay salaries and provide conditions comparable with what obtains in the private sector. Thus, schools lose their qualified staff to these other employment agencies, while vacancies are filled by unqualified and underqualified staff. This situation can be improved at the preservice stage by paying bursaries or special grants to students of education to assist them to provide books, clothing, food, and accommodation while they are in college or university. These trainees can be made to enter into bonds to teach for three to five years. This was part of teacher education policy in the 1970s. Funds were even provided to assist students while in practice teaching and to take care of their transport and teaching material expenses. The implementation of this policy made teaching attractive to young high school graduates.

The idea of a pedagogic university is not new in West Africa. The Nkruma government in Ghana established one at Cape Coast with a great benefit to the teaching profession in that country. In Nigeria, the need to generate the personnel required for development has moved the federal government to establish specialized universities, for example, the University of Agriculture and the University of Technology. But it is believed that the urgency with which this task is carried out depends on the vision with which the pedagogic universities tackle their task of training teachers for all the institutions responsible for preparing specialized personnel in agriculture, industry, law, and medicine. When the contribution of teacher education is conceived of and made functional at the tertiary level, teacher education can then be seen as very important and desirable at all levels of education. Teacher education for future school teachers could then acquire an unprecedented prestige and esteem that could make it attractive to high ability students.

### Issue 4: How to Meet the Special Needs of Schools

While the implementation of a strategy for accreditation may raise the standard of teacher education and, by implication, enhance the quality of the Nigerian teacher, there has also been a recognition of a need to improve the quality of the teacher education program. This improvement will not only affect the content of the subjects offered but also design an optimal mix of teacher training modes. This can be approached from either of two points of view: (1) striking an appropriate balance between imparting knowledge of specific subject matter, the professional components, and enrichment subjects such as music, fine arts, sports, and games; or (2) striking an appropriate balance between full-time and part-time teacher education programs through vacation courses or long-distance learning.

The first point of view concerns the proportion of teacher education time devoted to learning academic subjects vis-à-vis professional training and teaching practice or internship. As a result of expanding opportunities, most of those who enroll in teacher education programs are very young high school graduates. When they complete their programs, they are so new to their task in the classroom that they have to learn to swim in a sea to which they are not accustomed, receiving guidance from head teachers in areas where the teachers' own knowledge is severely limited. The time spent on the mastery of contents and on teaching practice is not well balanced to expose preservice teachers to models of effective teaching. This fact was sufficient motivation to carry out a national survey of modes of teacher preparation in the colleges of education (Avoseh, 1978). Three types were found: a general model; Alvan Ikoku College of Education, the Owerri model; and Federal College of Education, the Abeokuta model.

Most institutions have adopted the general model, which emphasizes the teaching of contents (general as well as specialized), professional courses (theories of education), and practice teaching in the ratio of 60:35:5. Teacher educators generally believe that this exposure is inadequate and that the program can be improved by spending four years on cognate and professional courses and an additional year for internship with very close supervision and guidance.

The second model originated from Alvan Ikoku College of Education, Owerri—one of the pioneer colleges in the preparation of middle-level teachers. This model has three distinct phases: the foundation, laboratory, and practicum. The foundation phase is characterized by the mastery of bodies of theoretical and professional knowledge. The laboratory phase is concerned with mastering instructional and interpersonal competencies under simulated classroom conditions. During this phase complex skills are identified and practiced under specified conditions. Advancements in technological devices for recording and reproducing behavior enable preservice teachers to observe and analyze their performance of a particular skill as it is played back. The practicum phase permits the demonstration of mastery of instructional, noninstructional, and interpersonal competencies under supervised actual classroom conditions.

The third model, the Abeokuta model, has emerged as a result of many years of experiments that enable prospective teachers to intervene meaningfully in the intellectual, emotional, and physical development of students. Its initial phase was characterized by providing real practical experience along with mastering theoretical knowledge. For example, home economics students have the experience of immediate practice by working in rotation in the catering department of the college. Practice teaching is organized in such a manner that preservice teachers spend a term in areas where there are shortages of teachers so that the third-year students are replaced in schools by the second-year students in the second term and the second-year students by the first-year students (freshmen) in the third term. Each cohort goes to schools for practice for two terms during the three-year program. The third stage of the development of the model is marked by two characteristics: the use of students from northern and eastern Nigeria to teach the Hausa and Igbo languages, respectively. It is compulsory that a child learn and attain functional competence in the mother tongue and other languages selected from Hausa, Igbo, and Yoruba in the senior secondary school. The implementation of this aspect of the National Policy on Education is fraught with many problems, one of which is the scarcity of teachers in the Nigerian languages.

The second part of this phase is concerned with the production of teaching materials in the three Nigerian languages. The pioneering effort of Professor A. B. Fafunwa and his associates at the University of Ife (now Obafemi Awolowo University) from 1970 to 1978 remains the most outstanding contribution which provides a model for training teachers in the Nigerian languages. Their newly published work (Fafunwa, 1989) reports the success of their experiment of teaching all subjects through the use of the mother tongue. Considering all the different facets of the Abeokuta model, many educators believe that this comprehensive approach is best for less developed countries.

Currently, teacher training institutions practice a combination of these training models. The accreditation requirements stipulate that every college or faculty of education should have an educational technology center. This has made it possible to incorporate some aspect of the laboratory phase into the teacher education program. Experience about the writing of textbooks and instructional materials is being shared through the organization of writers' workshops. This activity is elaborated on below.

## Issue 5: How to Reduce Teacher Education Costs

This next issue is concerned with how to make education meet the current and future demands of the society at minimum cost. On the one hand, the explosion in the school population has increased the participation of children from different socioeconomic groups. On the other, there is a downturn in the economy, resulting in the dwindling of budgetary allocation to teacher education. This development demands improvement in the organization, content, and methods of teacher education and has been embarked on to reduce the financial burden of federal and state governments. It is characterized by teacher education through distance learning, referred to as the Nigeria certificate in education by correspondence; and the Teachers In-Service Education Program (TISEP), or Teachers' Vacation Course.

The objective of these programs as alternatives to full-time residential programs in the universities and colleges of education is to organize teacher education as a continuous and coordinated process that begins with a low-level teacher preparation but continues throughout the teachers' professional career (Robinson, 1985). In many cases, these teachers upgrade themselves from a teachers' Grade II level to the NCE and bachelor's degree levels. This long process of upgrading underqualified teachers has the advantage of ensuring the commitment of graduates of the scheme to teaching in a situation where many capable teachers use teaching as a stepping stone to more lucrative professions.

Another objective is to make the beneficiaries of the teacher education program share the cost of their training with the government. In Nigeria there is a high level of unemployment of secondary school leavers and university graduates. Preservice college/university trained teachers are not certain about employment after graduation. Thus, it is of immense benefit for underqualified teachers to upgrade their competence and qualification on the job and so be assured of retaining their jobs. A benefit to their pupils is that, since correspondence and TISEP students are on the job, the knowledge gained on the program is immediately applied to classroom activities.

The strategy of upgrading teachers is directed at primary school teachers who entered teaching after ten years of education and are referred to as Grade II teachers (see Table 1). They are upgraded through a one-year university program for the associateship certificate in education. This course was first introduced by the University of Ibadan, Institute of Education. Centers were established in six out of the twenty-one states of the federation.

The teachers admitted to the course must have had at least five years of postqualification teaching experience and must have passed the Grade II teachers' certificate. While in the course, they are required to register for a minimum of twenty-one and not more than thirty units, including practice teaching and individual projects. The syllabus has been carefully written for all the subjects to ensure that the contents are suitable and challenging to experienced primary school teachers. A textbook writers' workshop has been organized for preparing small books suitable for each content area which make the course easier. These reading materials are intended not to limit the reading activities of students but to raise questions and give direction for reading more extended materials. The center in each state is located in an affiliated college of the University of Ibadan, Institute of Education, whose academic staff teaches the course on a part-time basis. In 1979 and 1980 more than two thousand primary school teachers graduated from the course. Successful graduates earn promotion to the next salary grade, and the more ambitious ones seek admission to colleges of education.

This example from the University of Ibadan is no longer the only one of its kind. More recently, the National Teachers' Institute, a federal government institution, has developed a five-year program for upgrading primary school teachers based on the University of Ibadan model (Osibodu, 1984, pp. 294–300).

The part-time, long-distance learning or correspondence program varies from state to state, but basically it is not a preservice program. It enrolls several types of teachers. Unqualified teachers enroll who have been employed to teach in the primary school because of a teacher shortage stemming from the introduction of universal primary education (UPE). The graduates of this program obtain an honorary teachers' Grade II certificate. The teachers who enroll in the courses leading to the honorary Grade II certificate are generally older than those who enroll in the conventional program and they must have had five to fifteen years of teaching experience. Such teachers are on the average about thirty to forty years old, and they have extended family commitments but extensive practical experience of teaching. They tend to be more committed to teaching, although they have little prospect of academic and career advancement. Since 1979 student enrollment in this type of in-service education for teachers has steadily declined. By 1985 hardly a student was enrolled in the honorary teachers' Grade II certificate.

The part-time and correspondence NCE and degree programs have now become widespread. They are run by colleges of education, the university's institute of education rather than the faculty of education, and in some universities by a special unit: the Correspondence and Open Studies Institute (COSIT) for example, of the University of Lagos. This program is designed for underqualified teachers in the primary level, but even more so in the secondary school. Three categories of teacher education programs are offered: (1) the associateship certificate in education, which is designed to provide instructional curriculum development and administrative leadership in primary education. This teacher education program is run by institutes of education of universities. (2) The NCE or degree programs to upgrade underqualified teachers in primary and secondary schools. The objective is to achieve comparable standards of academic and professional competence as those in the conventional full-time programs. (3) The degree program enrolls those who have already obtained the NCE in colleges of education. These programs appeal more to older students who have family commitments or lack adequate financial assistance to pursue a full-time program.

The part-time and correspondence programs have been criticized in terms of time spent on learning after a full day's job, demands made on the student by the African extended family, and the limitation imposed by lack of face-to-face interaction between teacher and student and among students (Tseja, 1990).

These constraints are being overcome by organizing contact periods during which time guidance and counseling sessions are held to help students plan their work and acquire helpful study habits. The staff also organizes workshops to develop the ability to cope more efficiently with the disadvantages of poor telecommunication and postal systems. Emphasis is placed on giving more assignments than is normal in a conventional system and on making copious and helpful comments on assignments.

These alternative modes in teacher education have been in practice since 1976; they somehow cater to more than ten thousand teacher education students. The problems of teacher shortage, cost, and standard are being resolved to some extent. But doubts remain as to whether some other problems identified can be solved by nonconventional modes. While long periods of training on the job may inculcate a habit of lifelong pursuit of knowledge in the teacher, engaging in a continuous process of discovery, disciplined by the scholarly modes of inquiry, is often better done through contacts and interaction with the teacher.

### Issue 6: How to Prepare Teachers to Write Their Own Textbooks and Instructional Materials

There is a growing concern about shortages of books owing to diminishing foreign exchange earnings (since most textbooks are foreign-produced), the scarcity of newsprint, and the absence of indigenous authors. The federal government has just formulated a book policy that will encourage the development of book and other instructional material production. This situation has created a new task for teacher education: that of imparting skills that are relevant in book production.

The demand for book writing and instructional material production skills is not new. Teachers have responded to this demand in creative ways, and teachers' professional associations have organized writers' workshops whose outcomes have been of great benefit to schools. The efforts made by the Science Teachers' Association of Nigeria, the Mathematics Association of Nigeria, and the Curriculum Organization of Nigeria have made textbooks in science and mathematics available and accessible to secondary school students. These books are either published by the federal government's Nigerian Educational Research and Development Council or by both foreign-based and indigenous publishers. Recently, indigenous publishers have satisfied most of the book requirements for primary and secondary schools by organizing writers' workshops in which teacher educators and classroom teachers were involved. The efforts being made in Abeokuta and Ibadan, mentioned earlier, are object lessons to students of teacher education.

The downturn in the economy and the government's structural adjustment program have encouraged self-reliance in all spheres and self-sufficiency in educational resources.

Thus, the government of the federation formulated the book policy to encourage local authorship by creating an organizational framework for curriculum and book development. Three autonomous organizations have been brought together in a new group known as the Nigerian Educational Research and Development Council. This bigger organization is responsible for arranging national workshops and identifying the kinds and areas of textbook needs. By regulating the life span for school textbooks, the government will ensure that poor-quality texts do not monopolize the book market, while young and creative writers undergo avoidable frustration. Teacher education programs are expected to provide opportunities for preservice and in-service teachers to acquire skills that can be readily utilized when they go into schools. It is assumed that serving teachers can write more useful textbooks than nonteaching writers. However, the solution to the scarcity of textbooks does not lie solely in developing innovative teacher education programs. Part of the solution lies in turning the economy around, including making print materials available as well as the hardware for book publishing. While this chapter was still in preparation, the federal government announced a drastic reduction in the duties on newsprint. Three large paper mills produce newsprint in the country which, if made to produce at full capacity, will satisfy about half of current paper needs.

## CONCLUSION

This country study shows that official attitudes toward teacher education have changed over the years. The current military administration has taken teacher education issues very seriously and above all has shown consistency and continuity in policy formulation and implementation. However, the relationship between teacher education and teacher performance is a complex one that requires a critical examination. Improvement in teacher education alone may not solve the problem of the shortage of qualified teachers unless the image of teaching changes drastically. Preservice teachers perceive teaching as an occupation for those who cannot succeed elsewhere. In other words, the old saying that "those who can, do and those who cannot, teach" is still very relevant in Nigeria.

The output of qualified teachers has increased, but the proportion of unqualified teachers has not altered appreciably (Ukejer, 1986) because governments are unable to pay the high salaries of qualified teachers, given the demand for teachers in a rapidly expanding education system. Teachers' conditions have improved appreciably but not in comparison with what obtains in other sectors of the economy. Concurrently, a high level of unemployment has created an army of unemployed qualified graduates and NCE teachers. Unlike other professionals, teachers have only slim opportunities for self-employment. The way out seems to favor an emphasis on teacher education by distance learning or part-time vacation courses. This process of gradual upgrading of knowledge and pedagogical skills keeps an underqualified teacher in continuous employment until he or she becomes fully qualified. By then, he or she is too old to shop around for alternative employment—a cruel choice for teachers, but perhaps one that will salvage the teaching profession in Nigeria.

Another area that needs attention is the national distribution of qualified teachers. Two patterns of distribution are in evidence: (1) a high concentration of teachers in urban areas to the disadvantage of rural communities and (2) regional differences in the distribution of qualified teachers. These disparities have given rise to a situation in which urban areas and some southern states have surplus qualified teachers who could have been employed in the north but are not. It has also made it impossible for educationally disadvantaged areas to break the vicious circle of educational poverty. The extent to which fresh initiatives to bring about improvement in teacher education will succeed will depend on the solution found to these nagging problems.

## REFERENCES

Adaralegbe, A. *A Philosophy for Nigerian Education.* Report of the Nigerian Curriculum Conference September 8–12, 1969. Ibadan: Heinemann Educational Books [Nigeria] Ltd., 1969.

Avoseh, O. "The Education of NCE Teachers: Critique and Proposal." A paper presented at the Conference of Educational Studies Association of Nigeria held in the University of Ilorin, Ilorin, Nigeria, 1978. Mimeo.

Fafunwa, A. B., J. I. Macauley, and J. A. Sokoya. *Education in Mother Tongue: The Ife Primary Education Research Project [1970–1978].* Ibadan: University Press Ltd., 1989, pp. xi, 1–166.

Federal Ministry of Education. "To Complete a 'Tripod' for Education Excellence in Nigeria—The National Commission for Colleges of Education Is Inaugurated!" *Newsletter* 10 (May 1989): 8–10.

Federal Ministry of Education. *Investment in Education: Report of the Commission on the Review of Post-Secondary Education in Nigeria.* Lagos: Government Printer, 1960.

Obiogun, O. O. "Education for Living." In A. Adaralegbe, ed., *A Philosophy for Nigeria.* Ibadan: Heinemann Educational Books [Nigeria] Ltd., 1990, pp. 152–169.

Osibodu, B. "The Part-time Associateship Certificate in Education of the University of Ibadan Institute of Education in Nigeria." In J. Greenland, ed., *In-service Training of Primary Teachers in Africa.* London: Macmillan Education, 1983.

Robinson, A.N.D. "The Nigeria Certificate in Education by Correspondence [NCE/cc] Programme." *Nigeria Educational Forum* 8, no. 2 (December 1985): 151–157.

Tseja, Gideon S. "Minimum Standard for NCE by Distance Learning and NCE Part-Time." A paper presented at the workshop organized by the National Commission for Colleges of Education on Minimum Standards, Zaria, March 21–25, 1990. Mimeo.

Ukeje, B. O. "Teacher Education in Nigeria: Problems and Issues in Teacher Education." In B. O. Ukeje, L. O. Ocho, and E. O. Fagbamiye, *Issues and Concerns in Educational Administration and Planning: The Nigerian Case in International Perspective.* Lagos: Macmillan Nigeria Publishers Ltd., 1986, pp. 44–61.

# 14

# SPAIN

## PILAR BENEJAM AND MARIONA ESPINET

The present country study deals with six of the most critical issues affecting teacher education in Spain: (1) Should all teacher education be unified at the level of higher education? (2) What relationship should there be between theory and practice in the teacher education curriculum? (3) How should future teachers be recruited? (4) What professional education should secondary teachers receive? (5) How should in-service teacher education be organized so that it meets the evolving demands of new educational reforms? (6) Should teaching be a professional career?

## GENERAL BACKGROUND

### Political, Economic, and Educational Background

The victory of General Francisco Franco, and the subsequent establishment of the dictatorship at the end of the Spanish Civil War in 1939, started a long period of severe cultural and educational deprivation. This lasted until the rapid economic growth of the 1960s, which forced the government to initiate educational reform.

The Franco educational administration requested financial support from the World Bank and received consulting services from Unesco (United Nations Educational, Scientific, and Cultural Organization) and OECD (Organization for Economic Cooperation and Development) in order to design the basis for an educational reform leading to the General Education Law of 1970. Although the law was approved, in principle, by the Franco government, it was not embraced by the majority of the dictator's allegiances which let it appear but denied support and financial resources for its implementation.

## THE EDUCATIONAL SYSTEM

### The General Education Law (1970)

The General Education Law of 1970 considered the following four positive changes, not all of which were completely implemented. First, primary education was to become compulsory for all Spanish citizens until the age of fourteen.

Second, education was to become more democratic by contemplating the participation of all those involved in it, such as teachers, students, parents, administration, and social representatives. This was clearly in opposition to the ideology of the social status quo, and thus it was never totally implemented.

Third, the quality of education was to be improved by considering the use of personalized and individualized teaching, freedom to participate in classrooms, the encouragement of creativity, and the use of continuous as well as holistic evaluation. However, several factors prevented the quality of education from changing satisfactorily, notably, the high ratio of students to classroom, lack of financial resources, inadequate teacher education, and Franco's intolerance of the new attitudes and values emerging from the pedagogical changes. Despite these impediments to change, the General Education Law gave moral support and a legal framework to a few progressive underground groups such as some teachers' associations and several private progressive schools.

Fourth, the education of primary teachers was transferred to higher education and delivered by the teachers' colleges. A new university institution called the education institute was created to educate secondary teachers, provide in-service education, and conduct research on education. Thus, three institutions dealing with the education of teachers at the level of higher education were established: teachers' colleges, education institutes, and university departments.

The General Education Law faced both the economic crisis of 1975 and a strong social demand for more schooling in rapidly growing urban and industrial areas. These two factors forced the government to allocate financial resources to provide fast but cheap schooling, and to hire teachers under poor financial and professional conditions. Teachers' dissatisfaction led to professional tensions, school conflicts, and strikes which added to the impediments to successful implementation of the educational reform.

### The Education System (1970–1990)

The General Education Law created a state-funded education system that lasted until 1990. The structure of this education system is shown in Figure 1.

Several structural changes introduced into the education system in 1970 mark a sharp contrast with the same system before 1970. First, preschool education was officially included within the public education system, although it was not made compulsory. However, funding limitations forced the government to allocate financial resources to primary education rather than preschool education.

Figure 1
The Evolution of the Education System in Spain

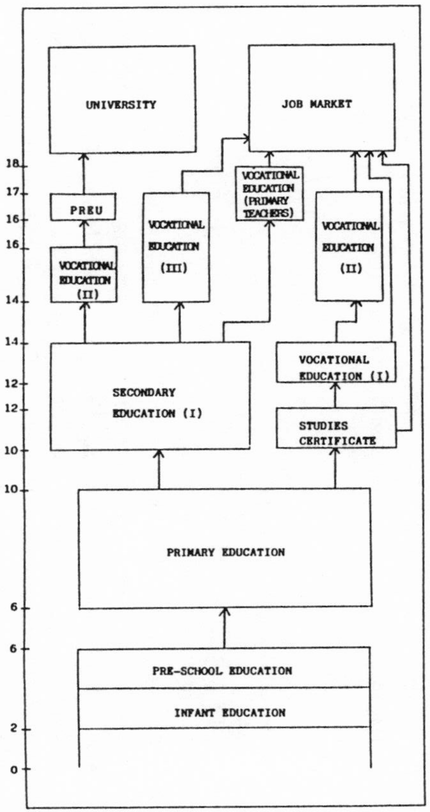

(a)
Spanish Education System
Before 1970

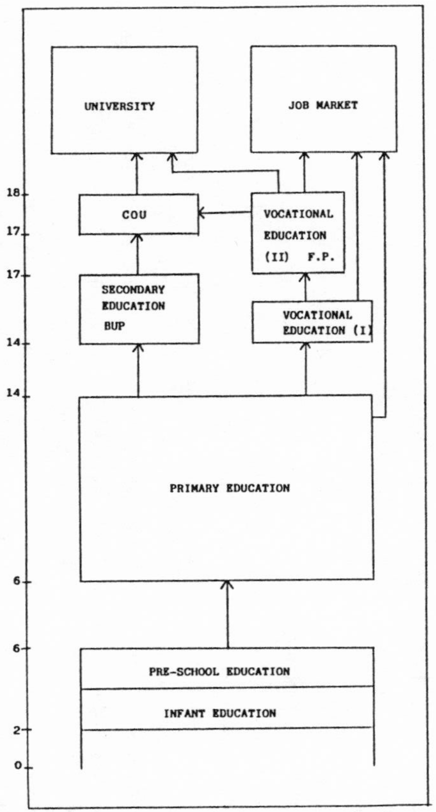

(b)
Spanish Education System
General Education. Law (1970)

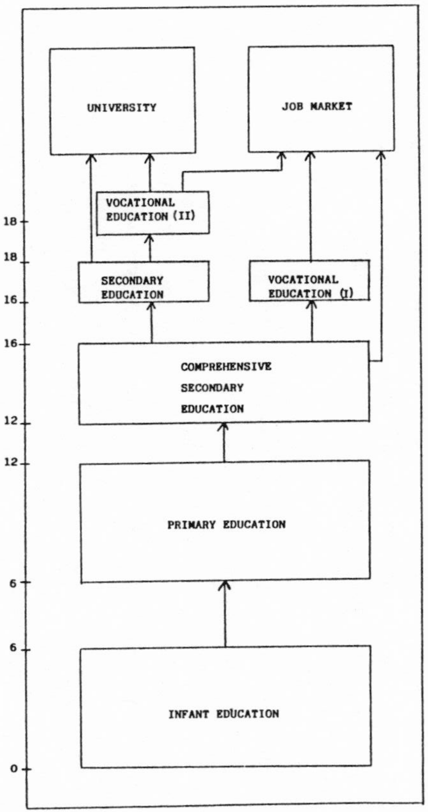

(c)
Spanish Education System
General Ordering Education System
Law (1990)

Second, primary education (Educación General Básica—EGB) was made compulsory for all children between six and fourteen years of age. Primary education was divided into two cycles. The first five years were taught by general teachers, whereas the last three years were taught by teachers with a subject matter specialty.

Third, at the end of primary school, there was a choice between vocational education (Formación Professional—FP) or secondary education (Bachillerato Unificado Polivalente—BUP). Students going into secondary education were required to have passing grades from all courses in primary education, whereas this requirement was not necessary for those going into vocational education. The purpose of secondary education was to provide students with both technical skills and basic academic knowledge. At the end of the secondary education period, students wanting to enter the university enrolled in a university preparatory year (Curso de Orientación Universitaria—COU) offered at the same secondary school. The purposes of vocational education I were to broaden students' basic knowledge and to provide them with practical skills for a basic level occupation. The purpose of vocational education II was to produce an intermediate-level working force. Although the law was inspired by the principle of equality between secondary and vocational education, this was not the case in practice. Vocational education became the redoubt of school failure.

Finally, the university system of higher education distinguished between the institutions leading to a five-year degree (facultades) and those leading to a three-year degree (escuelas universitarias) such as teachers' colleges. To enter the facultades, students needed to pass an entry exam offered by the university, whereas to enter escuelas universitarias students needed to have passing grades from a university preparatory year (COU), or to show a professional degree from vocational education II. Future primary teachers graduate from a three-year institution such as the teachers' college, whereas secondary teachers graduate from five-year institutions. In order for secondary teachers to get certified, they need to attend a one-year program (Curso de Adaptación Pedagógica—CAP) offered at the education institutes within universities.

### Private and Public Schools

The Spanish Catholic Church has always defended the citizen's right to create private educational institutions and the parents' right to choose the school for their children. A considerable proportion of Spanish schools are private.

The controversy between private and public schools has always been present in most parts of the capitalist world. However, Spain is one of the few countries in which public schools are the redoubt of the poorest segment of the population. The higher standards set by the General Education Law of 1970 in relation to school equipment and other educational services put private schools under such strong financial pressure that they requested state funding. Given the financial and political difficulties originating from a denial of such a request, the government agreed to fund private schools.

### In-service Teacher Education

In-service teacher education was brutally interrupted at the end of the civil war in 1939. It was not until 1965 that a few educators from Catalonia, with the support of some progressive political groups, created the educational institution known as Rosa Sensat. This private institution was established to provide in-service teacher education and to define the basis for pedagogical change according to both the pre-civil war educational tradition and the most progressive European movements. In 1975 several groups in Spain followed the Rosa Sensat experience by creating new pedagogical reform movements and expanding in-service teacher education. The most important activity organized by these teacher-based pedagogical reform movements was the Summer School. The courses, seminars, and conferences offered at the Summer Schools gave cohesion, strength, and direction to the new pedagogical reform movement.

Franco's administration initiated state-funded in-service teacher education in 1970 as a response to the demands of the new educational reform. Education institutes were created within each university to provide in-service teacher education and to conduct educational research. However, most of the education institutes were unable to define clear research and teacher development agendas, and lacked financial support from universities.

## EDUCATION WITHIN THE SPANISH DEMOCRACY

### Political, Economic, and Educational Background

The establishment of democracy in Spain after the death of General Franco in 1975 opened up a period of social, economic, and political changes. The economic crisis of the 1970s forced the democratic government to respond to the most urgent needs of industrial modernization and unemployment. Once the crisis was overcome, the government settled more diverse priorities such as change of tax policy and increase of social services and education budgets.

Education within the Spanish democracy was characterized by three main concerns: (1) decentralization of educational administration, (2) democratization of education, and (3) increasing compulsory education.

### Decentralization of Educational Administration

The approval of the Spanish Constitution in 1978 led to an autonomous government structure, so that the historical, cultural, and social diversity of Spanish territory was recognized. The decentralization of educational administration was a consequence of this new political order. The autonomous governments received full educational autonomy, including the regulation and administration of their own education systems. The Spanish government retained the power to issue educational and professional degrees, as well as guarantee citizens' right to receive and offer education.

When the old centralized model of educational administration was transferred to the new situation, however, the same administrative problems recurred. These problems were (1) the lack of citizen participation in the decentralized administrative decision making and (2) the rigidity of the civil servant personnel structure. However, several factors are still preventing educational administration from being totally decentralized; the fixed rights of civil servants, the lack of complete financial autonomy, and inadequate administrative competencies.

## Democratization of Education

Two laws were approved which regulated the democratization of education: the University Reform Law (1983), which gave more decision-making power to universities; and the Education Ordering Law (1984), which regulated school management within a more democratic framework. The 1984 law created the school council entity at the state, private, local, and school levels, in order to improve education management and to increase social control over education. Each Spanish school has a school council comprising the principal, the school coordinator, elected teachers, parents, and students, and one representative from the city educational administration. The functions of school councils are to select the principal, solve management problems, approve budgets, settle the pedagogical basis sustaining the educational project of the school, and supervise the general functioning of the school. School councils, with similar functions and wide social and educational participation, were created at the level of each city, in each autonomous community in which the Spanish territory has been divided, and at the state level. The school councils at the local level meet in the city halls, those at the autonomous community level meet in the capital of that area, and, finally, the school council at the state level meets in Madrid.

The implementation of these two laws has been slow and difficult partly because of the lack of democratic tradition within society, administration, and schools.

## Increasing Compulsory Education

The General Ordering of the Education System Law was approved in 1990, after a long and arduous period of deliberation, consulting, and experimenting. Although this law reiterates the basic aspects of the General Education Law (1970), others are modified. Two are the most important changes regulated by this law. The first is the extension of compulsory and comprehensive education from the ages of fourteen to sixteen. In doing so, students postpone professional decisions until age sixteen so that they reach the legal age to enter the job market.

The second is the integration of infant education within the education system. This change represented the first step toward implementing compensatory educational programs. Although infant education was not compulsory, the Ministry of Education anticipated a gradual increase of infant education schooling.

European economic factors brought pressure on the Spanish education system to increase compulsory education. The advancing European capitalism required highly trained professionals, with broad educational backgrounds, and short, flexible, quick, and reversible professional training. The adaptation of the education system to the systems in the European Community is necessary within the framework of imminent political and economic reunification. Although all social and political groups in Spain accepted the extension of compulsory education, the main problem that remains is how to manage a comprehensive school for all children until age sixteen.

## The New Education System

The new education system regulated by the General Ordering of Education System Law (1990) is shown in Figure 1. It integrates infant education, lowers primary education down to age twelve, and introduces state-funded comprehensive secondary education from age twelve to sixteen. At age sixteen, students choose between vocational education of diverse content and difficulty level, and secondary education with diverse concentration focus. The new educational reform introduces a basic prescriptive curriculum for the country, but it gives control over the different levels of curriculum definition to the autonomous educational administration and school communities. The new curriculum considers important pedagogical changes that are putting strong professional demands on secondary teachers. These teachers are the most ill equipped to handle the new educational reform because of their inadequate and insufficient initial professional training.

## New In-service Teacher Education

The consolidation of Spanish democracy and the growing intervention of both the central and autonomous administrations have forced the teacher-based pedagogical reform movements to rethink their action. The Ministry of Education admitted the failure of education institutes which became the redoubt of unmotivated teachers and educational administrators. New teacher-based institutions called teachers' centers were created, following the model of the British teachers' centers. The new teachers centers sought to facilitate teacher encounter, to provide educational resources to teachers, and to offer in-service teacher education. However, Catalonia, Pais Vasco, and Galicia have retained the education institutes. At present, in-service teacher education in Spain is rich and diverse. Several small-range projects are worth mentioning such as the School-Based In-service Teacher Education Project (FOPI) (Badia, 1984) and the

Education of Teacher Educators Project whose purpose was to prepare staff for the newly created teachers. Old and new institutions, as well as private initiatives, coexist in harmony. However, the educational administration has given preferential funding to new institutions while disregarding the already existing ones.

### Future Perspectives

Today Spanish education is in a state of turmoil. Although the General Ordering of Education System Law has been recently approved, policies regulating the functioning of the education system have not yet been issued. Thus, it could be anticipated that the implementation of the new educational reform is going to be a long and controversial process. However, new perspectives are now being anticipated as a consequence of the implementation of an open European common market in 1992. This imminent reality will force the Spanish education system to readjust to the new European demands. Among these demands is an increase in the range of compulsory education, better adjustment of education to the needs of the job market, and priority to research within and outside universities.

## ISSUES AND PROBLEMS

### Issue 1: Should All Teacher Education Be Unified at the Level of Higher Education?

The education of teachers in Spain differs in length, content, and structure depending on the level of teaching responsibilities. Teachers for infant education receive professional training in nonuniversity institutions. Preschool and primary teachers enter higher education for three years and receive a professional degree from a teachers college. Their education has both professional and subject matter components. Finally, secondary teachers attend the university for five years to receive a bachelor's degree in a specific subject matter, and they obtain their teaching certification at the education institute. As the age of students increases, the education of teachers in Spain lengthens and becomes more subject matter oriented. This education system is based on the strong belief that the essential core of teacher education is the volume and complexity of the subject matter taught in schools.

*Contextual Factors Challenging the Teacher Education System in Spain*

At least three important factors are challenging the teacher education system at present. The first is the growing impact on the educational community of the knowledge accumulated by educational psychologists, sociologists of education, and educational researchers. This knowledge is broadening educators' understanding of the role that contextual and psychological factors play in teaching and learning at all age levels. Consequently, the relative emphasis of subject matter knowledge versus professional knowledge in the education of teachers at different levels of teaching responsibility should be reconsidered.

A second important factor is the increasing awareness among teachers and teacher educators that early childhood education is important in compensating for individual differences. If effective compensatory education for disadvantaged children should start as early as possible, the education of preschool teachers should be reconsidered.

The third factor is the educational reform initiated by the Spanish Ministry of Education in order to increase the span of compulsory education. The need to provide comprehensive education for all Spanish children until age sixteen has forced teachers to face and treat the problem of student diversity. If future secondary teachers should be provided with concepts and tools for the understanding and treatment of individual differences among adolescents, the education of high school teachers should be reconsidered.

The national debate about the new educational reform has created a forum for reflecting on the adequacy of the teacher education system. The issue is formulated as follows: "Should all teacher education be unified at the level of higher education"?

*Alternative Teacher Education Proposals*

The more progressive groups within the educational community have formulated alternative teacher education proposals based on several assumptions from earlier progressive pedagogical reform groups including several teachers' unions and education specialists. The alternative Spanish teacher education proposals agree on the following assumptions:

1. All teachers are equally important. Consequently, they should have the same professional recognition and receive an equivalent teacher education.
2. The education of all teachers should be offered at the university, the educational institution that has the highest cultural, scientific, and professional standards. The best university setting for the education of all future teachers should be a new School of Education that integrates teachers' colleges, ICE, and foundational departments.
3. All teachers should complete the requirements for a university degree in a specific subject matter. The goal of university education should be to provide teachers with the intellectual skills derived from the process of learning a discipline.
4. All teachers should have a professional preparation that is both practical and theoretical. The goal of this education should be to provide teachers with the skills of facilitating students' learning processes and working with other teachers.

One of the most innovative alternative teacher education proposals was issued in 1984 (Gimeno and Fernández, 1980) by a commission under the supervision of the Ministry of Education. This proposal is shown in Figure 2. This alternative teacher education proposal suggested that all teachers graduate from a subject

**Figure 2**
**Teacher Education Proposal (1984)**

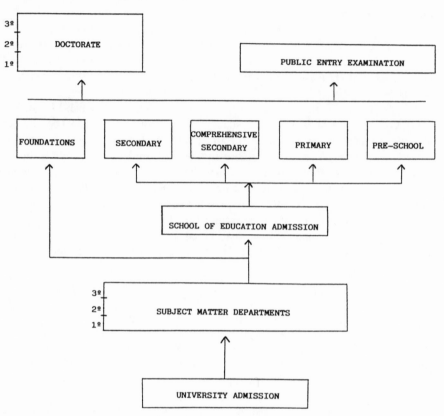

matter university department before applying to teacher education. After being admitted to the School of Education, future teachers select one teaching specialty among those available such as preschool, primary, comprehensive secondary, and secondary. At the end of two years of professional study, all future teachers receive the same university degree from the School of Education. Those students graduating from subject matter departments who want to play professional roles other than teaching apply to the Foundations Department. The studies offered in this department provide students with the core knowledge of educational theory.

The alternative teacher education proposal resolves in one way or another the challenges faced by the teacher education system at present. On one hand, it raises the status of preschool and elementary teachers, recognizing the importance of their task. On the other hand, it provides secondary teachers with practical and theoretical professional knowledge in order to face the changes emerging from the educational reform. Finally, it eliminates certification differences among teachers. In doing so, it sets the basis for more productive cooperation among teachers within the same school systems.

### Difficulties Associated with the Alternative Teacher Education Proposals

Although the alternative proposals constitute plausible solutions to the problems detected within the actual Spanish teacher education system, several professional groups find it difficult to accept and implement it. These professional groups are the following: the Spanish Ministry of Education, part of the educational community, high school teachers, subject matter departments within universities, and teacher educators.

*The Spanish Ministry of Education.* Spain's membership in the European Community has forced the Spanish Ministry of Education to allocate a considerable amount of financial resources to educational reform. This makes it virtually impossible to provide financial support to the alternative teacher education proposal at present. This proposal would, among other things, raise the salaries of all preschool and elementary teachers to those of high school teachers.

*The Educational Community.* The Spanish educational community is composed of teachers who differ in social status, salaries, and background education. High school teachers, of course, show resistance to the loss of any social and material privilege.

*High School Teachers.* The majority of high school teachers are opposed to the introduction of more professional courses and to the reduction of subject matter courses in their education. They see this change as lowering the academic standards of their educational background and diminishing their social prestige.

*Subject Matter Departments Within Universities.* Subject matter departments within universities are not offering to collaborate in the planning of teacher education. They show resistance to the loss of control over student candidates for teaching. In fact, the financial support given to university departments depends partly on the number of students registered.

*Teacher Educators.* A considerable number of teacher educators are opposed to becoming members of the School of Education faculty. On one hand, this professional change imposes strong demands on teacher educators to respond to higher university research standards. On the other hand, they foresee the eradication of small teachers' colleges, the reduction of teacher education positions, and the elimination of the dynamic role played by teachers' colleges in culturally deprived areas.

The educational community's support of the alternative teacher education proposals concerning the uniformity of teacher education across different levels of teaching responsibility has not been strong enough to reduce the resistance of the opposing professional groups. After several years of deliberation and discussion, the General Ordering of the Education System Law (1990) has partly closed the issue by not altering the structure of the Spanish teacher education system. In fact, comprehensive secondary and secondary teachers graduate from a specific subject matter university department, becoming certified afterward, whereas preschool and primary teachers receive their teaching certificate after three years of professional studies within a teachers' college.


## Issue 2: What Relationship Should There Be Between Theory and Practice in the Teacher Education Curriculum?

The primary teacher education curriculum is divided into two areas: subject matter courses and professional courses. Subject matter courses include general overviews of several areas such as language, mathematics, science, social studies, physical education, music, and art, as well as specific subject matter courses. Professional courses are divided into three areas: (1) Foundational and general education courses: educational psychology, sociology, pedagogy, general didactics, and school organization; (2) specific educational courses: subject matter teaching methods, curriculum; and (3) practicum in schools.

The practicum in schools is designed to provide future teachers with the opportunity to apply professional knowledge taught at the university to teaching in real classrooms. The practicum is usually offered during the last year of teacher education and lasts approximately three months. Student teachers work with a mentor teacher, and they are supervised once or twice by a university supervisor. The evaluation of student teachers is based mostly on the portfolios turned in at the end of the practicum. The portfolios collect all teaching materials used by student teachers and their own evaluative self-reflections.

The professional curriculum of Spanish teacher education is based on the conception that teaching knowledge is first transmitted from teacher educators to student teachers, and then applied by future teachers in practical situations. This conception assumes the unidirectionality between theory as provided at the universities and practice as experienced in schools. Thus, theory and practice are disconnected within the professional curriculum of Spanish teacher education.


### Consequences of the Disconnection Between Theory and Practice

Several problems have resulted from the disconnection between theory and practice. The first problem is that student teachers are required to choose a specific teaching level before having any chance to experience it in schools. Once future teachers reach the practicum, their professional choice has already become irreversible. The second problem is derived from teacher educators' needs to link theory to student teachers' practical problems. Teacher educators find it very difficult to motivate future teachers when the theory they teach has no experiential basis. The third problem is the lack of mentor preparation for the task of helping future teachers throughout their practicum. This problem is exacerbated by the communication barriers that exist between university professors and mentor teachers.

*Attempted Solutions to Provide a Balance Between Theory and
Practice*

Several teachers' colleges have recently attempted to provide solutions to the
above-mentioned problems. These solutions can be reduced to four different
proposals. The first proposal suggests lengthening the time devoted to the practicum in schools. The second spreads the practicum out along teacher education.
Many teachers' colleges have introduced a practicum during the second year of
studies, and some are negotiating with schools to do so in the first year of teacher
education. The third proposal suggests introducing an induction year for beginning teachers. The fourth and final proposal comes from the Ministry of Education
commission for the design of a new teacher education curriculum. The final
report of this commission assigns practical credits to all professional courses
within teacher education and lengthens the practicum in schools.

Despite the apparent diversity of the proposed solutions, their underlying
conception of the relationship between theory and practice remains the same.
All of them have attempted to increase in one way or another the amount of
time devoted to the practicum in schools. However, these proposals have not
modified the role of theoretical courses offered at the universities. In fact, theoretical professional knowledge is still first transmitted from teacher educators
to student teachers, and later future teachers apply it to practical situations.

Another emergent conception of the relationship between theory and practice
in teacher education has influenced the design of few teacher education curricula
and has inspired a small amount of the Spanish teacher education literature. This
conception is based on the idea that reflection instead of transmission should be
the link between theory and practice.

*Reflection as the Core of the Teacher Education Curriculum*

Teacher education curricula based on reflection advocate a more dynamic
relationship between theory and practice in the education of teachers. Practice
and the reflection on practice is the center of the teacher education curriculum.
Theory, as important as it is, is not thought to be delivered disconnected from
practice. Instead, it is provided through the communicative act of reflecting on
direct school experiences. This conception views theory and practice as intimately
related.

Although the number of implemented teacher education proposals based on
reflection is very limited, they are strong and interesting. An example is the case
of Sant Cugat Teachers College at the Universitat Autonoma de Barcelona.
Several teacher educators from this teachers' college have implemented a proposal based on reflection since 1976. Teacher educators teach in schools throughout the academic year. Student teachers prepare the lessons with the teacher
educator, attend each lesson taught by the teacher educator in schools, and finally
all together reflect on the experience after the class is over. This proposal does
not have many advocates among teacher educators given the strong demands

put on them. However, it provides the basis for a change in the relationship between theory and practice in teacher education.

## Issue 3: How Should Future Teachers Be Recruited?

The recovery of the Spanish economy at the end of the 1960s forced the Franco government to initiate an educational reform. This reform was a response to the need to provide a better qualified working force and more schooling for the rapidly growing urban areas.

The growing economy expanded the job market and thus made it difficult to recruit the necessary teachers. The Spanish Ministry of Education mandated the following two strategies in order to meet teacher shortages: (1) provide university status to teachers' college graduates, and (2) eliminate any admission requirements to enter teacher education.

As a result of these two strategies, although more students applied to teachers' colleges, a considerable percentage of them either failed the admission requirements at other schools, held a weak knowledge base, or were intellectually poor. The majority of students who chose teacher education were at the lowest rank of academic achievement. Today teachers' colleges are one of the least prestigious institutions within the Spanish university system. Spain has paid the price of disregarding teacher education quality in order to have an inexpensive and quick educational reform.

New social and educational factors are challenging the teacher recruitment system. On one hand, the Spanish birth rate started to decrease in the 1980s, producing surplus teachers. On the other hand, better qualified and more motivated candidates are needed in order to face the challenges of the Spanish educational reform in the 1990s. Several groups within the educational community have responded to these challenges.

### Guidelines for a Future Teacher Recruitment System

Several groups within the educational community used the general framework set by the Ley de Ordenacion General del Sistema Educativo (1990) to suggest guidelines for a future teacher recruitment system (Generalitat de Catalunya, 1982, Gimeno, 1984, and ICE Murcia, 1981). These guidelines had two underlying goals: to introduce higher standards for the admission of future teachers and to turn control of teacher education over to the professional community. These guidelines can be summarized as follows.

1. The process of candidates' admission to teacher education should be a priority. As much time as necessary should be allocated to it.

2. Admission to teacher education should be supervised by a team of teacher educators.

3. The maximum number of admitted candidates should be a political and professional decision.

4. The educational community is responsible for setting the criteria used to recruit future teachers.

5. Candidates should demonstrate a sufficient subject matter knowledge base and personal qualities for admission to teacher education. Candidates' previous experience with children should be especially noted.

6. Several quality controls should be considered during the education of future teachers in order to guarantee their teaching competence.

These guidelines were never used to design a future teacher recruitment system, given that the Ministry of Education decided to drop all requirements to enter primary teacher education and other three-year university institutions.

### The Selection of Teachers

Primary teachers are certified to teach in either private or public schools, once they graduate from a teachers' college. However, the procedure used to hire new teachers depends on whether the school is private or public. The principal is responsible for hiring new teachers in private schools. If private schools receive some financial support from the government, the decision to hire new teachers is made by the school council. New teachers who want to teach in public schools need to enter their names on a public waiting list. Public schools that need more staff must hire new teachers from the public waiting list in the order in which they appear.

Only public schools can provide tenure positions. All Spanish teachers are potential candidates for tenure positions provided they pass a public entrance examination. The public entrance examination follows national criteria and has both written and oral but no practical items. They are designed to evaluate the candidates' subject matter and foundational knowledge regardless of their practical and professional competence. There are no national specifications as to how much teaching experience is necessary before taking the public entrance examination. The scores on this exam are the only criteria for obtaining tenure provided that positions are available. The most important privilege of having tenure is that teachers become civil servants and get better pay than nontenured teachers.

The examination board for the public entrance examination consists of teacher educators, state supervisors, and teachers. They either volunteer to be members of the examination board, or they are recruited by drawing lots from the existing pool of tenure teacher educators, supervisors, and teachers. This system of screening teachers has been shown to have serious deficiencies. The first is that the hiring of new teachers lacks uniformity across private and public schools. The second is that the constitution of the examination board does not guarantee the academic and professional competence of their members. Finally, the public entrance examination does not allow adequate assessment of candidates' teaching competence. In sum, the screening of teachers appears inadequate to select the most able teachers.

*An Alternative to the Public Entrance Examination*

The public entrance examination has generated strong opposition within the educational community. Several proposals that have emerged since the 1970s provide an alternative to the public entrance examination. The most controversial alternative, known as Proyecto Otero, was issued in 1979 by the Ministry of Education. The Proyecto Otero recommended that both primary and secondary teachers be recruited, educated, and developed within a new institution directly dependent on the state administration. In order to enter this new public teacher education institution, candidates would be required to go through a process of selection and continuous evaluation. Those teachers graduating from this institution would be immediately hired by the public school system and would be given tenure. The teacher education curriculum was thought to be essentially professional, with a strong practical component.

The Proyecto Otero generated an intense but short debate on the quality of Spanish contemporary teacher education. However, because of the lack of extra financial resources, strong university opposition, and the impossibility of ensuring teacher education quality, the Proyecto Otero was not implemented.

*Improving Rather than Changing the Public Entrance Examination*

The debate over the Proyecto Otero led the educational community to suggest specific improvements to the public entrance examination rather than radical changes. One of several alternatives proposed to introduce an induction year after the public entrance examination and before teachers obtained tenure.

Several economic and educational factors are preventing this alternative from being implemented, including the lack of extra financial resources and the difficulties teacher educators, administrators, and school teachers have encountered in allocating extra time to teachers' induction. An additional factor is the communication barrier existing between the university, the administration, and schools preventing the induction year from being effectively implemented.

### Issue 4: What Professional Education Should Secondary Teachers Receive?

The secondary teachers' professional education was nonexistent before 1970. It was assumed that receiving a bachelor's degree from a subject matter department in a university was sufficient to teach in secondary schools. Recognizing the inadequacy of this assumption, the General Education Law (1970) regulated the professional education of secondary teachers. The government assigned the education institutes at universities the task of designing and offering a one-year program for the professional education of secondary teachers (Curso de Adaptación Pedagógica), having foundations, educational, and practical components. Students about to graduate or already graduated were eligible to enroll in the secondary teacher education program.

The implementation of secondary teacher education programs showed serious deficiencies. First, universities did not take this program seriously enough to ensure its quality. Second, public entry examinations for public teaching positions did not include professional or practical knowledge, thus making the secondary teacher education program almost irrelevant. Third, the majority of secondary school teaching still reproduces the prevalent teaching methods used in universities. Finally, dropout and school failure rates within secondary schools were and still are alarming. For instance, between 1975 and 1979 the percentage of students dropping out from elementary, vocational I, secondary, and COU (university preparatory year) was 15, 63, 46, and 21 percent, respectively.

The professional education of secondary teachers has been considered one of the key factors in the successful implementation of the General Ordering of Education System Law (1990). The changes included in this educational reform will put strong demands on secondary teachers who need more professional knowledge.

### An Alternative Secondary Teacher Education

The Spanish university council proposed the design of an alternative secondary teacher education to a group of specialists known as Comisión XV. This proposal distinguished between the education of comprehensive secondary teachers (for students twelve to sixteen) and secondary teachers (for students sixteen to eighteen). Thus, comprehensive secondary teacher education included a three-year university degree from a subject matter department and two years of professional studies within the school of education. Instead, secondary teacher education included a four-year university degree from a subject matter department and only one year of professional training. At the end of these five years of study, candidates would get certified as either comprehensive secondary teachers or secondary teachers.

### Future Perspectives

The university council rejected this proposal, adducing management difficulties, administrative problems, lack of financial resources, and loss of student enrollment in subject matter departments. Instead, the council decided to improve the quality of the existing secondary teacher education program (CAP) so that subject matter departments could slowly develop the necessary commitment toward it. The proposal maintained the old structure, but it increased the number of credits required for certification. In sum, future secondary teachers need a bachelor's degree from a subject matter department before they can enroll in a one-year program for certification (CAP). As with the previous model, subject matter courses take clear precedence over professional ones. Once more, the suggested improvements are too modest to meet the urgent demands for better prepared secondary teachers.

### Issue 5: How Should In-Service Teacher Education Be Organized?

In-service teacher education in Spain is free, voluntary, and diverse. The current state of confusion has forced the educational community to deal with the issue of how in-service teacher education should be organized so that it meets the evolving demands of new educational reforms. This issue is best expressed in the following three concerns: should in-service teacher education be controlled or free? should in-service teacher education be voluntary or mandatory? what content should in-service teacher education offer? These concerns are discussed separately below.

*Controlled Versus Free In-service Teacher Education*

The Spanish institutions offering in-service teacher education are (1) university institutions such as education institutions (ICE), education departments, and teachers' colleges; (2) institutions controlled by the state or the autonomous government such as teachers' centers, resources centers, and the Ministry of Education; (3) institutions controlled by the local administration such as local education institutes and education councils; (4) teacher-based groups such as teachers' unions, teachers' associations, and pedagogical reform movements; and (5) private institutions.

The variety of in-service teacher education is now under debate. Those within the education community advocating diversity argue that state, autonomous, or local administrations cannot effectively control in-service teacher education. Instead, they support free in-service teacher education because of its adaptability to changes and its ability to reach the maximum number of teachers. Those within the education community opposed to free in-service teacher education argue that this system does not ensure quality control, and it causes a draining of human and financial resources.

The most recent attempt to organize in-service teacher education from the Catalan government is the United In-service Teacher Education Scheme (Generalitat de Catalunya, 1982). Several factors explain the opposition to the scheme found within the educational community. On one hand, Spanish teachers have a solid tradition of independence, although they need financial support and professional recognition from the state or autonomous governments. On the other hand, the state and autonomous governments have built a heavy bureaucracy with a tendency to suffocate private initiatives.

*Voluntary Versus Mandatory In-service Teacher Education*

Teacher-based groups, teachers' unions, and the educational administration have taken the chief role in the debate about whether in-service teacher education should be mandatory or voluntary. Teacher-based groups and teachers' unions accept mandatory in-service teacher education, only if it is provided within their school schedules. Although the educational administration has partially accepted this proposal, it has claimed that the teachers' daily schedule already has provisions for in-service activities. Public opinion has contributed to this debate by supporting the idea that the educational administration has both the right and the obligation to define an in-service teacher education agenda.

The debate about whether in-service teacher education should be voluntary or mandatory has not yet been resolved. In-service teacher education has at present no possibility of being totally mandatory. The lack of financial and human resources is suffocating any attempt to implement such broad action. Today, in-service teacher education is mainly voluntary and occasionally mandatory.

*In-service Teacher Education: Content and Method*

Before the 1980s in-service teacher education offered traditional courses on subject matter, pedagogy, and subject matter teaching methods through a directive and didactic approach. The British educational tradition of action research has influenced the method and the content of Spanish in-service teacher education today. New school-based in-service teacher education projects are taking over the traditional courses offered outside the schools. The content of such projects is defined by the schools or by particular teachers following their local concerns. The most common methodology is problem solving, action research, or group interaction. Although this new approach is growing in acceptance, few educators have the skills to facilitate the process and ensure its continuity.

## Issue 6: Should Teaching Be a Professional Career?

Spanish teachers are promoted based on their years of teaching experience rather than their excellence. Thus, every three years all teachers, tenured and nontenured alike, are given a small salary increase. Neither educational research nor informed observation has established a correlation between teaching excellence and years of teaching experience. The most concerned groups within the educational community are starting a debate about other ways to reward teaching excellence in the promotion system.

Several impediments to improving the teachers' promotion system have been identified. The first impediment is the lack of tradition in evaluating the effectiveness of the Spanish education system. Another is the common belief of most educational administrators that teaching certification brings teaching excellence. Finally, teachers' unions reject policies that divide teachers, arguing that the educational administration is not able to guarantee the equity of any quality control in teaching. Despite these impediments, the Ministry of Education opened a debate over a proposal setting the basis for the design of a career ladder.

*Designing a Career Ladder*

In 1986 a group of educational experts from the Ministry of Education in Spain (Arango et al., 1986) designed a career ladder for teaching as an alternative to the teachers' promotion system. The group made the following assumptions.

A teaching career should be considered a profession with financial improvement for the majority of teachers; promotion criteria should be similar between elementary and secondary teachers; the span of time necessary to go from the first to the last level of the career ladder should be relatively short; promotion should not compel changing job placement; and promotion strategies should be diverse and multiple.

The proposal designed a career ladder with three levels. The first level corresponds to the induction into teaching and lasts two or three years. Teachers reaching the second level perform school functions such as department head. Teachers are required to spend at least five years in level 2 before they apply for promotion to level 3. The functions characterizing level 3 are school administration, school management, and supervision. Primary teachers are eligible to be promoted to secondary teaching, provided they hold a university degree and reach primary teaching level 2.

The evaluation committee includes teachers from the same level, teachers from higher levels, prestigious educators designated by the state school council, and educational administrators. The merits considered for promotion include years of teaching experience, in-service education, educational innovations, research and other publications, degrees, awards and scholarships, teaching experience in culturally deprived areas, and other professional activities.

*Opposition to the Teaching Career Ladder*

The opposition to the proposed teaching career ladder from several political parties, teachers' unions, and teachers' associations was so strong that the Ministry of Education was forced to abandon it. The main criticisms were as follows: it increased divisions among teachers; it made a clear distinction between primary and secondary teaching, attributing higher value to the secondary; the promotion criteria were essentially individual, disregarding school excellence; the proposal did not consider where to obtain the necessary human and financial resources; and more diversity of promotion strategies should be contemplated which were not based solely on economic rewards.

**CONCLUSION**

Since 1970 Spain has made a considerable effort to change its educational system. The most noteworthy results have been the following: (1) the progressive increase of compulsory education to reach European standards; (2) the inclusion of early childhood education within the education system; and (c) the transference of primary teacher education to higher education.

The priority of providing schooling for all Spanish children has forced the Ministry of Education to postpone qualitative reform of the education system. Several changes need to be considered in the near future. The first is to undertake a deep reform of the teacher education system, which in turn would enhance the status of teaching. The second imminent change is to redesign secondary teacher education so that it meets the demands of the new educational reform. Third, the process of admission to teaching needs radical reform in that it should represent only the first step toward a continuous teacher development process. Finally, it is of utmost importance to design new in-service teacher education programs so that they reach all teachers and reward teaching excellence.

The new educational reform issued in 1990 has lowered most expectations of deep structural changes within teacher education. However, some possibilities for change remain, given that most of the specific teacher education policies have not been issued yet.

## REFERENCES

Arango, J., et al. *Documento de bases para la elaboración del Estatuto del Profesorado.* Madrid: Ministerio de Educación y Ciencia, 1986.

Badia, J. et al. *Experiència Pilot de Formació Permanent de Mestres (FOPI) de Cornella. Balanç del Primer any de l'experiència.* Barcelona: Generalitat de Catalunya, Departament d'Ensenyament, 1984.

Benejam, P. *La formación de maestros: Una propuesta alternativa.* Barcelona: Cuadernos de Pedagogia, Laia, 1986.

CIDE. *El sistema educativo espanõl.* Madrid: Ministerio de Educacion y Ciencia, Centro de Investigación y Documentacion Educativa, 1988.

"El profesor, ese desconocido." *Cuadernos de Pedagogía* 161, (July-August 1988)

Generalitat de Catalunya. *Plà de formació permanent del professorat.* Barcelona: Department d'Ensenyament, 1989.

Generalitat de Catalunya. *Una proposta per a la renovació de la formació de mestres: Conclusions del seminari coordinador de les escoles de mestres de Catalunya 1981–82.* Barcelona: Generalitat de Catalunya, 1982.

Gimeno, J., and M. Fernández. *La formación del profesorado de EGB. Análisis de la situación española.* Madrid: Ministerio de Universidades e Investigación, 1980.

Gimeno, J., et al. *Informe técnico del Grupo XXV sobre la reforma de las enseñanzas universitarias relacionadas con los títulos sobre educación y profesorado.* Madrid: Consejo de Universidades, 1988.

Gimeno, J., et al. *Proyecto de reforma de la formación del profesorado.* Madrid: Ministerio de Educación y Ciencia, 1984.

ICE Murcia. *Las escuelas universitarias del profesorado de EGB.* Murcia: Universidad de Murcia, Instituto de Ciencias de la Educación, 1981.

MEC. *La reforma de la formación de profesores de educación.* Madrid: Ministerio de Educación y Ciencia, 1982.

"Profesionalidad y profesionalización de la enseñanza." *Revista de Educación* 285 (1988).

Villar, L. M. *Formación de profesores. Reflexiones para una reforma.* Valencia: Prom-olibro, 1986.

# 15

# Union of Soviet Socialist Republics

## JOAN B. WILSON

The public teacher in our country must be raised to a height where he never stood, does not stand now, and could not stand in bourgeois society. . . . We must get to this state of affairs systematically, undeviatingly, with diligent work *on* his spiritual/intellectual enhancement, *on* his comprehensive preparation for his truly high calling, and, the chief thing, *on* the enhancement of his material position.

—V. I. Lenin

As the process of disintegration of what was once the Soviet Union progresses, each political entity, whether or not it is separated, inherits the same issues and problems in teacher education described here.

This chapter discusses three issues that must be resolved for the Soviet Union to achieve basic reform in the professionalization of the teaching force. First, a trifurcated teacher training model has produced classroom teachers with marked differences in professional commitment and in abilities to fathom pedagogical abstractions. Few have attained truly professional status with the competency skills and self-actualizing behaviors this denotes. Many become on-the-job teacher dropouts, cynical and unfocused, who either vainly seek alternative livelihoods or patiently put in their time to earn a meager pension.

Second, the current formalistic professional training programs stifle creativity, initiative, and independence in the teacher candidates. This perpetuates rote learning and authoritarianism in the schools as the graduate practitioners teach as they have been taught. The appeals to innovate, to humanize, and to democratize the teaching-learning process have met stiff resistance from teachers who want business as usual. Those who can be persuaded to reorganize classroom activities often complain that they are castigated by parents, administrators, and the very students they teach. An enormous amount of human effort must be expended by these courageous reformers to overcome the status quo which comforts the unmotivated student body, the absentee parent(s), and the ubiquitous hacks in administration. Each contributes powerfully toward undermining the national goal to restructure the system so that it has the capability to reshape Soviet society.

Third, the low status of teachers in the USSR has impaired the recruitment and retention of a quality professional staff. One of the underlying problems in the Soviet Union, as in most other places in the world, is that fiscal support for education has too low a priority as other important sectors in the economy make successful bids for resources. A profile of those who are presently in the teaching cadre presents a grim picture. Absent are those talented and bright graduates with a lifetime dedication for their chosen work. A precarious social position undergirded by a pitiful wage and benefit structure can only attract and keep a marginally proficient staff or brighter women whose low status prevents them from entering other occupations. The ragged general working and living conditions for both rural and urban staffs add to the dismal picture which turns away well-qualified teacher candidates who seek positions that offer greater public esteem and personal satisfaction.

Sporadic efforts are being made to address these issues, for they are seen as crucial to empowering national imperatives. However, the magnitude of non-educational domestic and foreign policy crises continues to collectively fracture the long-established facade of Soviet unity and, so far, to dwarf the importance of educational reforms (Brzezinski, 1989).

## THE IDEALS OF SCHOOL REFORM AS BASIC TO PERESTROIKA

Observers of the world scene as well as students of comparative international education are aware of the well-publicized efforts underway in the Soviet Union to restructure its major institutions. Many of the intelligentsia believe that crucial to the success of these efforts is the power of educational policymakers to change as well as strengthen the kinds of educational opportunities available both to the young and adult populations. President Mikhail Gorbachev's many compelling arguments in his best seller *Perestroika* popularized this view. He zeroed in on education as a key determinant of the direction and rate of change. Two traditional high priorities which he cited as imperative for an integrated curriculum included polytechnic and humanistic education. In the first case, the rigors of polytechnic education with its main focus on training youth for the world of work consistent with the demands of scientific and technological have to be mastered for the nation to achieve its economic targets. In the second case, the moral and ethical goals in humanistic education establish the proper guidelines for the upbringing of youth within the ideological and cultural framework of Communist society (Gorbachev, 1987).

The failure of both strands in Soviet education has become a *cause celebre*. Reformers from all quarters began publicly to express long-held private concerns that both teachers and students throughout the country had diminished motivation, curiosity, and purpose, and that the educational system had sunk into the same morass as the political and economic system. Clearly, those teachers in service needed to upgrade their teaching skills, general level of education, and sense of national purpose. On a longer term basis, a more sophisticated and professional workforce would have to be recruited, trained, and retained to create an educational environment with the potential to check the chaos in which this great nation has found itself.

## ISSUES AND PROBLEMS

### Issue 1: Inadequacies of a Trifurcated Teacher Training Model

Policymakers in the USSR are pondering the dilemma created by the national practice whereby teachers enter the profession from three educational segments. Each curriculum prepares candidates for the classroom with a range of knowledge, skills, and abilities that vary from basic pedagogical practicalities to advanced levels of professional and academic erudition. Such a diversified influx of practitioners undercuts the national effort to improve the quality of instruction in the classroom. It also accentuates the problem found in many countries around the world which is that the system, in general, attracts less able individuals to it. Furthermore, talented teachers leave after a few years.

*The Trifurcated System for Preparing Teachers*

Secondary institutes that specialize in preschool and elementary education train a majority (55 percent) of the elementary teachers in the field today, thus perpetuating a normal-school model. These programs are scheduled to phase out for apparent reasons: their graduates begin practice at age nineteen with minimal qualifications. The better trained 45 percent of the elementary teaching force are graduates of the pedagogical institutes with four or five years of higher education to their credit, a national long-term goal for all elementary staff.

For their part the universities also add to the teaching force, although their primary mission is to train future scholars and scientists. This has come about because the university entrance examination system does not screen adequately for the kinds of intellectuals capable of inductive thinking and the production of original work. Rather, the exams rely heavily on rote learning of facts and textbook definitions. On this basis, many students gain entry and do graduate, but do not complete postgraduate and/or doctoral study. In addition to having "Historian" inscribed on their diplomas, they will have the added entry, "Teacher of History" (Privavorov, 1989).

This situation further diffuses the teacher pool in the schools. Most university graduates have not mastered any teaching-learning strategies, although the university offers pedagogical courses. Rather, they have concentrated on becoming research-based professionals in a specific discipline. When the university graduates begin their public school assignments, they typically stress the rigors of content mastery through memorization of facts and applied deductive thinking. With minimal formal knowledge of how best to motivate the immature learner or appropriately impart knowledge, these university-trained teachers are part of the hard-core resistors to change. In contrast, pedagogical institute graduates have a thorough understanding of subject matter and the training in pedagogy sufficient to impart this knowledge, however imperfectly, to elementary and secondary learners.

### Pedagogical Institutes, an Inconsistent Source of Teacher Candidates

In view of this state of affairs, one would expect to find most pedagogical institute graduates in the schools. However, data indicate that 94.9 percent *plan* to work in the schools immediately after receiving their job assignments, but only 43.4 percent *plan* to do so in the long run (Ziiatdinuva, 1990). Unlike the misplaced university graduates who teach in the schools and live according to a modest standard of living, many institute graduates who have teacher of mathematics diplomas are happily employed in high-paying jobs as mathematicians or as computer programmers. This reversal of expected graduate placement has occurred for at least two reasons. In terms of learning basic subject matter, prestigious pedagogical institutes are quite comparable to less prestigious universities. During the pre-Gorbachev stagnation period, quite a few pedagogical institutes became universities at "the insistence of local leaders who needed another status vignette." For all intents and purposes, they remain pedagogical institutes in that they offer fewer specializations than universities, and often these are of poorer quality (Pivavarov, 1989). Thus, many high-powered students graduate from pedagogical institutes and pursue nonteaching careers; many mediocre students matriculate at the universities and enter the public school teaching force as other more prestigious occupations are closed to them.

Each of the three levels of teacher training discussed here has made a unique contribution to the rough mixture of practitioners in the field whose subject matter mastery, pedagogical know-how, and professional interests vary widely depending on educational opportunities and personal disposition. Token remedial efforts are underway, but the educational system is so vast and complex that nothing short of a major campaign for quality education, waged on many fronts, can begin to make the desired impact. Refresher courses on a grand scale, improved standards of certification, and the reorganization of preservice education stand out as imperatives.

## Issue 2: Liberalizing a Formalistic Teacher Training Plan

Because pedagogical institutes predominate as the primary trainer of teachers, their internal challenges and turmoil illuminate important ideological positions currently under debate. Two issues are being contested hotly. The first deals with the proper balance between academic courses and pedagogics, the general principles and philosophy of education. The second focuses on substantive issues in the pedagogical teacher training curriculum itself.

## An Academic Curriculum Versus Pedagogy

Students in pedagogical institutes are told from the beginning that the goal is to train future teachers, even if *their* main objective is to learn a discipline rather than to teach it in the schools. (Note that 50 percent of the graduates do not end up working in education, despite their announced plans to do so and the teacher shortage.) However, the balance in the course of study between classes in pedagogics (13.5 percent) and in subject matter (72.3 percent) appears to belie the institutes' purpose. To many policymakers, a realignment must take place so that a much greater emphasis can be given to courses in the bare essentials of the school curriculum and in strengthening professional teaching skills. According to this argument, it is irrelevant for future teachers to acquire expertise in the complexities of academic subjects if they cannot survive in a classroom setting of unmotivated children who will not profit from such erudition.

The reformers also hold that a more professional education will contribute to an enlightened school climate and will promote learning outcomes. It will therefore become unnecessary for teachers to engage in the many deceptive practices now associated with grade manipulation and the signing of false certificates and diplomas to cover up the alleged incompetence, immorality, and powerlessness of administrators who hold onto their positions at the expense of the teacher's professional honor. Indeed, there is an obvious gap between the proclaimed universal compulsory education and the actual level of training of most students, a condition resulting from pressured teachers having to meet 100 percent pass standards for their students. In 1987 the USSR State Statistical Committee reported that 4 million students were given a secondary education. In fact, this number of certificates was issued, but the number of those who received a general secondary education was at least 30 percent lower (Amonashvili, et al., 1989). No doubt a rebalancing in the current course of study in teacher education could produce a more effective teacher and contribute to mastery learning. This assumes that the professional curriculum features pragmatic courses based on research, psychology, and enlightened instructional strategies.

## Scholasticism Versus the Pedagogy of Cooperation

No longer acceptable in Soviet schools is the command-administrative, sternly authoritarian style of instruction that has been so destructive to mutual respect. In its place the reformers want the teacher's style of work and the curricula changed so that mutual cooperation between teachers and students in the classroom will foster creativity, individual differences, and honesty. An important contributor to this new thinking about school reform and the kinds of practitioners who will implement these changes is the Pedagogy of Cooperation. So labeled by the Teachers' Gazette (*Uchitel' skaia gazetta*), the Pedagogy is a loose association of teacher-scholar innovators around the USSR who gained public notice when the spirit of *glasnost* freed them to speak out against the establishment, the Ministry of Education. Basing their ideas on positive relations between teachers and students, the Pedagogy's restructuring principles have strongly supported the camp demanding more pedagogics in a teacher-training, clinical-based model.

Such a shift in emphasis will have to include a reevaluation of the current pedagogical curriculum which has been built around a preponderance of pedantic, uncritical dogmatism presented in a scholastic fashion. As it stands, students almost unanimously refer to pedagogy in its current form as "the least useful subject of the entire course," "a waste of time," "a collection of banal assertions not confirmed by classroom practices," and so on. (Pivavarov, 1989).

Progressive students and professors want to eliminate the current unpreparedness of beginning teachers by giving them large doses of some very practical skills, such as how to apply psychology to everyday classroom situations. This would seem to necessitate a new model in higher education pedagogical institutes in which the curriculum would become saturated with courses geared toward on-line clinical activities. To deal with these tasks plans are on the drawing board to create a new generation of syllabi, curricula, and textbooks. The old-line theoreticians in education have countered that such an emphasis on the practicality of teaching would weaken the alleged fundamental soundness in teacher education. However, even in view of their willingness to include more practical training skills while not compromising the time allocated to theory, these purists are hard pressed to defend the dogma on which the last seventy years has rested. Their critics point out that the prevalance of these abstract-theoretical courses has produced institute graduates with no knowledge of the schools, no confidence or enthusiasm for their new assignments, and no skills in making the necessary adjustments to the schoolroom (Ligachev, 1989).

Hence, the debate has taken at least two turns: (1) that the balance between subject matter courses and pedagogics must shift more to the latter; and (2) that the study of pedagogy must move from its present theoretical base to more practical applications.

Some very practical solutions remain open to the Soviets. In the first instance, a rebalancing of the course of study to reduce the overemphasis on content can still guarantee that graduates have an excellent command of the social sciences, humanities, arts, and sciences. In the second case pedagogical institutes may be able to find an agreeable compromise between the theoreticians and the pragmatists in education as they do have the autonomy to offer their own electives and options. With added time in the curriculum, opportunities would emerge for newer, more relevant courses that could reduce the "turf" warfare so familiar to academicians. However, this will not excuse the fundamentalists from the imperative to present the most cogent and compelling professional theories as handmaidens to classroom practice.

## Issue 3: Low Status of Teachers Which Impairs Recruitment and Retention of a Quality Professional Staff

It is doubtful that the Soviet economy can fully address a seventy-year buildup of educational needs, exacerbated by stronger competition from other Soviet institutions and power bases (e.g., the party and governmental bureaucracy, the military establishment, heavy/light industries, and agriculture).

### The Underlying Problem: Limited Financial Support for Education

The statistics tell their own story. Over the past quarter century expenditures on education have grown 470 percent and now add up to a total of 40 billion rubles. Yet, for many years the share of educational expenditures in the state budget has declined. In 1970 that share totaled 11 percent; in 1986 it was a modest 8 percent. The state budget has now reduced this meager allocation. The present share of expenditures on education is only two-thirds that of the United States, for example. In 1986 the secondary schools had equipment worth 58 rubles per student compared to 119 rubles in the German Democratic Republic and in Sweden, 750 rubles.

A common problem for all schools—from kindergarten to higher education institutions—is the low technical equipment level. Just to meet all the needs of the education system annually requires school supplies, equipment, and furniture worth approximately 2 billion rubles. In many schools today the basic equipment is a blackboard and chalk. Money spent on educational technology amounts to 56 rubles per student—which is half as much as is required by today's modest standards. Old equipment that has been dismantled by industry is being installed in vocational-technical schools, even those newly built. University, medical, and pedagogical institutes have been meeting only 15 percent of their requirements for specialized equipment (Ligachev, 1989).

The costs for new and improved school facilities are staggering. Although exact projections from the USSR are not readily available, comparable figures from California which projected a new student population of 780,000 over a five-year period (1986–1991) provide a scale. The Department of Finance estimates that twenty-six thousand new classrooms will cost at least $3.8 billion and that the deferred maintenance requests will total more than $2 billion by the end of that period (California Coalition, 1986). Since the U.S. and the USSR school population is approximately the same size, and California represents one-tenth of that population, it is clear that funds for facilities will present an ongoing challenge for both countries.

To these costs must be added the tremendous expense associated with elevating teacher salaries and fringe benefits, which can account for more than 70 percent of an education budget. Available statistics show that salaries for Soviet educators have simply not kept up with those for other professional groups. In 1982 the average monthly salary of instructors, including highly paid instructors in higher education, was 137.5 rubles. This ranked in fourteenth place among comparative groups and reflected a slippage from ninth place in 1965. Preliminary steps were taken in the middle 1980s to improve the wages of teachers in hard-to-staff assignments with as much as a 35.7 percent overall increase. More recent statistics (1988) report an average salary for the education sector of 195 rubles, which is still under the 203 rubles that is average for industrial workers and white-collar employees (Yagodin, 1988).

These statistics may paint a more favorable picture than actually exists in many of the separate republics. In 1988 the average aggregate per capita income in the families of workers and employees that are systematically studied by the USSR State Statistical Committee came to 152 rubles per month. A survey conducted in late 1988 among teachers in the Tatar ASSR (Autonomous Soviet Socialist Republic) showed that 40.5 percent of teachers' families had per capita incomes of over 100 rubles; 12.6 percent had per capita incomes of 120 to 150 rubles; and 6.6 percent had per capita incomes of more than 200 rubles. The minimum living standard is no rarity among teachers' families (Ziiatdinova, 1990).

These factors have seriously impaired recruitment and retention efforts for the most able teacher trainees/practitioners. Cognizant of this worldwide problem, twenty-five years ago the Intergovernmental Unesco Conference on the Question of the Status of Teachers (Paris, 1966) recognized "the crucial role played by teachers in the development of one of the most basic human rights—the right to an education—and the importance of the contribution teachers make to the development of the human personality and contemporary society" and passed a recommendation to assure teachers the status consistent with their role.

Status in that recommendation meant (1) a social position that reflected the respect due teachers because of the importance of their work and their ability to carry out their responsibilities, and (2) the working conditions, remuneration, and other material benefits as favorably compared to other professional groups (Ziiatdinova, 1990). If the prestige of the teaching profession is an accurate indicator of a country's development, the USSR must do more than catalog the extent of the disparities and deprivations. Policymakers must also calculate the impact that the new liberalization in economic activities will have on the talent pool as it will be drawn to new entrepreneurial/capitalistic opportunities.

*The Teaching Cadre's Place in the World of Work*

The most discussed topic of the extraordinary All-Union Congress of Workers in Public Education (1988) was the serious decline in the material and social prestige of the teaching profession. This decline was most graphically illustrated by a recent comprehensive survey (1989) conducted by the Department of Social Sciences of the Tatar Teachers' Refresher Institute. It questioned over eight hundred teachers, students, and parents on the theme, "Your opinion of the social status of the teacher in Soviet society." Respondents were selected by quota, taking into account the urban and rural populations of the Tatar ASSR. They included teachers who had taken institute qualifications courses to upgrade their skills, students in the ninth and tenth grades of city and rural schools, and parents in their workplaces or at the sites of their children's schools.

Highlights from this attitudinal questionnaire cast a deep shadow over the hope that the many unresolved social and economic problems of teachers in the USSR can or will be resolved expeditiously. The profession seems grounded in a field of negativity so dense that it defies the imagination as to how it can galvanize public opinion into supporting the mission of the schools and the unique contribution of the professional staff. For example, in the Tatar survey the respondents were asked, "In your opinion, how prestigious is the teacher's profession in society?" The rankings: "highly prestigious" by 4.6 percent of the students and 2.5 percent of the parents; "average prestigious" by 61.5 percent of the upper grade students and 46.0 percent by the parents; "low" or "very low" by one-third of the students (32.8 percent) and over half by the parents (51 percent). Characteristically, because of the primitive conditions prevailing in the rural schools, students from the rural areas gave a resounding negative assessment of 43.6 percent.

The survey probed teachers' attitudes toward their profession through questions referring to a second choice of profession. "If there was occasion to choose a profession over again," 60.6 percent would remain in their profession, 32.6 percent "would think about something else," and 9.3 percent "would certainly be repeating a mistake by choosing the teaching profession." Thus, almost 40 percent of experienced teachers are ready to change professions if offered the opportunity. The representativeness of these data is substantiated by research carried out in Krasnoiarsk, which found that only 57.4 percent of urban and 62.2 percent of rural teachers intended to remain in their profession.

Questions concerning "professions which society values *more highly* than the teaching profession in terms of social significance" graphically revealed the hierarchy of social values in the USSR. The majority opinion of the adult respondents (62.6 percent of the teachers and 57.0 percent of the parents) placed at the top people working in trade, public food services, and consumer services. Physicians followed as ranked by 34.6 percent of the teachers and 46.5 percent of the parents. Next preference went to highly qualified professional workers, journalists, and economists. In assessing the least prestigious profession, teachers and parents again agreed. They singled out the engineer's profession (5 percent of the teachers and 10.5 percent of parents). Students surveyed had substantial differences in their value orientations in ranking the above categories but were consistent in placing the teaching profession below those mentioned.

Student responses to several questions add a unique dimension, for it is from this group that future recruits to the profession must be drawn. Only about 15 percent of the upper grade students definitely linked their own life plans to the teaching profession. Nearly one-half (54.1 percent) of the school graduates "would not choose the teaching profession," and 24.6 percent of them "would not choose it under any circumstances." To the question, "What factors evoke negative attitudes toward the teaching profession in you?" almost one-half (47.2

percent) cited in the first place "the absence of human contact between teacher and students."

The Tatar survey categorized the reasons for student negativity toward the teaching profession: the unsatisfactory material-technical base of the schools (33.4 percent), teachers' low salaries (29.7 percent), neglect of the material and living conditions of teachers (28.8 percent), the absence of appreciable results in public education (26.3 percent), the absence of any help to teachers on the part of the public (24.6 percent), the policy (*diktat*) of the administration of public education (23.8 percent) and, as a result, the lack of prestige of the schools themselves in society (21.7 percent), and the unattractive image of teachers in mass consciousness (17.1 percent) (Ziiatdinova, 1990). Parents' responses paralleled those of the youth to this question and many others that attempted to characterize the esteem in which the teaching profession is held by the clientele and parents it serves.

The discouragingly low overall ratings to questions about the political, cultural, and intellectual character of today's teacher, about the imperative to provide teachers with the opportunity to acquire books, journals, and newspapers in scarce supply, and about family support for the teacher's authority confound any foreseeable basic restructuring of the professional image. As parents counsel their bright and motivated offspring on vocational/professional career choices, their failure to consider the teaching profession as an option will perpetuate the failures and weaknesses so well documented in the present system.

The Politburo, cognizant of the difficulties facing the teaching profession, is seeking to turn the system around through a dedicated effort to enlist the best intellectual resources of society to teach and bring up school- and college-age youth. It intends to recruit "the most outstanding scholars, cultural figures, and specialists in the national economy" through an early identification plan which is to become the common concern of all councils of educational institutions, their administrators, and party organizations to implement, nurture, mentor, and support. "Young people who are inclined to go into teaching should be spotted early, while they are still in school or college; they should be given good advice and recommended for enrollment in higher educational institutions; they must be provided with jobs and organized, (given) internships; mentors should be selected early on. Without all this, it will be impossible to achieve genuine renewal" (Ligachev, 1989).

*Conditions of Employment: The School and Community*

The Tatar survey also explored the reasons for teacher dissatisfaction with the profession and discovered the following as most crucial in their opinion: lack of attention to material conditions of life (56 percent), absence of public education's appreciable success (41.3 percent), the unsatisfactory material-technical base of the schools (38.6 percent), the low level of scientific and methodological support for the teacher's efforts (37 percent), the dictatorship of public school administration (25.6 percent), low salaries (20.6 percent), and lack of the necessary conditions for creative endeavor (17.3 percent). It is clear that teachers are most dissatisfied with their social position and the environment in which they work (Ziiatdinova, 1990).

Aware of the general level of discontent, the USSR Ministry of Education has spoken out on the necessity to redress the social injustices borne by the profession that suffers by comparison with workers in other fields. At present, 84,000 teachers live in private apartments, but more than 200,000 need improved housing. By contrast, in industry, several times more housing is built annually per worker than in public education. According to data released by the USSR Central Statistical Administration, in 1986 the loss of work-time by workers in public education owing to illness and child care added up to 775 work-days per 100 workers. However, only two sanitorium vouchers (*putevki*) and three vacation home vouchers were allotted per 100 workers. There are further inequities: only 15 out of 193 teacher refresher institutes have preventive sanatoria, and the profession has no Pioneer camps, a major benefit for urban workers in particular (USSR Ministry of Education, 1989).

Thousands of children and teachers are on double and triple sessions to accommodate the new intake of six year olds as well as to compensate for the ravages to existing facilities where there has been no deferred maintenance. Long hours, many in the darkness of early morning and evening, crowded conditions, large classes, and the overuse of frayed materials and equipment add to the daily burdens of teachers who labor in full view of a critical public.

Despite a national school construction campaign, investigations undertaken by the USSR Central Statistical Administration uncovered in the early 1980s numerous cases of figure padding to bolster the number of schools built. Existing on paper only were 25 percent of the claimed school accommodations in Kirghizia, 17 percent in Uzbekistan, 14 percent in Turkmenia, 13 percent in Belorussia, and 11 percent in Moldavia. Currently, 1.25 million school students (3.3 percent of the total school population) and their teachers attend schools that should have been demolished, and 8.4 million (22 percent of the total school population) are attending schools that need major repairs. In Tadzhikistan and Kirghizia up to 9 percent of the students and their teachers are attending schools housed in dilapidated buildings, and 40 percent are going to schools requiring major repairs (Denisova, 1990).

A closer look at classroom conditions around the USSR detail the work environment of the teaching profession which repels all but the most robust or desperate. From every part of the Soviet Union, letters of protest from teachers, parents, and concerned citizens have bombarded major newspapers, journals, the USSR State Committee on Public Education, and party authorities up to and including the CPSU Central Committee which graphically describe the situation. Anxious teachers from the Kirov Region wrote to *Pravda* in June 1987 as follows: "Our school in the village of Lekma, Slobodskoi District, is in an old wooden building. It was built back in the last century. The roof sags and the rafters are pulling apart. The district sanitation and epidemiology station has issued an official document certifying that the school is in hazardous condition. The school's troubles are also affecting people's moods.''

The journal *Krest'ianka* received a letter from the village of Tsvitna, Aleksandrovskii District, Kirovograd Region: "Youngsters in the secondary school are cold from early autumn until spring. The temperature in the room never rises above 10 degrees C. When the cold season sets in, the youngsters have to sit in class with their coats on, on cold benches. If they are wet when they come to school, there is no place for them to dry out. It's cold in the gymnasium. In the cafeteria also. The youngsters are always getting sick." Despite the humane slogan, "Children Are Our Common Concern" and reports about more and more new, modern schools with computers, video technology, swimming pools, and cafeterias, official data announced at the February 1988 Plenum CPSU Central Committee paint a contrasting picture.

Nationwide, 21 percent of the students and their teachers attend schools in buildings lacking central heating, 30 percent in buildings lacking plumbing, and 40 percent in buildings lacking a sewer system. More than 40 percent of general education school students (more than half in the countryside) are not provided with gymnasiums. In the rural schools attended by 16 million children and taught by 1.5 million educators, 4,000 lack electricity, 72,000 do not have indoor plumbing, and nine out of every ten lack a sewer system.

The new intake of six year olds has further exacerbated the facilities crunch. Many schools have converted dressing rooms, teachers' lounges, and hallways into classroom space. In Estonia, in 1988, only twenty-five out of fifty-three new classrooms for six year olds passed inspection. In Chimkent Region, in 1989, 634 schools announced they were accepting six year olds, but the sanitation officers authorized only 26 schools. In Kazakhstan inspectors recently came upon an appalling case. In the Georgievsk School in Lengerskii District, two lavatories with tiled walls had been converted to classrooms. Of course, such conditions have a negative impact on how youngsters feel. Out of 4,000 six-year-olds questioned in different areas of the country in 1988, about 80 percent complained of fatigue and 30 percent complained of headaches. By the end of the school year many youngsters' eyesight had deteriorated. Motivated by pedagogical research to begin formal instruction at age six instead of seven, the state has failed to plan or provide the necessary instructional support for such an immediate and dramatic student intake. The resulting ordeal for both students and teachers has been destructive to morale and learning (Denisova, 1990).

Teachers and students work with outdated technology, which compounds the misery of everyday working conditions. An exhibit at the USSR VDNKH (Exhibition of Achievements in the National Economy) in 1988 with the theme "Technical Means of Instruction in Public Education," occupying 10,000 square meters of exhibition space, showed visitors physics instruments that were developed in 1937 and are still being used to acquaint school students with the principles of modern physics. It also displayed primitive and mediocre visual aids and Soviet-made computers whose outstanding feature is their record number of breakdowns per minute of operation. The situation is especially critical in the rural areas where the lack of technology, electricity, and plumbing adds to the woes of the staff which tries to instruct in classrooms with dirt floors and no ceilings. "Is it any wonder that a woman teacher from Tadzhikistan, taking the speaker's stand in the 'Rural Schools' section at a recent teachers' congress, could not utter a single word but burst into tears?" (Denisova, 1990 p. 10).

Many other problems plague the schools and affect the vitality of the teaching profession. Grade inflation, plummeting educational standards, moral turpitude in the classroom, low proficiency in the Russian language, and lack of professional competence among school administrators stand out as major detriments.

## CONCLUSION

In the age of *glasnost'* many of the truths of the past are being examined and have been found to be false. As the purging continues and the public at large begins to grasp the enormity of the problems facing education, it has to be obvious that the system cannot by itself rectify the situation. It will take the full commitment of the state to overcome the discrepancies that have stood in the way of education's power to transform the Soviet society and to meet the proclaimed expectations for the twenty-first century.

The limitations in the trifurcated system of teacher training are both obvious and subtle. The reformers agree that the secondary institutions which are specializing in teacher training courses must be phased out, for the young and unsophisticated graduates with minimum pedagogical training cannot meet basic professional standards. Yet, if the history of teacher training in the United States is any measure, it will take decades to convert from the normal school model to the college/university teacher-candidate design.

A more difficult dilemma is that of vocational misplacement for the pedagogical institute and university graduates who do or do not elect to work in education. Appropriate changes in the certification system may provide a substantive and qualitative leap in enhancing teachers' professional skills and might guarantee certain proficiencies in the classroom regardless of the candidates' formal training. More precise vocational counseling could insure that more teacher trainees gain entrance to the pedagogical institutes and eliminate students with noneducational goals who account for substantial numbers of place holders.

For the Soviets it is an alarming fact that today the system of pedagogical education is only weakly oriented toward the formation of creative, broadly erudite, competent teachers. The requisite commitment to the package of programs for the reform of teacher education has been lacking. The old formalism persists, with its reliance on the dogmatism prevalent for the past seventy years. However, significant breakthroughs are evident, especially in urban institutions which have had better technology, trained instructors, and access to the ideas of the reformers.

The financing of education must be given high priority if the status of teachers is to be improved so that it attracts a more talented cadre. Conditions in the schools detract from a positive working environment to the extent that only a few able men and women accept teaching as a long-term commitment.

## REFERENCES

Amonashvili, I., et al. "The Methodology of Reform." *Soviet Education* 31, no. 7 (1989): 44–76.

Brzezinski, Z. *The Grand Failure. The Birth and Death of Communism in the Twentieth Century*. New York: Macmillan Publishing Co., 1989.

California Coalition for Fair School Finance. *Facilities and Students: The Issues* 10 (1986): 1–6.

Denisova, L. "Let Us not Sin Against the Truth." *Soviet Education* 32, no. 5 (1990): 7–31.

Gorbachev, M. *Perestroika. New Thinking for Our Country and the World*. New York: Harper and Row, 1987.

Ligachev, E. "On the Course of Restructuring the Secondary and Higher Education System and the Party's Task in Carrying it Out." *Soviet Education* 31, no. 4 (1989): 6–67.

Pivavarov, V. "Teacher Education in the Soviet Union: Processes and Problems in Context of Perestroika." In E. Gumbert, ed., *Fit to Teach: Teacher Education in International Perspective*. Atlanta, Ga.: Center for Cross-Cultural Education, Georgia State University, 1989, pp. 8, 87–103.

USSR Ministry of Education, Summaries. "Place School Restructuring on the Level of Today's Requirements." Soviet Education 31, no. 3 (1989): 24–49.

Yagodin, G. "Through Humanization and Democratization, Toward a New Quality of Education." *The Current Digest of the Soviet Press* 40, no. 52 (1988): 3.

Ziiatdinova, F. "The Teacher's Social Position." *Soviet Education* 32, no. 5 (1990): 32–42.

# 16

## UNITED STATES

### WILLIS D. HAWLEY

Since the early 1980s the United States has been involved in major efforts to improve its public schools. Improving the quality of teacher education is a central goal of this educational reform movement. After briefly describing the context within which changes in teacher preparation are being called for, we turn to an examination of eight issues or general proposals for reforming teacher education in the United States, the assumptions and research that relate to these ideas, and how policymakers and teacher educators have responded. The final sections of this chapter seek to predict what new changes are likely to be widely adopted in the near future and to suggest what the rationale for more fundamental reforms than those now receiving much attention might look like.

### GENERAL BACKGROUND

Americans always seem to be involved in efforts to reform their schools, and it is not easy to say just when these efforts become national movements. Most observers agree that the current reform movement began no later than the spring of 1983, when the federal government's National Commission on Educational Excellence issued a report in which it declared that the quality of American education rendered the country *A Nation at Risk*. There is little doubt that the educational reform movement in the United States was energized primarily by the conviction that the quality of schools had declined and was inferior to the quality of education in other countries, with which the nation is competing economically.

The belief that the United States had fallen from some previously acceptable level of school quality and the realization that most of the world's educational systems were more centrally controlled and more uniform in their definition of educational goals and content than were American schools led to a "first wave" of reforms that sought to specify goals and standards for student achievement, limit curricular diversity, require tests of teacher candidates and teachers, and reward teachers based on performance. In general, control of educational decision making shifted from local communities to state governments.

The previous major call for educational reform in the United States was triggered in 1957 by the Soviet Union's success in sending Sputnik into outer space. This led to experimentation and efforts to enrich the core curricula of schools, especially courses related to mathematics and science. In contrast, the reform movement of the current decade sees experimentation as part of the problem and demands that students take more core courses and that these courses push students to learn those things that can be tested on so-called standardized tests. Both reform movements saw teachers as part of the problem, but the earlier effort sought ways to cope with the perceived limitations of many teachers and notions like teacher-proofing the curriculum gained some currency.

Contemporary reformers have seen teachers as a big part of both the problem and the solution. As the nation became increasingly convinced that the academic ability of the average student was declining, concern for the academic ability of teachers gained increasing attention. Research reported the low scores on college entrance tests of students wanting to teach, showed that many education majors had weak high school and college courses, and revealed that even among those wanting to teach when they entered college, the most academically able chose other careers (Schlechty and Vance, 1983). These findings fueled concerns about standards being applied in teacher education programs and about the ability of the "profession" to attract talented people given new career opportunities available to women and racial minorities. Many teachers, perhaps reacting to the decline in their earning power, to the bashing they were receiving by some policymakers and by the popular media, as well as to the greater diversity of students in their classrooms, added credibility to the idea that teaching had lost its appeal to able people by asserting, in response to national surveys, that they would not now recommend that others choose a career in education.

While Americans were losing faith in the academic ability of the nation's teachers—despite the absence of evidence that those who were actually hired to teach in recent years were any less qualified than those teachers hired earlier—researchers were finding increasing evidence that teachers' mastery of various instructional strategies explained variations in student learning and that effective schools were characterized by certain working conditions that fostered effective teaching (Hawley and Rosenholtz, 1984).

Growing recognition of the importance of good teachers, concern that the academic abilities of prospective teachers were declining, mounting concern over an impending teacher shortage, and the overall conviction that the nation's public schools were failing combined to make teaching and teachers focal points of the reform movement of the 1980s.

## THE IMPROVEMENT OF TEACHING AND TEACHER EDUCATION

The initial reforms designed to improve teachers and the profession emphasized teacher evaluation and higher teacher salaries. Evaluation and pay were to be linked through merit pay or career ladders in a number of states and localities. These proposals were followed by a so-called second wave of reforms emphasizing the importance of improving the conditions under which teachers worked.

Once the quality of teachers and teaching was on the policy agenda, efforts to reform teacher education proliferated. It is, of course, quite sensible to believe that improvements in teacher education would improve teaching, and the available research supports this assumption. On the other hand, teacher education had few defenders, and not a single study was available to demonstrate that variations in the content and process of teacher education made a difference in how well teachers taught. Indeed, teachers themselves seemed to rank their preservice preparation to teach rather low when asked what accounted for their professional expertise. However, while the potential contributions of teacher education reform to the improvement of schools were uncertain, other considerations made teacher education a popular target of educational reformers. These considerations also shaped the nature of the teacher education reform proposals that have been most widely adopted.

There are at least five reasons why preservice teacher education has attracted the interest of reformers. First, teacher education programs are generally held in low esteem on their own campuses. Thus, not only did few leaders in higher education come to the defense of teacher education programs, or at least oppose regulation of them, but a number of prominent academicians joined the call for reform. Although these calls for reform from within were not prescriptive, they gave implicit support to the premise that intervention by state governments or university governing boards was justified.

Second, the perception that college students pursuing teacher education were, in general, very weak academically made it easy to argue that various constraints should be placed on who should be admitted to teacher education and to the profession itself. The assumption that teacher education students were weak academically reinforced the belief that teacher education curricula were not very rigorous or worthy of considerable investments of student time.

Third, teacher educators were engaged in extensive self-studies, and those advocating change sought to build support for their proposals by pointing to the weaknesses of "conventional strategies" for preparing teachers. Although many teacher educators were seeking reform themselves, there was little agreement about the directions of change, at least little agreement that others could discern. Moreover, the most visible calls for change—by the American Association of Colleges for Teacher Education (1985), the Holmes Group (1986), and the

Carnegie Forum (1986)—directly or indirectly argued for eliminating or diminishing undergraduate teacher preparation, and this led to considerable rancor among teacher educators. This internal division may have confirmed the idea that change from within colleges and universities was unlikely.

Fourth, teacher education was already heavily regulated by states. Most states had specific course requirements for teachers, for example, and had had them for some time. Indeed, teacher educators themselves regularly advocated state policies that would ensure that prospective teachers would take the courses they believed were essential to effective teaching and that they, it happens, taught.

Fifth, teacher education reforms did not cost much money. Thus, one could require more or fewer courses, more fieldwork, teacher candidate testing, and other provisions without having to make tradeoffs with other reforms. Even if one did not think teacher education reform was a high priority, establishing policies to bring it about seemed to cost less than other ways to express a commitment to educational improvement. Not surprisingly, the states with the most restrictive teacher-entry policies typically made relatively small investments in public education.

None of this is to suggest that the reasons for reforming teacher education are wholly opportunistic. As noted earlier, it is intuitively sensible to believe that improvements in the way teachers are taught would have a positive effect on teaching. Moreover, it was not difficult to find support for the proposition that most teacher education programs needed improvement or for the conclusion that many programs were so weak that the best thing to do was to abolish them. But the vulnerability of teacher education to demands for change from outside of colleges and universities contributed to easy victories for reformers. Thus, few efforts to study the relevant research or otherwise to think through the consequence of proposed reforms or to experiment with alternative models of teacher preparation have emanated from state agencies. Colleges and universities themselves have not infrequently looked beyond the teacher education program itself for ways to improve the education of teachers.

## THE AGENDA FOR REFORMING TEACHER EDUCATION
## IN THE UNITED STATES

Since the mid–1980s, a host of government-sponsored and privately financed studies and reports on teacher education have been issued and an unprecedented number of reform proposals have been introduced by state legislators. Dozens of different prescriptions have emerged from all of this activity. Most of those that have received continuing consideration can be encompassed by one of eight general issues and themes:

1. Various measures of intellectual capability and academic achievement should be used to control entry to teacher education and to teaching so as to increase the quality of the teaching corps.

2. Prospective teachers should have a strong grounding in the liberal arts and should have substantial coursework in the subjects they will teach.

3. Professional education courses, especially those related to teaching methods, should be more sophisticated and more demanding.

4. Professional education should involve more field experiences and semester-long practice teaching experiences.

5. The teachers of prospective teachers should model effective and varied teaching practices.

6. College or university-based preservice teacher education should be extended to one full year of coursework beyond the time the person receives the bachelor's degree.

7. Induction programs for first-year teachers or special schools for teacher training within public school systems should be developed in order to ensure that new teachers are able to put into effect and build on what they learn about teaching in college.

8. States should develop ways that individuals can be certified that would not require attendance in conventional preparation programs.

These eight issues and themes represent the public agenda for teacher education reform in the United States. In the next several pages, we will examine the assumptions that underlie these general proposals, whether they can be supported by evidence or grounded theory, the extent to which they have been or are likely to be implemented, and their probable consequences. To the extent that hard evidence and specific examples exist, we will try to use them, but we acknowledge that some of the conclusions reached are based on rather long inferential leaps. When such speculation is not obvious, an attempt will be made to label it accordingly.

Before examining the issues of greatest interest to those who would reform teacher education in the United States, it may be useful to briefly describe the basic characteristics of teacher preparation.

## THE SYSTEM OF TEACHER EDUCATION

Describing teacher education in the United States is not a simple task. More than other educational programs at colleges and universities, teacher education programs are shaped by state government regulations. These regulations, which are reflected in both requirements for teacher certification and standards for program approval, vary enormously in content and in their specificity. Variations in policy are, of course, reflected in the structure and content of programs. Within states, teacher education programs vary considerably owing to differences in the missions, students, and resources of the institutions. Despite this variability, it is possible to identify some general characteristics of teacher education in the United States.

• Over 1,200 four-year institutions of higher education (more than 70 percent of all four-year colleges and universities) educate teachers. Despite declining enrollments in teacher education in the 1970s, the number of institutions offering teacher education programs has increased.

- While more than half of the institutions educating teachers are private, public colleges and universities prepare about 80 percent of the teachers.

- Less than half of the teacher education programs are accredited by the National Council for the Accreditation of Teacher Education (NCATE), although some of the institutions not accredited are among the most prestigious. All programs, however, are approved by state education agencies, and the institutions in which they are housed are accredited by regional accrediting bodies.

- Most of the coursework prospective teachers take is not in pedagogical subjects or professional studies. Students preparing to teach in secondary schools typically take less than 25 percent of their courses in professional studies and major in one or more academic disciplines taught in the schools. Students wanting to teach in elementary schools take almost 45 percent of their course credits in subjects related directly to teaching and learning.

While variations in state requirements account for variations in teacher preparation programs across states, most of the states participate in "reciprocity agreements" that allow teachers certified in other states to teach in theirs. Teacher certification and licensure are typically linked, and requirements differ by teaching specialty. Most states provide for dozens of different certification fields.

Most new teachers in the United States receive their initial teacher certification in the context of undergraduate college programs. Typically, completion of undergraduate teacher education programs requires a bachelor's degree and 135 credits (or nine conventional semesters) for prospective secondary teachers and 125 credits for those preparing to teach in elementary schools.

As students move through their college years, they become increasingly engaged in professional coursework and field experiences. The first two years of college are spent primarily in general education, mainly arts and science courses. Often, some teacher education courses are taken in the first two years, but formal admission to the teacher preparation usually occurs after the sophomore year. Practice teaching is undertaken for all or most of one of a student's last two semesters in college.

With this brief overview of teacher education in mind, let us turn to the proposals for change that comprise the agenda for teacher education reform in 1988.

## ISSUES AND PROBLEMS

### Issue 1: The Academic Ability of Teachers Should Be Enhanced

Various measures of academic capability, subject matter knowledge, and professional competence should be used to control entry to teacher education and teaching so as to increase the quality of the teaching corps.

## Assumptions

There has been an extraordinary increase in the use of formal testing and other preservice screening procedures to influence the quality of teaching in the United States. This movement derives its energy from at least four assumptions:

1. A significant proportion of the students preparing to be teachers and who enter teaching in the United States are not very bright or academically able.

2. A significant number of would-be teachers lack fundamental knowledge and competence related to effective instruction.

3. Many teacher educators and institutions of higher education cannot be counted on to provide prospective teachers with the knowledge and skills they need or to screen out of teaching those among their students who fail to meet acceptable standards of performance and achievement.

4. A person's performance on written tests or in college courses is a valid measure of potential teaching effectiveness.

## Relevant Evidence

Assumptions about the limited academic ability of teachers appear to be based largely on a handful of highly publicized studies and stories that report the poor performance of teachers or prospective teachers on written tests and the relatively weak performance on college entrance examinations of high school graduates who *say* that they *intend* to teach. However, studies that focus on college entrants tell us very little about teacher education students, much less about teachers. More than half of the students who initially express interest in teaching never receive a teaching certificate, and those college students who transfer into teaching programs from other fields are more able, on the average, than those who "drop out." Moreover, many of those certified—roughly 30 percent—do not become teachers.

College students who are engaged in teacher education, on the whole, appear to be as able academically as other college students. A national sample of teacher education students surveyed in 1985–1986 reported their grade point averages and admission test scores at levels that place them in the middle of the distribution of scores and performance of all students and in the top third of their high school graduating classes. The Scholastic Aptitude Test (SAT) scores reported by these students were roughly 100 points higher than the scores reported for prospective freshmen interested in teaching that have received so much attention. While elementary teacher candidates had lower SAT scores than secondary teacher candidates, they had slightly higher grade point averages *before* entering teacher education. This relatively positive picture of the comparative academic capability of prospective teachers is similar to the findings of an analysis of data from a 1985 national survey of college graduates conducted by the U.S. Department of Education.

A number of studies compare the academic ability of students in teacher education with that of arts and science majors. Some of these studies examine many colleges and universities within the same state, and more look at a particular campus. All these works suggest that teacher education students compare favorably with arts and science students, although it seems reasonable to conclude that there are more very weak education students than very strong students on most campuses.

But to say that students preparing to be teachers are average may be unsatisfying. And to know the average capability of prospective teachers does not tell us about the distribution at the low end of the achievement spectrum where parents presumably want none of their children's teachers to reside. Moreover, it may be that teacher education graduates with higher scores on the National Teachers' Examination are less likely to enter teaching than those with lower scores (Schlechty and Vance, 1983). Do various tests and do college grades predict the performance and effectiveness of future teachers? Scores on tests of subject matter knowledge and grades in the subjects a teacher teaches appear to have a small but consistent relationship with teacher performance and student achievement. This relationship is stronger when the courses being taught focus on more sophisticated content matter and learning objectives (e.g., the acquisition of higher order skills). Although college entrance tests apparently do not predict teacher effectiveness, there is some reason to believe that scores on tests of teachers' verbal ability are related to student achievement (Hawley and Rosen-holtz, 1984).

What has been the impact of these assessments and standards? National longitudinal data on the academic quality of teacher candidates are limited. While it seems likely that there has been no great change over time in the *relative* ability of teacher education students, fluctuations in teacher salaries and the availability of jobs will no doubt explain some changes. But the full impact of the large-scale introduction of new constraints on the composition of teacher education programs and on entry to the profession that took place in the 1980s has yet to be assessed adequately. In the South, where state policies have been most restrictive, teacher educators agree that the quality of teacher candidates has risen and, perhaps because job opportunities and salaries for beginning teachers have improved, overall enrollments have not diminished.

Nationally, enrollments in undergraduate teacher education increased significantly in the mid–1980s. However, one consequence of the new screens to teacher education and to teaching has been the reduction in the number of black, Hispanic, and Native American students who are interested in and eligible to enter the teaching corps.

*Implementation*

As of fall 1989, forty-five states had mandated some form of testing for prospective teachers. This includes basic skills tests, usually administered prior to formal entry to teacher education; tests of general knowledge; tests of subject matter knowledge; and tests of professional knowledge and skills. Many states employ two or more of these types of tests, and the most commonly used are those developed by the Educational Testing Service. Following the lead perhaps of the NCATE, an increasing number of states are requiring minimum grade point averages for entry to teacher education programs. Even where these requirements are not mandated by state governments, many institutions have established them or raised their requirements.

The quality assurance measures that may have the largest effect on teacher education in the long run are on-the-job tests of beginning teacher performance. In some states, the performance of new teachers on such measures is tied to either or both state approval of the teacher education program or to teachers' opportunities for certification or merit pay. Such performance assessments may be particularly influential because their implications for curriculum design and content are clear.

## Issue 2: Teachers Should Be "Better Educated"

Prospective teachers should have a stronger grounding in the liberal arts and substantial coursework, in most cases a major, in the subject(s) they teach.

*Assumptions*

This proposal actually embodies two separable ideas, but they invariably are proposed together. First, let us examine the call for liberal arts-focused teacher education. Seemingly almost everyone in the United States believes that teachers should have a strong liberal arts education. The issue is: what does "strong" mean? There appears to be substantial agreement that at least half of a teacher's undergraduate education should be in the liberal arts and that this coursework should be broadly distributed in the natural sciences, humanities, and the social sciences. The assumption underlying this belief is that such a background will allow teachers to call on a broad range of knowledge in making judgments in general and in giving context and depth to their teaching.

Many critics of conventional teacher education, including some teacher educators, have argued that the equivalent of two years of liberal arts coursework leaves teachers undereducated in comparison to other professionals who often have three years of general education and one year or more of a disciplinary major (Holmes Group, 1986).

Just as few would oppose liberal arts-based education for teachers, hardly anyone would argue that teachers need not know the subjects they teach. But, again, the issue is: what does it mean to know one's subject? There appears to be near consensus that secondary teachers should essentially major for at least a year's worth of courses in the subject to be taught (even though a fourth to a third of universities did not have such a requirement in the 1980s). But there is much less agreement about whether elementary and middle or junior high school teachers should be required to major in a single subject or in an interdisciplinary major other than education. Despite this lack of agreement, all the states tend to require that all teacher candidates major in a field or fields other than or in addition to education.

The assumption underlying the idea that secondary teachers should major in the subject they teach is obvious enough: such study is seen as essential to prospective teachers' effectiveness to teach the content that students in their courses will be expected to learn. A corollary of this assumption is that the more teachers know about a subject, the easier it is for them to learn new things about that subject. The importance of this notion to teacher effectiveness is presumably greatest in those fields whose content changes rapidly, like the sciences. However, many high school teachers teach more than one topic (e.g., math and physics), and there is little demand among would-be reformers of teacher education that teacher candidates complete a major in the subjects for which they receive so-called secondary endorsements to teach (though the Holmes Group report calls for this level of coursework to be completed subsequent to initial certification).

The absence of a demand that prospective secondary teachers major in every subject they teach may represent an accommodation to the reality that such demands would significantly reduce the supply of teachers. It may also reflect another assumption about the usefulness of a major in an academic discipline, an assumption that seems to motivate many of those who advocate requiring prospective elementary teachers to major in a single subject. This assumption is that learning one subject in some depth is itself a source of intellectual development and gives the person confidence that he or she can gain a sophisticated understanding of a field. This expertise, it is argued, is part of being "well educated." Another view of the utility of studying one topic in some depth is that it is a form of mental exercise and that the intellectual strength that develops therefrom can be applied to other intellectual tasks independent of their content.

Behind the idea that teachers should have more coursework in the liberal arts and in a given subject than many teachers have had in the past is the view that these courses are more challenging intellectually than are education courses. This assumption links the notion of "better educated" to these reforms. As the Holmes Group (1986, p. 93) asserts in its statement of the need for extended teacher education programs (those that exceed the conventional undergraduate curriculum): "The curriculum for prospective career teachers does not permit a major in education during the baccalaureate years—instead, undergraduates pursue *more serious* general/liberal study and a standard academic subject normally taught in the schools" (emphasis added).

*Relevant Evidence*

To have a firm grounding in the liberal arts may mean different things at different colleges and universities, and the systematic study of the impact of variations in the content and number of liberal arts courses on the performance or effectiveness of prospective teachers is virtually nonexistent.

A number of studies seek to determine the relationship between the subject matter knowledge or background of teachers and their effectiveness in teaching that subject. The findings from these studies are somewhat inconsistent, but it seems reasonable to conclude that the number of courses a person takes in a subject or a person's grades in these courses are unrelated to teaching effectiveness; and knowledge of subject matter measured by tests is modestly associated with student learning, especially in more advanced courses. Studies from which these generalizations are derived deal almost exclusively with the teaching and learning of secondary subjects. Thus, we can obtain no lessons here for the redesign of certification programs for elementary school teachers.

As noted above, implicit in the argument that more preservice coursework should be required in the liberal arts and in academic disciplines is the belief that education courses are not very challenging. The U.S. Department of Education's report (1987) advocating alternative certification programs for liberal arts graduates reflects this conviction when it cites a teacher's conclusion that "Most education courses are cheap hoops through which one must jump in order to enter the classroom." There are no content analyses which examine the relative rigor, by whatever standards rigor might be defined, of education as compared to that of other courses. It appears that when students majoring in liberal arts fields are not constrained by specific requirements, they do not elect courses because those courses would add depth to their knowledge of a given topic or because the courses are known for their rigor.

*Implementation*

Several states have increased the number of liberal arts courses that teachers must take before they can be certified. In addition, there appears to be a trend among states to require that teachers, at least secondary teachers, major in a field taught in high school.

The requirement for an academic major has not always been applied to primary or middle school teaching candidates, and in some states a multidisciplinary major is permitted in lieu of a single subject field. It is not·yet clear how or even whether these requirements will be applied to persons seeking certification in special education, vocational education, or other specialty fields. These requirements, when they are accompanied by a reduction in specific state requirements for education-related courses (as they have been in some states), might have the effect of reducing the number of education courses required by colleges and universities for teacher certification—but not necessarily.

At many institutions of higher education, teacher candidates are being required to take a broader range of courses than was required a few years ago. At the same time, requirements in education courses are also being increased. Thus, undergraduate students seeking certification are finding it increasingly difficult to graduate from college in four years. Perhaps in response to this situation, or perhaps because they value pedagogy less than other states, the legislatures in some states (e.g., Virginia and Texas) have substantially limited the number of education course credits that can be required for certification.

### Issue 3: The Teacher Education Curriculum Should Be More Rigorous

Professional education courses, especially those related to teaching methods, should be more sophisticated and more demanding. While the terms *sophisticated* and *demanding* are not very precise, when applied to the teacher education curriculum, they connote three tests of curriculum reform and student evaluation: the material taught should reflect the latest and best research on teaching and learning; the content of education courses should require just as much intellectual effort to understand as do other courses; and the standards by which student performance is judged should be at least as rigorous as the standards applied in other courses.

*Assumptions*

An obvious assumption that gives rise to this proposal is that teacher education is not academically rigorous. This belief seems to follow from other beliefs relating to the alleged academic weakness of most teacher education students, and it is sustained by recurrent reports by teachers that their teacher education courses were not demanding. The prescription of greater rigor seems to assume that the three aspects of rigor noted above will result both in screening from teaching students who are not academically able and in enhancing the contributions teachers can make to student learning.

*Relevant Evidence*

There are no studies of course content which examine the relative rigor of education courses in terms of the level of intellectual effort required or the currency and quality of the research they cover. However, in a recent survey of a national sample of teacher education students, a majority of those preparing to teach in high school ranked their teacher education courses as more time consuming than other courses. When asked to compare the rigor of their methods courses with courses in various content areas, these students saw English and history courses to be no different, on average, than methods courses, but they regarded courses in foreign languages, math, and science as more demanding. A review of college transcripts of southern students shows that teacher education students tend to keep their distance from foreign language, science, and math courses that are not required.

*Implementation*

As noted, the academic quality of teacher education students is increasing because of screening mechanisms and increases in teacher salaries. There is some anecdotal evidence that this change is allowing some education faculty to make greater demands on their students.

It appears that teacher educators throughout the United States are revising methods courses in light of recent research on teaching and learning. The American Association of Colleges of Teacher Education (AACTE) has published a series of authoritative reviews of research to facilitate these curricular changes, and the U.S. Office of Educational Research and Improvement (OERI) has been supporting thirty-three models of how research can improve teacher education.

If it is desirable that students preparing to be teachers receive a stronger grounding in the liberal arts so that they can bring what they learn from these courses to their professional performance, we would expect that efforts would be made to integrate or at least align liberal arts and education coursework. But few such efforts appear to be underway. In 1988 the Carnegie Corporation initiated a project involving thirty colleges and universities to promote the attainment of this goal.

### Issue 4: Preservice Preparation Should Be More Practical

The amount and quality of field-based (in-school) learning opportunities prospective teachers have should be increased before they are certified to teach. This should include a semester-long practice-teaching experience.

*Assumptions*

The drive to increase the amount of time prospective teachers spend in schools, both in practicums and in practice teaching, is motivated fundamentally by the belief that the best way to learn to teach is to learn from outstanding teachers in "real-world" situations. Furthermore, the commitment to field-based teacher training is motivated by the notion that the "teachable moment" occurs when student teachers experience the complexities of teaching and are given direct feedback, which, in turn, they can test by making the suggested correction and learning what happens as a result. Another assumption undergirding the push for more school-based time for students preparing to teach is that teaching is basically an art that should be structured less by scientific principles than by intuition, common sense, and lessons derived from experience. It follows from this assumption that practitioners, that is, current teachers, have more useful knowledge to share with those learning to teach than do college professors.

Advocacy for greater field-based instruction comes mainly from teachers themselves and from school administrators. These practitioners often get a friendly hearing from policymakers, almost all of whom seem to know at least one teacher who has complained that he or she was inadequately prepared in college for the reality of the classroom. Many teacher educators appear to share the view that field-based instruction, in which they see themselves playing a major role, is a productive source of teacher learning. In its guidelines, NCATE, which represents both teachers and teacher educators, calls for standards that would increase the amount of school-based learning that teachers-in-training now receive.

*Relevant Evidence*

When asked to choose the most valuable aspect of their preparation for teaching, new teachers more often point to practice teaching and other practical experiences than to their courses in teaching methods, psychology, or other college subjects. This emphasis on practical lessons is greater among elementary than secondary teachers.

Despite this widely held conviction about the efficacy of field-based teacher preparation, the available research suggests that practicums and practice teaching are often not very effective and may be counterproductive in many instances. On the whole, early (pre-practice teaching) field experiences seem to have a small positive effect on teacher candidates' attitudes. In many cases, they have negative effects. In his 1985 synthesis of quantitative findings on field experiences, M. Malone (1985) concluded, "Students receiving a few to a moderate number of field experiences seem to benefit from them. When students are exposed to more than three or four courses involving a significant field experience component, desired outcomes may not be affected and may, in fact, decline" (p. 19). Similarly, in their synthesis of findings from thirty-eight studies on the relationship between early field experiences and prospective teachers' attitudes toward teaching, G. E. Samson et al. (1984) found no consistent effects of the amount of time involved in such experiences.

There also is little evidence to support the investment of greater time in practice teaching. Of course, some studies and descriptions of field-based teacher education programs and practice teaching situations report positive outcomes; some field experiences are obviously better designed and implemented than others. But why do most field-based courses and practice teaching experiences fail to demonstrate the effect that the advocates claim for them? A number of answers to this question can be offered. First, the lessons prospective teachers are taught in the college classroom are not reinforced and may indeed be contradicted by the lessons they learn explicitly and implicitly from classroom teachers. Sometimes this derives from problems of coordinating what is going on in practice with the subjects being taught in college. Sometimes the inconsistency comes from differences between professors and "cooperating" teachers about what is worth knowing. In many cases, colleges and universities have little, if any, influence on the selection of the cooperating teacher.

Second, classroom teachers who are to serve as role models and coaches often have no training in how to facilitate learning among adults.

Third, cooperating teachers often lack the time and the motivation to play a major role in the education of teachers. Among the explanations of this are the absence of economic or career advancement incentives for exerting the extra effort; the absence of release time from already heavy burdens of teaching; or the absence of support from principals or fellow teachers for teacher training activities.

Fourth, college faculty often have only limited involvement in most practice teaching experiences. One study shows that college professors may see student teachers for only 2 percent of the time they are involved in their practice teaching assignment. This low involvement appears to be related, in part, to a perception by college faculty that the supervision of field experiences is more time consuming and is less likely to be rewarded by their institutions than other activities (e.g., research).

Fifth, preservice teacher candidates may think of themselves as college students involved in episodic learning in transit through the college curriculum rather than as persons preparing for a job.

Finally, prospective teachers may not be ready cognitively to benefit from intensive field experiences. This may be particularly true when student teachers experience different lessons within their colleges taught in different ways, inconsistent lessons being taught in schools and college classrooms, and the trials of first-year teaching which cause many novices to focus on student control and to dismiss practices that complicate classroom management or require extensive information processing.

*Implementation*

In general, teacher preparation programs embodied more field-based courses and longer periods of practice teaching at the end of the 1980s than they did at the beginning of the decade. The problems associated with investing more preservice teacher preparation time in school-based learning are not new, and some efforts are underway to cope with them. Several colleges and universities are experimenting with interactive video as a substitute for some practicum experiences. Other universities are working on strengthening the training and compensation of cooperating teachers and otherwise are working more closely with school sites in which students are placed for practice teaching.

The most far-reaching plan being considered is to establish year-long interships in special schools, sometimes called Professional Development schools. These schools, in effect, would give practicing teachers a greater role in preparing new teachers and might shift some of the teaching of methods instruction and other topics involving specific competencies from colleges to school systems.

## Issue 5: The Teaching of Teachers of Prospective Teachers Should Be Improved

College and university professors should effectively model the exemplary teaching practices they expect of beginning teachers.

*Assumptions*

It is widely assumed that teachers learn a lot about teaching by observing those whom they assume know how to teach. This assumption, of course, is the reason given for having prospective teachers engage in substantial observation of exemplary teachers during practicum and practice teaching experiences. It follows that those with the formal responsibility for preparing teachers would affect what teachers learn as much by what they do as by what they advocate teachers should do. The primary advocates for this reform appear to be teacher organizations whose leaders assert that at least some of the weaknesses in the preparation of beginning teachers is related to the poor teaching students experience in college and to the lack of practical knowledge among teacher educators (National Education Association, 1986).

Such criticisms of the professoriate by practicing teachers invariably focus on education faculty members. Teacher candidates, however, take most of their courses from faculty in fields other than education. Recently, teacher educators have sought to point this out and to draw attention to the fact that few faculty in colleges and universities think about the ways they teach as a source of student learning or, for that matter, take responsibility for the education of teachers.

*Relevant Evidence*

There appear to be no systematic studies of the fit between the teaching practices college professors employ and the pedagogy being taught to prospective teachers, or how the teaching practices of college professors influence the teaching style or effectiveness of their students who become teachers. There is evidence that new teachers do not use the full range of the competencies they learn in college. One explanation could be that prospective teachers did not experience the effectiveness of the teaching strategies they were being asked to learn. Another explanation for this underutilization of learning is that student teachers and first-year teachers dismiss the lessons they learned in college when confronted with ''practical advice'' from fellow teachers, the complexity of classroom management, and other realities with which teachers, especially new teachers, must deal.

A recent survey of students preparing to be teachers shows that such students identify education professors (over all other teachers and professors) as the type of persons who had been most helpful in modeling teaching styles and strategies worthy of emulating, although these students had not yet experienced practice teaching. Overall, students preparing to teach believe that they are being well prepared.

Students preparing to be teachers assert that teacher educators provide them with helpful and positive models. Yet, once they begin practice teaching, student teachers appear to rely heavily for cues about effective teaching on classroom teachers. One study concluded that students look forward to field experience. They value it, and after they leave college they recount it as the most significant part of their program.

*Implementation*

Despite the absence of evidence related to the need for this reform or its efficacy, few would argue that the goal is not worth pursuing. But if the goal is not yet fully met and is being sought, the quest is unmapped at present. One recent study of universities and colleges in southern states found little evidence of explicit efforts by faculty to change their teaching behaviors. One reason why policymakers have given little attention to the improvement of instruction for prospective teachers is that teaching behavior is difficult to specify and monitor.

Three conditions could foster improvements in how teacher candidates are taught: measures of student learning that professors recognized as valid and that were available to their peers and to prospective students; greater institutional rewards for effective teaching in colleges and universities; and opportunities for higher education faculty to learn new ways of teaching.

A few states are exploring better ways to measure what prospective teachers know and are able to do. California and Connecticut, for example, are engaged in such efforts. The assessment of effective college teaching remains a primitive enterprise. Thus, the rewarding of exceptional teaching that models the pedagogy that teacher candidates should be taught, is not probable. State reforms in teacher education almost never include resources that are targeted at enhancing the competencies or knowledge of the professoriate.

## Issue 6: Teacher Preparation Programs Should be Extended to Five Years

Teacher preparation programs should require a minimum of one year of post-baccalaureate study before initial certification to teach is granted. Programs for so-called extended teacher preparation come in different shapes and sizes. The two most common general types are (1) five-year programs in which teacher education-related courses are distributed throughout the undergraduate experience and in a year of graduate study at the same institution; and (2) fifth-year programs in which all requirements for certification are to be met and a master's degree is often, but not always, awarded.

### Assumptions

The five-year teacher preparation movement, which encompasses many programmatic variations, has influential proponents. Among them are a special task force of the American Association of Colleges of Teacher Education, the majority of the members of the National Commission on Excellence in Teacher Education (1985), and the Carnegie Forum on Education and the Economy (1986). The Holmes Group (1986), which includes the deans of schools of education at most of the nation's research universities, calls for would-be teachers to complete five years of college *and* an internship before entering full-time teaching. Many leading schools of education (e.g., Chicago, Stanford, and Teachers' College, Columbia) now offer teacher training opportunities only at the postbaccalaureate level.

Among the most commonly held assumptions about the effectiveness of extended programs that motivate support for this proposal are the following:

1. Teachers will be more knowledgeable about the subjects they teach, and this knowledge will make them better teachers.
2. Taking more liberal arts courses will make prospective teachers more effective when they begin to teach.

3. There is too much to know about teaching to be learned in four years of college, given the other things students must learn in order to be well-educated professionals. A corollary to this assumption is that what students learn in college about teaching will be reflected in their on-the-job classroom performance.

4. The teaching profession will gain in status, and this enhanced position will, in turn, increase salaries and the attractions of teaching to able students.

5. Extended programs will enhance the status of schools of education.

### Relevant Evidence

The first of these assumptions imagines that students in extended programs will take more courses in the subjects they will teach. However, as noted earlier, the number of courses one has taken in the subject one teaches is not related to teaching effectiveness.

The idea that prospective teachers in extended programs will take more liberal arts courses than students in four-year programs assumes that five-year students will be substituting liberal arts electives for education electives. This assumption would be irrelevant if the professional curriculum, rather than the liberal arts curriculum, filled up the time gained by extending the program. And this is what some teacher educators advocating five-year (not fifth-year) programs have in mind. In any case, there is no evidence that the number of liberal arts courses teachers have taken will increase their effectiveness. Although we could identify a set of liberal arts electives that might enhance teaching, students do not typically select their electives with the idea of challenging themselves or building on their strengths. Moreover, the transfer of knowledge from one topic (e.g., philosophy) to another (e.g., classroom management) is very problematic.

The assumption that extended preparation programs are necessary because of an exponential increase of new knowledge about teaching implies that students in such programs would not have more liberal arts courses than they have had in baccalaureate programs. In any case, to say that there is more to learn and that beginning teachers can learn it in ways that they will put to use in classrooms is not the same thing. There is considerable evidence (discussed later) that teachers do not use all the knowledge and skills they have when they enter teaching after four-year programs.

Some research suggests that teachers with master's degrees are more effective, or at least are judged to be more effective. In these studies, the vast majority of teachers did their graduate work after they had begun teaching.

The assumption that requiring a graduate degree, or at least postbaccalaureate study, for initial certification will enhance the status of the profession, thereby increasing both its intrinsic and extrinsic attraction for potential candidates, appears to be based on references to some other professions, especially law and medicine. However, such reasoning overlooks the recent experiences of other professions whose members have unsuccessfully sought higher status from advanced degrees—such as librarianship and social work. In fact, the majority of

American teachers have a master's degree and, although the number of master's recipients was growing rapidly, the earning power of teachers was declining.

One way to test the argument that extended programs will lead to higher salaries and higher status is to look at what has happened in California, where completion of a fifth year of college before would-be teachers can be fully certified has been required for many years. Teacher salaries in California trailed those of many non-southern states until very recently. Many cities in California cannot fill open teacher positions, teaching candidates have ranked very near the bottom of thirty occupations with respect to measures of verbal and quantitative abilities, and a third or more of the teachers statewide are hired with temporary credentials because not enough students seek full certification before entry. In short, the lesson to be drawn from California's long experience with extended programs is that they do not increase the status or attractiveness of the teaching profession.

Finally, what about the assumption that extended programs will enhance the status of schools of education? When we look at the low-status academic units in universities, along with education schools, we will find library schools, schools of social welfare, schools of public health, and schools of nursing. What all these schools have in common is that they prepare persons to pursue relatively low-paying careers, most of which are in the public sector.

*Implementation*

Although interest in extended programs seems to be growing in institutions of higher education, the movement is slow and the players, on the whole, are tentative. The only national data available on teacher education enrollments in postbaccalaureate teacher education programs show little change between 1985 and 1986, while undergraduate enrollments were increasing 20 percent.

In the last few years, policymakers in several states—including Colorado, Tennessee, North Carolina, Virginia, and Texas—have considered joining California in requiring a fifth year of college before granting initial certification. Each of these states has decided not to mandate postbaccalaureate programs. Apparently, public policymakers have rejected a five-year preservice requirement out of concern for the impact on the supply of teachers, political demands by institutions of higher education that might not be able to offer five-year programs or attract students to them, and skepticism that the claims made by five-year advocates regarding increased teacher quality would be realized. Indeed, states seem much more ready to *reduce* the amount of preservice teacher education (through limiting the number of courses, prohibiting a major in education, and authorizing alternative certification routes) than they are to increase the educational demands on prospective teachers.

## Issue 7: The Way Teachers Are Inducted into the Profession Should Be Improved

Induction programs for beginning teachers or special schools for continued teacher training within public school systems should be developed in order to ensure that new teachers are able to put into effect and build on what they learn about teaching in college.

## Assumptions

It is widely recognized that first-year teachers often have experiences that are unsatisfying professionally and that new teachers fail to implement much of what they learned in their preservice preparation. It is assumed that induction programs that provide support for new teachers will both increase teacher effectiveness and reduce teacher attrition. The need for induction programs is not seriously questioned in the United States, but some observers believe that most induction programs, which invariably seek to link new teachers with more experienced ones, are usually inadequate. Leading advocates for induction argue that the transition from college to solo teaching requires a year-long internship in schools that are especially structured to foster the novice teacher's professional development. Apparently, there is growing interest in professional development schools—regular schools serving diverse populations and thus different from the university-based lab schools of the past—as the way to achieve effective entry to the teaching profession.

## Relevant Research

A large body of research indicates that beginning teachers often have a very difficult time applying the full range of what they know and are able to do in "their own classrooms." This, of course, constrains their professional expertise and limits the positive effects they can have on students. Moreover, many new teachers have such a difficult first year that they decide that a career in teaching will not have the rewards for them that they thought it would. This leads to decisions to leave teaching. Some studies of teacher attrition estimate that as many as 20 to 25 percent of new teachers leave a school district after their first year.

Large-scale induction programs have only recently gained attention. Therefore, there is little research in print which links such programs to teacher performance or attrition. However, anecdotal evidence suggests that such programs are making a contribution to a more productive and satisfying transition from college to work for many teachers. At the same time, there is reason to believe that most programs would be more effective if mentor teachers had more time and training to undertake this task and if university faculty had more involvement aimed at linking what is being learned on the job with what is being learned in the classroom. Recent research on teacher mentoring suggests that this role is difficult to perform and that it takes time and specific training before most teachers feel comfortable with and are competent in the role. Moreover, the idea that experience is a good teacher of teachers, despite the testimony of many teachers that experience has been their most influential teacher, is increasingly being called into doubt. This research suggests that people learn best from experience when they have been trained to learn in that way and when they have the support from one or more persons who can provide objective feedback, discuss alternative behaviors, and facilitate interpretation of an action on their perceptions.

*Implementation*

Many local school systems in the United States have induction programs. Most of these programs involve pairing a beginning teacher with a senior teacher or a team comprised of teachers and administrators. In some communities, orientation seminars are held for new teachers. Widespread implementation of induction programs seems to require state mandates and financial support. Most states require some form of induction program, and some of these programs provide state funding to support the active involvement of faculty from institutions of higher education. Many programs rely on especially selected teachers to perform a mentoring-type function for the new teachers, such as those in Virginia, North Carolina, and California. It seems very likely that induction programs will become universal in the near future, although it is also clear that these programs will differ dramatically in the resources devoted to them and in their quality.

Establishing professional development schools is much more expensive than establishing conventional induction programs. Among the advocates of professional development schools is the Holmes Group, and variations on this idea can be found in scattered sites throughout the United States. Thus far, however, the costs of this strategy and problems associated with developing different roles in teacher education for both institutions of higher education and school systems have limited the number of professional development schools. The development of such new arrangements is also complicated by the unwillingness of teacher educators to relinquish "final" responsibility for teacher preparations and by the historic assumption by most school systems that teacher training is the job of institutions of higher education.

The financial expense, as well as the costs of political, administrative, and interorganizational activity necessary to establishing professional development schools, is high enough that we can expect to see such schools introduced only in some communities where they will meet other needs of the school system—such as staff development (as is the case in Louisville) or the need for magnet schools—or on a pilot basis.

## Issue 8: Alternative Certification

New ways to certify teachers should be found that reduce the time and specific requirements of college-based teacher certification programs. Before discussing this proposal, it will be useful to define some terms. Alternative teacher certification (ATC) is not the same as provisional certification or extended teacher preparation. Almost all the states authorize the issuance of provisional or emergency teaching certificates to college graduates when school systems cannot fill teacher vacancies with certified personnel. For example, about 50 to 60 percent of all new mathematics and science teachers were not certified when they entered teaching in 1981. Persons who fulfill the requirements of alternative teacher certification programs are fully certified and, in effect, are assumed by the states to have all the qualifications that persons completing traditional preparation programs have.

### Assumptions and Advocates

The interest in ATC seems to be motivated by at least three beliefs. First, a concern about the quality and quantity of teacher candidates has led many policymakers to conclude that the hurdles presented by and the low status of teacher education programs are one source of these problems. They reason that if it were possible to reduce the costs—in terms of time and money—and the specific requirements imposed on those who would teach, more talented people could be attracted to the profession, including recent college graduates and persons in the workforce interested in changing careers.

Second, as noted in previous sections, it is widely believed (1) that courses in the foundations and methods of teaching are unnecessary and/or (2) that one can best learn how to teach by learning on the job from outstanding practitioners. Implicit in these assumptions is the proposition that research holds few lessons that could enhance teacher effectiveness. Those who hold these beliefs have advocated alternative programs not because of their expedience but because of their presumed efficiency and effectiveness.

A third rationale for ATCs is related to the first two: the requirements of the various states have become increasingly restrictive and indefensible. This view holds that reform of these state requirements, which have dubious relationships with teacher effectiveness, is not likely to bring about sufficient change to justify the effort. Thus, some people regard bypassing the current system as a way to cope with current inadequacies of certification processes and to develop new models that will attract more and better qualified students.

### Relevant Evidence

Two kinds of evidence seem to relate to ATC. The first deals with the assumptions that drove the move to such programs; the second is information relating to effect on teacher recruitment and effectiveness.

There appears to be no research that adequately links variations in teacher education programs with variations in teacher effectiveness. Available research, even though most studies have serious weaknesses, shows that those teachers who were certified in traditional programs perform better in classrooms than those who were provisionally certified or not certified at all. But it is not known whether taking certain courses or any given number of courses makes much difference. We have no evidence that the real and anticipated shortages of qualified teachers can be traced to "unnecessary barriers that block [the] way into the teaching profession," as the U.S. Department of Education (1987) claims, rather than to the limited attractions of the career itself.

Studies of the relative effectiveness of ATCs are limited in number. With the exception of New Jersey, and some urban districts, ATCs produce a small proportion of the new teachers hired. They do, however, seem to be gaining in enrollment.

The limited evidence available on the effects of ATC suggests that most teachers prepared through ATC are judged to be as effective in their initial teaching as are teachers prepared in conventional programs. The evidence also suggests that participants often have stronger academic records, do somewhat better on written certification tests, and are more likely to be male and nonwhite, than those teacher candidates with whom they were compared.

*Implementation*

ATC programs differ significantly from one another, and the content and strategies embodied in some of these programs may not be very different from some ''conventional'' internship programs. While ATCs comes in many shapes and sizes, most are one of two general types: joint programs between districts and institutions of higher education; or programs authorized by states and administered by districts without formal college or university involvement.

ATC programs vary considerably in the amount of instructional time related to pedagogy that they entail and in the ways these lessons are taught and learned. Almost all alternative programs allow college graduates qualifying for certification to teach at full pay before being fully certified and to begin teaching with no more hours of instruction in pedagogy than would be experienced in three or four courses, often considerably less.

At least thirty-three of the states had established alternative teacher preparation programs by 1990. Many of these programs focus on specified fields with continuing teacher shortages (such as mathematics, science, and foreign languages) or on secondary education.

Clearly, the dependence of states on ATCs for the supply of teachers differs widely from state to state. In most southern states that have adopted ATCs, less than 2 percent of those certified to teach came through ATCs. In New Jersey, on the other hand, whose program may be the best known nationally, about 20 percent of all newly hired teachers were certified through the alternative route.

As noted, early reports on the effects of ATC are basically positive, given rather modest tests of effectiveness. For this reason, and because criticisms of teacher education and shortages of teacher candidates in certain fields and in certain communities are unlikely to dissipate, the popularity of alternative teacher certification is likely to continue to grow.

## Other Issues on the Teacher Education Reform Agenda

The eight general proposals for reforming teacher education in the United States just discussed are not the only ones receiving attention, but they do seem to be the ones receiving the most consideration. At least three other developments are related to possible changes in teacher education.

First, there is a continuing search for incentives that will attract able people to fields and locations with chronic teacher shortages. These fields include the physical sciences, mathematics, foreign languages, bilingual education, and special education. It is also difficult to recruit persons to teach children who live in central cities and rural areas. This search for incentives increasingly is emphasizing the need to attract students of exceptional academic ability generally and minority students in particular.

Second, several states are actively considering the establishment of professional standards boards, whose membership would be dominated by teachers, that would set and oversee teacher education policies. This development has gained increased attention as a result of a highly visible effort supported by the Carnegie Corporation and many leaders of American education to establish a National Board of Professional Teaching Standards for certifying experienced teachers. While it is too early to assess the effects of the Carnegie effort, it is raising fundamental questions about the governance of teacher education and the ways teacher knowledge and competence should be assessed.

Third, the search for ways to reward teachers for performance and to differentiate teacher roles within schools is yielding new methods of assessing teachers and, implicitly, more specific definitions of good teaching. This will affect the curriculum of teacher education. In addition, the differentiation of teacher roles is creating a cadre of teachers, such as the mentor teachers in California and master teachers in Tennessee, who are potential teacher educators in both colleges and universities.

## CHANGES IN TEACHER EDUCATION: 1980–1991

Recognizing that there are many variations in the way teachers are educated in colleges and universities in the United States, we can still point to several changes in the 1980s.

1. The academic capabilities of students preparing to teach have leveled up. That is, people with the qualifications of the bottom 20 to 30 percent of the would-be teachers in 1980 were pursuing other careers in 1990.

2. Increasing proportions of students preparing to teach are satisfying the same general education requirements that liberal arts students must satisfy. All prospective secondary teacher candidates, and a significantly larger proportion of elementary and middle school teacher candidates, have a major other than, or in addition to, teacher education.

3. The proportion of courses taken by teacher candidates that are "professional" is less, and course content is based more on research related to learning, teaching, and effective schools. There is not much difference, however, in the extent to which the professional curriculum explicitly embodies the theory and knowledge students are exposed to in their major or in other liberal arts courses.

4. Prospective teachers are spending more of their time in the field, although most such field experiences are not very different from those provided in 1980.

5. More teachers of teachers, especially those who think of themselves as teacher educators, model effective teaching practices. On the other hand, teacher educators are playing a relatively smaller role in the education of teachers.

6. A slightly higher, though growing, proportion of new teachers are being certified in five-year or fifth-year programs, but most such programs are not mandated by state authorities.

7. Almost all states have some form of induction programs for new teachers, but these differ considerably in quality from district to district. Professional development schools or centers have been initiated in several local districts, some with state support, to continue the training of graduates from collegiate preparation programs, to retrain teachers who are returning to active service, and to facilitate the transition of new teachers from college to work.

8. An increasing number of states have some form of alternative certification, and this, especially in those states that have improved teacher salaries significantly, has reduced the number of emergency certificates. The increase in alternative certification programs has been accompanied by a reduction of the limitations on the types of teachers that can be certified in this way.

Will these changes significantly improve the quality of teaching in America's schools? There is little reason to believe that these changes are significant enough either to attract a very different group of applicants to teaching (once the bottom 20 percent are excluded) or to change how much beginning teachers know and are able to do. This pessimism about the teacher education reform movement in the United States is based on (1) a conviction that the ''reforms'' receiving the most attention are not coming to grips with some of the most fundamental problems, (2) a recognition that significant reforms in teacher education are dependent for their success on changes in schools that do not seem very likely to occur widely, and (3) a concern that we will run out of energy for reform and faith in the potential of teacher education before we get to the basics.

Let us conclude, then, by briefly examining each of these concerns.

## CONCLUSION

### Fundamental Issues in the Reform of Teacher Education

The issues that have dominated public debates over teacher education in the United States, though important, do not address the most significant problems of improving the education of teachers *and* increasing the impact of teacher preparation on teacher effectiveness. Like most reform agendas, current teacher education reform proposals have focused on what might be called structural matters and have done so largely within the context of the way teacher education has been organized and the roles it has played historically. If we were to step outside this context and these roles and ask why it seems so difficult to change teacher education in ways that enhance its effects, we might ask questions such as: How can the concomitant demands that teacher education be more rigorous and more relevant be reconciled? How do teachers learn? What can teachers best learn in what contexts and in what ways? What are the appropriate roles for institutions of higher education and for schools in fostering the professional development of teachers?

### The Rigor versus Relevance Conundrum

Teacher educators in the United States are recurrently confronted with demands from teachers and administrators (who rally others to this call) that teacher preparation be made more relevant to the needs of everyday practice. In addition, they are continuously confronted with demands from within the institutions of higher education and from others that the curriculum for prospective teachers be made more rigorous. Demands for relevance usually imply a focus on skills training taught in the field, with only enough theory to give the practice the semblance of credibility within the college or university. Demands for academic rigor usually focus on the need for more discipline-based theory, more sophisticated knowledge of the ecology of teaching (e.g., philosophical traditions and conflicts, sociocultural influence on learning, etc.), and greater emphasis on the development of capacities for systematic inquiry that transcend the immediate needs of teaching and have seldom been part of the training of the teaching corps now in the field.

The failure to respond to demands for immediate relevance runs the risk of criticism from practitioners and policymakers that schools and departments of education presumably serve and on whose support teacher educators depend for political support and public deference. Failure to meet the tests of rigor brings low status within universities and colleges and, often, low professional self-esteem among teachers and teacher educators.

Quite naturally, most teacher educators profess to be pursuing both relevance and rigor—and often attain neither goal. Teacher educators in research universities, however, tend to emphasize their commitment to rigor, and those teacher educators at institutions with a strong history in teacher education tend to emphasize their contributions to skill development. Most teacher educators, however, first and foremost want to improve schools and see their students' competencies rather than their own scholarship or their students' scholarly dispositions, as their way of influencing improvement. Not surprisingly, then, teacher educators overwhelmingly believe—or say they believe—that they are producing teachers who are ready, upon certification, to be effective in the classroom.

The desire to improve practice, and the conviction that this can be done through teacher training, makes teacher educators relatively responsive to relevance demands. For example, as we have seen, the amount of field-based coursework that prospective teachers experience has increased significantly in recent years.

However, despite efforts at relevance—which, in addition to more field experiences, include greater use of simulations, microteaching, and the integration of research on effective teaching into practice-oriented lessons—criticism from practitioners has continued and, perhaps, increased.

The more practice oriented the teacher education program becomes, the more vocational and unrigorous it appears to other professors and to administrators within institutions of higher education. The resultant disdain might well be a price worth paying if the contributions teacher educators make to the quality of schools were recognized and rewarded. But they seldom are. Thus, many teacher educators find themselves constantly on the defensive and with few allies when educational reformers go looking for easy targets. Reforming teacher education is a popular sport in the United States, and one consequence is that teacher educators are the most regulated of all academicians (which further diminishes their lot within academe) to the point that some state legislators have ordered education professors into the schools on a regular basis to learn "what schools are really like." (Imagine a legislature requiring that law professors observe in courtrooms.)

Most teacher educators complain about the rigor versus relevance conundrum in which they seem to be inextricably caught and seek to walk the fence, or perhaps build gates in the fence, between academe and schools. We can conclude, however, that the demands on teacher educators for both relevance and rigor are not very compatible without concluding that the balancing act often attempted is as productive as would be the reduction of this role ambiguity. We might look for such clarification in the search for the reasons why greater efforts to achieve relevance do not seem to translate into greater support for teacher education. That search, in turn, might start with a concern for how teachers learn.

### Toward an Understanding of Teacher Learning

The search for improvements in teacher education has frequently focused on the number of courses of different types to be taken rather than on the content of what is to be learned. As with the rest of higher education, however, attempts at improvement often do deal with curriculum. In the search for content, the usual process has been to try to identify what good teachers know and do. It appears that when designing a curriculum for children, reformers have not asked, how does the type of person to be taught learn at different stages in her or his development?

Therefore, teacher education reform has proceeded on the assumption that if we could determine the most important things teachers should know and be able to do, then teacher candidates could and should be taught at least much of this in their preservice programs. The sense of efficacy related to teacher education embodied in this assumption is reinforced by a substantial body of research indicating that efforts to teach teacher education students particular competencies are often effective when the learning is assessed in the context of controlled preservice settings.

On the other hand, there is also good reason to believe that teachers do not implement much of what they are taught. There has been a tendency to explain this reality by suggesting that the schools are often hostile to new ideas or that the pressures under which a new teacher works causes her or him to focus on a narrow repertoire of teaching skills. Another explanation is that teachers don't really know what they learned to the extent that they can perform the skill or use the knowledge in different settings—when they must deal with many competing objectives at once and when it is necessary to modify the previously studied behavior to make it effective enough to warrant its continued use. Moreover, it may be that much about teaching cannot be learned effectively until the person has actually taught and unless the behavior is learned in context and subsequently reinforced. To put this notion another way, it seems likely that teachers go through stages of cognitive development in which teaching itself, and variations in the conditions within which teaching occurs, play a critical role in how and what a teacher can learn. The bases for a theory of teacher learning that supports this hypothesis are now being developed (Berliner, 1987; Thies-Sprinthall and Sprinthall (1987). Almost certainly this work will suggest the limited impact that preservice education can have on first-year teachers' *competencies* and usable knowledge about teaching.

The prospect that a focus in college on practical teaching skills is, at best, inefficient and, at worst, doomed to failure (measured by the expectations of teachers, principals, and parents) is very unsetting for teacher educators. On the other hand, precisely because teaching is so complex and because its hectic pace does not suit the learning of some things teachers should know, prospective teachers would be well served by preprofessional education focused on the facilitation of learning and how to learn how to teach. In this realization lies the way out of the rigor versus relevance conundrum.

*A Changing Role for Higher Education in Preservice Teacher Education*

If greater knowledge of how teachers learn is likely to call into question the efficacy of much of what is now being done in conventional preservice teacher education programs, what role can institutions of higher education perform in preparing teachers? One way to answer this question is to identify the topics teachers cannot learn easily or are not likely to be taught, even under the best of circumstances, on the job. Such topics include theories and research about child development and learning; knowledge about the effects of class, race, and ethnicity on learning and behavior; how to learn from experience; how to engage in quantitative and qualitative analysis; the uses and misuses of various types of measurement; and complex problem solving.

Why couldn't these things be taught in arts and science courses? Some of them could, but most of them are not, at least not in a way that would facilitate their transfer to teaching behavior and to learning about teaching. It is very difficult to transfer knowledge from one domain to another, and in order to do so it must be planned for and the necessary capabilities must be consciously developed. Indeed, if we expect teachers to be able to make effective use of the knowledge they gain from education courses, it will be important either to restructure some of those courses or explicitly design education courses. In this way teachers will use the theory, methods of analysis, and insights derived from arts and science courses most directly relevant to teaching. This is particularly true for subject matter courses—not so much those at the introductory levels but those at the advanced levels where the development of content pedagogy seems important.

If it is difficult to achieve the transfer of knowledge, it follows that preprofessional teacher education is not likely to directly affect teacher learning and behavior unless bridges are built between institutions of higher education and schools. As mentioned earlier, experimentation with such bridges is now underway in the United States.

## The Reform of Schools and of Teacher Education

As the Holmes Group, the Carnegie Task Force on Education and the Economy, and others have pointed out, the limited attraction of teaching as a profession and the conditions of teaching in many schools significantly constrain the effects that the reform of teacher education can have on effective teaching. Moreover, the reform of schools would almost certainly reduce teacher attrition and thus reduce the amount of preservice teaching that occurs. This, in turn, would allow institutions of higher education to pursue new roles in the continuing education of teachers and would likely increase the ease with which preservice learning was transferred to professional performance.

Perhaps the most important way to improve schools and preservice teacher education would be for school systems to take real responsibility for the professional development of teachers. As noted above, teacher educators seem all too willing to say that they can ready their students to be effective teachers. School systems have been all too happy to sustain that myth because it serves as the rationale for the minuscule investments made in teachers by states and localities. It seems ironic that schools—which exist because of the social need to develop the individual's cognitive capabilities, knowledge, and skills—assume only marginal responsibility for the development of their own workers on whose expertise the successful performance of their mission depends. It is interesting to speculate how good America's schools could be, and how good teacher education could be, if the nation invested half as much in the growth of teachers' capabilities as it does in the professional skills of its military personnel.

## It May Be Over Too Soon

In education reform, the energy necessary to bring about basic changes can get used up on symbolic struggles and less important issues. This is particularly true when the well-meaning policymakers focus their attention on the things they can affect most easily by passing laws that constrain error rather than creating options and capacities that would facilitate movement in new directions. The teacher education reform effort in the United States will likely spend its energy before it gets to the fundamentals. The changes that have occurred will be seen to be sufficient by those dissatisfied with the way things were, and those who feared change most will issue a collective sigh of relief and assure one another that it could have been worse.

## REFERENCES

American Association of Colleges for Teacher Education. *A Call for Change in Teacher Education*. Washington, D.C.: 1985.

American Association of Colleges of Teacher Education. *Educating a Profession: Extended Programs for Teacher Education*. Washington, D.C.: 1983.

Atkins, J. M. "Preparing to Go to the Head of the Class." *The Wingspread Journal*, 1, no. 3 (1986).

Berliner, D. C. "In Pursuit of the Expert Pedagogue." *Educational Researcher* 15, no. 7 (1987): 5–13.

Bransford, J. D. *Human Cognition: Learning, Understanding and Remembering*. Belmont, Calif.: Wadsworth, 1979.

Carnegie Forum on Education and the Economy. *Task Force on Teaching as a Profession. A Nation Prepared: Teachers for the 21st Century*. New York: 1986.

Coleman, J. S., T. Hoffer, and S. Kilgore. "Cognitive Outcomes in Public and Private Schools. *Sociology of Education*, 55, no. 23 (1982): 65–76.

Darling-Hammond, L. *Beyond the Commission Reports: The Coming Crisis in Teaching*. Santa Monica, Calif.: Rand Corporation, 1983.

Darling-Hammond, L., A. E. Wise, and S. L. Pease. "Teacher Evaluation in the Organizational Context: A Review of the Literature." *Review of Educational Research* 53, (1983): 285–328.

Edelman, M. J. *The Symbolic Uses of Politics*. Champaign/Urbana University of Illinois Press, 1964.

Good, T. L., and J. Brophy. "School Effects." In M. Wittrock, ed., *Handbook of Research on Teaching*, 3rd ed. New York: Macmillan, 1985.

Griffin, G. A., and H. Hukill. *First Years of Teaching: What Are the Pertinent Issues?* (Report No. 9051.) Austin: University of Texas at Austin, Research and Development Center for Teacher Education, 1983.

Grissmer, D. W., and S. N. Kirby. *Teacher Attrition: The Uphill Climb to Staff the Nation's Schools*. Santa Monica, Calif.: Rand Center for the Study of the Teaching Profession, 1987.

Hawley, W. D. "The High Costs and Doubtful Efficacy of Extended Teacher Preparation Programs: An Invitation to More Basic Reform." *American Journal of Education*, 95, no. 1 (1987): 275–298.

Hawley, W., and S. Rosenholtz. "Good Schools: A Synthesis of Research on How Schools Influence Student Achievement." Special Issue of the *Peabody Journal of Education* 4 (1984): 1–178.

The Holmes Group. *Tomorrow's Teachers*. East Lansing: Michigan State University, 1986.

Jencks, Christopher et al. *Inequality: A Reassessment of the Effects of Family and School-ing in America*. New York: Basic Books, 1972.

Malone, M. "A Quantitative Synthesis of Preservice Teacher Field-Experience." Paper prepared for the annual meeting of the American Educational Research Associ-ation, 1985.

National Commission on Educational Excellence. *A Nation at Risk*. Washington, D.C.: U.S. Government Printing Office, 1983.

National Education Association. *Excellence in Our Schools, Teacher Education: An Action Plan*. Washington, D.C.: Instructional and Professional Development Com-mittee, National Education Association, 1986.

Rodman, B. " 'Alternate Route' Said a Success." *Education Week*, February 24, 1988, p. 7.

Samson, G. E., J. B. Borger, T. Weinstein, and H. J. Walburg. "Pre-teaching Expe-riences and Attitudes: A Quantitative Synthesis." *Journal of Research and De-velopment in Education* 17, no. 4 (1984): 52–56.

Schlechty, P. C., and V. S. Vance. "Recruitment, Selection, and Retention: The Shape of the Teaching Force." *Elementary School Journal* 83 (1983): 469–487.

Schlechty, P. C., and V. S. Vance. "Do Academically Able Teachers Leave Education? The North Carolina Case." *Phi Delta Kappan* 63 (1981): 106–112.

Southern Regional Education Board. *Alternative Teacher Certification Programs: Are They Working?* Atlanta: SREB, 1988.

Thies-Sprinthall, L., and N. A. Sprinthall. "Preservice Teachers as Adult Learners: A New Framework for Teacher Education. In L. Katz and J. Raths (eds.), *Advances in Teacher Education*. Norwood, N.J.: Ablex, 1987.

U.S. Department of Education. *Opening Alternative Routes to Teaching: A Strategy for Increasing the Pool of Qualified Teachers*. Washington, D.C.: 1987.

Veenman, S. "Perceived Problems of Beginning Teachers." *Review of Education Re-search* 54, no. 2 (1984): 143–178.

Weaver, W. T. "Solving the Problem of Teacher Quality. Part I." *Phi Delta Kappan*, 66 (1984): 108–114.

Weaver, W. T. "Solving the Problem of Teacher Quality. Part II." *Phi Delta Kappan*, 66 (1984): 185–188.

Wright, D., M. McKibben, and P. Walton. *The Effectiveness of the Teacher Trainee Program: An Alternate Route into Teaching in California*. Sacramento: Com-mission on Teacher Credentialing, 1987.

# APPENDIX: COMPARATIVE STATISTICAL TABLE: FACTORS RELATING TO TEACHER EDUCATION

Teacher education is an elusive entity to capture in statistics. This explains why data on this type of training do not appear in the standard, international statistical, reference books on education, the most important of which are the annual statistical reports produced by Unesco and the World Bank.

Teacher education is a very broad term, covering the many variations of training activities that fall between formal, university degree-granting programs and short-term, informal, in-service programs for unqualified or underqualified teachers.

To add to the ambiguity of the term, teacher education takes place, often simultaneously, in many different types of institutions; university, college, pedagogical institute at the higher education level, pedagogical institute at the secondary education level, and training program at the high school level. In addition, each of these institutions may be private or public, and many countries do not gather statistics on the private.

Finally, the relationship between the number of students in teacher preparatory programs and those who actually end up teaching for the short, medium, or long term is tenuous. Thus, the number enrolled in various types of programs is misleading.

For these reasons, the use of international statistical comparisons of systems for teacher preparation per se is not encouraged. However, statistics on factors relating to the social and economic context of teacher education are both available and useful. Examples of these appear in the comparative statistical table.

For valid statistics on teacher education, it becomes necessary to turn to individual country studies that describe how certain educational statistics are used and also present the larger educational and social setting. Only a few books present these data for countries, worldwide. For example:

Gimeno, Jose B., and Ricardo M. Ibanez. *The Education of Primary and Secondary Schools Teachers*. Paris: Unesco Press, 1981.

Holmes, Brian, ed. *International Handbook on Educational Systems*. 3 vols. New York: John Wiley and Sons, 1983.

|  | GNP Per Capita (1988) | Life Expectancy (1988) | Fertility Rate, Births Per 1000 (1988) | Infant Mortality Rate Per 1000 (1988) |
|---|---|---|---|---|
| Arab Gulf States | 15,770 | 71 | 4.9 | 25 |
| Australia | 12,340 | 76 | 1.9 | 9 |
| Brazil | 2,160 | 65 | 3.4 | 61 |
| Canada | 16,960 | 77 | 1.7 | 7 |
| China | 330 | 70 | 2.4 | 31 |
| Egypt | 660 | 63 | 4.5 | 83 |
| Great Britain | 12,810 | 75 | 1.8 | 9 |
| Germany | 18,480 | 75 | 1.5 | 8 |
| Israel | 8,650 | 76 | 3.0 | 11 |
| Japan | 21,020 | 78 | 1.7 | 5 |
| Malawi | 170 | 47 | 7.6 | 149 |
| Malaysia | 1,940 | 70 | 3.7 | n.a. |
| Nigeria | 290 | 51 | 6.6 | 103 |
| Spain | 7,740 | 77 | 1.6 | 9 |
| United States | 19,840 | 76 | 1.7 | 10 |
| U.S.S.R. | n.a. | n.a. | n.a. | n.a. |

| Illiteracy Rate (age 15+) (1990 est.) | Educational Expend. as % of GNP (1986-87) | % of Age Group In Primary Education (1989) | % Of Age Group In Secondary Education (1987) | % Of Age Group In Higher Education (1987) | Primary Pupil/ Teacher Ratio (1987) |
|---|---|---|---|---|---|
| 89.9 | 2.4 | 99 | 60 | 9 | 25 |
| n.a. | 5.5 | 106 | 98 | 29 | 17 |
| 18.9 | 4.5 | 103 | 37 | 11 | n.a. |
| n.a. | 7.3 | 105 | 104 | 58 | 26 |
| 26.7 | 2.4 | 132 | 43 | 2 | n.a. |
| 51.6 | 5.9 | 90 | 69 | 20 | n.a. |
| n.a. | 5.0 | 106 | 83 | 22 | n.a. |
| n.a. | 4.4 | 103 | 94 | 30 | n.a. |
| 7.0 | 5.8 | 95 | 83 | 34 | 19 |
| n.a. | 4.9 | 102 | 96 | 28 | 29 |
| 5.7 | 3.2 | 66 | 4 | 1 | n.a. |
| 21.6 | 6.9 | 102 | 59 | 7 | 22 |
| 49.3 | 1.5 | 77 | n.a. | n.a. | n.a. |
| 12.9 | 3.2 | 113 | 102 | 30 | n.a. |
| 0.5 | 6.8 | 100 | 98 | 60 | 25 |
| 1.6 | 7.5 | n.a. | n.a. | n.a. | n.a. |

Sources:    -UNESCO
            -World Bank

Kurian, George T. *World Education Encyclopedia*. New York: Facts on File Publications, 1988.

Postlewaite, T. Neville. *The Encyclopedia of Comparative and National Systems of Education*. New York: Pergamon Press, 1988.

# BIBLIOGRAPHIC ESSAY

Very few books have appeared on issues and problems of teacher education per se, and few, if any, have dealt with the topic in more than just a few countries. However a number of key references provide background information on the topic, and in a number of books that analyze teacher education in different countries, issues and problems are referred to or can be inferred.

Edgar B. Gumbert, ed., *Fit to Teach: Teacher Education in International Perspective* (Atlanta: Center for Cross Cultural Education, Georgia State University, 1990). This book deals with the structure of teacher education in four liberal democracies and three communist countries. Many issues and problems, though for the most part not dealt with directly, can be identified. However, most of the chapters are written from the school perspective, with little attention to the social factors affecting the shape of teacher education.

Val Rust and Per Dalin, *Teachers and Teaching in the Developing World* (New York: Garland Publishing Inc., 1990). This work, several chapters of which were written by non-Anglo writers, deals with topics in teacher education, for example, preservice education, who teaches, in-service education, communication technology, all in cross-national perspective. Although issues and problems can be inferred, they are largely generalized and thus are removed from their national contexts.

Eric Hoyle and Jacquetta Megarry, eds., *Professional Development of Teachers: World Yearbook of Education 1980* (New York: Nichols Publishing Co., 1980). Major topics in teacher education are examined utilizing examples from various countries. Since only three of the twenty-six chapters are written by non-Anglo writers, the perspective is that of Canada, the United Kingdom, the United States, and Australia. This volume covers issues and problems in teacher education, but considerable effort is required to identify them because they are dealt with incidentally as part of other descriptive material.

Richard Goodings et al., eds., *Changing Priorities in Teacher Education* (New York: Nichols Publishing Co., 1982). This book deals with changes in teacher education world-wide and the resulting issues and problems. Of special interest is the chapter on the developing countries. Since the topics are dealt with cross-nationally, there is an absence of country backgrounds, which is so essential for a deeper understanding of the dynamics of teacher education systems.

Donald Lomax, *European Perspectives in Teacher Education* (New York: John Wiley Publishers, 1976). Although this book focuses mostly on Europe, it also includes an informative chapter on European models of teacher education in developing countries. Although issues and problems are not highlighted as such, the chapters are set in the context of the social, economic, and political processes that accompany rapid change.

John Goodlad, *Teachers for Our Nation's Schools* (San Francisco: Jossey-Bass Publishers, 1990). Although this book deals exclusively with teacher education in the United States, it is included in this bibliography for a special reason. The issues and problems of teacher education in the United States are typical of those in many countries of the world and in all likelihood will become central in other countries in the future as they reach more advanced stages of development. The carefully considered recommendations for reforming teacher education, based on exhaustive analytical data of current practices, merit worldwide attention.

# Index

# ABOUT THE EDITOR AND CONTRIBUTORS

OLUSOLA AVOSEH is currently deputy vice-chancellor of Lagos State University in Apapa, Nigeria, where he was formerly dean of the Faculty of Education. He earned graduate degrees in sociology and the sociology of education from Canadian universities and has written extensively on educational development in Nigeria. He is currently editor of the *Nigerian Journal of Comparative Education*.

PILAR BENEJAM is head of the Social Sciences Education Department in the School of Education, Autonomous University of Barcelona, Spain, the institution from which she earned her advanced degrees. Her writing has focused on the area of teacher education reform in international perspective, and she is the author of *La Formación de Maestros: Una Propuesta Alternativa*

MIRIAM BEN-PERETZ is dean of the School of Education at the University of Haifa, Israel. As visiting professor, she has taught in German, Canadian and U.S. universities. Her extensive writing has focused on the role of teachers in curriculum development and cross-cultural research in teaching.

MAE CHU CHANG is currently a general educator at the World Bank, having served as an expert on China in such organizations as the Organization for Economic Cooperation and Development (OECD), the U.S. Information Agency (USIA), and the U.S. National Institute of Education. She is the author of *Coverage of the U.S. in Chinese Textbooks,* and her extensive articles have focused mainly on Chinese and bilingual education. She was born in Taiwan and did her graduate studies at Boston University.

JOSÉ MARÍA COUTINHO is an associate professor in the Department of Educational Foundations and Counseling, Division of Teacher Education, at the Federal University of Vitoria, State of Espiritu Santo. Brazil. His advanced degrees from the University of California, Los Angeles, are in the fields of history, social sciences, and comparative education. His publications are in the areas of teacher, comparative, and global education.

YUVAL DROR is head of the Department of Education in the University Division of Oranim, the School of Education of the Kibbutz movement at the University of Haifa, Israel. His advanced degrees in sociology and education are from Hebrew University.

MARIONA ESPINET holds a joint position in the Departments of Pedagogy and Science as well as Mathematics Education at the Autonomous University of Barcelona, Spain. Her advanced degrees are from Barcelona and the University of Georgia. Her publications are in the field of science education and research methodology.

VALERIE-DAWN RUDDELL GIRHINY is currently an education officer in the Centre for Teacher Education, Ministry of Education, Ontario, Canada. She holds graduate degrees from McMaster University and the University of Toronto. She has held academic positions at Toronto Teachers' College, Hamilton Teachers' College, and the Ontario Teacher Education College. She has served as ministry inspector of private schools and has held other administrative posts in the Ministry of Education.

CHRISTA HÄNDLE is on the staff of the Max Planck Institute for Human Development and Education in Berlin, Germany. As a researcher in the field of education, she has completed studies on proposed teacher education reforms in what were once East and West Germany, thus placing her among the educational experts attempting to reconcile the two former systems of teacher education and form one unified system. Her publications have focused on such topics as the professional socialization of young teachers as well as on teacher education in institutional and social contexts.

WILLIS D. HAWLEY is director of the Center for Educational Policy and Human Development, the Vanderbilt Institute for Public Policy Studies, as well as professor of education and political science, Vanderbilt University, Nashville, Tennessee. He is dean, emeritus, of Peabody College, Vanderbilt University's School of Education. He has taught at Yale and Duke universities and holds an advanced degree from the University of California at Berkeley. His extensive list of published books, articles, and book chapters has dealt with teacher education, education reform, urban politics, and organizational change.

HARRY JUDGE is a senior research associate of the Oxford University Department of Educational Studies (of which he was director for fifteen years). He is also professor of teacher education policy at Michigan State University. His numerous publications have focused on teacher education in international perspective and his recent book, American Graduate Schools of Education, has been widely credited with contributing to the reform movement in U.S. teacher education.

HOWARD B. LEAVITT is an adjunct professor of social foundations of education at the School of Education, the University of Massachusetts, Amherst, and is the director of the Council on Global Perspectives for the Professions. He has worked for the U.S. Agency for International Development and the World Bank in the area of overseas educational development. For six years he was the editor of the annual international yearbook on teacher education published by the international division of the American Association of Colleges for Teacher Education. His advanced degrees are from Columbia University.

RUSSELL J. LESKIW is director of International Services Consulting, a Canadian firm specializing in management and educational consulting. He was acting president at the formation of the University of Lethbridge and was the founding dean of the university's first Faculty of Education. He has served as chairman and executive director of the Joint Board of Teacher Education in British Columbia as well as senior superintendent of educational personnel in that province's government. His advanced degrees are from the University of Oregon. His numerous publications have centered on teacher education.

A. LOURDUSAMY is an associate professor at the School of Educational Studies, Universiti Sains Malaysia, Penang, Malaysia. His advanced degrees are from Malaysian and British universities. His area of research interest is individual differences and their influence on learning behavior.

J. B. KUTHEMBA MWALE is head of the Department of Educational Foundations at Chancellor College, the University of Malawi, Zomba, Malawi, and coordinator of the university's Centre for Educational Research and Training. His degrees are from Canadian and British universities. His extensive publications focus on teacher education policy and practice in Malawi.

LYNN PAINE is a member of the Department of Teacher Education, Department of Sociology, Michigan State University. She has served as China expert in a number of institutions and has written extensively on Chinese education and teacher education, utilizing information gathered from frequent visits to the Far East. Her advanced degrees in education as well as sociology are from Stanford University.

TAHER RAZIK is a professor in the Faculty of Educational Studies at the State University of New York, Buffalo. He was born in Egypt, and his professional career has concentrated on educational policy and research in developing countries, with emphasis on the Middle East. He has served as educational adviser to many of the ministries of education of the region and as senior researcher at Unesco in Paris. He is a prolific writer and the author of eight books, including *A Systems Approach to Teacher Training and Development: The Case of Developing Countries*, published by Unesco. His advanced degrees are from Ohio State University.

MANABU SATO is an associate professor in the Department of School Education, University of Tokyo, from which institution he holds advanced degrees.

He has also taught at Mie University. His major interests lie in the areas of curriculum history and clinical research on teaching. His numerous publications, including three books, deal with such topics as educational reform in Japan and the United States, as well as research on teaching and in-service education.

SOK KHIM TAN is a lecturer at the School of Educational Studies, Universiti Sains Malaysia, Penang, Malaysia. Her areas of interest lie in teacher education and the teaching of science, especially physics, as well as the teacher as researcher. Her advanced degrees are from the University of Malaysia and Cornell University.

R. D. TRAILL is professor of education and head of the School of Education at the Canberra College of Advanced Education in Belconnen, Australia. His extensive publications focus on teacher education and curriculum development. His advanced degrees are from the universities of Tasmania and California at Berkeley. He is widely published in the areas of teacher education and curriculum development.

JOAN B. WILSON is professor of educational administration at the California State University at Los Angeles. Previously, in various California schools, she has served as teacher, department chair, high school principal, and finally superintendent of the South Pasadena school system. She has written on the subject of educational reforms in the Soviet Union based on first-hand experience in that country. Her advanced degrees are from Columbia University and the University of California at Los Angeles.

DIAA EL-DIN A. ZAHER is an associate professor of the foundations of education at the College of Education, Ain Shams University in Cairo, Egypt. He holds advanced degrees in educational planning from Ain Shams University. His publications deal with educational planning for many different aspects of the educational enterprise. He has also served as education planning consultant to various organizations in Egypt as well as in other Arab countries.